About this book The starting-point of this study was the discovery that Goya's most famous series of etchings, the *Caprichos*, was published on Ash Wednesday in 1799. The Spanish artist waited until the 'last Carnival of the century' to bring his celebrated work to light because his aim was to give a personal vision of the 'world turned upside down'. This book reconstructs the link between Carnival, Revolution and the turn of the century in Western culture and analyses the way in which Goya's late work vividly illustrates this triple link.

The Marquis de Sade is a second emblematic figure in this fascinating adventure into the reversal of all values. Topics such as inversion and perversion, violence and transvestism, folly and the triumph of the flesh, techniques of ambiguity and the symbolism of laughter are illustrated by means of a wide range of examples. The authors shed new light not only on the work of one of the world's great artists but also on the birth of the modern world as a whole.

About the authors Victor I. Stoichita was educated in Bucharest, Rome and Paris. He is currently Professor of History of Art at the University of Fribourg, Switzerland. His publications include *Visionary Experience in the Golden Age of Spanish Art* (Reaktion, 1995), *The Self-Aware Image* (1997) and *A Short History of the Shadow* (Reaktion, 1997).

Anna Maria Coderch was educated in Barcelona and Madrid and taught for many years as Assistant Professor at the University of Gerona, Spain.

GOYA

The Last Carnival

Victor I. Stoichita and
Anna Maria Coderch

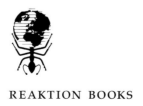

REAKTION BOOKS

Published by Reaktion Books Ltd
79 Farringdon Road, London EC1M 3JU, UK
www.reaktionbooks.co.uk

First published 1999

This book was published with the assistance of the
Council of the University of Fribourg, Switzerland.

Series design by Humphrey Stone

Colour printed by BAS Printers Ltd, Over Wallop, Hampshire
Printed and bound in Great Britain by Biddles Ltd, Guildford
and King's Lynn

British Library Cataloguing in Publication Data

Stoichita, Victor Ieronim
Goya: the last carnival. – (Essays in art and culture)
1. Goya, Francisco de, 1746–1828 – Criticism and interpretation
2. Painting, Spanish 3. Painting, Modern – 19th century.
4. Painting, Modern – 18th century – Spain.
I. Title II. Coderch, Anna Maria
759.6

ISBN 1 86189 045 1

Contents

Preface and Acknowledgements

The subject of this book is the world of the imagination at the turn of the century. Not our turn of the century – there are other books that have already dealt with this subject and there will no doubt be more to come from the maelstrom as we hurtle into the new millennium that awaits us. The turn of the century this book deals with is no ordinary one, but one that witnessed the death of one world and the birth of another. This threshold and this journey, crucial to our understanding of the modern world, have no precise date, but are located somewhere between the Revolution of '1789' and the year that appears in our calendar as '1800'.

However, our book – and this must be clear from the outset – is the story not of a journey but of its imaginative world. We look at the birth of modernity as a final surge of what had, in the shape of the Great Festival, constituted the ancient rite of the rebirth of time, a rite that reached – at the threshold of modernity, around 1800 – one of its most difficult (but also one of its most significant) moments. We are therefore looking at the birth of the modern imagination in Western culture as a final carnivalesque surge. Our debt to such cultural anthropological studies as Mikhail Bakhtin's *L'oeuvre de François Rabelais*[1] will no doubt become clear, as will the areas of thought we have broken away from.

Bakhtin drew attention to the importance of the periodic inversion presented by the Carnival and to the aesthetic of licentiousness and the culture of laughter that derived from it. The Middles Ages and Renaissance therefore come across in his study as being richer than they do in academic studies focused almost exclusively on élitist culture. The history of aesthetics and literary theory in turn were enriched by the new category of the 'carnivalesque'. Bakhtin continued to develop this theme, among others, in another work, as well as through the interpretation of literary techniques up to the nineteenth century.[2] But despite his theory regarding the permanence of the *carnivalesque*, he was fully conscious of the fact that, as an historic reality, the *Carnival* inevitably had its temporal limits. In fact, he observed that:

> From the second half of the seventeenth century, we witness a process of progressive decline, degeneration, and impoverishment of the ritualistic forms and carnivalesque attractions in popular culture (. . .). The distinct carnivalesque view of the world together with its universality, its brazenness, its utopian character and predilection for the future begins to transform itself into a mere festive mood. The festival has *virtually* ceased to be the second life of the people, its temporary renaissance and rebirth.[3]

It is a pity that Bakhtin did not go into the subject of this 'virtual' end of the historical Carnival in greater depth. To do this, he would no doubt have had to cross the eighteenth century so as to arrive at the great turning-point around 1800. Our book intends – albeit partially – to bridge this gap. It is 'Bakhtinian' only insofar as it endeavours to answer a question that Bakhtin either considered unnecessary or did not wish to address. It is anti-Bakhtinian inasmuch as it tackles unstable, hybrid and disintegrating structures rather than solid categories like those discovered and set in motion by the author of *Rabelais and His World*.

Given the enormity of our task, our perseverance was sorely tested. Exploring the imagination of the last Carnival led us into research whose interdisciplinary nature transcended the norm. We had to confront not only the artistic manifestation of a complex historical reality but also such problems as the relationship between playful reversal and revolution, between carnivalesque festival and the turn of a century, between eschatological obsessions and myths of regeneration at the crossroads of modernity. Fortunately, there was help to be had from significant existing research.[4] We made a conscious decision not to be tempted to make an exhaustive study of the subject or to make any claim that it was exhaustive, preferring to focus our research on the imagination of the disintegrating carnival, concentrating on examples and key personalities. The most important of the latter is certainly the Spanish artist Francisco Goya, with the Marquis de Sade a close second.

A few words need to be said about this book as a collaborative work. It is the result of a joint venture that has taken several years to come to fruition. All the ideas are the product of discussions and lengthy debates, which makes it impossible (and pointless) to establish paternity. On the other hand, the authors are jointly responsible for the end results. Whilst the first draft was undertaken by the author listed first on the title page, reciprocal readings and re-readings have left their mark.

Research material was gathered in Fribourg, Los Angeles, Madrid and Munich; our thanks go to Anita Petrovski and Christelle Marro (in Fribourg), Catherine Schaller and Acacia Warwick (in Los Angeles) and Antonia Fernandez Valencia (in Madrid). The working environment provided by the National Library in Madrid, the Zentralinstitut für Kunstgeschichte in Munich and the Getty Research Institute in Los Angeles contributed greatly to our research and to the development of our ideas. Conversations, bibliographical information and encouragement from colleagues and friends brought the joy of communication and the sharing of knowledge to an otherwise solitary occupation. We should also like to thank Rocio Arnaiz, Andreas Beyer, Catherine Candea, Andrea Carlino, Charles Dempsey, Jutta Held, Klaus Herding, Thierry Lenain, Elena Lupas, Sergiusz Michalski, Michael Roth, Jean-Claude Schmitt, Salvatore Settis, Barbara Maria Stafford, Jean Starobinski, David Summers and Susann Waldmann. Work on the final draft was facilitated by the granting of a sabbatical term from the University of Fribourg, and a clean manuscript was created with the help of Pauline Audren de Kredrel. The manuscript was checked during a visit to the Institute for Humanities at the University of Michigan (at the invitation of Thomas R. Trautmann and Celeste Brusati). At the invitation of Fernando Marias, a truncated version of Chapter 7 was read during a seminar entitled 'The Imprint on the Canvas: Concepts and Images of the Spanish Artist', organized by the 'Duques de Soria' Foundation, Soria, in July 1999. We would like to thank colleagues and students who took part in the seminar for their questions and comments. We would also like to thank students at the University of Fribourg for their interest during the course and seminars that accompanied the writing of the book, as well as the members of the 'Representing Passions' team at the Getty Research Institute and those of the 'Form and Pattern' group at the Institute for the Humanities at Ann Arbor, who followed our research right up until the final stages.

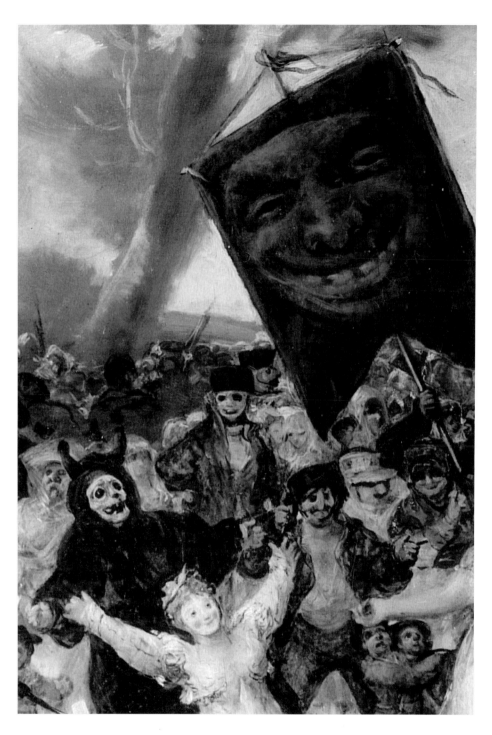

1 Goya, *The Burial of the Sardine* (see illus. 8).

1 The Turn of the Century as a Symbolic Form

A CARNIVAL THAT NEVER TOOK PLACE

'A feeling of melancholy reigned deep within their souls as they entered the city of Rome.'[1] So ends book VIII of *Corinne ou l'Italie* by Madame de Staël (1807). It is necessary to read the beginning of book IX in order to understand how a powerful antithesis is created, without any breaking off:

> It was the day of the noisiest festival of the year, the end of the carnival, when, like a fever of joy, like a lusting after entertainment, it takes hold of the people of Rome in a manner that does not exist anywhere else. The whole city is in disguise, at the windows there is barely a spectator left without a mask to watch those who wear them, and this merriment begins on a particular day and at a given moment; and no public or private event in the year would normally prevent anyone from enjoying himself at this time. (. . .) During the carnival, class, manners and minds are all mixed up; and the crowd and the shouts, and the repartee and sugared almonds that indiscriminately flood the passing carriages, mix all mortal beings together, creating a jumbled-up nation, as though there were no longer any social order. Corinne and Lord Nelvil, both dreamers and thinkers, arrived in the middle of the hullabaloo. At first they were stunned by it, for there is nothing more strange than this bustle of noisy pleasures, when the soul completely withdraws into itself. They stopped off at the Piazza del Popolo, went up into the amphitheatre, next to the obelisk, from where they could see the horserace.[2]

The detailed description that ensues, and to which we shall return, is the most important outcome of the fundamental split described in Madame de Staël's novel. There is on the one hand, those who observe (Corinne, Nelvil) and, on the other, the objects of their observations (the race, the festival). As a result, the Carnival, which should in principle have erased all boundaries between spectators and actors ('at the windows there is barely a spectator left without a mask to watch those who have them') has lost something of its all-encompassing power and therefore, implicitly, something of its innermost being. Hence the festival is turned into something it was not: a show. This fatal transformation signals the death of the Carnival and had been anticipated by Goethe in *Das Römische Carneval* (1788/9): 'When one ventures to describe the Roman carnival, one must expect to be reproached and told that such a festival cannot in fact be described.'[3] Despite this instinctive reproach, Goethe proceeded to write his famous and important description. Madame de Staël followed suit. By describing what cannot (or must not) be *described* but only *experienced*, the Carnival, through the observer's perfect magnifying glass, reveals what is at stake and the poet becomes hermeneutic.

Despite their similarities, Goethe's and Madame de Staël's texts describe two different ways of approaching the Carnival at the time of its transformation. To Goethe (whose description of the 1788 Roman festival was published in the spring of 1789), the Carnival was a symbolic Revolution:

> If we are to be allowed to continue to speak more seriously than the subject warrants, we would observe that (. . .) liberty and equality can only be sampled in the vertigo of madness, and that the greatest of pleasures can only seduce at the highest point when it courts danger and when it delights in its proximity to voluptuous sensations that are both disturbing and sweet.[4]

As for Madame de Staël , the situation was more complicated though no less significant. She wrote her novel (set in 1795) at the beginning of the nineteenth century, in 1805. By describing what her heroes would have seen from the top of the stands erected in the Piazza del Popolo, the writer consciously or unconsciously employed poetic licence: we know for sure that there was no Carnival in Rome in 1795. For reasons that Goethe had intuited so efficiently, the Roman Carnival had been banned immediately after the French Revolution.[5] When (in 1805) permission was granted for it to resume, it was no longer the same, as the author of *Corinne* implied: '. . . a kind of universal petulance made it more like the bacchanals of the imagination, but only of the imagination.'[6] While it could even be said that for Goethe, in 1788, the Carnival heralded the Revolution, for Madame de Staël, in 1805, it was no more than a memory or, at the very most, a dream of the *Ancien Régime*:

> . . . night is falling; slowly the noise diminishes, it is followed by the most profound of silences; all that is left of the evening is confused mental images which, by turning the life of each into a dream, for a brief moment, let the people forget their work, the scholars their studies, great lords their idleness.

Multiple rites of passage[7] take place in this imaginary projection of the festival. The first involves the very essence of the Carnival. This, by definition, is a festival that celebrates the periodic rebirth of time.[8] It unleashes energies, reverses hierarchies, mixes individuals together to create a dynamic mass. It affects time, by turning itself into an intermediary time, a kind of between-the-two. The second rite of passage, implicit in Madame de Staël's nostalgic description, is born of the event that had put the festival on hold, an actual historical inversion that recognized its symbolic (and imaginary) double in the carnivalesque festival: the Revolution. We can add a third rite of passage: that of the end of one century and the beginning of another. This one shifts the closing ceremonies to the apparently abstract plane of the calendar. It brings about and introduces a reflection on transitional time, time which reverses so that it can begin again in the dialectic that founded this same calendar (the Christian one) that hangs in the balance between the 'first century' (and first year) of a new era (first century and first year of the Incarnation) and, according to the same belief system, the fast-approaching horizon of Judgement Day. In short, the Revolution squeezed itself in between the last actual Carnival described by Goethe and the first imaginary Carnival described by Madame de Staël. The turn of the century squeezed itself in between the imaginary time of the story entitled *Corinne* (1795) and the actual time it was written (1805). The ramifications of this double overlap are such that her text can be considered to have the richness of an allegory. Let us therefore use it as the point of departure for a search that is likely to go much further. For, in effect, throughout the eighteenth century, carnivalesque rebirth, revolutionary inversion and a gap in the calendar would appear to have been the different ways of acting upon and reflecting on time, and where they meet up is where we can place the birth of the modern world.

The easiest way to define the Carnival is to say that it is a period that begins with the Epiphany (6 January) and ends at the beginning of Lent (Ash Wednesday). This last day signals the renunciation of the flesh, or to be more precise, the con-sumption of flesh is forbidden (*carne levare*) during the 46 days that lead up to Easter.[9] But it is when it reaches its climax that the Carnival becomes truly itself. This takes place in the final days of the cycle, between Quinquagesima Sunday and Shrove Tuesday, when, traditionally, all manner of excess is permitted in the name of the period of abstinence due to begin the following day. Carnival and Lent vie with one another during February, but the actual dates vary from year to year. These – like Easter – are calculated on the lunar cycle, Easter falling on the first Sunday after the first full moon of spring. At the other end of this period of fasting, Shrove Tuesday is therefore the day when the last moon of winter wanes, while the night that precedes Ash Wednesday is marked by the moon's temporary absence.[10]

The archaic, indeed ancestral nature of this kind of calcula-tion has been repeatedly emphasized by ethnologists. At times they have drawn attention to parallels with other similar fes-tivals which, in the pagan world or in 'primitive' societies, also celebrated this pivotal time,[11] at other times they have preferred to stress the event's Christian characteristics, inas-much as carnivalesque debauchery can only be properly understood in relation to the asceticism of Lent.[12]

It is neither our intention nor within our powers to review the details of this debate. However, we do feel that it is neces-sary to provide a brief résumé of how the Carnival functions within the framework of Western culture with a view to fur-thering an understanding of its final evolution and crisis.

To begin, we can summarize the main characteristics of the Carnival as *licence, excess, inversion, dressing-up* and *joy*. We are conscious as we pause to examine these terms that they are limited and arbitrary in nature. At this point, two criti-cisms could be levelled at us. The first is that we could have added other characteristics; the second stems from the fact that licence/excess/inversion/dressing-up/joy are notions which have a complementary relationship because they either cut across or partially overlap with each other.

To be more precise, only the last term stands out from the others, inasmuch as it is a consequence of them. The latter, through their reciprocal, complementary relationship and through their common relationship to the joy they bring, reveal the possibility of an all-encompassing term. The joy brought by licence, excess, inversion and dressing-up is a reaction to the *mise-en-scène* of otherness. Hence the Carnival could be defined as the *festival of joyful otherness*. It celebrates the period when the universe drifts as a result of order collapsing. Its opposite – disorder – triumphs, and the cosmos itself is vanquished by chaos. The Carnival is joy in the face of triumphant difference (joy in the face of disorder and chaos, seen as the reverse of order and the cosmos). A consideration of these issues brought us into contact with an anthropological discourse that, some several decades ago, through a study of 'primitive' cultures, drew attention to the existence of *destructuring ceremonies* and proposed that the carnival be considered in the light of the concept of '*anti-structure*'.[13]

The notion we are advancing, that of the *festival of otherness*, has, we believe, the advantage of leaving intact the paradoxical coherence of the Carnival founded on structuring opposites rather than destructuring ones. The terms that define Carnival (licence, excess, inversion, dressing-up) vindicate joy not as an attitude in the face of necessity, nothingness or the abyss (in the face of the abyss, not joy but only anguish is possible), but as a positive perception of otherness. Carnivalesque disorder is relative, not absolute, and it is no coincidence that it was in fact *structuralist*-based philosophy (mainly Bakhtin's) that best defined it. A particularly crucial aspect should be emphasized, however; it was when the Carnival was in crisis that joy in the face of relative chaos came under threat and at times – as we shall see – even changed into anguish when faced with absolute chaos.[14]

Let us examine in greater depth the descriptive terms we have suggested, taking their intrinsic complementarity into account. The first of them, licence, gives carnivalesque time its characteristic of opposition to normal time. Permissiveness is a temporary 'law', however. The saying 'Anything goes' is only applicable to 'meat days' (Sunday, Monday, Tuesday before Ash Wednesday); hence the desire to take advantage of them as much as possible and the frenzy to be as licentious as possible to the bitter end. Excess (of food, sexual appetites, liberty, joy) is born of the latent fear of the imminent approach of the permissive period's end.

Licence and excess are a direct response to the prohibitions during the Days of Abstinence (it is the imminent threat of Lent that automatically justifies the Carnival) and an indirect response to all the rules that govern normal time,'normal' time being time structured and regulated in accordance with the rhythm and necessities of everyday life. This structuring is of course dependent on social order, which is temporarily suspended by carnivalesque licence. What is significant here is the fact that licence comes, as it were, from 'nowhere' but itself. In the eighteenth century, it was Goethe who once again expressed this in a famous formula: 'The carnival of Rome is a festival that is not actually given to the people, but one that the people give themselves.'[15] Madame de Staël, who preferred allegory to Goethe-style aphorisms, developed the same idea in a tract that describes the climax of the Roman festival, although in reality it is a huge metaphor for it:

> The People's Square, which was crowded with people, is now empty. Everyone is in the amphitheatres that surround the obelisks, and countless heads are turned towards and dark eyes fixed on the barrier from which the horses will speed. They arrive unbridled and without a saddle, (. . .) rear up, whinny and stamp their hooves. (. . .) The impatience of the horses, the shouts of the grooms become, the moment the barrier is raised, a truly dramatic sight. The horses are off (. . .). The streets spark beneath their hooves, their manes fly, and their yearning to win the prize, to which they now abandon themselves, is such, that there are those who, upon arriving, are dead from the swiftness of their race. We are amazed to see such free horses so spurred on by personal passions; it is frightening, as though thought had taken on animal form. The crowds leave their places once the horses have passed, and follow on in disarray.[16]

We are witnessing a time when the perfect circle of self-accorded liberties, still valid in Goethe's time, broke up, taking the Carnival with it. From the stands, the public watched the great show of licence and excess in the form of animals racing 'unbridled and without a saddle'. Here Madame de Staël is playing with the double register. The first has already been mentioned: the horserace is the Carnival '*mise-en-abyme*'. The second is aimed at the metaphysics of the mask. If the race frightens 'as though thought had taken on animal form', this fact can be attributed to the disturbing totemism created by the wild spectacle of otherness. There was no schism in the traditional Carnival: everyone wore a mask, and no-one was him- or herself. In its enormous complexity, the mask was the richest symbol of metamorphoses, the violation of natural boundaries, the transfer of power from human to animal and vice versa. Together with licence and excess, it formed a common cluster ('anything goes under cover of the mask') being – as a fundamental carnivalesque principle – only one aspect of dressing-up. Transvestism is above all the form that characterizes otherness. The joy it brings comes from the dialectic between otherness and identity, dialectic that is extremely flexible in fact. 'To present oneself as an other' induces laughter only when true *identity* is revealed, and the significance of this laughter can vary for a wide variety of reasons and allusions, ranging from the *mise-en-scène* of similarity to the spectacle of difference.

Next to the animal mask, the most widespread carnivalesque form of expressing otherness was cross-dressing. Once again, it is Goethe who paid this special attention:

> Masks now begin to become more varied. Young men dressed in the carnival clothes of women from the lowest of the classes, with their chests bared and an air of shameless self-importance, generally begin by fooling around. They fondle the men they encounter and are brazen and familiar with the women as if they were their equals; and furthermore, they do whatever their fancies, minds and mischief tell them to do.[17]

It is significant that the poet captures sexual reversal in a form that implies social debasement as well, which is not always the case in the secular tradition of carnivalesque transsexuality. He also drew attention to the fact that the change of sexual roles becomes one with licence and that both laughter and joy are in the offing. With Madame de Staël, on the other hand, there is no mention of this archaic form of transvestism. Her melancholic gaze 'historicises' the Roman Carnival or, to be more precise, isolates it in its historicising elements:

> Often a grotesque seriousness contrasts with the vivacity of the Italians, and one might be tempted to think that it was their bizarre clothes that were bringing out a dignity unnatural to them. At other times, through the disguises they create, they reveal such a peculiar knowledge of mythology that one might well believe the ancient fables to be still popular in Rome. (. . .) There is a kind of mask that is to be found nowhere else. These are masks based on the faces of ancient statues, which, from afar, imitate perfect beauty: women often lose much when they abandon them. And yet this motionless imitation of life, these roving wax faces, however beautiful they are, are just a little frightening.[18]

We shall have occasion to return, but in another context, to the extraordinary implications and significance of this 'neo-classical' festival described by the author of *Corinne*. For the present, we shall limit ourselves to emphasizing once more the changes that took place after 1800. Madame de Staël examined the figures of carnivalesque otherness on two occasions. On the first occasion, the dynamic form of the wild horserace represented it, on the second, the motionless form of the statuary masquerade. But on both occasions, and despite their being diametrically opposed, neither joy nor fear is to be found in the perception of the dressing-up game, so awe-inspiring is the human mirrored in the animal that moulds itself into the superhuman forms of classical perfection.

It is difficult, if not altogether impossible, to separate completely the theme of transvestism from that of reversal; both are at the heart of the carnivalesque tradition. Both play with the idea of otherness, and their complementarity is perfect. Human disguised as animal implies a reversal of kingdoms; man disguised as woman and woman disguised as man implies a reversal of sexual roles that – as we have seen in Goethe – becomes one with a reversed social order (oppressed disguised as oppressor and vice versa). All these shifts from same to opposite have as their aim the symbolic abrogation of the norm and the joyful establishment of the non-norm. Consequently, it is a reversal of the comic order that is being targeted, with kingdoms, sexes and classes taking on the roles of figures.

Within this context, it would be illuminating to examine the iconography of 'the world upside down' as it was codified in the sixteenth century in Western culture, where it was to survive in its different versions until the nineteenth century.[19] The oldest broadsheets known today had a double centre (illus. 2). In the upper part of the sheet, an upside-down globe floats in the sky. The lower level of the image, which is, as a rule, a selective, enlarged and exemplary view of what is hidden by the upside-down globe at the top, is organized around a second centre, a woman dressed in the clothes of a warrior, an enormous spear in her right hand. At her feet, in a position of submission, is a bearded man dressed as a woman and holding a distaff. In case this exchange of symbols was not explicit enough, the man's staff and the woman's sword cross. It is no doubt significant that the sexual reversal we find here establishes the themes of social reversal and power games. It is also significant that, apart from a 'strong centre' that polarizes the cosmology of the world turned upside

2 Italian, *'And This Is the World Upside Down'*, c. 1660, print.

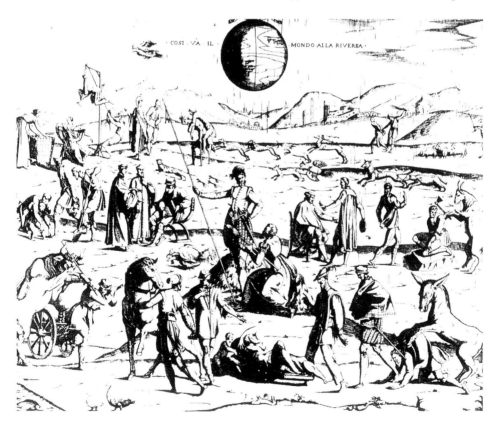

· COSI · VA · IL ·   MONDO ALLA RIVERSA ·

down into the metaphor of reversed sexual difference, there is no mandatory order in which the print should be read. The choice is clear: to dispel, through the denigration of the traditional mechanisms of reading, any suggestion that the upside-down world could have an 'order'. Thus the images are perceived through blocks which are more or less arbitrarily sequenced and paths which intersect. What is important is that, throughout the alternating and complementary representation, the triple complexity of the three essential reversals (sex, kingdom and society) in the image of the 'other world' is brought to light: the hen mounts the cockerel, the donkey climbs onto the peasant, the peasant oversees the lord, the wolf minds the flock, the victim tortures the executioner, the cockerel hunts the fox, the hare chases the greyhound, the mice run after the cat and so on and so forth.

In eighteenth- and nineteenth-century broadsheets, things changed only in appearance (illus. 3). Artistic quality deteriorated, and it is obvious that the sheets were destined for a public now accustomed to reading. Organized into small, numbered pictures, each benefiting from a caption, these broadsheets do not, however, give a clearer indication as to the order of the whole, which, moreover, has no unifying narrative structure. The flexibility of the sequencing suggests a multitude of permutations. In first position, we frequently find the image of the inverted world, which gives the sheet its title, and the change of sexual roles is still in a central position, as can be seen in frames 28 and 38 of illustration 3.

The distribution, in the form of popular prints, of the iconography of the upside-down world raises the problem of the relationship between this topos and Carnival. From the time of their emergence in the sixteenth century, the prints did not illustrate a festival but the world. The temporary reversal proposed by the Carnival became a permanent law; the world had become carnivalized, and the prints, through their wide-ranging examples, present us with an image of this world. Not just an invitation to experience joy (so crucial to the Carnival), the world turned upside down was on the one hand utopian and on the other a criticism of society. In the Spanish print illustrated here, only the final image still evokes the carnivalesque origin of the whole. As to the rest, from the first square with the initials of the inverted globe to the last square, which illustrates the carnivalesque motif of clothes

20

EL MUNDO AL REVES.

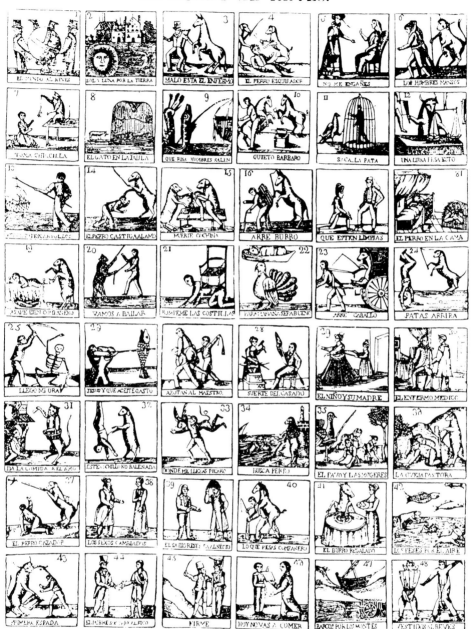

3 Catalan, *The World Upside Down*, early 19th century, print.

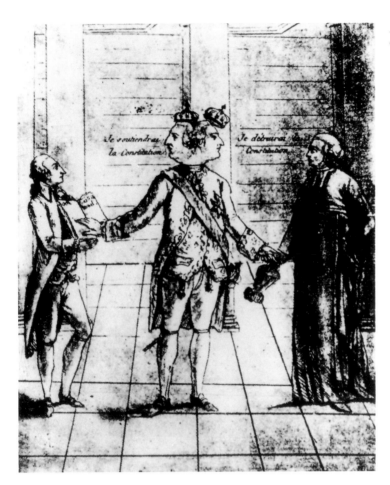

worn upside down, the scenes have lost their ceremonial character. By fixing what in the Carnival was no more than fleeting – substituting high for low and low for high – the carnivalization of the world is offered as the sum total of a series of acts of reversal. Their nature is unreal, dreamlike and utopian, and the intrinsic impossibility of their ever happening results in laughter: the hen will never mount the cockerel; the donkey will never climb onto his master.

Carnival reversals fulfilled their functions inasmuch as they were temporary and insofar as their violence was relative. Their very obscenity had a purifying importance that was toned down during the eighteenth century: as a rule people clouted one another with sugared almonds and confetti, sprinkled perfumed water on one another and proclaimed a fool or beggar 'king' for a few days. If anyone was

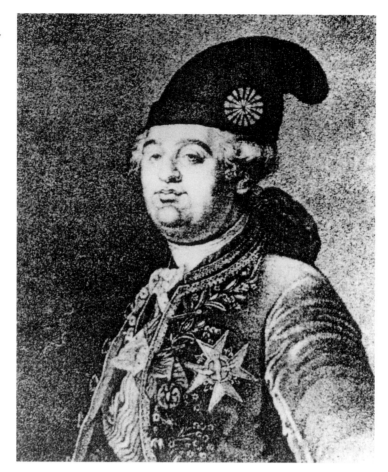

5 French, *Louis XVI Wearing Liberty Hat*, 1792, print.

executed, this was done 'in effigy'. It is said that latent violence has been tolerated by the powers that be since the Middle Ages, since it has been acknowledged as a 'safety valve', a symbolic manifestation whose function has been to replace or avert genuine social upheavals.[20] However, symbolic violence did at times turn into genuine revolts: some of the best-known examples include the 1580 Carnival of the Romans, which ended in bloodshed,[21] and the many Carnivals during the German religious wars, when people smashed images, burned down castles and joined the peasant revolts.[22] In this context, a phenomenon that is perhaps more interesting than the actual transition from Carnival to revolt is the communicative relationship established between the two.[23] By seeking to recoup the symbolic elements crucial to its own celebration, revolt can itself become Carnival. In an exaggerated way, this is what happened during the French Revolution, when the inversion of the ancient order followed a rhythm quite similar to the ancient rites of termination. We can follow the shifts in the forms concealed by such violence, when symbolic became real, without losing anything of its ritual impact. This will become clearer when we examine the imaginative world of the Revolution and, more particularly, the proliferation of anti-monarchic caricatures. Here the animal mask was dominant: Marie-Antoinette was often a panther, the Count of Artois a tiger, the Duchess of Polignac a vixen, the King himself always a pig.[24]

24

The Monarch, whose power was diminishing, took on an essentially carnivalesque role. In his capacity as a cuckold, he was already a deposed king; however, in traditional Carnivals, as we have seen, the cuckold (the ousted king) symbolized winter in retreat. He was divested of his finery, beaten and mocked.[25] The carnivalization of the figure of Louis XVI was rich in implications, and it is interesting to note how the image we have of him, from Revolutionary documents, is characterized by a form of mockery that focuses increasingly on his crowned head. He is sometimes depicted as being double (illus. 4) to indicate political duplicity (it should be pointed out that in this case, only one of the crowns is falling, the one 'under' which the king is declaring himself to be anti-constitutional, while the other remains firmly on his head).[26] In another hypostasis – the 'disguise' here could not be more significant – the head has none of the symbols of monarchic power but only a red hat (illus. 5). In a third (illus. 6) – mockery has been replaced by actual violence – the head of the executed king has become 'food for thought for crowned jugglers'[27] – the transition from Monarchy to Republic has united Revolution and Carnival. Something of the ambivalent relationship that equates symbolic and real violence is, as we have seen, to be found in Goethe's description of the Rome Carnival (1788), which turns the vertiginous appeal of freedom into the madness of the festival. In Madame de Staël (1795/1805), the die is now cast: 'During the carnival, class, manners and minds are all mixed up; and the crowd and the shouts, and the repartee and sugared almonds that indiscriminately flood the passing carriages, mix all mortal beings together, creating a jumbled up nation, as though all social order had disappeared.'[28]

The Carnival has become a pure metaphor.

REVOLUTION, TURN OF THE CENTURY, CARNIVAL

In its original meaning, the term 'revolution' was part of the special vocabulary used by astronomers, astrologers and chronologists. It referred to the return (*revolutio*) of a star that had completed its orbit. In the Middle Ages, it went on to mean the completion of a cycle and the end of any period of time. In this way, after a 'revolution', a fragment of time – a period – is presented as something completed by having 'revolved'. Recent studies have shown the slow but steady way in which this word evolved from its original meaning ('cycle', 'return') to signify 'completion' or 'end', arriving eventually at the present-day notion of 'change' or 'mutation'.[29] In French, Furetière's *Universal Dictionary* (1690) already contained the definition used by historians in which 'revolution' meant 'extraordinary change that occurs in the world'.[30] Although this meaning predominated throughout the eighteenth century, the polysemy of the term remained valid for a long time.[31] Stars, the globe, ideas, society and politics all are subject to upheavals; people attribute these in vain to the will of a benevolent creator now replaced by the agnostic *fatum*, by cyclical fate from which nothing and no-one can escape: 'When terrible revolutions, floods and earthquakes wreak havoc over a large part of the globe I inhabit, where is this God's benevolence, where is the beautiful order that in his wisdom he placed in the universe?'[32] The same author goes on to say:

> In the terrible convulsions that sometimes shake up political societies, and which often result in an empire being turned upside down, there is not a single action, a single word, a single thought, a single wish, a single passion among the agents who, as destroyers or victims help bring about the revolution, that is not necessary, that does not act as it should act, that does not unfailingly produce the effects it must produce, in accord with the place these agents occupy in the moral maelstrom. This would appear obvious to an intelligence capable of grasping and appreciating all the actions and reactions of the minds and bodies of those who contribute to this revolution.[33]

To the philosophers of the Age of Enlightenment, all social and political cataclysms bore the inevitable marks of cosmic upheaval and were subject to the same implacable laws. To some writers – the first being Rousseau – the inevitability of revolution is superimposed on the topos of the world turned upside down:

> You rely on the present social order, never thinking that this order is subject to the inevitability of revolution, and it is impossible for you to predict or to warn against something that will only affect your children. Large becomes small, the rich man becomes poor, and the monarch

becomes subject: are the blows dealt by fate so rare that you think you can escape them? We are fast approaching crisis point and the century of revolutions.[34]

With such ideas in the air, it should have come as no surprise when the Bastille fell on 14 July 1789 nor that (almost) everyone soon found the right word to describe the occasion: it was neither a revolt nor a riot; it was well and truly a 'Revolution'. It should have come as no surprise either that one of the priorities of this 'Revolution' was the control of time and its symbolism. The notion of 'century' had already been challenged in the pre-Revolutionary era.[35]

> ... the length of a century is essentially arbitrary, but we are obliged to give each century a hundred years solely to facilitate the chronological order of calculations and quotations. No physical revolution in nature is completed in the space of a hundred years, in the same way that a physical revolution in nature is completed over the course of one year, this being the revolution of the sun that we call annual.[36]

Once the Republic had been proclaimed (on 22 September 1792), there was very little doubt that the eighteenth 'century' had come to an end. To some, this end had perhaps come somewhat early; to others, it had arrived not a moment too soon, and in accordance with a law that had nothing to do with geometric centenaries (which, as we have seen, had already been challenged) but with reversals of a cosmic-historic order. The solution to this discrepancy was, as we know, radical: to change the calendar.[37] The new Republican Calendar, established by order of the Convention in October 1793, decided, after a good deal of experimentation, that the New Year would begin on 22 September 1792. This date marked not only the day the Republic was proclaimed but also that of the autumn equinox. Two processes were involved in this attempt to restructure time: the de-christianization of the calendar (Year 1 being no longer the year of Christ's birth but the year the Republic was proclaimed) and the harmonization with 'natural' rhythms (nothing of importance happened on the cosmic plane on 1 January, whereas on 22 September a 'revolution' took place).

We know that the Republican calendar was not altogether successful and that it was abolished by Napoleon in 1805–6.

Moreover, it was never really embraced by the population at large, who never broke completely from the old temporal order. The most difficult moment in this cohabitation of the Gregorian and Republican calendars probably occurred in 1799 (year VIII). After the 18 Brumaire (9–10 November) uprising, during the real last year of the century, it became clear that the Revolution had 'revolved'. The old calendar had had its cruel revenge on the new. The gap between the two temporalities grew, and the two worlds found themselves side by side. Then the one slid over the other almost without touching it.

The changes to the calendar were only one aspect, albeit the most abstract and intellectual one, of a growing awareness of the emergence of a 'new time as opposed to the old time'. By 1789, the end of one time and the beginning of another was lived in such a direct, violent and blatantly obvious way as to make all symbolic representation highly problematic, indeed pointless. The desire for celebration remained, and, immediately after the fall of the Bastille, there was a desire to have a new national holiday 'for a revolution without precedence'. The history of this national holiday, which hoped to replace the Carnival and all festivals associated with it, is that of total failure.[38] The reason for this is that the Carnival, as we have seen the traditional festival that marked the rebirth of time, had been replaced by the Revolution itself. The relationship between the Revolution and its symbol is complex and the removal of the festival can be explained on several levels.[39] First and foremost, there was 'enlightened' thought, which considered the Carnival to be 'a festival fit for enslaved peoples'.[40] Following on logically from this was a perception of the Revolution as a 'real' reversal, one which was immediately overtaken – and this is significant – by a feeling of fear in the face of the Carnival as both strong principle and potential threat. The wearing of masks was strictly prohibited during the Terror, and 'any man disguised as a woman' was immediately condemned to death.[41] By way of compensation, a revolutionary dress code was created, but the Phrygian cap was soon replaced by the top hat of the 'independents' (illus. 7).[42]

Paradoxically, the *Ancien Régime* had already attempted to curb the Carnival before it was finally banned in 1790, though on neither occasion was it abolished completely. The Carnival

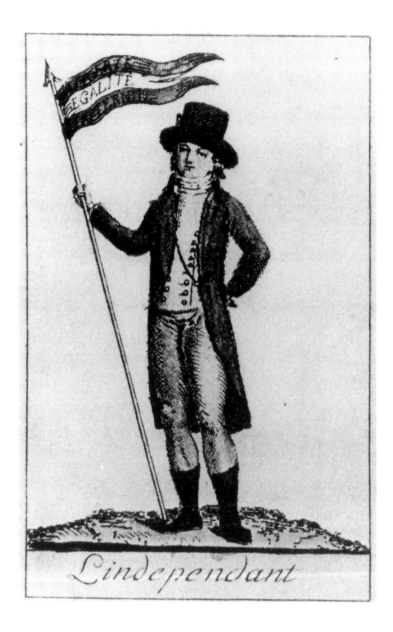

found other ways of manifesting itself, the most significant of which was through the popular press. Thanks to this new *medium*, there appeared a truly 'literal Carnival' in the guise of pamphlets published on the Sunday, Monday and Tuesday before Ash Wednesday.[43] These were quite dangerous, as it was not Reaction that was speaking through them but the Revolution that was mocking itself. We read: 'The folly of nations can change in name and face, but it always reverts to the character that best suits it.'[44] Or:

> For the people, carnival has been banned; but ever since the revolution first began you have established one for yourselves, that you enjoy showing neither modesty nor restraint. You forbid, under pain of fine, merchants to display masks and character costumes in their shops, but you do not blush to wear them yourselves on the most serious and important of occasions.[45]

Or again:

> At the time when Louis XVI was eating like a horse and drinking like a Knight Templar – and this time continues still; it is in the juice of the grape that the French monarch drowns his decadence – when Marie-Antoinette was engaging in the worst excesses of prostitution, when the depravity of the Court knew no bounds, Shrove Tuesday had a major role to play in the Palace of our Kings and at the heart of the Capital. At the time the Royal Sceptre was no more than a fool's bauble, and Parisians were at one and the same time drunk on pleasure and stooping under the weight of servitude and misery. Today the name of Shrove Tuesday appears pointlessly in the calendar; it no longer presides over madness and foolishness. However, France has never been as much disguised as it is at present; everyone is dressed-up. What now presides over these new costumes, clothes, hearts and faces? It is the Revolution, yes, the Revolution that has taken over the principles of Shrove Tuesday, and since 1 July 1789, we have seen the reign of perpetual carnival.[46]

In their unmistakable irony, these lines contain a truth. The Revolution was the 'making' of the Carnival just as, in its turn, the Carnival was the 'un-making' of a Revolution. Between 1789 and 1799, the rites of passage poured in, multiplied, jostled, and the end of a time was hidden behind masks whose symbols had to be deciphered.

2 The Carnival is Dead, Long Live the Carnival!

The putting to death of the Carnival was in itself a ritual. At the heart of the festival, the symbolic elimination of its principle signalled a climax. In its historical perspective, another death, no less ritualized, took place at the end of 1800. We shall endeavour to follow the Carnival's manifestations in the figurative representations of this period. This is not an easy process, being littered with clever traps. The first of these was the proliferation of the carnivalesque in eighteenth-century art, which could be found in its different forms virtually throughout Europe, from Italy (Tiepolo, Pietro Longhi) to England (Hogarth, Rowlandson). We find this proliferation less interesting for the simple reason that it signals the Carnival's taking root rather than its demise. What caught our attention instead was the terminal carnivalization at the turn of the century. Here the figures are fewer in number but richer and more complex. They have the added advantage of expressing themselves through such giants as Goya.

Experts have acknowledged the carnivalesque theme in Goya's work for a long time, but it is generally considered as particular to his art and indicative of a dialogue with popular Iberian traditions.[1] Without wishing to challenge this notion, which is no doubt an important one, our examination will focus on the ideological issues of a symbolic introduction already broached in the first chapter of this book. It strikes us that it is in this context that Goya's great strength lies. On the 'margins' of Europe and straddling the century (he was born near Saragossa in 1746 and died in Bordeaux in 1828), he best incarnates the figurative reflection of the major rites of passage.[2] We are convinced that it is only by giving it a central place in the artist's thinking and by outlining its inner core that we can fully appreciate its impact. Moreover, we shall only succeed in understanding the ritualization of the terminal Carnival that took place

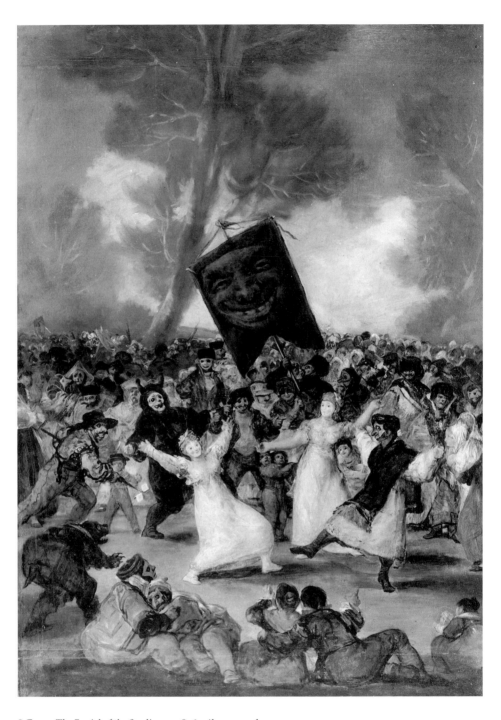

8 Goya, *The Burial of the Sardine*, c. 1816, oil on wood.

around 1800 if we undertake a detailed examination of the way Goya portrayed it.

We shall begin with the most complex and best-known painting the Spanish painter devoted to the theme (illus. 8).[3] The difficulties surrounding the picture's dating are symptomatic; it varies from 1793 to 1819, though experts have recently tended to favour the latter.[4] Its posthumous title – *The Burial of the Sardine* – gives rise to another difficulty. The fashionable Madrid ceremony that bore this name was held on Ash Wednesday and celebrated the end of the Carnival and the beginning of Lent. Both the ceremony and the Goya painting that depicts it were already creating problems at the end of the nineteenth century:

> What is this sardine that is being buried on Ash Wednesday at the precise moment when its reign is supposed to begin, that is to say at the beginning of the holy days of fasting and abstinence and when fish unseats meat? It is perhaps an antiphrasis created by the merry spirit of the people, a symbolic manifestation of a farewell that must be addressed, at the onset of Lent, to gastronomic delights.[5]

An answer already exists in this question, which places the solution within the context of a rhetoric that is both popular and sophisticated. As anthropological studies have demonstrated, the 'burial of the sardine' was one of the ceremonies held at the end of the carnival or, to be more precise, at the death of the Carnival.[6] The custom was widespread in Spain and also in the Western Pyrenees, but the story of what actually took place is ambiguous and not without contradictions. According to tradition, it was not a 'sardine' that was buried (for sardines would become essential nutrients during the days of abstinence to follow) but half a pig. This half-pig was shaped like a giant sardine, and the resulting formal and symbolic games of opposition between 'lean days' and 'fat days' initiated a whole network of propitiatory inversions and ironies. Hence what was *said* was 'sardine', but what was *meant* was pork, as though attempting to make the Carnival last longer, at least on the level of linguistic untruths. The untruth expressed with the help of the antiphrasis (the sardine is, *in reality*, a half-pig) alleviated the sadness prompted by the farewell. On the other hand, if we take the expression 'burial of the sardine' literally (as was often done, it would

33

appear),[7] this gives the disturbing impression that the Carnival triumphed over Lent on the very day when the latter should have begun, and that the 'meat' principle was therefore triumphant at the very moment when it should have been buried.

What is certain is that there was no easing off, on the part of ordinary people, of the pressure to continue the Carnival beyond Shrove Tuesday into Ash Wednesday.[8] And it is in this context that the ceremony of the Burial of the sardine became the final subterfuge: better a sad festival than no festival at all! It is here that the shift performed by Goya's small painting becomes both striking and troubling. This will become much clearer if we can trace its origins with the help of the preparatory drawing in the Prado (illus. 9). It was never Goya's habit to make preliminary sketches to be developed later on, so the existence of this drawing is in every way exceptional. It is as though there was an urgent need in this case – and in this case only – to have two versions. We see that his first idea was to create a scene that depicted the triumph of Religion, and thereby the triumph of Lent. It is monks and nuns who express their joy at the death of Carnival beneath the Papal insignias that decorate their banner. X-rays have revealed that in the painting, the large, dark, grinning face was added later, thereby covering the word MORTU<U>S, which had been there, just as it is in the drawing.[9]

An internal antiphrasis would therefore appear to have governed the inception of this painting, which now falls into place with the help of an important change in meaning. If in this drawing Goya was seeing the 'burial of the sardine' as the victory – grotesque or burlesque, it does not really matter – of religion over the festival, in the final painting mourning becomes a triumph and is projected onto an overcast sky, as though to deconstruct it. In place of the insignias of power and death, the banner displays a broad smile. A delirious heaving crowd carries this new banner, which seems not to want to remain upright. Its oblique position at the centre of the image underscores its instability and highlights the erratic dynamism of the human mass. In truth, this is neither a circle dance nor a procession, but rather a distant memory of both. The movements of the participants are unsteady; the dance is disorganized and ungainly; the crowd's progress has turned into drunken confusion. Masks still cover faces; the sexes are

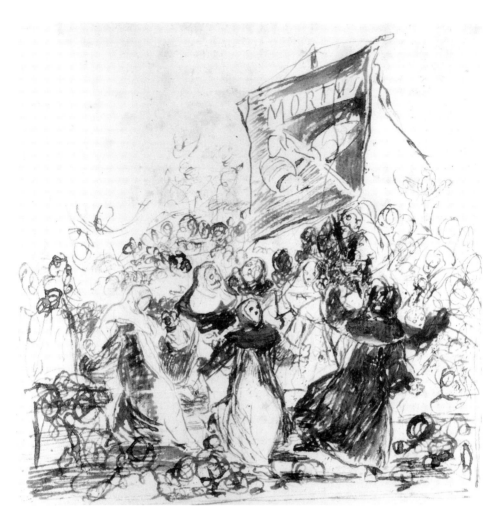

9 Goya, *The Burial of the Sardine*, c. 1816, pen and sepia ink.

muddled up; children rub shoulders with adults; animals (real and pretend) are in amongst the people. Two menacing creatures appear at the left of the image under the inquisitive eyes of the spectators seated on the ground and hungry for entertainment: a man wearing a large black hat armed with a spear and a bear with long claws and a gaping jaw. Their attention is focused on the dancing women.

Anthropological studies proved extremely useful when it came to interpreting this image, since attention had for a long time been focused on the many versions of the Carnival that tackled the *topos* of the bear emerging from the cave over the period when this particular festival reaches its climax. In some cases, the bear (or man in a bearskin), known as Martin,

35

throws himself on the young women or, more often than not, on just one of them. Usually called Rosette, she is actually a young man disguised as a woman whose blonde plaits have been braided into a crown, whose face is powdered white and whose tight bodice is ready to burst.[10] It is difficult to ascertain the exact role played by these ancient rites of spring in Goya's work. However, what can be said is that even if his interest was more than purely documentary, he was certainly no ignoramus. It is interesting to note that within the context of the most detailed literary description of the Madrid festival of the burial of the sardine by the author Ramon de Mesonero Romanos (1839), the festival is referred to as 'a burlesque and profane parody revealed in all'.[11] Asked to give his opinion about the relationship between his literary description, Goya's pictorial description and reality, Romanos said:

> With reference to Goya's painting (with which I am not familiar), I think that neither he nor I know any more about this Bacchanal, which is not the monopoly of Madrid, and which comes from very far away. (. . .) But I think that Goya has done what I have done, that is to say, he has taken possession of a fact, and he has embroidered around it all the necessary decorative details in order to produce an artistic or literary painting. Besides, I am convinced that it is no more than I have painted or Goya imagined and that everything can be reduced to a simple formula or to a pretext to break the fast for another day rather than the representation of the death of the sardine.[12]

This account is extremely valuable because it highlights the fact that shortly after Goya produced his painting, its fictional nature, which reinterprets a transgression by accentuating its contractions, was acknowledged. The transition from preparatory drawing to painting, with the implied change of mood, would appear to confirm this impression. It shows that the artist was interested in depicting the confusion and paradox of the 'carnivalesque' disorder that prevailed over the first day of Lent. Disorder as a sin was a common theme in anti-carnivalesque sermons and usually referred to the abuse that went on during meat days. Ash Wednesday would finally come along to put a stop to it: 'Compare these sacred ceremonies and sad thoughts to the impetuous torrent of disorder, debauchery and outbursts that engulf Christian folk during this period,'[13] one of these sermons stated before going on to say: 'What madness is this, that having so surrendered oneself to debauchery, to disorder and to greed, the Church must have recourse to penitence and fasting?'[14] This sermon (given in 1783) never once mentioned the idea that disorder (*el desorden*), depravity (*la disolución*), debauchery (*el desenfreno*) and entertainment (*la diversión*) might continue even into the first day of Lent.

Once again, Goya's transition from drawing to painting proves to be significant. In the drawing, the portrayal of disorder can be found in the actual freedom with which the lines of ink create a large and spectacular tangle, but when it comes to showing due respect to the theme – the triumph of Lent – the artist was more 'conformist'. In the painting, the disorder is that of a carnival that does not want to die. The formula is original on both the level of content and that of form. We should perhaps draw attention to this second level, since there were no great models to help Goya. Apart from a few exceptions,[15] the indistinct moving mass had not yet become a codified subject in art, neither had disorder become a theme to be depicted. It is highly likely that this is why the artist himself did not refer to his *Burial* as a painting (*quadro/cuadro*), (although, as we have seen, his early commentators did), but rather as a *borrón en tabla* (something like a 'blot', 'rough draft' or 'doodle on panel'). In other words, like something quite contradictory, since it brought together the solidity of the traditional support of a painting and the stylistic and conceptual 'disorder' of a new representation.[16] The 'doodle', as the true and proper carnivalization of 'painting', is an idea that emerged late in Goya's thinking, and the painting we have just analyzed is the most complete manifestation of this, for it brings together form and content in an exemplary way.

If we wish to go into this subject in greater depth and examine its sources, we shall need to consider the alternative modes of expression used by the artist rather than the 'great paintings' he worked on for most of his life. It is the etcher, the author of the small, quick sketches, who will make his beliefs known more readily. An examination of such sketches reveals that the carnivalesque theme of reversals was constant and that it accompanied Goya throughout his long and turbulent career. The later formalization of the relationship of reversal can only be understood once a thematically structured study

of his work has been undertaken. Only within the framework
of such a study will carnivalesque 'disorder' reveal its figures.
Let us begin with the most important.

THE THIRD SEX (OR NEITHER AND BOTH)

There is an early piece of work produced by the young Goya
(by this we mean produced before his 1792/3 crisis and illness)
that anticipates the reversal of sexual roles, which became a
much more frequent theme in his later drawings and prints
(illus. 10). We do not know what inspired the creation of this

10 Goya,
Mythological Scene,
1784, oil on canvas.

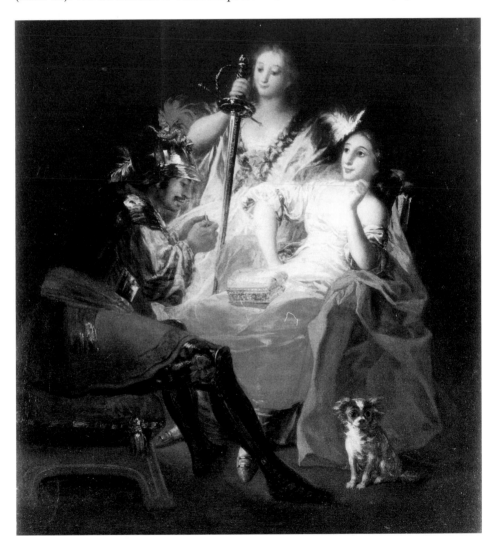

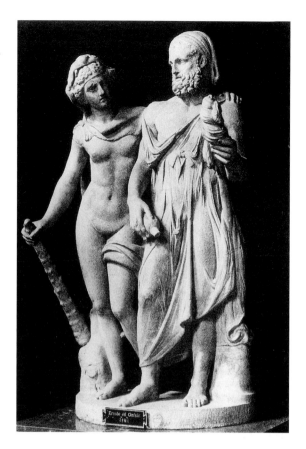

11 *Hercules and Omphale*, 1st century BC.

work, and experts have found it extremely difficult to interpret.[17] The title, and therefore the theme, is problematic, and
the tradition from which it comes uncertain. According to tradition, the story illustrates a secondary episode in the adventures of the great Greek hero Hercules, who, carrying out the
orders of the Oracle of Delphi, set off for Lydia, where he
became the slave (in keeping with other slave-spouse variants) of Queen Omphale. There he was forced to wear
women's clothes and do women's work, while Omphale wore
his lion skin and carried his club.[18] This tale of castration is all the
more powerful as the hero is the very symbol of masculinity.

As far back as the classical period, the story of Hercules and
Omphale was depicted as a parable of transsexuality.[19] A
small neo-Attic statuary group dating from the first century
BC (illus. 11) shows the hero dressed in a chiton and wearing a
woman's headdress that contrasts with his curly beard. In his
left hand, he carries a distaff and in his right hand, a shuttle.

39

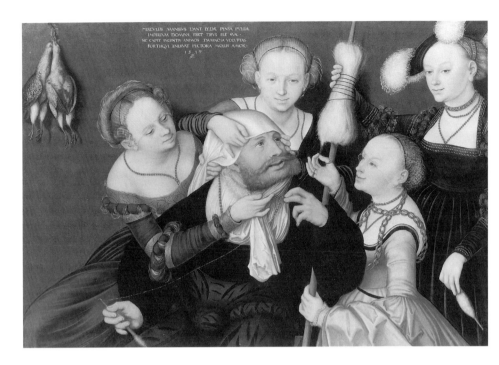

Omphale, on the other hand, is as naked as a Greek athlete of the same period. She puts a protective arm around the great hero, gazing tenderly at him as she clutches his club in her other hand. This reversal of traditional roles, very simply expressed, can also be found in art of the Renaissance. Lucas Cranach, for example, tackled the theme on more than one occasion.[20] A brief examination of one of Cranach's works might shed light on Goya's work. In one of Cranach's versions (illus. 12), Hercules is portrayed as a German knight, whose beard and – in the preparatory drawing[21] – other manly attributes have been highlighted by the painter. Hercules is in the process of being dressed in women's clothes by three young women with plunging necklines, while a fourth, the most elegant of all (probably Omphale herself), looks on. Two of the women are covering the hero's bearded face with a shawl, while another is teaching him to spin, having already placed the distaff under his arm. A Latin inscription illuminates the scene and connects with the eyes of one of the girls who stares at the spectator. In this way, the latter is given to understand that there is a message in the painting that is of direct concern to the viewer: to give in to the charms of voluptuousness makes a man look ridiculous and strengthens the power of

12 Lucas Cranach, *Hercules and Omphale*, 1537, beech wood.

women. It is interesting to note that while Cranach portrayed the burlesque feminization of man, he was rather more restrained and extremely respectful when it came to depicting the masculinization of woman, which ancient texts and the tradition of the 'world upside down', already in existence in Cranach's time, would have permitted him to stress. Through the use of interacting allusions, he thematized the inversion of sexual roles that the intelligent spectator would understand to be at the heart of the new power relationship established in the Hercules/Omphale dyad. It was the woman who now had to hold the spindle (an ancient phallic symbol) and the man who had to work with the distaff (an ancient symbol of the female sex). But the spindle (*phallos*/phallus), the only object to have a double function in this painting, is also directly related to the name of the one who now possesses it (Omphale), thereby personifying her castrating role. So the spectator, in order to understand the painting completely, had to have some knowledge of Latin and maybe a bit of Greek, but most certainly an understanding of euphemisms and popular puns.

Goya's approach was different, and his innovations were significant, so much so that we might well ask ourselves if we are in fact dealing with a mythological scene (illus. 9). There is no direct appeal to the spectator as there is in Cranach's painting, no moralizing inscription and no looks of admonition – that of the small dog in the foreground is just a last caricatured remnant. The three characters are preoccupied by the unusual activity of the moustachioed, armoured warrior in the left foreground: he is threading a needle. The feminization of Hercules (as we shall refer to him for the sake of convenience) takes place not through transvestism, but through the activity he is engaged in. The exchange of symbols corresponded to the topoi of the upside-down world, where women had weapons and men had women's tools (illus. 2). The significance here is to be found in the exchange of distaff and sword (or spear or, later, rifle). Goya's solution is an extremely personal one. It can be found neither in the iconography of Hercules and Omphale, nor in that of the upside-down world. It points to the antithesis between 'tiny' and 'gigantic', between sensitivity and strength, between sewing implement and weapon of war. The position of the two main characters' feet might indirectly suggest an erotic interpretation in which the inverted male/female dialectic is brought to light through the central role played by the sword, its phallic verticality and transfer.

The mythological handling of the theme of symbolic castration is an anomaly in Goya's work, but the theme itself is a constant. To follow its mutations would no doubt prove enlightening. We shall limit ourselves to a single example. *Capricho* 35 (illus. 13) depicts life in Madrid at the end of the eighteenth century, through a mix, typical of Goya, of the concrete (clothes) and the abstract (space). The artist is thereby suggesting that the scene we are witnessing is both dated and timeless, particular and universal. A young man is allowing three women to shave him; one holds the razor, the other two hold the barber's instruments. The young man's face is almost as smooth as a young girl's. Furthermore, the sheet wrapped around his shoulders makes it even more difficult to identify his sex, so much so that we might even be led to believe that this is just women having fun. However, the grammatical form of the inscription (*Le descañona*) proves the seated person is indeed a man. It can be interpreted in at least two ways ('She is shaving him the wrong way'/ 'She is plucking him'), whereas the ambiguity of the text-image binomial is even more complex. What we have in effect is not only a reformulation of the very same situation illustrated in the Classical repertoire through the Hercules/Omphale theme (illus. 12) but also the same pyramidal compositional blueprint that establishes women 'on top' and man 'underneath'.[22]

All that Goya's misogynous as well as misanthropic *Capricho* does is give an ancient *topos* a new form: that of the feminization of man under the control of women. The eighteenth century was full of people bemoaning this fact (has there ever been a time when they were not?). In *L'Année merveilleuse ou les hommes-femmes* (1754), for example, the author, Father Coyer, predicted a time of 'great change' when 'men would be changed into women, and women into men'. He went on to say:

> So that we shall therefore no longer be surprised to see male individuals wearing earrings, making tapestries, entertaining from their beds at midday, interrupting a serious conversation to talk with their dog, speaking to their own faces in a mirror, fondling their lace, losing their tempers

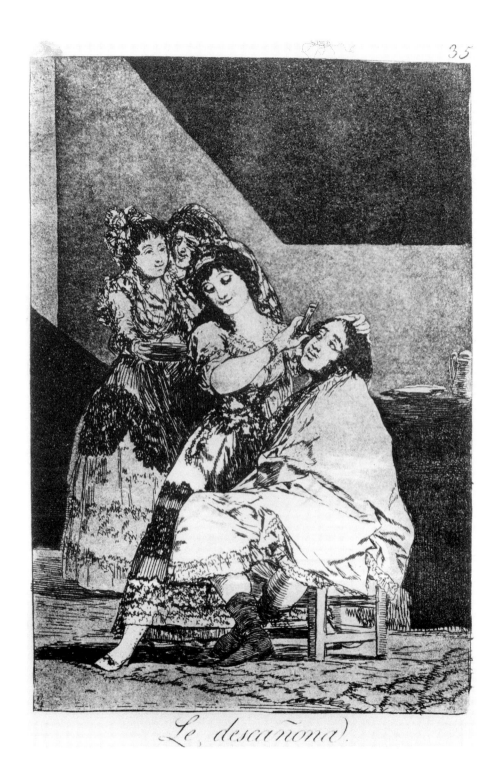

Le descañona.

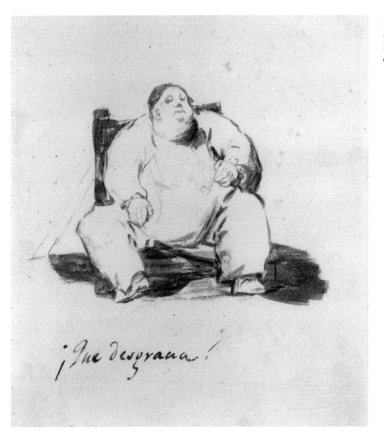

over a broken maggot, swooning over a sick parrot, and finally revealing all their charms to the opposite sex.[23]

The specular relationship between the mythological painting (*Hercules and Omphale*) and the criticism of social customs (*Capricho* 35) is echoed in Goya's work by the position the artist gives in his drawings to the theme of gender-role reversal. The drawings appear to be a coarse and direct experience in which the carnivalesque emerges clearly. It is in this light that a whole series of images, involving the traditional canons of masculinity, must be examined.

Several of these images are to be found in what the experts refer to as the *Sketchbook Journal*,[24] a rich collection of drawings by Goya, which is full of short and sharp observations. In one of these (illus. 14), we see an extremely fat man with a double chin, seated on a bench. The inscription at the bottom of the page is an exclamation: *Que desgracia!* (What a disaster!). In

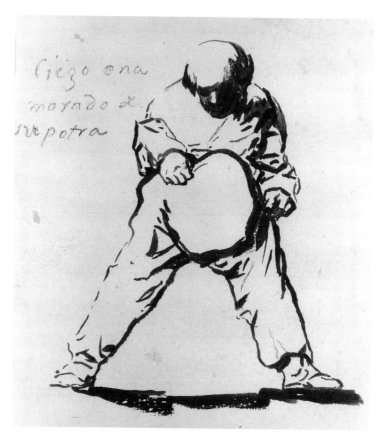

15 Goya, *'Blindman Enamoured of His Bulge'*, c. 1800, sepia wash drawing.

another (illus. 15), we see a person standing, legs apart, looking at his round belly. The inscription identifies him as a 'blindman enamoured of his bulge' (*ciego enamorado de su potra*). A third (illus. 16) shows a paunchy individual of indeterminable gender (because of the raised skirt, it was for a long time thought to be a woman);[25] the inscription here reads 'Aunt Gila's little queer' (*El Maricón de la tia Gila*).

These drawings are three variations on the originally carnivalesque motif of the grotesque body. Bakhtin and others[26] have come up with detailed explanations as to how the distended and exaggerated-out-of-all-proportion belly (which in particular contexts has even spawned such pseudo-divinities as St Pansart, Sancto Pança, Zanpanzar or Mardi Gras) was the exemplary incarnation of the very spirit of the Carnival. Exuberance, the adulation of worldly goods, the vindication of fertility and the importance accorded the human body's lower regions – are all elements that make these 'round-bellied'

45

El Maricón de la tía Gila

figures indispensable to the carnivalesque world. And yet
there are times when the pure grotesque gives way to tragi-
comedy. This is what we believe happens in Goya's drawings,
where certain elements give rise to the hypothesis that
another carnivalesque motif emerges next to the image of the
grotesque body, in order to present us with a reversal that is
both hilarious and dramatic: the motif of the man-woman in
its most powerful version, that of the 'pregnant man'. A fourth
drawing, from the *Bordeaux Sketchbook* (illus. 17), portrays the
theme of cross-dressing and can help us further in this connection. What its caption refers to as a 'malicious fool' (*loco
picaro*) (today we would be more likely to refer to a 'malicious
queer') is a man dressed as a woman. Pierre Gassier described
it well:

> Wearing a hat, earrings and dainty shoes, he disguised
> himself as a woman, and then just to complicate matters, he

made for himself an impressive pregnancy with the help of a few thick cushions tucked under his shirt, the corners of which he tied behind his back, and went so far as to bend his knees so as to make his enormous abdomen stick out as far as possible.[27]

Cross-dressing was very much part of the carnivalesque ritual and formed its own system with its companions licence and reversal. The protruding stomach was also a figure of excess which, in this instance, became part of the system in a dialectical manner – that is to say, as excess in reversal and in licence. Goethe, with his usual sharpness, in fact captured this relationship in a performance given by a Carnival 'queer':

> At that moment, having had a fright, the pregnant woman feels unwell; a chair is brought, the other women see to her,

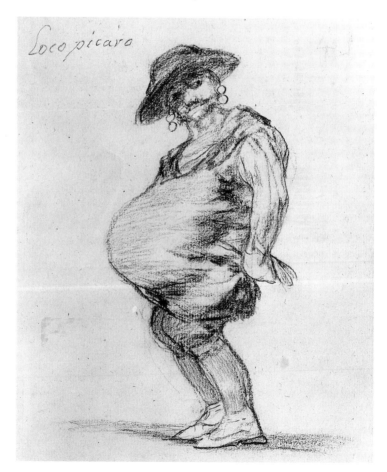

17 Goya, 'Malicious Fool', c. 1824–8, black chalk.

she thrashes about pathetically, and, to the delight of her assistants, unexpectedly gives birth to a nondescript, shapeless being. Having given their performance, the troupe sets off to play the same farce, on another fellow-creature, in another venue.[28]

If we do not find similar scenes in Goya, despite the fact that the myth of the man giving birth was fairly prevalent in Spain,[29] it is because his work is more than an illustration of the Carnival; it is a study of comic reversals. It is this aspect of the drawings in the *Sketchbook Journal* that make them so valuable. They cannot be considered as sketches *per se* depicting carnivalesque situations, nor can they be considered as studies of social mores. Rather, they are a critical gloss around the *topos* of the pregnant man.

This *topos* has its own history, of which Roberto Zapperi made an in-depth study.[30] Zapperi demonstrated the importance of the part played by the debate that surrounded sexual customs and the roles given the partners in sexual union. Within the framework of this debate, even male masturbation, regarded as sex without a partner, is a symbol of erotic otherness which can give rise to such phenomena as self-impregnation. In all probability, this is the variant Goya had in mind in drawing 64 of the *Sketchbook Journal* (illus. 15). The *potra* (usually translated as 'bulge') with which the character is enamoured is nothing but a euphemism. The man is enamoured of his 'beam', and his pregnancy is a solitary and reprehensible pregnancy. We shall have occasion to return – in another context and in greater detail – to the ways in which Goya made use of puns in images that were erotic in nature. For the present, we shall limit ourselves to pointing out that the explanatory inscription is an important feature: the 'lover' (*enamorado*) is named with a broken and poorly written word that reveals him to be an *ona-morado*. The phoneme *Ona-* needs no explanation. The moneme *morado*, however, is polysemantic: it refers to the colour violet-red, but also signifies 'full', 'stuffed', 'bursting'. To love one's 'beam' too much, to love it blindly, produces an outlandish character – a 'onen-amoured' – whose fat belly is both a sign of his disgrace and also his punishment.

The misdemeanour of 'Aunt Gila's little queer' is quite different (illus. 16). Here, and in a way that is much more overt than in the drawing just analyzed, the cause of the male pregnancy is the result of homosexuality. Impregnation 'that goes against nature' was a theme that had been portrayed a century earlier in Rubens's great *Drunken Silenus*, which has been copied and interpreted many times over the centuries (illus. 18). The anal coupling of the obese Silenus and the muscular black man is only one of the narrative elements of this painting. The event is treated with a certain restraint, but it is clear enough to leave us in no doubt as to what is going on.[31] It is interesting to note how the classical bacchanalian theme became carnivalized at the approach of the eighteenth century. A drawing by Watteau after Rubens (illus. 19) transforms the bacchic festival into a carnival procession and the central character into a true and proper 'queer'. His sexual organ has disappeared into his bushy pubic hair, and his companion is no longer clutching his hips, as is the case in Rubens's painting, but his breasts, thereby increasing the sexual ambiguity of the scene.[32]

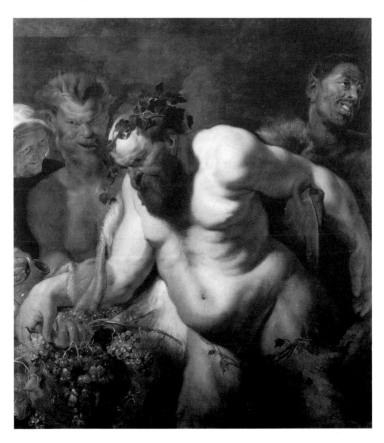

18 Studio of Peter Paul Rubens, *Drunken Silenus*, first half of the 17th century, oil on wood.

49

19 Jean-Antoine Watteau, *The March of Silenus*, c. 1715, coloured chalks.

We must now examine the significance of drawing 21 of the *Sketchbook Journal* (illus. 14), particularly the 'disaster' that has befallen its hero. This misfortune is nothing to do with obesity, as one might at first suspect (at the time, obesity was still a sign of prosperity), but with the disgraceful pregnancy, the product of a reversal of positions during the sexual act, long anathematized by the Church. Zapperi recalled how the polemic surrounding male/female coital positions came up against that of the more general theme of *on top* and *underneath*.[33] Indeed in Spain, the erotic horse was condemned *expressis verbis* in the treatise by the Jesuit Thomas Sánchez entitled *De sancto matrimonio sacramento*, where the only position considered to be natural was *mulier succuba, vir autem incubus*. Sánchez condemned the reversed position as a mortal sin:

> This way of going about things is absolutely contrary to the laws of nature because it prevents the seed from the male ejaculation from being received and retained by the female vase. Moreover, it is not only the position of the person that is being reversed but also their condition: and it is in the nature of things that the male should perform and the female submit. The very fact that the male places himself underneath makes him passive while the woman by

putting herself on top becomes active. Who could deny seeing that nature is filled with horror at such a turning upside down?[34]

Despite its simplicity, Goya's drawing reveals its sources of inspiration. These are not found in 'reality' ('in reality' there are no pregnant men), but in the study of sexual distinctions as bequeathed us by tradition. Anatomical pictures whose aim it was to illustrate the effects of pregnancy on the female body, or the broadsheets on empirical sexology readily available – it would appear – from apothecaries and healer-barbers, can be considered as possible models for drawing 21 of the *Sketchbook Journal*.[35] Goya's reversal is executed with an irony that is unmistakable, but whose moral intentions are difficult to establish with any precision. The flexible relationship between irony and moralism has in fact been one of the main problems involved in interpreting two of his major series of etchings: *Los Caprichos* (Caprices) and the *Disparates* (Absurdities). Rather than go into the subject at great length here, it would seem more appropriate to concentrate once again on the carnivalesque forms tackled by Goya. In this context, there is an indirect response to the question just formulated. In effect, in the world of the Carnival, morality does not have a great role to play, since it is also, and above all, a time of absolute permissiveness, a time for gaiety when the world is turned upside down. In the drawings just analyzed, carnivalesque examples and situations are the object of short but careful observations. They are extra-temporal examples and situations that can be found in any Carnival and at any period in history.

It is interesting to note that Goya carried out these observations fairly late in his career. In his major series of etchings – first in the *Caprichos* – as well as in the accompanying drawings that are the product of the same mind, the carnivalesque is integrated into more specific and more codified social situations. This claim can be corroborated with the aid of a drawing from what, for the sake of convenience, we will refer to as the *Madrid Sketchbook* (illus. 20).

Pierre Gassier remarked that this drawing is a genuine preview of the grotesque or caricatured representation of man and his body.[36] What strikes us as even more significant is the fact that the centre of the drawing is a dialogue around the male

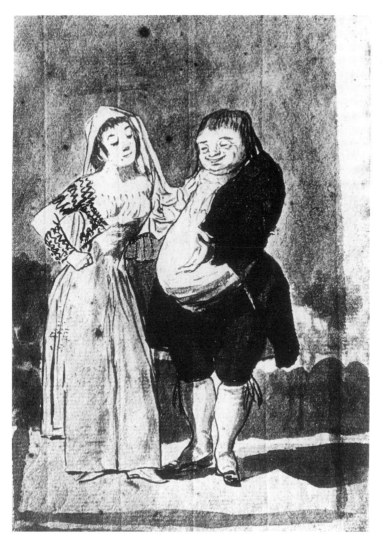

20 Goya, Drawing
B. 49: *Young Woman
with a Paunchy Man*,
1796–7, wash on
paper.

character's protruding stomach. The motif is carnivalesque,
but the image conceals its sources. Let us examine the language. Several elements draw attention to the grotesque nature
of the distended stomach – first the woman's expression and
then the man's gesture. Other signs, less obvious but no less
important, can be added: the woman's slender waist creates a
counter-curve that accentuates the protuberance of the male
stomach. In the absence of further information and especially
for want of any explicit or implicit inscription, our interpretation must stop here. Nevertheless, we can quite legitimately say
that this drawing illustrates a situation of reversal (the man has

a stomach that the woman does not have). If there is carnival-ization, it is not obvious (as was the case with the other draw-ings). What Goya is showing us instead is a reversed society and, implicitly, a carnivalized world.

What is so striking in this context is how frequently, in Goya's work, the theme of the feminization of man comes up and how rarely the masculinization of woman, especially since in contemporary thought on the decline in mores, this particular theme was recurrent: 'These days they wear men's clothes, a frock coat with three collars, hair tied back in a ponytail, a cane in their hand, shoes with flat heels.'[37] Father Coyer wondered whether: '. . . if they removed the coat of colour they apply, would we not detect the signs of strength on their faces, their skin thickening, their features growing coarse and their beard sprouting?'[38]

In Goya's work, there is a unique example – once again a drawing – that tackles the theme of masculinization in the form of the motif of the bearded lady (illus. 21). The context of the *Black-edged Sketchbook* from which this drawing is taken shows that the artist was more interested in depicting 'fair-ground freaks' than in criticizing particular social customs.[39] The contrast with the quotation from Father Coyer could not be stronger. Like many other eighteenth-century authors, Father Coyer used the 'bearded lady' motif to be ironic about the emergence of a new type of being, the thinking woman – indeed the philosophical woman[40] – whereas Goya was attracted by the otherness of this spectacle. The inscription that accompanies the drawing provides it with a historical foundation: 'This woman was painted in Naples by José Ribera known as the Spagnoletto, *c.* 1640.' The inscription is probably more recent and of doubtful authenticity – a false inscription therefore, given the object of the representation. It is nevertheless significant because of the way in which the drawing was perceived, as a gloss on a 'portrait' that already existed. The similarities between Goya's drawing and Ribera's canvas (illus. 68) are, despite their common theme and despite the inscription, extremely weak. Ribera left us a double portrait, commissioned in 1631, we know, by the Spanish Viceroy to Naples.[41] We see (as the conspicuous inscription tells us with its many details) the bearded lady Magdalena Ventura, at the age of 52, carrying her third child in her arms and accompanied by her husband. It is not the

53

21 Goya, Drawing
E. 22: *'This Woman
was Painted in
Naples by José Ribera
Known as the
Spagnoletto'*, c. 1640,
1803–12, India ink
wash.

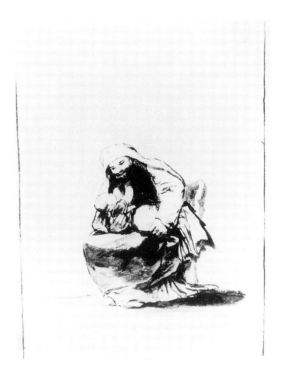

22 Giovanni
Battista Gaulli
(known as
Baciccio), *Saint
Joseph with the Child
Jesus*, c. 1670–85, oil
on canvas.

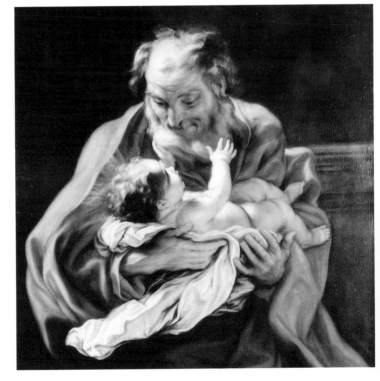

first time that an artist has left us a painting of this kind; others were recorded as early as the sixteenth century, the best known being the portrait of the famous Brigida del Rio (known as *The Bearded Lady of Peñaranda*) by Juan Sánchez Cotán (illus. 23). Both examples deal with images of 'miracles' (the inscription that accompanies Magdalena Ventura speaks of a *magnum naturale miraculum*); artists made their own contributions to depicting 'truthfully' that which was unbelievable. Admittedly, compared to Sánchez Cotán, Ribera had made some progress. Brigida del Rio could very well have been a man dressed as a woman, and the painting could be seen as having been created under the sign of Hermaphrodite. Indeed, as has been demonstrated recently,[42] the scholarly Sebastián de Covarrubias returned to this painting in one of his *Emblemas morales* (Madrid, 1610), where he transformed it into an *imago* (illus. 24) accompanied by an *inscriptio*: *Nevtrvmque et vutrvmque*. This direct quote from Ovid (*Metamorphoses*, IV, 379) refers to the mythical Hermaphrodite as a double being who was *neither* or *both* sexes at one and the same time. The *subscriptio* develops this idea ('I am hic, & haec, & hoc. I declare myself to be both man and woman and a third . . .') and ends on a moralizing note: 'any man who looks at me will be – if he lives in an effeminate manner – another myself.' The 'miracle' could not have been turned more completely – or more wrongly – into a sermon.

Ribera's painting also depicts a double being – that is, both masculine and feminine – but it is different from the Brigida del Rio portrait inasmuch as it shows the co-presence of combined characteristics – beard and breasts – and emphasizes an existential situation to which the infant and the astounded husband also belong. In order to fully understand the issue, we need to delve deeper into its comparison with the 'bearded lady of Peñaranda'. Let us read one of the seventeenth-century texts that refers to it:

> Hippocrates wrote of the Eretruse woman whose voice, when her periods stopped, became masculine, husky and deep, and who grew a beard, enough for her to pass as a man, a fact that, according to Aristotle, happens to many women, as we have seen in Spain in the case of the woman from Peñaranda, whose voice became deep and whose beard grew so great that it covered her chest.[43]

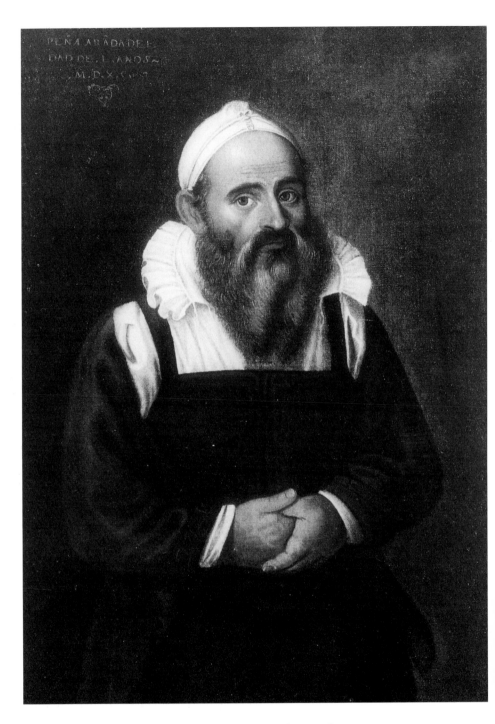

23 Juan Sánchez Cotán, *Brigida del Rio, the Bearded Lady of Peñaranda,*
1590, oil on canvas.

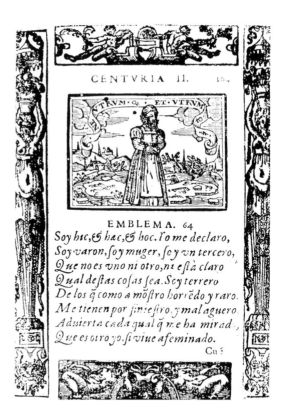

24 Sebastián de Covarrubias, *Emblem 64*, from *Emblemas morales* (Madrid, 1610).

CENTVRIA II.

EMBLEMA. 64

Soy hic, & hac, & hoc. To me declaro,
Soy varon, foy muger, foy vn tercero,
Que no es vno ni otro, ni eſtà claro
Qual deſtas coſas ſea. Scy terrero
De los q̃ como a mõſtro horrẽdo y raro.
Me tienen por ſinieſtro, y mal aguero.
Aduierta cada qual q̃ me ha mirad.,
Que es otro yo. ſi viue afeminado.

By basing himself on the 'experts', the author of this text is endeavouring to find a scientific explanation for the phenomenon of facial hair and its direct link with the cessation of menstruation. It is when we compare Ribera's painting to this scientific explanation that its *magnum miraculum* nature is revealed: according to the inscription, Magdalena Ventura's beard began to grow when she was around 37 years old, which (as the picture testifies) did not prevent her from giving birth to a child whom she breast-fed herself. Magdalena Ventura was therefore not a woman who (like Brigida del Rio) became masculine at the onset of the menopause, but a woman whose maternal functions were still active (adds the inscription) even at the age of 52.

And yet the painting is a mixture of docu-evidence and symbolic imagery. The emblematic insertions leave it wide open to a more complex interpretation: on the pedestal (which also acts in support of the edifying inscription) is the shell of a sea snail, a distaff and a spindle. The snail is traditionally the bisexual being par excellence,[44] and the spindle/distaff dyad,

57

as we have already seen, also had well-defined sexual connotations. The presence of these symbolic objects in Ribera's painting on the one hand, and in the prints depicting the world upside down on the other, rules out the possibility of any similarities being attributed to coincidence in order to establish a system of symbolization common to both representations. But in the Ribera painting, there are also allusions which still have to be deciphered, whereas in the prints of the world upside down (illus. 2), whose didactic nature is evident, the symbols are organized into coherent systems; the reversal of the husband/wife roles, the portrayal of double beings (the bearded mother with breasts displayed) and the emblematic snail can be placed on the compositional axis.

We would at this point be quite justified in wondering what Goya had absorbed of this whole tradition. In all probability, his bearded lady is not the same as Ribera's, and the message contained in the drawing is also quite different. It is difficult to believe that the drawing could have been the first notation for a painting. The only element that might suggest this is the double frame surrounding the pictorial field. It should be noted, however, that this is a feature common to all the drawings in the *Black-edged Sketchbook* and that none of them ever ended up as actual 'paintings'. On the other hand, the integration of Goya's bearded lady into the context of 'miracles-images' and of the imagination of a world of exceptions and transgressions remains justifiable. What Goya emphasized in this particular drawing is this mother/father's splendid beard, which is an object of fun for the child who buries his hands in it. It is imperative that, in this context, we examine the striking iconographic similarities between the drawing and certain religious paintings of the Counter-Reformation that portray bearded saints (Joseph, Felix, etc.) fussing over infants (illus. 22).[45] There are several ways of approaching these similarities. The first is to attribute them to chance. The second is to see them as products of a 'reversal of signification' (*Bedeutungsinversion*), a fairly common process in the eighteenth century in general and in Goya's work in particular, and a mechanism through which a sacred theme provides the compositional solution for a profane scene.[46] Finally, the third approach, an extension of the second, looks for the significance behind the reversal of the sacred into the profane.

Let us look for a moment at this last option. In his study

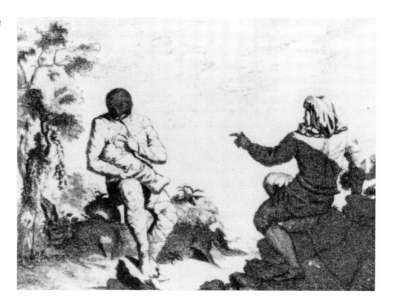

25 Italian, *Harlequin Suckling His Child*, 18th century, print.

devoted to the theme of 'paternal milk' and to its significance in traditional cultures, Roberto Lionetti draws attention to points of contact between this motif and that of the pregnant man and its carnivalesque ramifications. He also draws attention to the archaic nature of the figure of the breast-feeding father, which, he says, goes at least as far back as the mythical saint Mammes of Caesarea (also known as Mammas or Mammet), none other than the counterpart of the ancient mother goddess Ma (i.e. Cybele). He considers this early reversal to be one of the oldest manifestations of 'breast envy' on the part of men, the others being indulged during carnivalesque festivals in the form of cross-dressing.[47] In this last context, the best-known ludic incarnation is that of Harlequin as mother (illus. 25), which was certainly extremely popular during the eighteenth century.

In light of these considerations, we can place Goya's drawing at the junction of several interpretative codes. The 'bearded mother' has something of the 'paternal saint' about her as well as something of the comedy of the fair. This duality shows that transgression creates complex iconography at the heart of which the sacred and profane can communicate.

ON GOYA'S BESTIARY

In *Dialektik der Aufklärung*, Max Horkheimer and Theodor Adorno emphasize the central role played by the man/beast

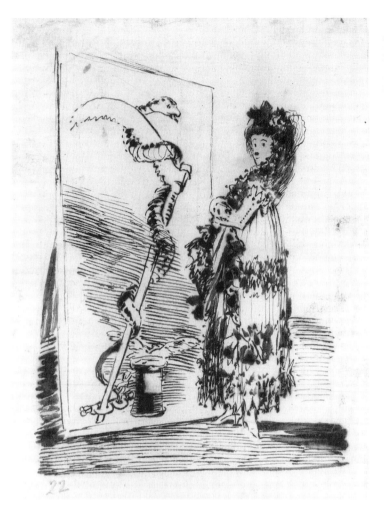

26 Goya, *Woman
and Serpent*, 1797–9,
pen and sepia
wash with reddish
scumble over entire
sheet.

relationship, in an attempt – essential to the spirit of the
Enlightenment – to define the idea of 'man'.[48] No artist has
been able to define the fluctuating nature of this relationship
better than Goya; to study it in all its complexity is a task that
goes far beyond the limits of this book. We shall therefore
limit ourselves to examining only one aspect, which we could
refer to as 'the specular relationship and its mutations'. Here
the artist himself comes to our assistance, with a series of
drawings in which this relationship is described in detail. The
series, generally known to as *The Magic Mirror*,[49] is not part of
any 'sketchbook' and is usually considered to have been produced around 1797–9 – i.e. at the same time as the *Caprichos*.
The drawings in it have no pre-established order, so our

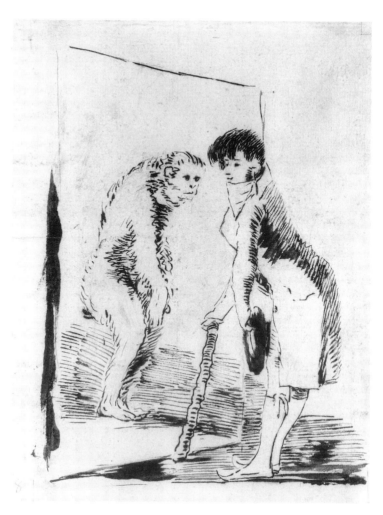

27 Goya, *Dandy and Monkey*, 1797–9, pen and sepia wash with reddish scumble over entire sheet.

analysis will follow a possible but not mandatory sequencing.

In the first drawing (illus. 26), we see a woman dressed in the clothes of a *maja* standing in front of a mirror from which a serpent coiled around a scythe gazes out at her (an earlier version in sanguine shows a crutch rather than a scythe). The second drawing (illus. 27) depicts a similar situation, although the protagonists are a young man and a monkey (there is a variant in red ink wash and sanguine (illus. 34) in which the monkey is replaced by a creature being tortured by an iron collar). The third drawing (illus. 28) shows a student wrapped in a cape[50] in front of a giant frog. Finally, in the last drawing, we see a policeman (*alguazil*) with a cape and sword in front of a cat standing on its back legs (illus. 29).

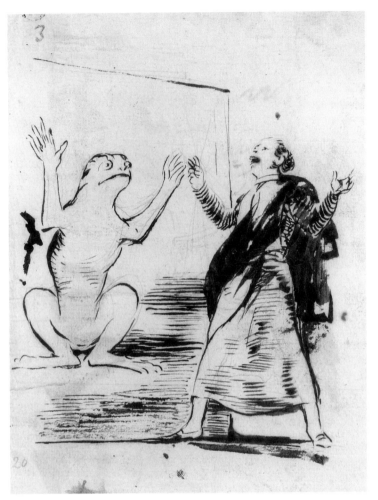

28 Goya, *Student and Frog*, 1797–8, pen and sepia wash with reddish scumble over entire sheet.

This series has long been the subject of conflicting interpretations. López-Rey, the first to have paid it particular attention, saw it as a direct reaction to the success in Europe, especially in Spain, of Lavater's *Essays on Physiognomy*. In fact it is a gloss on the concept, dear to physiognomy, of the relationship between the physical and the moral. The magic mirror reveals in animal form the human's true psychic nature.[51] To Folke Nordström, however, the series illustrates the four temperaments: melancholic (woman/serpent), sanguine (young man/monkey), phlegmatic (student/frog) and choleric (policeman/cat).[52] René Andioc, who, in a well-argued study, highlights allusions to contemporary fashions, which were the most significant butt of Goya's satire,[53] has recently

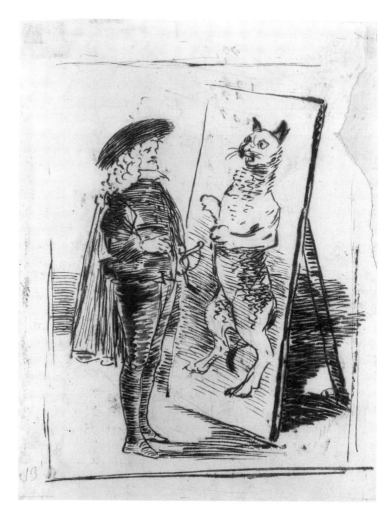

29 Goya, *Policeman and Wild Cat*, 1797–8, pen and sepia wash with reddish scumble over entire sheet.

cast doubt on this interpretation. We shall put it on hold while we re-examine the series from López-Rey's and Andioc's points of view.

We need to bear in mind that Goya had, since the 1770s, been interested in the metaphor of animal physiognomy. It was at times quite explicit in the rural scenes of the tapestry cartoons he worked on. In *The Washerwomen* (*Las lavanderas*, illus. 30), for example, everything – Goya specifies this in a letter – takes place in the form of a game: '. . . several washer-women are resting on the banks of a river. One of them has fallen asleep, her head resting on the lap of another. Two of the women are trying to wake her by touching her face with the muzzle of a sheep. Another, seated, is laughing at the scene . . .'[54]

63

This picture has attracted the attention of several art historians, who have detected in it allusions to the symbolism of
Melancholy[55] or Lust.[56] It would seem, however, that both
painting and Goya's letter are fairly clear in their underscor-
ing of the proximity of the woman's and the sheep's heads.
We may wonder at the significance of this closeness, but one
thing is certain: the image as much as the text stresses that
laughter is the obligatory response to this union. This reaction
is part (Goya's letter states as much) of the story itself: the
woman is sleeping (and dreaming), and when she wakes her
friends will have played a nasty trick on her; the image from
her dream will have been reversed. Instead of Prince Charming,
she will be surprised to see a sheep. For the moment, however,
the animal's 'kiss' that will 'wake her' is an opportunity for a
confrontation of a physiognomic kind, in which a dialogue
between the two kingdoms is produced through adjacency.
Goya's *mise-en-scène* allows us to compare the young woman's
face with that of the sheep, thus bringing out the ancient theme
of the similarity between human and animal physiognomies
(illus. 31).[57]

It is, however, crucial to emphasize the role played by the
'comparison' made through the proximity of the two 'faces' in
the absence of the specular metaphor that was to be fundamental in the drawings Goya produced between 1797 and
1799 (illus. 26–9). This metaphor has its own complex history.[58] Suffice it to say that in the Middle Ages it had already
evolved iconographically in a moralizing direction that Goya
was to develop further. In the medieval examples (illus. 32), it
was usually the woman who, questioning her beauty in a
mirror, received a cruel response in the form of the devil's
backside. One element must be emphasized here: namely the
radicalization of the reversals (beauty/ugliness, face/back-
side, high/low).

Armed with these reminders, we can examine the particular attributes of Goya's discourse on the man/animal relationship. The first thing we notice is that Goya handled this
relationship differently in each drawing. In the first, it is the
serpent that is looking at the woman, while she herself would
appear to be somewhat preoccupied (illus. 26). In the second
drawing, it is the mimetic scene between monkey and young
man that is the most amusing (illus. 27), it is so highly developed that we wonder who is mimicking whom. Furthermore,

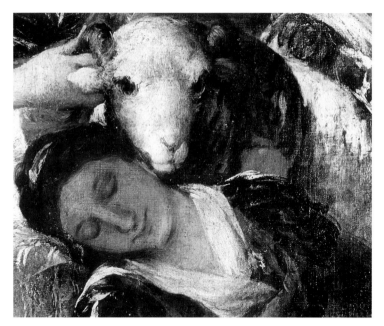

30 Detail of Goya, *The Washerwomen*, c. 1779, oil on canvas.

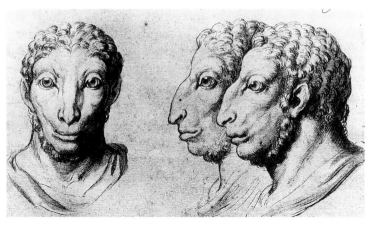

31 Charles Le Brun, *The Ram Man*, engraving from Morel d'Arleux, *Dissertation sur un traité de Charles Le Brun* (Paris, 1806).

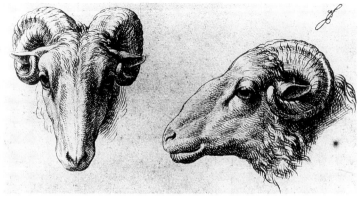

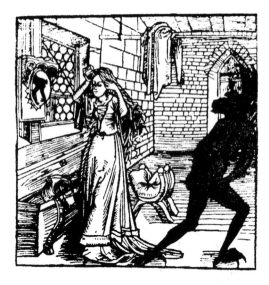

32 German, *The Devil and the Woman*, woodcut from *Der Ritter von Turn* (Basel, 1493).

to underline the transgression of reality, Goya has placed a club in the dandy's hand that does not quite go with his ultra-modern outfit. Its real place is on the other side of the mirror.

The third drawing (illus. 28) recalls the dialogue of the second, except that this time the two beings, instead of coming closer so as to study each other better, seem to be equally scared of one another. Here the mime-show plays with certain similarities in body language and physiognomy. The mime is underscored by adjacent elements, such as the quasi-contact of the student's right arm and the frog's left, or by the psychological aspects expressed formally, such as the parallel lines of ink that link the area of the mirror to the student's clothes and vice versa.

Structurally, the last drawing is less clear (illus. 29). Unlike the others, the mirror looks more like an enormous painting, and the reflection is transformed into a contemplation of the image. And yet the way Goya placed projection screens in his drawings gives them a common trait which recalls Della Porta's observations on distortions produced with the help of oblique mirrors:

The appearance of the one who is looking will vary depending on the location. If you place the mirror at an obtuse angle, the face of the one looking at himself could become so distorted as to make him look as though he had a donkey or a pig's face. If he bends down, it looks as

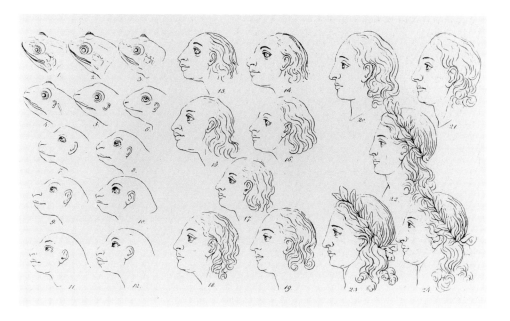

33 Johann Caspar
Lavater, *From Frog
to Apollo,* engraving
from *Essai sur la
physiognomie,* vol. 1
(The Hague, 1781).

though his eyes are coming out of their sockets, like those
of the grasshopper. If the angle becomes progressively
bigger, the nose and the mouth will become distorted and
look like a dog's mouth.[59]

It is difficult to know exactly how Goya came to know about
this tradition but we may suppose that he was familiar with it,
since he combined it with that of the specular reversals that
evolved during the Middle Ages (illus. 32).

The drawing of the student and the frog (illus. 28) was
López-Rey's strongest argument in support of his hypothesis
regarding the influence of the Lavaterian physiognomy on
Goya. In fact, Lavater had on several occasions presented a
diagram outlining human evolution from 'original frog' to
'perfect human being' (illus. 33).[60] What was so innovative
about Goya (and what has been ignored by critics) is not his
obvious copying of the idea but his interpretation of it. Step by
step, face by face, and with a minimum number of variations,
Lavater's diagram shows the gradual transformations leading from batrachian to human. The changes between one head
and the next are barely perceptible. Yet the distance between
the end of the series and its beginning is almost metaphysical.
It was precisely at this point that Goya came in. Suppressing
all intermediary elements, he placed the first and last compo-

nents face to face, and then he underlined the fear caused by this terrible confrontation. Like Lavater's 'perfect man' or just like his Apollo, the student (in theory) represents the human individual at the top of the evolutionary ladder. Goya's interpretation stresses a consequence of the process: the magic mirror shows not only that the 'real nature' of the young man is animal, but also removes the distance between the beginning and the end of evolution, revealing the gap between 'illusion' and 'truth'. While Lavater emphasized the sense of gradual transition and the sublime end of the journey, Goya featured its emptiness.[61]

Let us pursue this line of thought by analyzing *Dandy and Monkey* (illus. 27). Andioc has shown that the young man with the untidy hair, black hat and pointed shoes personifies a social type that was ridiculed around 1795 and known as *currutaco* – that is to say, young man following the latest fashion. The Spanish *currutaco* is in fact a *sui generis* transposition of the French *Incroyable* (a Directoire 'beau'):

> It was the height of elegance to appear shortsighted, disabled and deformed (. . .). The frock coat was deliberately pleated at the back to create the silhouette of a hunchback; the trousers were attached at the knees with a button to give the illusion of knock-knees. The enormous cravat, wrapped several times around the neck, covered the chin, and reached as far as the lower lip. A huge cocked or cone-shaped hat covered the dog-eared hair. Court shoes with pointed toes, a thin cane in the hand (. . .) completed the outfit.[62]

All these distinctive elements appear in Goya's drawing, together (as we have seen) with the extra touch of the cane 'magically' transformed into a club. The specular dandy/monkey dialogue features the same type of reversal of extremes as that of the frog/student. But this time, the dialogue is between 'primitive' and 'modern': the mirror states that there is harmony, equivalence and, indeed, identity between the hairy beast and the super-elegant.

Having arrived at this point, we must examine the significance of the second version of this drawing (illus. 34). The first thing we notice is that here, Goya did not follow the same symmetry of movement that had the short-sighted dandy and his ape-like *alter ego* confronting each other. There are other

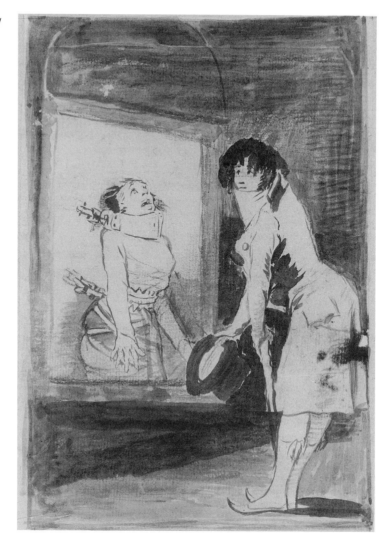

differences: the club is no longer there, and the top hat is important. However, the main difference is to be found in the strange figure of the tortured creature who, through his presence, removes the drawing from the cycle of 'wildlife fables' in order to give it another interpretation.

It strikes us that, by accentuating another contemporary fashion in his satire, Goya was attempting a *mise-en-scène* of another kind of reversal. By highlighting the top hat, he drew attention to the ideological implications of the clothes. These, it must not be forgotten, were imported from neighbouring France, where – this was the middle of the Directoire – they were the symbolic 'clothes of Liberty' (illus. 7).[63] Goya's satire becomes easy to understand: when 'clothes of Liberty' become the 'tyranny of fashion', 'independence' becomes 'torture'.[64]

The drawing that features the woman and serpent (illus. 26) also has two versions. In the first, abandoned before it was finished,[65] the serpent coils around a crutch, not a scythe. If the crutch is a *memento* of old age, then the scythe is a *memento* of death. The changes Goya made in the second version underscore the relationship of reversal through radicalization. The woman, whose true nature is sin (Goya might seem to be preaching), is not conscious of the imminence of old age (first version) or the inevitability of death (second version). In this way, beauty, youth and life become, in accordance with an ancient topos, their absolute opposites. To underline the connection between woman and serpent (and therefore the latter's originally sinful nature), Goya has given her a snake-like movement that forces her to turn her head towards the spectator. The disadvantage of this pose is that there is no specular image; the advantage is that the spectator is presented with a face lit by tiny eyes – a veiled reminder of the 'serpent's eyes'.

The cycle of the 'magic mirror' is contemporaneous with the *Caprichos*, where the animal metaphor is permanently present. Other drawings from the same period show how Goya worked the human face into both caricatures and animal metamorphoses. Following an ancient tradition, the most representative of these drawings (illus. 35) whose carnivalization is more than obvious, was produced during a social gathering.[66] In it, we find several grotesque profiles executed in a style that might well go back as far as Leonardo da Vinci, as well as several heads that reveal the animal nature (dog, monkey) of the portraiture. In the upper right-hand corner is a round face bisected by a broad grin. Some elements[67] lead us to believe that this is a self-portrait. Other factors make it very similar to the beaming head that dominates the *Burial of the Sardine* (illus. 8). We must not draw any hasty conclusions from this, of course, but we can at least note the complexity of the work undertaken by Goya to carnivalize the world, and maybe also note a few allusions to his position at the heart of this world.

There is another drawing that leads us to believe that Goya's thoughts on his own place in a universe of masks was more complex than we might think. It is the most enigmatic

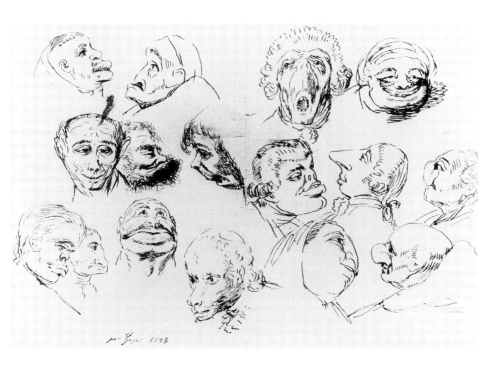

35 Goya, *Sixteen Caricatured Heads*, 1798(?), pen and sepia.

of his many self-portraits, also produced during the 1795–6 transitional period (illus. 36). We see Goya in a completely frontal pose, a strange expression on his face, eyes staring as if he is lost in space. His untidy hair, symmetrically parted in the middle, falls down into a beard that encompasses his face. This spectacular growth (never before or after did Goya portray himself with a beard, and there is no evidence that he ever had one) is no coincidence; indeed the whole self-portrait is made up of unknowns. We can find only one likely explanation for this. This drawing is – we believe – an attempt at animal self-physiognomy, in which Goya imagined himself (or saw himself in his mind's eye, in the mirror of his imagination) as having a lion's features. A look at images and texts from ancient treatises (illus. 37) dispels any doubts as to the significance of this self-projection onto a *sui-generis* bestiary. The lion-man is strong, dominant and regal, like the king of the beasts, say the texts; like Jupiter himself, adds Le Brun. This is how Della Porta describes him: 'His hair tumbling down onto his brow, half-straight, half-wavy, is of average length. His nose is straight, the colour of the lion. The curved eyebrows are often in a frown. The beard is bushy. The neck thick.'[68] Compared to the prints that illustrate the

71

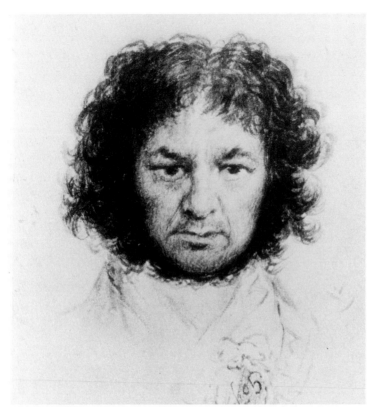

36 Goya,
Self-portrait,
c. 1795–7, India ink
wash drawing.

37 Charles Le Brun,
Leonine Head,
engraving from
Morel d'Arleux,
Dissertation sur
traité de Charles
Le Brun.

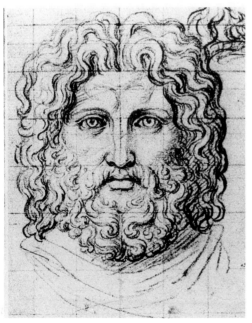

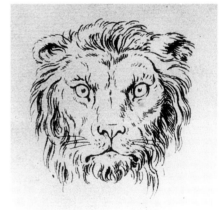

De Humana physionomia, the grin in Goya's drawing is softer and the seriousness of the expression is more accented. Compared to Le Brun's print (probably studied by Goya in the 1781–6 French edition of Lavater's *Essays on Physiognomy*), this self-portrait tones down the mythological allusion without negating it altogether. If we compare it to what we have presumed to be a distorted self-portrait of the mocking artist (illus. 35), we find two diametrically opposed masks produced in the same period, 1795–7. Faced with (and encompassed in) a world of symbolic dressing-up, carnivalesque laughter and Olympian gravity both defy and complement one another.

3 Vertigo

External bodies that are naturally at rest appear to move in circles, to fall from high to low, or to rise from low to high. We think we fall from Heaven to earth or to the sea, that we rise from there up into the clouds, that we turn like a whirlwind in the air, and that we are then cast down with the whole of the Universe, into the deepest of abysses.[1]

In describing these symptoms, La Mettrie (in *Traité sur le vertige* [Treatise on Vertigo] [1737]) was expressing the diagnostic of a genuine *mal du siècle*, or 'world-weariness'.[2] Few of his contemporary artists or fellow thinkers could have added anything to this image. Condillac, for example (in 1787), introduced his reflection on human thought as a whirlwind-thought,[3] while Rousseau narcissistically projected vertigo onto his own self and, thus, onto the human condition in general, writing: 'I am on the earth as though on a foreign planet onto which I fell from my own.'[4] In Spain, in 1795, Cadalso generalized:

Everything changes, alters and perishes in this world; there is nothing that is stable and solid in the universe apart from the actual sight of the Universe. Everything else varies, changes, is reversed, falls and vanishes under the inescapable sickle of time, which indiscriminately destroys human beings as well as all the works made by their hands and minds.[5]

The *topos* is baroque, its manifestation enlightened. In the iconosphere, the one who would best express it was Goya, once again. Not only because of the crisis that struck in 1792–3, which La Mettrie could have described as a 'natural, brooding and symptomatic' vertigo,[6] but because of the assimilation, on the level of the creative imagination, of a 'world-weariness' of which real illness was but a pale reflection.

Goya's vertiginous imagination passes through that of the fall. Its first manifestation is to be found in carnivalesque form in *The Straw Man* (*El Pelele*; illus. 69), where everything would still appear to be a game. What we are witnessing is a rite of ludic reversal, which is also a rite of punishment *in effigie*. Four young women are tossing a puppet with broken joints up into the air by means of a sheet. They do not, it is true, allow him to crash to the ground and break, but neither will they allow him to rest. Flying so as not to be destroyed, the simulacrum will always be in a state of between-the-two, a perpetual state of unco-ordinated reversal: he can no longer control his limbs; his masked head has swung round his neck, but, dumbfounded, still gazes up at the sky. It is quite obvious that the puppet will soon fall, face down, legs pointing into infinity, even though for the present they still form a large circumflex accent highlighted by the huge grin of one of the women mocking him. There is voluptuousness in this derision and even a degree of violence alluded to in the simulated torture.[7] The iconographic programme for the royal tapestries, for which this painting was a preliminary study, came straight from the King, who insisted on the need to tackle 'rural and ludic' scenes.[8] Slight variations, probably made by the painter himself, raise questions about an idyllic and imaginary world, which should, in principle, have been that of the perpetual festival.

It is easier to understand *The Straw Man* if we compare it to another important painting in the series, a slightly earlier one, *Blind Man's Buff* (illus. 38). The comparison is viable and illuminating since the two works have a common theme although they expressed it differently. 'Blind man's buff' as it was played in Madrid in Goya's time[9] was based on a circle dance and combined with a game of identification and elimination. As with all circle dances, it was highly symbolic of time, especially of time that is renewed when it spins around.[10] In Goya's painting, we see a group of *majos* and their *majas* forming a circle with members of the upper classes on the banks of the Manzanares River, a favourite spot for Madrid festivals. The circle turns, and elimination is part of the role-play. The role of the victim in the game is to symbolically represent the misfortunes that can befall each and every one of us in a universe that spins faster and faster. It is now imperative that the blind man, who has spun around or has been pushed until he is dizzy, identify the people spinning perpetually around him, each taking the place of the other. In this game, *otherness* and *identity* have a dialectical and complex relationship. The puppet-like rigidity of some of the figures and their attempts to escape identification create a strange impression of perpetual and infinite permutations. Through its perfect circularity, the movement of the dance is transformed into immobility.

Despite the originality and 'modernity' of this painting, it is easy to identify what it owes to tradition. An early example (illus. 39) is instructive, especially as text and image throw light on one another. This is how, in 1499, Francisco Colonna described the dance of time, which illustrates his famous erotic novel *Hypnerotomachia Poliphili* (*The Dream of Poliphilus*):

> ... dancing men and women each with two faces, one laughing and the other crying. They danced in a circle, holding hands, man with man and woman with woman, the arm of the man passing in front of the woman, the other passing behind, in such a way that a happy face would always be turned towards a sad one (...). This dance was in the shape of an oval, formed by two continuous semicircles of two lines above and below. Under the story was written: TEMPUS which means 'time'.[11]

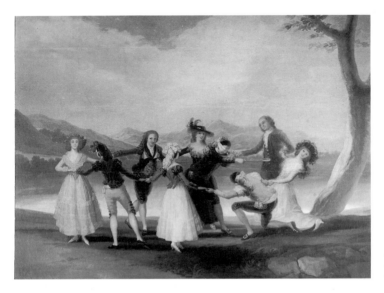

38 Goya, *Blind Man's Buff*, 1788–9, oil on canvas.

We should note the very particular nature of Colonna's metaphor. It can only be fully comprehended if it is seen in the context of the hero's fictional itinerary, as an enigmatic portrayal that needs to be deciphered. It is the final word (*TEMPUS*) that gives the allegorical picture its significance. Humanist culture and its games only provided Goya with a formula on which to construct his own allegory, which is also an outdoor festival. It is difficult to ascertain, without falling prey to spurious hypotheses, how and by what means he knew of and then transformed this ancient formula. We feel it is more important to focus on *how* he did this – that is to say, which representational means he used to present his own thoughts on time. In this respect, Goya would appear to have chosen an extremely simple route that combined symbolic implications with the fundamental elements of painting as a means of expression. In *Blind Man's Buff*, there are in fact two allusions to time which he skilfully superimposes by virtually forcing them to dialogue. One is the dance, the other the river. Circle dancing, particularly popular during festivals that marked the summer solstice, has a significance well known to anthropologists as a symbolic celebration of the *sol-stitium* when the sun's predetermined path reached one of the points on its ecliptic.[12] The river, on the other hand, marks a linear and unidirectional temporality, different from that of the dance, which is the

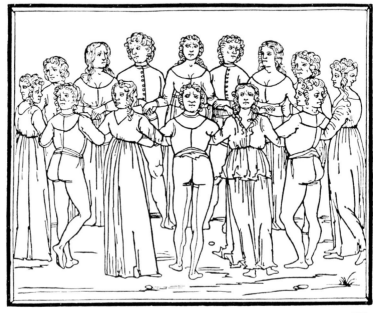

39 *The Dance of Time*, engraving from Francisco Colonna, *Hypnerotomachia, Poliphili* (Venice, 1499).

circular and dynamic symbol of the eternal return of the same.[13] Through a minor modification, Goya has shown us the dialogue of two Times: cut by the frame, the river reaches for the circularity of the dance and the calm of the lake. The painting tells us that at the solstice, river-time spins around and the game of circularity leads it into an infinite return.

Another rite of passage is depicted in *The Straw Man* (illus. 69): the carnivalesque (and equinoctial) rite of radical reversal through which low is replaced by high and vice versa. Furthermore, the puppet is the symbol of the old time that is dying or, to be more precise, of time spinning around itself so that it can be turned into its opposite, the young time of new beginnings. There are inherent differences between these two paintings, springing from the fact that they celebrate the passage of two rites whose singularity is well defined: that of circular return and that of reversal. But there are also other differences, just as important, which require explanation. In the form of a game, *The Straw Man* contains the germ of a symbolic violence that is much greater than the mocking of the blind man's search thematized by *Blind Man's Buff*. It might be only a coincidence, but, between the dates when these two works were produced, extremely important events took place in Spain and the rest of Europe. *Blind Man's Buff* was begun in 1788 – the final year of the reign of the philosopher-king Charles III, who was personally involved in the iconographic and ideological planning of the 'rural and ludic'

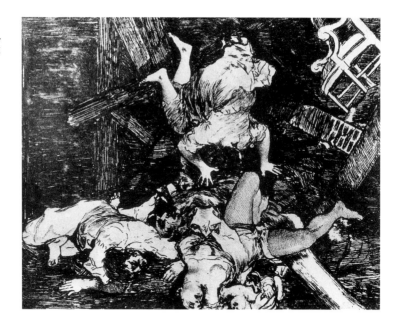

41 Goya, *The Disasters of War* 30, *c.* 1800–11, etching and wash.

cycle – and completed in 1789, when his son, Charles IV, was already on the Spanish throne. The new reign signalled the end of the period of rural idylls. This is why *The Straw Man*, produced in 1791–2, can be considered as the last remnant of the rural and idyllic cycle and the first evidence of a new iconosphere. In this mixture is a *mise-en-scène* of the sublimated dialectic between festival and violence, in a country that was still experiencing the uncertainties of an interregnum. On the other side of the Pyrenees during this very same period, the game was being replaced by seriousness, and the festival/violence dialectic was also moving in the same direction. This swing would ultimately lead to the putting to death, in 1791, of 'old time', not through an effigy, but via the guillotine.

Between 1788 and 1792 – of this there is very little doubt – time turned round, time turned upside down. However, what is difficult to ascertain with any accuracy is whether we are justified in interpreting Goya's works as allegories of this double process, or whether it would not be wiser to see them as the products of an act of imaginary projection and filtering of a thematic whose ideological actuality is irrelevant. We favour the second hypothesis because of the recurrence of certain motifs and their transformations through time. In a later series of etchings, known as the *Disparates* (Absurdities), both

79

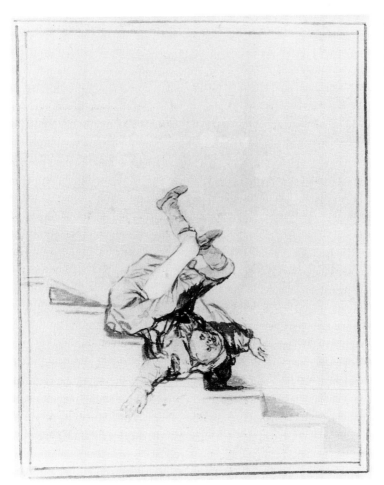

42 Goya,
Drawing E 38:
Feats? Be Your Age,
1803–12, India ink
wash.

circle dance and puppet reappear. However, they are transformed and partially combined (illus. 40, 70). The dance has
broken up, the circle has collapsed, and the 'eternal return of
the same' has become a caricature of itself. As for the puppet
game, this is the last carnivalesque manifestation of the
victim/torturer relationship, but one that is taken to such an
extreme that any spectator would, one way or another, understand that the festival, as Goya describes it in the *Absurdities,*
is the ludic as well as pathetic commemoration of a partially
transfigured sacrificial crisis.[14] Between the mannequins that
fly up to the sky in the *Absurdities* (c. 1814–20) and the free-
falling victims of the *Disasters of War* (c. 1820–4; illus. 41) is a
relationship that is both substitutive and complementary. It
is a relationship that is difficult, indeed tricky, because it

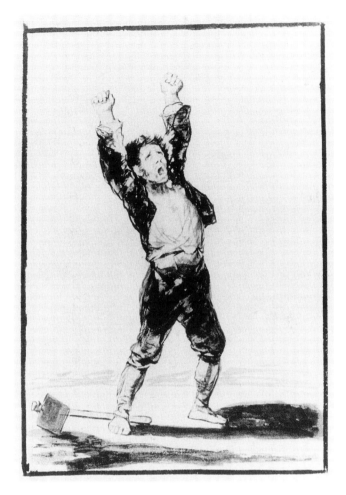

43 Goya,
Drawing E 39:
*Shouting Will Get
You Nowhere,*
1803–12, India ink
wash.

challenges the boundaries that separate comedy from tragedy. Let us examine them.

We propose, as our point of departure, to look at two neighbouring drawings from the *Black-edged Sketchbook* both of which date from between 1803 and 1812 (illus. 42, 43). Even though they are not directly linked with *The Absurdities* or *The Disasters of War*, these drawings strike us as being significant inasmuch as they portray the painter's secret laboratory during the period of gestation of the two series. In the first, we see an old woman falling down the stairs. The page setting is extremely simple, and the blank spaces play a crucial role. The staircase and the inverted person cross the page diagonally. The woman's legs are up in the air, and her feet wave helplessly in the void; she is shouting and one can read fear on her face. And yet the reaction it provokes is not compassion but uncontrollable laughter. Thomas Hobbes and, after him, Henri Bergson, to recall the most famous examples, gave a detailed description of how the ancient and fundamental mechanisms of mockery make an involuntary fall into an event that triggers laughter: 'A man runs down the street, trips and falls; the passers-by laugh. I do not think they would have laughed at him if he had suddenly decided to sit down on the ground. It is therefore not his sudden change of position that makes people laugh, but what is involuntary about the change.'[15]

The man who falls is therefore a puppet knocked down by an alien force. When the *low* takes the place of the *high* (as is the case in this drawing), when the backside is exhibited and

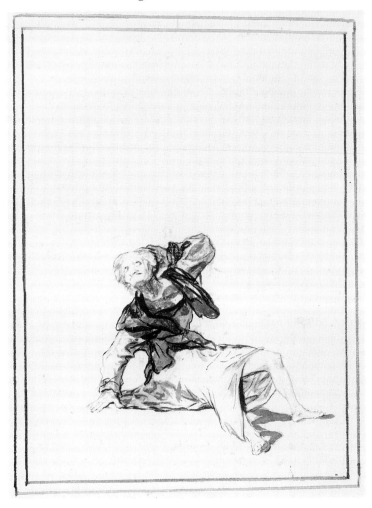

44 Goya,
Drawing E 6:
Complain about the Weather, 1803–12,
India ink wash.

the face contorted, this force reveals its own strength and reminds us of the weakness of the other. Although Bergson rationalized the relationship between fall and laughter, we would be quite justified in thinking that Goya might not have found this kind of determinism particularly satisfying. He would probably have been more comfortable with another gloss, made by Baudelaire in 1855:

> It is a fact, if we wish to see things from the point of view of the orthodox mind, that human laughter is closely linked to an accidental ancient fall, to physical and moral degradation. Organs manifest laughter and sorrow, where the rule and science of good and evil reside: the eyes and the mouth. In the earthly paradise (that we presume to be past or yet to come, memory or prophesy, like theologians or socialists), that is to say in the milieu where it seemed to man that all things created were good, joy was not to be found in laughter.[16]

Within this perspective, the fall at which we laugh – and the one depicted by Goya is such a one – is 'a fall within the fall',[17] a comic and apparently innocent reminder of the human condition and its limitations.

Since we can get closer to Goya's thinking only if we examine all his sketchbooks and drawings, we feel it is necessary to explore at least a few more examples, also taken from the *Black-edged Sketchbook*. Should we compare drawing 38 (illus. 42) with the one that bears the number 6 (illus. 44), we would not find any significant differences between them. Once again, an old woman falls down as a result of having stumbled or having been knocked down.[18] The most notable difference in this drawing is to be found in the fact that the victim is trying to attribute her misadventure to the action of an exterior invisible force. Experiencing vertigo, she places the accident of which she has just been the victim under the cover of an 'ancient fall', petitioning a higher authority in the hope of receiving an explanation for it. Goya's genius as an observer is apparent in the body language and mimicry. The old woman rests her right arm on the ground, in an attempt, as we understand it, to stand up. Looking up at the sky, she raises her other hand to her head. But the sky is empty, and – at least in Goya's picture – no one can provide her with an answer.

We should once again emphasize the importance of the empty space and its functions in Goya's work. If it takes up practically half a page, this is because it thematizes an absence. Admittedly, Goya could have framed his drawing differently, making it more compact. In so doing, he would probably have saved paper, but the depth and impact of what he was proposing would have been lost. In certain cases, however, he chose other ways of suggesting the same idea. In drawing 39 from the same sketchbook (illus. 43), for example, he created a scene based on an ascending movement. The contrast between this composition and its neighbour, number 38 (illus. 42) could not be greater or more significant, but everything suggests that their sequencing is no accident. It is the dialogue between the high and the low that gives them their dialectic unity. Let us therefore study this man who is bemoaning his fate. Having dropped his spade, he raises his arms to the sky and opens his mouth to shout, but nothing and nobody can answer him. In this instance, absence is thematized by 'outside-the-frame'. It is expressed not by blank space but by the notion of *boundary* implicit in the way Goya framed the picture. This time, the black edge is not only the false frame of the drawing, it is also a frontier between world and sky, between *here* and *elsewhere*.[19]

THE EMPTY SKY

It is in effect the great theme of the 'Death of God'[20] that Goya confronted as much in his two final series of etchings as in the drawings of his later sketchbooks.[21] Or, to be more precise, their real theme is the world in the absence of God. Whereas the *Disasters of War* mark a surfeit of the sacrificial symbolic (illus. 41, 48), the *Disparates* (illus. 40, 70) proclaim the absurd to be a structure that carries the universe. The Carnival is very much present in the two series; God is not there at all, however. This accounts for the fact that what we now find is a significant thematic split: the therapeutic violence (temporary or comic) of the Carnival is always accompanied by what could be referred to as 'pathological violence' (constant and dramatic), which is characteristic of humanity and human presence in the world. Goya tackled the same themes (the fall, the reversal) either comically or dramatically, but from 1792–3 on the differences between carnivalesque symbolism and rites of violence began to fade, so much so that it was virtually impossible to see them.

84

The sense of disenchantment with the world[22] that went hand in hand with its carnivalization developed slowly; Goya probably worked in this vein from the time of his illness in 1792–3 until the end of his life. By embarking on such a wide-ranging exploration, he was, as an artist, confronting a complex problem. Western artists had already perfected a rhetoric able to express the 'nouminous', the sacred. Goya now had to find (and herein lay the challenge), a way to express not its presence but its absence. This challenge already existed, though between the lines, in the famous letter dated 14 October 1792 that he sent to the Academy of Fine Arts in Madrid.[23] This is a truly anti-academic manifesto, probably the most important European demonstration against the arts of the 'Cultural Revolution of Year II' that had broken out on the other side of the Pyrenees.[24] One vital aspect of its contents must be underlined: the very clever shift Goya performed in the area of religious art:

> I shall bring proof so as to demonstrate with facts that there are no rules in Painting and that the oppression or servile obligation to which young artists are subjected, to study and to follow altogether the same route is a great hindrance to those who wish to make of this difficult art a profession which has more in common with the Divinity than all the others since it deals with everything that God has created.[25]

Reading between the lines, this is what Goya was saying: there is a traditional art fettered by the rules of the Academy. Of all its different manifestations, the representation of the Divine poses the greatest problems, as this is where the inflexibility of norms is the most oppressive. The freedom demanded by the younger generation should be seen (and this is where Goya's ingenuity comes in) not as a revolt against God but as a recognition of his presence in all things created by him. Goya is therefore inviting us (though with understandable caution, given the Spanish context, in which the influence of the Inquisition was still considerable) to a change of direction and thematic repertoire. The sky (or the heavens) will no longer be the subject of painting; the earth will or, to be more precise (and to follow Goya's reasoning and language), the subject of representation will no longer be the Divine (*lo divino*) but, as he says two lines later, 'divine nature' (*la divina naturaleza*).

85

The replacing of the 'Divine' by 'divine nature' was in itself an enlightened project and, within academic circles, a symptom of a cultural revolution in its own right. Goya's second step was to prove even more difficult: to challenge the characteristics of 'divine' and their true relationship with 'nature'. It goes without saying that – in Spain – such a challenge could not be freely expressed in discursive form. However, through more or less veiled allusions, it was apparent in Goya's imagery. Looking at the *Disasters of War* (illus. 41, 48), we are left in no doubt that 'human nature' could actually contain something of the 'divine'. Looking at the *Caprichos* or *Absurdities*, however, we might well wonder what the divine/madness ratio was here on earth.

A comparison of the 'first' and the 'second' Goya – that is to say the work produced before his illness (and the anti-Academic manifesto) in 1792–3 and his later work – reveals the part played, in this change of paradigms, by the process of reversing the ancient forms. This process was brought about in several ways. One was the way mentioned by Goya in his letter to the Academy where he asks that this new art be more direct and less polished (*de menos cuidado*) than major formal works (*de mayor esmero*). Drawing, graphic techniques, the 'doodle' (*el borrón*), produced a kind of 'anti-painting'.[26] The freedom of this new form can also be found if we go down other avenues, particularly those where the reversal of ancient artistic norms is executed through its carnivalization. We have already had occasion to give one likely example of this, when we referred to the links connecting one of Goya's drawings (the bearded mother) to the Counter-Reformation iconography of the saints and child (illus. 21, 22). We would now like to examine other forms of the carnivalization of earlier art in Goya's work.

If we look through the so-called 'Italian Sketchbook' (*El Cuarderno Italiano*) – the most important collection of pictures documenting Goya's travels in Italy (1770–71)[27] – it is possible to see that he had two favourite areas in which he worked during his stay there. On the one hand, there are copies and versions in the style of the Ancients, and on the other, copies in the style of Renaissance and Baroque religious art. One of these drawings (illus. 45) depicts a vision. In accordance with this type of composition, very much in fashion at the time of the Counter-Reformation,[28] Goya shows a man kneeling on

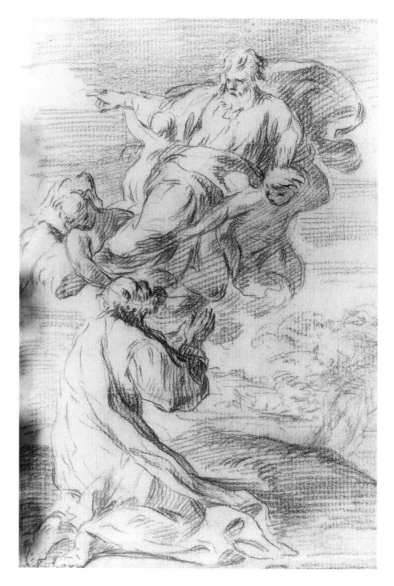

45 Goya, *A Vision: God the Father and Abraham*, fol. 33r from the 'Italian Notebook', 1770–73, sanguine and black wash highlights.

the ground in prayer. The drawing is constructed as a well-defined diagonal that highlights the ascending character of the scene. The man's naked feet are at the bottom of the drawing, while God the Father's head and his coat, flapping in the sky, are at the other. The contact between lower and upper levels is achieved through prayer or, more precisely, through a dialogue concretized in the codified body language of prayer and reply. Other details, such as the line of the ground or the tree on the right, underscore not only the earthly setting but also the fact that, as a miracle, the scene depicts an opening, indeed the heavens erupting into the world. Given the fairly traditional oversimplification of this drawing, there is no reason why we should be unduly surprised to rediscover it, virtually unchanged, in the religious paintings Goya was to produce ten years later. He remembered it, for example, when he was asked to paint an altarpiece for the church of San Pedro in Urrea de Gaén (Teruel).[29] The iconographic changes he introduced were minimal: in the lower part St James is on his knees praying, but in the sky it is Our Lady of the Pillar who emerges from the clouds. If we call to mind the empty skies in some of Goya's later drawings (illus. 43, 44), we can see just how traditional his early paintings were.

However, we also have visual documents which speak to us of the task of deconstructing ancient religious images begun by Goya soon after 1792. The most important of these is probably from *Los Caprichos* (1799). In its final version, this etching bears the inscription *Lo que puede un sastre* (Fine feathers make fine birds). The explanation contained in the Prado manuscript, which probably reflects Goya's own interpretation, adds: 'How often a ridiculous animal suddenly transforms itself into a ghost who is nothing even though he pretends to be much. That much a tailor's skill can accomplish, and the stupidity of those who judge of things from their appearances.'[30] In the preparatory drawing to this *Capricho* (illus. 71), there was no inscription, no explanation; the composition as a whole spoke so clearly through its apparent simplicity that Goya, probably fearing censure from the Inquisition, had to modify it for the etched version.[31] If, in the print published in 1799, the title and certain additional features turn this final version into a mockery of superstition, in the drawing it is religion and religious practices that are being directly challenged. The formula adopted by Goya is similar to those found in Counter-Reformation paintings that portray apparitions (illus. 45, 47), except that the theophany is shown to be an illusion; the divinity is a scarecrow made from a monk's habit and a shrivelled-up old tree. As for the visionary, she is just a poor frightened girl, and the vision is a simple optical illusion.

Other eloquent examples of reversal can be found in the *Sketchbook-Journal*, where the theme of the grotesque body (illus. 14–16) significantly coexists with that of the tortured and martyred body. In one of these drawings (illus. 46), we see an old man, bound and hanging upside down from a complicated instrument of torture. His bared legs and lower abdomen are a sign of humiliation that also appears in Goya's carnivalesque drawings, though in a very different way (illus. 42, 44). The inverted body can be represented either in ludic and comic mode or in tragic mode. In both cases, the same paradigm, that of the *Straw Man* (illus. 69), is used, except that a split has taken place. If in the *Straw Man*, ridicule and punishment coexist symbolically, in the later drawings they go their separate ways to become extreme.

Manifestations of violence subject the spectator to a terrible ordeal, and Goya explained this quite clearly with the

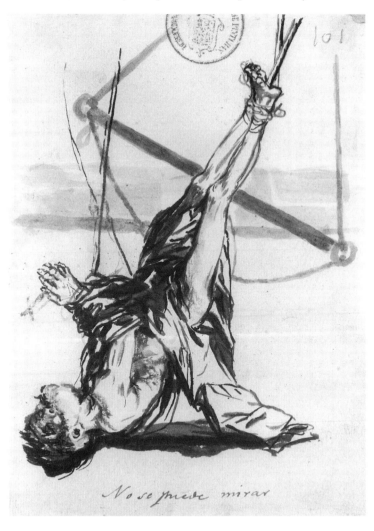

46 Goya, Drawing C. 101: *We Cannot Look at This*, 1814–24, India ink wash.

89

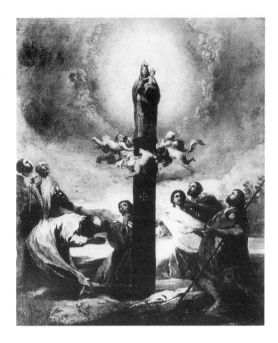

47 Goya,
*Apparition of the
Virgin of the Pillar to
Saint James and His
Disciples, c. 1775–80,*
oil on canvas.

inscription that accompanies drawing 101 of the *Sketchbook-Journal* (illus. 46): 'We cannot look at this' (*No se puede mirar*). We are therefore encountering a theme that will reappear time and again, either directly or indirectly, in Goya's work: that of the almost unbearably violent image, the image that, instead of attracting the spectator, drives him away.

In the drawing in question, the unbearable nature of the image is heightened by the fact that the torture victim, bound and hanging upside down, is still imploring the heavens. But, despite his crucifix and aposcopic expression,[32] he finds no salvation. As with *Capricho* 52 (illus. 71), this drawing takes an anticlerical stance and contains a fairly transparent allusion to a type of representation – Baroque paintings of apparitions – that Goya had himself painted in his youth. By exposing this allusion, Goya is implicitly distancing himself from his own beginnings.

We can also find in his etchings instances in which ancient religious images are denigrated through simulacra. There Goya's mockery is directed at statues and processional imagery. The series in question is the later *Disasters of War*. Etching no. 67 (illus. 48) shows two statues being carried. The one in the foreground represents the 'Virgin of Solitude' (*La Virgen de la Soledad*), an extremely popular image considered to be miraculous.[33] In this case, however, the statue is not being carried in triumph, and processional verticality has been replaced by a horizontality that destroys the sacred aura. The allusions in this etching are even more glaring when we compare it to a work Goya produced in his youth. In the religious paintings produced between 1770 and 1780 for clients from his native Aragon, he on many occasions tackled the theme of the adoration of holy images in the shape of the apparition of the Virgin of the Pillar. In one of these paintings (illus. 47), we see the miraculous statue of the Virgin and Child projected against the sky, surrounded by a huge halo and a double ring of dancing cherubs. St James and his disciples are in ecstatic prayer below. The dual nature of the Virgin of the Pillar – miraculous statue and apparition – is underscored by both form and iconography. The radical verticalization and projection against the dazzling background of the open sky are just two of its most important features.

It is crucial to note at this point that in the eighteenth century the miraculous image of the Virgin (still in the Iglesia del Pilar in Saragossa) and, more particularly, its *mise-en-scène* and exaggerated cult, were mocked by enlightened (and Protestant) travellers from abroad. One of them wrote:

> I think that the reason why we are not always able to look upon the miraculous image, is that this Image, which is extremely small and almost completely hidden behind the rich ornaments with which it is bedecked, is extremely high up. It can only be seen in perspective, through an infinite number of lights that dazzle the eyes like the sun, when you try to gaze at it. Furthermore, these lights are reflected on all sides in the gilding, the precious stones and the gold plating, which only increases the confusion of the viewer. This small Image is on a column of very fine jasper. Part of it can be seen from outside the chapel through a small hole expressly made for the purpose, so that the devout whatever their status or condition may have the consolation of being able to kiss it; or like some to lick it.[34]

We know of no reason why Goya should have turned against this image that had marked him so deeply during his youth in Aragon; moreover, any direct attack would have been hard to imagine given the prestige accorded this Virgin. However, as we can see in etching 67 from the *Disasters of War*, he was sceptical when it came to the cult of images in general. What

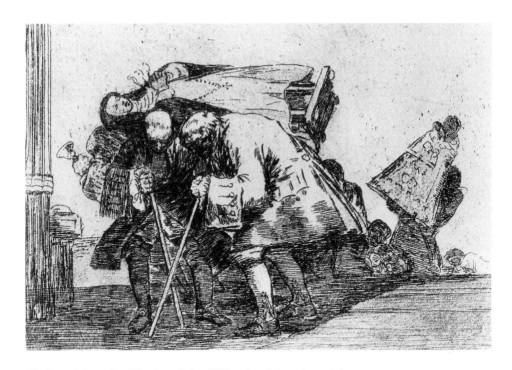

distinguishes the Virgin of the Pillar (and its pictorial representations) – that is to say its radical verticalization – is rejected here; a reversal and the destruction of the surrounding sacred aura replace the elevation. In this etching, the horizontal position reduces the statue to a mere object, an object no different from any other. It is in effect a deposed, toppled image, stripped of its powers and its sacred connotations. Through being inverted, the idol reveals its true nature: it is a simulacrum, a mere empty habit on a pedestal on wheels, a poor papier mâché mannequin and nothing more. We would be justified at this point in drawing a parallel between this mockery of the sacred image and the revolutionary iconoclasm in France that led to famous incidents of vandalism.[35] But the differences are significant. Goya was drawing attention not so much to the dangers of the destruction of images (it was 1814–29) but rather to their restoration.[36] The people carrying this statue are representatives of the nobility and clergy, and the artist is telling us that their efforts to support and restore the ancient imagination were illusory since what they proposed was nothing more than the adoration of an empty form.

48 Goya, *The Disasters of War* 67: *This One Is No Less,* 1815–20, etching and aquatint.

The criticism of religious art contained in Goya's letter of 14 October 1792 to the Madrid Academy of Fine Art was primarily a plea for replacing the 'Divine'. His letter also stated his opposition to the teaching of Ancient Art:

> To those not familiar with either Greek statuary, or nature, it might appear scandalous to belittle the former in favour of the latter (. . .). He who would detach himself from it without seeking what is best in nature is bound to tackle Painting and Sculpture in a monotonous manner, as all have done up until now.[37]

The development of an anti-classical poetics and palate is a phenomenon in Goya that has been much explored by experts.[38] Within the context of our study, it assumes a particular importance and therefore demands our full attention. Most important are the transformations, indeed inversions, of classicism that he executed. The 'Italian Sketchbook' is only relevant in part. Although Antiquity is represented in it, it seems to have been of limited interest to Goya – with one notable exception. One of the few models – repeated at least three times in the 'Sketchbook' and from three different angles – to have had any intrinsic appeal to him was the famous *Belvedere Torso* (illus. 49). We must examine the reasons for this.

The seminal work on the neo-classical art conception, Winckelmann's *Geschichte der Kunst des Altertums* (*The Origins of Art History*) (1764, 1776), leaves us in no doubt that this sculpture had a unique place in the historical and critical structure of neo-classicism:

> Despite being quite mutilated, having no head, no arms and no legs, this statue of Hercules, such as we see it today, is still a masterpiece in the eyes of all those who understand the mysteries of art, and who can visualise it in all its beauty. (. . .) The bones would appear to be enveloped in a glowing skin; the muscles are firm, nothing is superfluous and in no other work of art can we find flesh that is so alive. We could even say that this Hercules is closer to the pinnacles of art than the Belvedere Apollo himself. (. . .) It would appear that the Torso of Hercules is one of the last perfect works produced by Greek art before it lost its freedom.[39]

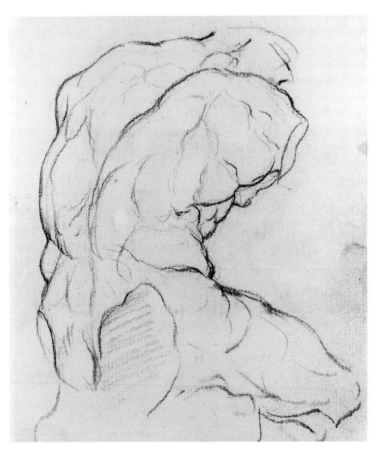

49 Goya, *The Belvedere Torso*, fol. 61r from the '*Italian Notebook*', black wash drawing.

This famous description is a most eloquent *mise-en-scène* of a masterpiece from Antiquity that keeps locked away inside itself the dialectical relationship between the rise and fall of the classical form. The physical degeneration of the statue, as thematized by the text, can be interpreted in several ways. It highlights the relationship between fragment and totality, between ugliness and beauty, and proclaims that perfection can be reconstituted from its fragmentary state through the reaction to the work. It is the insightful reaction that reconstructs, on the level of the imagination, the body of the representation in full, as well as its beauty. With all its physical defects, adds Winckelmann, the *Torso* is, paradoxically, the very incarnation of the mimetic idea of classical art, whose strength is to be found in the exemplary way in which *life* is presented through *stone*. But the fall from this pinnacle is fast approaching, and if the *Torso* is a masterpiece it is also (and

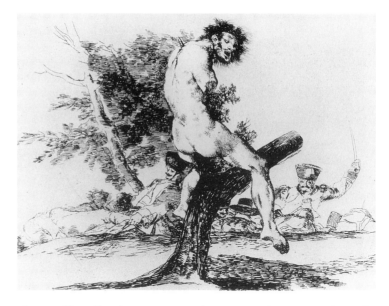

above all) a 'final masterpiece', or even *the* masterpiece. In the final sentence of the description – commentators have quite rightly pointed this out – the statue becomes an image that personifies the final erosion of the integrity of Greek civilization itself.[40]

That said, it should come as no surprise that it was *this* statue to which Goya was constantly drawn.[41] For him, it characterized the distorted classical form, a hyperbolized and at the same time denigrated human body. And this was the direction he would take when executing his most brilliant version of it, as etching 37 from the *Disasters of War* reveals (illus. 50).

Etching 37 is an unusually violent image: the mutilated body of a rebel is impaled on a tree, whose pointed branch pierces his body from anus to shoulder blades. This is a powerful image, in the category of those 'we cannot look at'. The visual impact was clearly anticipated as the body, tortured in the most humiliating of ways, was placed in the centre foreground of the representation. It is not difficult to recognize in Goya's mutilated man a direct transposition of the *Belvedere Torso* as shown in one of the studies he made while in Rome (illus. 49). This unusually violent scene results from a modification of the formal classical repertoire by means of a radical carnivalization. The humiliation of the victim by anal piercing is also a consequence of a rhetoric of degradation and denigration that

95

has always been prevalent in injurious body language and punishments *in effigie* of carnivalesque origin.[42] By impaling the *Belvedere Torso* on a dead tree, Goya chose the most disturbing way to produce a link between the degradation of the notion of the human and that of classical form. It is interesting to look for a moment at the processes used by Goya in the execution of his version of the *Belvedere Torso*. The latter was transposed into the etching only after having been subjected to processes of completion and integration. We notice at once that Goya completed the legs and buttocks and added a portion of the right arm, without for all that compromising the image of violent mutilation. The victim's head, turned towards the spectator, is another important addition. His contortion and the image's 'unbearable' nature are thus

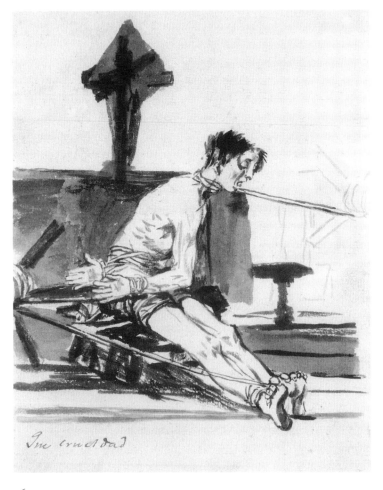

51 Goya, Drawing C. 108: '*Such Cruelty!*', 1815–20, sepia wash.

accentuated. But the major transformation is that the *Belvedere Torso*, the 'living statue' of neo-classical aesthetics, becomes an exposed corpse in Goya's drawing.

There are few examples in Goya's work of the violent transformation of an ancient model that can rival the power and eloquence of this etching, even though, in his later work, Goya was obsessed with the theme of the contorted body (illus. 51). Like reversal (illus. 46), contortion involves an examination of the body and its 'normal' state.[43] This examination can be carried out either on the violent level of human degradation and debasement or on the level of the carnivalesque rhetoric of joyous reversals.

It is striking to note that when Goya tackled the comic torsion of the body, he once again embarked on a dialogue with Antiquity and its famous models. One of the drawings in his earliest 'Sketchbook' proves this (illus. 52). However, this drawing, usually referred to as 'Back view of young woman raising her skirts',[44] might appear to have nothing 'classical' about it and would seem merely to be a simple comment on the language of obscene gestures, common to the Carnival: the exposing of the backside. The head turned to look at the spectator creates a curious face/back duality which is also no stranger to the ancient rites of renewal, as is proved by the print of the Dance of Time that appears in Francesco Colonna's erotic novel (illus. 39). But this is an unusual case of bi-frontality rather than an actual torsion. In fact, the pose was aptly criticized from the point of view of classical aesthetics in Leon Battista Alberti's treatise on painting:

> The head of a person standing cannot tip backwards beyond the point where the eyes see the middle of the sky and he can only turn it sideways until the chin touches the shoulder; and as for this part of the body where we put a belt, we can practically never turn it so that the shoulder is positioned to form a straight line from the navel. (. . .) [it is necessary to avoid] representing movements that are so violent that, in the same figure, chest and buttocks (*et pectus et nates*) are visible at the same time which is impossible to do and most indecent to see (*indecentissimum visu est*).[45]

What must be stressed is the fact that Goya, precisely by tackling this kind of torsion, both breaks away from Renaissance aesthetics and rekindles the dialogue with classical models. His drawing contains clear allusions to the only classical model to feature, before it was invented, the Albertian interdiction. This is the famous Greek statue, of which there are so many versions and copies, depicting *The Callipygean Venus* (*Aphrodite Kallipygos*) (illus. 53).[46] There is no sign of this model in the Italian Sketchbook (as was the case with the *Belvedere Torso*), but it is more than likely that Goya was familiar with it, either directly from his trip to Italy, or indirectly through the prints that illustrated the most important inventories of ancient statues. The best account of the origins of this statue is the one found in Vincenzo Cartari's book on mythological iconography (1556):

> Two young women, the beautiful and graceful daughters of a peasant, were arguing in vain one day as to which of them had the most beautiful buttocks. And so they decided to go to a public road where they came upon a young man they had never met before. They showed him the object of their dispute so that he could be the judge, promising him that they would accept his decision. The young man, having carefully examined and considered with much application the part that had become the object of dispute, judged that the oldest of the girls had the most beautiful buttocks and, having fallen in love with her, took her home, where he told his brother what had transpired. The latter wished to reassure himself with his own eyes and went to the place where his brother had told him he would find the other sister, distressed because her buttocks had been judged to be less beautiful. When she showed them to him, the young man found them so beautiful he instantly fell in love with her and while consoling the young woman he persuaded her to go with him, which she willingly did. And thus the two brothers took as their wives the two sisters with the beautiful buttocks, who not long after became extremely wealthy (we do not know how, but it is not difficult to imagine). They decided to erect a temple to Venus, giving her the name of Callipyge which means 'with the beautiful buttocks', since it was from that part that their happiness had come.[47]

This story, which for Cartari had Boccaccio-type overtones, performs a situational reversal: it is not the face which, in the

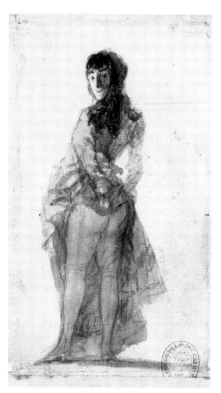

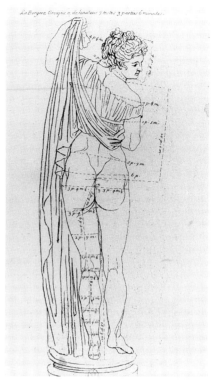

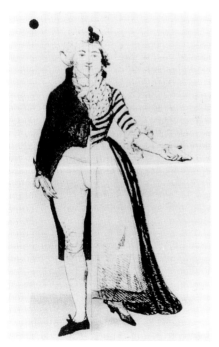

52 Goya, Drawing
A. b (2): *Back View
of Young Woman
Raising Her Skirts*,
1796–7, India ink
wash.

53 Girard Audran,
*The Callipygean
Venus*, engraving
from *Les Proportions
du corps humain
mesurées sur les plus
belles figures de
l'Antiquité* (Paris,
1683).

54 English, *The
Man-Wife*, 18th century,
engraving.

tradition of the love story, is the part of the body where the beauty of the beloved is first manifested; neither is it the whole body that attracts and is fallen in love with, but what is found diametrically opposed to the face, and at the lower extremity of the body. Consequently, the statue of the Callipygean Venus whose creation marks the end of the story shows the goddess in the process of baring her buttocks and contemplating them over her shoulder. And so it came to pass that one of the rare ancient works of art to make its theme the act of undressing, also tackled the awkward, but oh so expressive, simultaneous exhibition of face and backside. The exposing of the lower regions of the body (*anasyrma*) was considered to be an erotic gesture (*schema erotikon*) in Antiquity and was consequently often used by hetaerae as an orgiastic movement.[48] It is to this act that Alberti probably alludes, at the end of the excerpt from the treatise quoted above, when he advises against the representation of indecent torsions, as they 'imitate the movements of histrions (*histrionum motus*), to the detriment of the dignity of the painting'.[49]

Goya's version is significant for all of the above reasons. We can in fact consider the Callipygean Venus (and its variants, *Aphrodite Hetaira* and *Aphrodite Porné*) to be a divinity of the carnivalesque type. If the *Belvedere Torso* was used by the Spanish artist to express the drama of the tortured, split body, the *Venus with the Beautiful Buttocks* is used as a model to represent the comedy of erotic exposure. If it is true, as Madame de Staël claims in her description of the Roman carnival (see Chapter 1), that at the turn of the century it was fashionable to dress up to look like the most famous 'ancient statues', then it is certainly true that no work of art lent itself to this new role more readily than the *Venus with the Beautiful Buttocks*. Let us now study what Goya made of it.

In his drawing from the *San Lucar Sketchbook* (illus. 52), it is not so much the beauty of the proportions that we find in the foreground, but rather the obscenity of the gesture. The lifting of the skirts reveals the person's legs, whose pose is different from the classical counterpoise of the Callipyge (illus. 53). The other major difference is that the head does not turn to look at the buttocks but at the spectator. There is an erotic appeal in this look, as well as a greater twist of the neck that, to put it in Albertian terms, accentuates the representation's 'indecent' nature. The face that gazes out at us is so intensely shaded that some experts believe it could be partially covered by a black mask.[50] This hypothesis is difficult to verify no matter how carefully one examines the drawing, which has many other ambiguous features. The thick hair of Goya's Callipyge also differs from the classical bun. Tumbling over her shoulders as it does, it actually surrounds her face and part of her chin on the shaded side of the head, while the other side of her face remains white and luminous. The artist thus created the impression of a double being in the tradition of ancient festive bi-frontality (illus. 39), but he did so by resorting to the carnivalesque parti-coloured.[51] The duality of the contrasting black/white face is to be found (though differently expressed) in the lower part of the drawing, where the raised skirt reveals not only the buttocks (as was the case in all statues of Callipygean Venus), but also the tight trousers worn by this ambiguous, devious, deceptive person. Comparing this drawing to other contemporary prints (illus. 54), we might well wonder if, for it to be understood properly, it should not be integrated into the discourse on carnivalesque bisexuality, as the 'fools' (or 'queers') documented in other, later drawings have been (illus. 17).[52] The fact that we cannot give a clear-cut response to this question can be attributed to the figure's structure: this double being is precisely double because he or she is full of ambiguities from head to foot.

This small drawing conceals Goya's thoughts on the function of the dual and inverted image. The general framework within which this motif should be placed has been outlined by anthropologists and religious historians:

> Morphologically, cross-dressing and symbolic androgyny are akin to ceremonial orgies. In both of these cases, there is a ritual 'totalisation', a reintegration of opposites, a regression to the primordial indistinct. All in all, it is the symbolic restoration of 'Chaos', of the non-differentiated unity that preceded Creation, and this return to the indistinct is translated by a supreme regeneration, by a prodigious expansion of power.[53]

In Goya, torsion, inversion, the fall and reversal (and the resulting intrinsic vertigo) are therefore figures of a radical renewal *in actu*, where violence alternates with mockery, carnival with revolution, and everything is turned upside down and nothing is put back where it belongs. It is precisely this

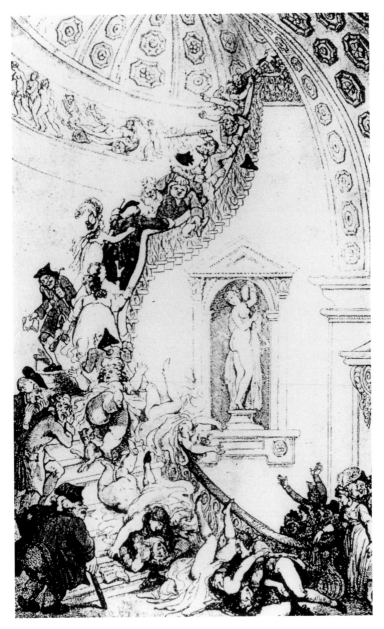

complexity that gives his work its interest. Here we should
mention contemporaneous attempts to tackle the problem of
the reversal of values through that of classical form.[54] One
eloquent example uses the same formal repertoire as Goya,
though in a far less complicated way and with the help of a
particular rhetoric.

56 Detail from William Hogarth, Frontispiece of *The Analysis of Beauty* (London, 1753).

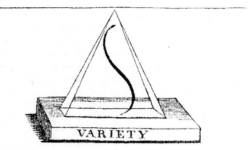

The Englishman Thomas Rowlandson produced a print (illus. 55) in which he mocked the exhibitions held at the Royal Academy in London, thereby poking fun at contemporary art.[55] In the print, we see a typical open-day crush during one of these exhibitions. The staircase is crowded with assorted members of the public who, Rowlandson seems to be telling us, go to view exhibitions as if they were fairground attractions. This image carnivalizes contemporary art and its public[56] with unmistakable allusions to contemporary aesthetics which had declared the serpentine to be a 'line of variety and of beauty'.[57] Here the sinuous line, which in the frontispiece of Hogarth's *Analysis of Beauty* (1753) took on an emblematic importance (illus. 56), is reversed. Everything takes place around a spiral path that reverses the initially ascending direction taken by Hogarth into a ludic *mise-en-scène* of a fall. The staircase is transformed into a sinuous toboggan, and the exhibition is preceded by a symbolic exhibition of the inverted ladies' posteriors that the middle-class gentlemen, who have managed to remain upright, do not hesitate to examine through their lorgnettes. Through the alliterative *exhibition staircase/exhibition 'stare' case*, the caption to the print emphasizes the burlesque transformation of the art exhibition into a house of prostitution. The divinity beneath whose protective smile this metamorphosis takes place is none other than the Callipygean Venus, who, exhibiting her serpentine beauty, towers above the inversion on her pedestal.

Rowlandson did precisely what Goya did not do: he endowed the vertigo of novelty with a particular form, that of caricature.

4 Clinic of Pure Reason

Rose Keller, 'widow of Charles Valentin pastry cook', was the first known victim of Donatien-Alphonse-François, Marquis de Sade. Begging for alms in front of a church on Easter Sunday, she was accosted by and persuaded to go home with 'a young man dressed in a grey frock coat, a hunting knife at his side, a cane in his hand'. There things turned ugly.[1] Here is an extract from the report the surgeon Le Comte made the following day:

> The third of April in the year, seventeen hundred and sixty eight (. . .) I the undersigned Pierre Paul Le Comte Master Surgeon. Permanent corresponding member of the Royal Academy of Surgery Residing in Arcueil. Went to Arcueil castle in order to visit a woman who had been mistreated whom I learned was called Rose Kailair, whom I found to be ailing in several parts of her body, whom I examined and discovered the whole area of the buttocks and a part of the loins whipped and excoriated with cuts and deep and long contusions to the spine of the back, and furthermore a contusion and tear to the top of the right hand, the whole of which appeared to me to have been made by some heavy and sharp instrument, also noticed melted wax in some of the wounds. Made at Arcueil this third of April seventeen hundred and sixty eight.[2]

In the cross-examination headed by the King's councillor, the same surgeon gave the following details:

> (Lecomte) said that what he understood by excoriation, was that only the skin had been removed in different places over the whole area of the buttocks, and a part of the loins, and that with regard to the contusions they were none other than those resulting from a whipping; that with regard to the cuts, he only saw places where the skin had

been removed, and that he felt he could not describe them any better than he already had . . .[3]

The following pages do not in any way claim to deal with the problems of the sexual psychopathology resulting from the Marquis de Sade's taste and actions and documented by eye-witness accounts. This has been done and extremely well.[4] Our deliberations concern Sade the writer and the links between his perverse sexuality and his transgressive literature. The transition from one to the other brings into play a whole net-work of symbolic relationships that we shall endeavour to address. The first is the possibility of discovering within the fantasized act (the torturing of Rose Keller being one of these) a symbolic world that found textual expression and, as it were, fulfilment through literature. The kind of scenes depicting what took place between the Marquis and Rose Keller abound in the novels Sade began to write much later during his long years in prison. So as not to stray too far from the event already quoted, which takes on an initiatory importance in the career of the libertine Sade, we shall examine the reasons why he treated Rose Keller's lower regions as he did.

A man beats a woman, methodically concentrating on the buttocks, whose skin he ruptures and peels off in order to expose the flesh. Thus far, perverse pleasure would seem to have gained the upper hand over any kind of symbolic issue. The fact that 3 April 1768, the day the event took place, was Easter Sunday inevitably leads to speculations on the signifi-cance of the Sadistic ritual that cannot be ignored. In her deposition, the victim made a clear reference to this:

> . . . in her suffering which she says lasted for over an hour and a half she had made him several remonstrations on Religion, begging him to save her soul, and not to give it to the Devil, to spare her because she had not been to confes-sion or done her Easter duties, and he said he would hear her confession, took a chair, and sat down next to her to hear her confession, and she told him that she was asking him if he wanted to make her suffer death and passion as the Jews had done to Jesus Christ, he said yes, that he was developing a taste for it and that this gave him pleasure, she remonstrated with him that it was necessary to think of God, of the Holy Virgin and the Holy Spirit; he left her at that moment grinding his teeth like one possessed.[5]

Anthropological studies have enabled us to find answers to our questions. Arnold van Genepp in his *Manuel de folklore français* points to the existence of customs that link the Carnival-Lent cycle with that of Easter. He reveals that sometimes, the end of Lent coinciding with Easter Sunday is marked by a very simple gesture such as, for example, eating bread and a nice piece of bacon. However, at other times, a more complex ritual takes place although it has the same significance: that of *unlenting oneself* (*se décarêmer*), regaining possession, sometimes violently, of the flesh.[6] This return to licence can also involve a return to quite pronounced primitive brutality, kept in check by Lent, and by an awakening of primitive humanity with its basest instincts. Perhaps we are not mistaken in regarding this episode with Rose Keller as a concrete manifestation of these rites. Van Genepp, who never wrote on Sade but who was probably one of the greatest authorities on popular ancient customs, referred to one, no longer practised nowadays but common in the late Middle Ages, according to which on Easter Sunday men and women would beat one another with birch sticks. He also described the special mass celebrated early on Easter Thursday and known as the *blue mass*, held on behalf of women beaten by their husbands.[7] This violent epilogue of Lent corresponds perfectly with carnivalesque or pre-carnivalesque violence as documented by Ovid in the description he gives of the Roman feast of the Lupercales (15 February), when naked young men, belonging to wolf-men brotherhoods and armed with lashes made from the skin of a sacrificial goat, beat any women they encountered.[8]

One should not, of course, jump to the misguided conclusion that on Easter Sunday 1768, the Marquis de Sade was displaying some obscure folkloric intent or the mysterious prototype of a new ethnographic upsurge or, for that matter, his knowledge of Latin literature. His actions are nonetheless disconcerting (or even more disconcerting) once we are aware of this coincidence and when we come to examine his motives. The fact that sadism, with its metaphysics of martyrdom, sacrifice and expiation, is 'a bastard of Catholicism' has been acknowledged for a long time, and there are excellent studies on the subject.[9] The area where this explosion of erotic or Sadeian cruelty links up with the Carnival-Lent dialectic has remained outside the scope of interpreters, a quasi-paradoxical fact given, on the one hand, the recent upsurge of studies on sadism and, on the other, those linked to the Carnival. If this fundamental aspect, on which we now propose to focus, has never received the attention it deserves, it is probably due to the fact that, despite their common ancestry, a gulf is being created between the Sadeian world and that of the Carnival, as a result of there being an absence in Sade of one of the principal terms of carnivalesque phenomenology. What Sade lacks is neither licence nor excess nor reversal nor transvestism. What he misses is that which is created in reaction to the others: joy, real joy. The ludism found in the ancient rites of violence has been replaced by the seriousness with which they are carried out in a sad, grey world devoid of smiles and laughter. If, as some commentators have stressed,[10] there is humour to be found, it is involuntary, just like the absurdity of gravity, the hilarity of solemnity.

We shall endeavour to examine a mutilated carnivalesque structure by initially tackling the reasons for and significance of its unsatisfactory functioning, in order then to concentrate on the creation of the Sadeian imagination in relation to contemporary imagination. Our first statement is that the 'philosophy' underlying Sade's works and thoughts is extremely straightforward. Maurice Blanchot defined it as 'first and foremost a philosophy of interest, then of integral egoism. Each must do as he pleases, each has no other law than his own pleasure'.[11] But what Blanchot does not say is that this premise (which only partly explains Sade) is in fact none other than that of the Carnival and that it comes directly from Rabelais, of whom we know the Marquis was an avid reader.[12] Carnivalesque licence and permissiveness are traditionally restricted, as Carnival itself was restricted to the festival period or (in the case of Rabelais) to a favoured spot (the utopian Abbey of Thélème). In Sade, the enclosed area as the space-time of the orgy is found in the detailed description given of the castle of Silling in *One Hundred and Twenty Days of Sodom* (1782). But by combining it with the theme of travel, which reaches its climax in *Juliette's* (1797/9) European journey, Sade proclaims debauchery as an eternal law and an element of the world's supporting structure. Sadeian rituals, of which we have so far given only one example, copied ancient practices into a literary structure, repetitive and stereotypical *ad nauseam*. Alongside the licence and transgression that this literature heralded as a universal law, it is necessary to high-light the immediate consequences of the anguish that pervaded the last days of the Carnival: to revel in flesh as though there were no tomorrow. But if traditional people were content with the Carnival/Lent alternation, and were able to find in its rhythm an equilibrium by which to live, in Sade the anguish of *carne levamen* is constant, and Carnival is perpetual. In this way, the festival loses not only its exceptional character but also its popular aspect. Endless, Sade's carnival is also highly individualistic. Despite the frequent and complicated orgies described in Sade's novels, the ritual violence is no longer concerned with the pleasure of the masses, but with that of the individual. Revolution is no longer on the horizon; murder is.

And yet despite its exaggerated egotism, Sade's literature can be viewed against the backdrop of the Revolution, the Terror and the Consulate. The chronological landmarks are unmistakable. In July 1789, having been incarcerated for twelve years for debauchery, Sade was hiding in a hole in his prison wall in the Bastille the twenty-metre long roll containing the *One Hundred and Twenty Days of Sodom* (begun in 1782). Free at last, in 1791 (Year 1) he published *Justine or the Misfortunes of Virtue*. In the middle of the Terror, he wrote *The Philosophy of the Boudoir* (published in 1795); in 1797, it was the turn of *The New Justine followed by the Story of Juliette, her Sister*, in 1800 that of *Crimes of Love, preceded by an Idea on Novels*. Maurice Blanchot has underlined the fact that if Sade was able 'to recognize himself' in the Revolution, it was 'only insofar as, exchanging one law for another, it represented for a while the possibility of a regime without laws'.[13] It should be pointed out, however, that Sade's years of freedom between 1790 and 1801, preceded by twelve years' imprisonment and followed by another thirteen, were not the years when he wrote his books, but when they were circulated. These writings, produced in the bowels of prisons and brought to light by the whim of an author who, in the case of his most obscure (*The Story of Juliette*), denied his own authorship, are paradoxically and essentially unreadable.[14] Not only because, as Sade himself said, the story is 'impure' or because certain passages are 'unpleasant', but because the written word is like an instrument of torture directed against the reader.[15] Like some of Goya's plates that 'cannot be looked at', certain passages in Sade 'cannot be read'. Sade's text is violent and carnivalesque insofar as it attacks the reader and reverses the very idea of literature:

> It is now dear reader, that you must adjust your heart and your mind to the most impure story that has ever been written since the world began, no such book can be found either among the ancients or among the moderns. Imagine that all the pleasures that are honest or prescribed by that animal of which you constantly speak though you do not know it and which you call nature, imagine, I say, that these pleasures are excluded from this collection and that when you happen upon them, it will only be when they are accompanied by some crime or coloured by some infamy. No doubt, many of the transformations you will see painted will displease you we know, but (. . .) it is up to you to take them or leave them . . .[16]

Two observations must be made at once. The first refers to the awareness of the reversed 'norm'/'transformation' relationship, and therefore to the awareness of the reversal performed (in Sade's vision) by the literary act. The second refers to the artificial freedom his text is likely to give to whoever will read it, and which we might call the carnivalization of the author/reader pact. In reality, the reader *faced with* Sade's pages is no more 'free' than the people bound *in* and *by* his texts. Indeed Sade sees himself as indebted to a generalized carnivalesque practice that reverses values, turns habits upside down and becomes permanent from being cyclical. Before being a perverse erotic practice, sadism was an attack on established hierarchies:

> In the eyes of nature all form is equal, nothing is lost in the huge crucible in which its variations function, all the portions of matter that throw themselves into it are incessantly renewed into other forms and whatever we do to it, none would offend it directly, none would be able to affront it, our destructiveness would rekindle its power, strengthen its energy and would not weaken it.[17]

Hence transformation becomes the norm, and vice that triumphs over virtue is nothing more than a 'reconstitution in the order of things'.[18] One of Sade's great ambitions was to outdo the ancient dialectic 'world upside down/world right way round' by proclaiming the unique truth of a 'perverse world'[19] where differences were either cancelled out or merged.

Let us therefore examine the rhetoric on which Sade's universe is based. It is – as we might well expect – carnivalesque. Should we summarize it, this is the picture we will get: humans are animals; what is low prevails over what is high; pleasure is to be found in inversion, indeed in perversion; transgression is the norm; normality is transgression; vice is virtue; virtue is vice.

Other terms could no doubt be added to this synopsis and each term developed one by one with ramifications and a plethora of examples. But we will take a shortcut. To begin with, we shall examine the vice/virtue and fortune/misfortune binomials in relation to each other. Such an analysis strikes us as being imperative given the importance attached to these pairs of notions in the titles chosen by Sade. Then, we shall tackle the techniques of reversal that involve human beings by concentrating on the elements of carnivalesque reversal to be found in the formation of names and description of bodies.

MORAL DISTORTION

The Marquis de Sade wrote (rewrote) the story of his virtuous heroine Justine three times: in 1787 under the title *The Misfortunes of Virtue*, then four years later expanded into *Justine or The Tragedies of Virtue, followed by the Story of Juliette and her Sister or The Prosperities of Vice*. The third date is uncertain. Experts have repeatedly drawn attention to the possibility of an edition in 1799 or 1800.[20] Whichever is correct, it is obvious that the theme of the 'tragedy of virtue' was always with him, whereas that of the 'prosperities of vice' was presented as a gigantic 'appendix' (six volumes in-folio with prints).

It has not been sufficiently emphasized that here Sade was returning, by reversing it, to one of the great themes of Christian philosophy; the struggle between vice and virtue, which had already been given a literary voice in vernacular Latin. As far back as the beginning of the fifth century, Prudentius's *Psychomachia*, to cite the best-known example, featured in allegorical form the moral conflict between Faith and Idolatry, Modesty and Lust, Patience and Anger, Pride and Humility and so on. The Virtues always won in the end.[21]

Through their titles, Sade's novels announce the assimilation of this tradition, as well as the transformation they perform, because this time Vice prospers and Virtue founders. The very first version of Justine's adventures embodies in fact the misadventures of Justice, a personification that, alongside Prudence, Strength and Temperance, gave Christian tradition its highly codified system of Cardinal Virtues. Sade's explanation is unambiguous:

> It is not whether a man chooses vice or virtue that he will find happiness, for virtue like vice is only a way of behaving in the world; it is therefore not a question of following the one rather than the other, it is only a question of paving the general way; he who strays will always be in the wrong. In a world that is entirely virtuous, I would recommend virtue because it comes with rewards, happiness will inevitably follow; in a world that is totally corrupt, I would never recommend anything but vice.[22]

In the shadow of this reversed morality, the title of the story from which this quotation is taken contains an allusion to a notion that, in subsequent versions, becomes progressively more blurred. This is the notion of 'fortune' as opposed to 'misfortune'. This binomial was to be replaced by 'prosperity/tragedy', a process by which Sade confused the issue and which once again leads us back at least to the Christian Middle Ages.

Goddess of Fickleness in Antiquity, randomly distributing her favours, Fortuna was soon given as her symbol a wheel that never stopped turning, toppling – in an instant – those who thought they were on top, raising those who thought they were cast out forever.[23] This iconography soon split, however, and two divergent ways of regarding luck appeared. According to one of these, Fortuna's blindness is evoked by a wheel turned by winds blowing from the four corners of the universe (illus. 57). Their concerted efforts produce a movement that is uninterrupted and has no pre-established order, thus leading to spectacular reversals: the king seated at the top will fall at any moment; another will take his place and will fall in turn. The second interpretation acknowledged the assimilation of this ancient motif into Christianity, because the 'prime mover' of the wheel of fortune was none other than 'the hand of God' (illus. 58). In this way, 'Fortune'

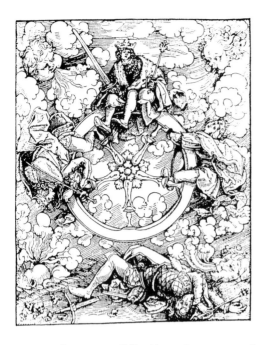

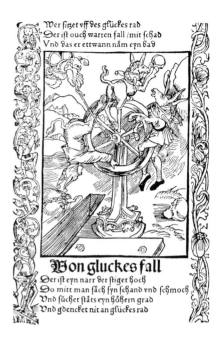

was no longer as 'blind' as she was at the beginning of her iconographic career and was able to assimilate a whole system of moral values.[24] This structure was extremely simple and amalgamated the high/low dialectic with Christian values: the last would be the first, the high (*Superbia*, for example) would be vanquished by the low (*Humilitas*), etc. Hence the implicit moral: to try to climb to the top of the Wheel of Fortune is tantamount to Folly. This is in fact Sebastian Brant's message in *The Ship of Fools* (1494):

57 The Petrarca-Master, *The Wheel of Fortune*, c. 1500 –25, woodcut.

58 Attributed to Albrecht Dürer, Engraving from Sebastian Brant, *Das Narrenschiff* (Basel, 1494).

> Whoever follows the wheel of fortune
> Exposes himself to tumbles and troubles
> Could fall into the brink.
> The Fool who climbs to the top,
> May the seat of his pants be clean!
> Whoever always wants to go up a grade
> Should remember that whoever rises
> To the top falls back to the ground.
> None reaches that high on earth
> May he be sure of his tomorrow
> May his luck never change.[25]

It comes as no surprise that this expansion of the ancient motif transformed the Wheel of Fortune into one of the emblematic objects of carnivalesque processions.[26] The print and accompanying text of *The Ship of Fools* (illus. 58) were already a reflection of this. Not only are they a reminder of human destiny in the face of God, but they also illustrate in allegorical form the symbolic social reversal established by the Carnival.

At the end of the eighteenth century the most important interpretations of this reversal came from Goya and Sade. In the former case, *Capricho* 56 (illus. 59) conforms to a vision of the metaphysics of the fall as well as to the traditional moral imperative. The title of the plate is *Ups and Downs* (*Subir y bajar*). It depicts a giant with the legs and feet of a goat, seated on a curved surface (which could be that of the globe itself) supporting like an intrepid gymnast a man whose hair is on fire and who is holding fire in both hands. The instability of his position is reinforced by the characters in free fall to the giant's left and right. A moment earlier, it was they who were where the giant now finds himself, for an instant, in front of the viewer. An atmosphere vaguely reminiscent of a fair where acrobats and fire-eaters interact would appear to reveal the etching's distant origins. The other source – moral and historic – can be found in the explanatory inscriptions, the one in the Prado commentary being the closest to the spirit of Goya: 'Ups and downs. Fortune is unkind to those who court her. She rewards with smoke the trouble of climbing, and punishes with downfall him who succeeds in rising.' The inscription points to the fact that this etching was conceived (or that it was considered very early on) as a new variant of an old motif. It underlines the futility of all ambitions to elevation and introduces the notion of 'fall' as a 'punishment'. Two other ancient commentaries on the *Caprichos* introduce other elements.[27] They identify the goat-man as the personification of Lust and the precariously balanced person as Charles iv's Prime Minister, Godoy. More important than these political allusions (which are possible, but always debatable), is the fact that the notion of 'Vice' (as Lust) is integrated into the structure of the Wheel of Fortune, which is our prime concern here. The wheel is none other than the Earth itself, and Vice the monster who inhabits it.

This is where the Marquis de Sade – indirectly, of course – comes in. For him too, Vice is the mainstay of the world, except that it now unequivocally moves in the same direction

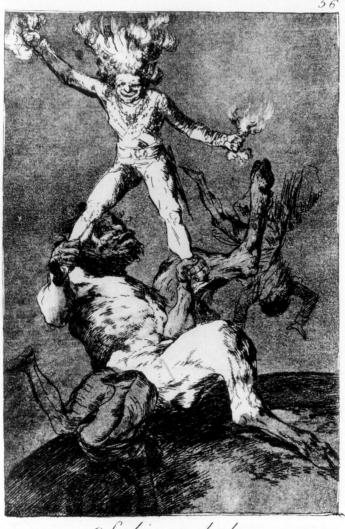

56

59 Goya, *Capricho 56: Ups and Downs*, 1797–8, etching and aquatint.

Subir y bajar.

as Fortune. This reversal is to be found on two levels. The first is in Sade's meticulous descriptions of perverse debaucheries, sometimes illustrated with explanatory prints (illus. 60). These can often be seen as particular cases in which the unwavering mechanisms of the ancient 'moral wheels' are concretized. Great Pan is there, as a symbolic presence, in the form of a 'God of the Gardens' who supports a complicated structure created so that the debaucher can satisfy his lust and the virtuous can suffer.

60 Illustration for D. -A. -F. de Sade, *La Philosophie dans le boudoir* (Paris, 1795), engraving.

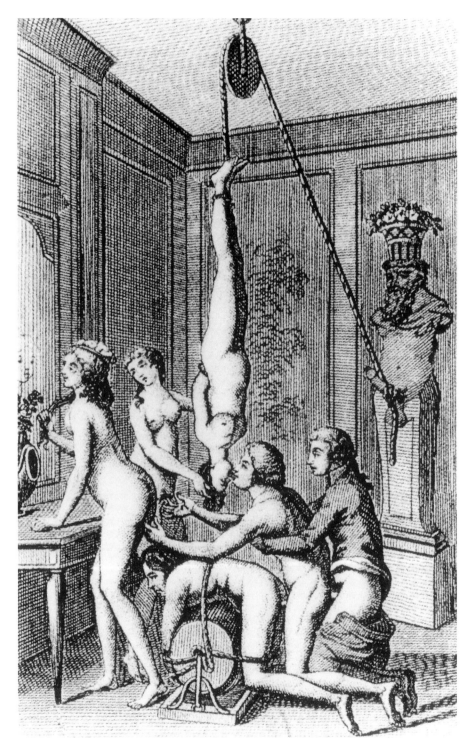

The second way of accessing Sadeian reversal is by means of the countless discursive passages where, through the words of his characters, the author communicates his new 'moral philosophy'. By way of an example, here is an extract from the lesson given by Mme Dubois to her perverted pupil:

> Thirty years ago, an uninterrupted succession of vices and crimes led me step by step to fortune, I touched it; another two or three happy blows and I passed from the state of misery and mendacity into which I had been born to an income of fifty thousand pounds. Do you think that at any time during this brilliant career of mine, I was ever once pricked by an instant of remorse? Do not believe it, I never was. A dreadful reversal would suddenly have driven me from the pinnacle into the abyss so I could not accept it any more; I might complain about men and my mistakes, but I will always be at peace with my conscience.[28]

In this excerpt (and others like it), it is not difficult to recognize the direct dialogue that is established with the ancient symbolism of the gyratory mechanisms of the rise and fall, a dialogue whose function is to transform the ancient *topos* into a form stripped of ethical constraints in the name of the power of Nature. All virtue is, from this point of view, 'bad' because it is 'against nature'. Of all Sade's characters, the 'just' Justine is the one who is the most aware of this: 'Oh! Just heavens, I exclaimed with bitterness, it is therefore impossible for any virtuous action to be born in me, without it being instantly punished by the cruellest of misfortunes most dreaded by me in the universe!'[29] And so, each time Justine invokes the heavens, they remain silent or, at the very most, signal their anger. The worst probably being the moment that brings her life (and the novel that tells her story) to a close. The scene is famous. To protect her vicious sister, Juliette, Justine endeavours, in a desperate final attempt at virtue, to close a window blown open by the storm, but:

> . . . a flash of lightning knocked her back into the middle of the drawing room leaving her lifeless on the floor (. . .) struck down so that even hope itself could no longer remain in her. The lightning had entered through the right breast, it had burned her chest, and had come out through her mouth, disfiguring her face so much that she was a horror to behold.[30]

There is no such thing, Sade tells us, as 'Divine Justice', only – at the very most – 'Natural Injustice'. Even in the details of Justine's death we find the presence of a superior force, a universal power that is blind but equipped with a 'quasi-conscience' that punishes the good and saves the bad. The piercing of the virtuous body and its 'dis-figuration' reveal the 'perversity' of this force in relation to all dreams of universal justice.

This conclusion makes any detailed approach to the ancient system of virtues and vices, still functioning in Sade but the other way round, completely redundant. We should like to give one further and, in our opinion, important example, because it reveals that the justification of lust and violence, usually thought to represent the uniqueness of the Sadeian discourse, is, in the final analysis, no more than a synecdoche of a much greater reversal. This time, the example is taken from the *Story of Juliette*:

> . . . modesty is a chimera; sole product of mores and education, it is what we would call a fashion of habit; nature having created man and woman naked, it is impossible that she would also have given them an aversion or a shame at being so. If man had always followed the principles of nature, he would not know modesty; a fatal truth that proves that there are certain virtues that have no other cradle than the complete ignorance of the laws of nature. What distortion we would give to Christian moral, if we were to examine in this way all the principles of which it is made! But we shall talk of all this. Today let us speak of other things, so get undressed, like us.[31]

It is crucial to understand the significance of the order in which this diatribe ends: Sade's characters undress in order to speak. In the Sadeian Carnival, man does not mask himself; he unmasks himself, and nudity is nothing other than the cruel unveiling of his innermost being. What we have here is probably a radically transformed reflection of the philosophy of the Enlightenment: naked man is essential man, which is to say, nasty, lecherous, vicious and bestial. Roland Barthes quite rightly observed that Sadeian orgies were deprived of the slow eroticism of the *strip-tease* and that the victims' bodies as well as those of the torturers were immediately undressed.[32] His ingenious explanation (that strip-tease is an epiphanic narrative and that the atheist Sade destroyed the sacred aura surrounding everything including sex) needs to be reformulated. In fact, Sade's novels are full of such phrases as 'get undressed', 'bare yourselves', 'he/she bared him/herself', 'he/she was instantly naked', 'here he/she/they is/are completely naked', etc. The speed of command and action is, we believe, the consequence of a wish (quite literally) to expose man. There is a second command, which, from a statistical reading of Sade's books, could be even more advantageous than the stereotype 'get undressed'. This order, more obscure but no less significant, is: 'hitch up', 'tuck up', indeed 'take off!' This order also leaves no room for the teasing slowness of amorous preambles, because it is generated by the same imperative as the more generic 'get undressed'. The only difference being that following the order 'hitch up!' that is so frequent in the Marquis's accounts, the body is only partially exposed, though enough for it to uncover – and as quickly as possible – the most important part of man and his body, that is to say his backside. In the *schema erotikon*, as well as in the tradition to which Sade was still attached, uncovering the buttocks had a tendency to become a gesture (perhaps even '*the gesture*') that best defined 'distortion'. In answer to the great question that emerged during the Enlightenment, 'What is man?',[33] Sade responded with reductions that followed on from one another: man is reduced to his body, the body to its seat, the seat to its centre – that is to say, to a void or, worse still, to the simple passing of waste. All this probably took place indirectly, beginning with the originally carnivalesque apotheosis of the ancient *anasyrma*: '. . . she (Madam Brentôme) sometimes contented herself with tucking up rather than removing their clothes, finding in the action of raising or gathering up their skirts, even more pleasure than in the too great a facility afforded by their complete nakedness.'[34] Or (it is Juliette that speaks): 'She has the most beautiful arse in the world, said the great vicar, the moment he saw me all naked.'[35] This sentence is significant since it highlights the synecdoche: all naked, for only one part of Juliette's body is being admired, that which defines her essence.

Sexual inversion, of which there is no lack in the Marquis's novels, is no more than a continuation (or maybe even the emblem) of a reversal that is much more important and more wide ranging, where what is behind takes the place of what is in front (the anus surpasses the sexual organs), what is low takes the place of what is high (the posterior surpasses the head). This is probably why, in the middle of one of the sodomite orgies in *Juliette*, when Ducroz exclaims 'it's *a question of taste*', Volmar promptly replies (and Sade emphasizes this with italics), 'It's *philosophy*, it's *reason*.'[36] It is also why one of the darkest characters in Sade, Saint-Fond (whose name of course lends itself to several alliterative and homophonic games), at the very moment that he is exposing his post-Termidor utopia, proposes a counter-revolutionary law that begins as it were 'at the bottom':

> 'And what are, say I, the laws that you propose?'
>
> 'Firstly I wish to work on public opinion through fashion: you know the influence it has on the French':
>
> *First Article*: I would create clothes for men and women that leave almost completely uncovered all the lustful parts and the buttocks in particular.[37]

The driving force behind the Sadeian 'Revolution' is fairly straightforward: in Western tradition, the backside – its name, its use and of course its exhibition – was (is) absolutely forbidden. It was (is) a wretched part of the body and, as the orifice for the passing of shameful waste, profane lowness par excellence.[38] In the Christian West, it was only during the licentious period of the Carnival that it could be named and exhibited.[39] But by the end of the eighteenth century, the Carnival was dead. Sade returned once again to some of its functions through the 'distortion' that makes the body's nether regions the very ersatz of the sacred: 'I shall therefore see it, this divine and precious arse that I aspire to so ardently! . . . Good God! Such plumpness and freshness, such lustre, such elegance! I have never seen such a beautiful one!'[40] This ludic sacralization, found in the orgiastic descriptions and accompanying prints, spawns a very real and complex iconography, in which the Christian rite overlaps with its opposite number, and where adoration blasphemes (illus. 61). The backside is, in this context, multi-purpose. It can, as an idol of a new religion, replace the crucifix and, as a place of sacrifice, be a substitute for the altar. The moment the theme of the black mass (or counter-mass) is tackled in contemporary prints (in this instance by Goya), the ritualization of the backside is more cautious though no less significant. The witches' Sabbath in *Capricho* 71 (illus. 62) brings the anti-beauties together under the starry vault of a 'cosmic temple'. They are like the excrescence of the earth, whose very crust bulges before the spectator's eyes, looking like the allusive form of an immense backside. The same totemic device is produced in a diametrically opposed way: in Sade, the backside replaces the sky/heavens; in Goya, it is a substitute for the earth.

The Sadeian search for an iconographic support system to blasphemously make the posterior sacred inevitably leads Sade to the pagan iconography of the naked goddess. She is the idol who, whether implicitly or explicitly, holds sway over most of the orgies:

> My friend was as naked as I was. In an instant we were examining one another in silence at first for a few minutes. Clairwil was fired up at the sight of the beauty that nature had lavished upon me. I could not get my fill of admiring hers. (. . .) Those buttocks! Dear God! It was Venus's arse so adored by the Greeks. Never had I seen more delicious cheeks.[41]

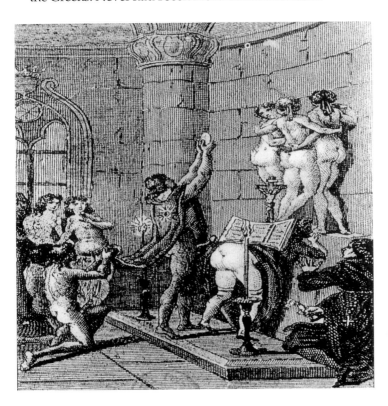

61 Illustration for D. -A. -F. de Sade, *La Nouvelle Justine* (Holland, 1797), engraving.

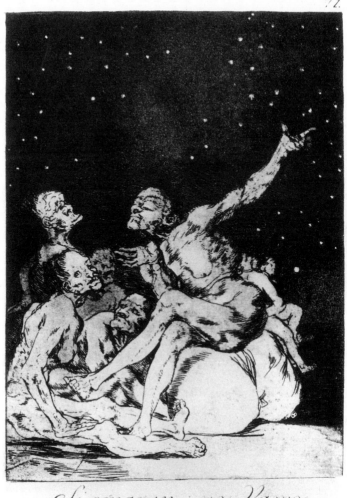

62 Goya, *Capricho 71: We Must Be off with the Dawn*, 1797–8, etching and aquatint.

Si amanece; nos Vamos.

And again: 'There is not one single corner of the earth that did not have temples and spectators to this so-called crime of sodomy. The Greeks, who made *so to speak a virtue* of it [our italics] erected a statue to it under the name of The Callipygean Venus.'[42] In *The Philosophy of the Boudoir*, from which this quotation is taken, the union of the emblematic image of distortion and its actual naming put the final seal on the reversal, now achieved, of the system of vices and virtues. The *Callipygean Venus* is the tutelary image of the *mundus perversus*.

Reversal is the driving force behind Sadeian anthroponymy. Mme de Lorsange is a she-devil and, like Saint-Fleurent, the only 'saint-like' thing about her is half her name. Saint-Font is in truth a bottomless ('*sans fond*') pit of nastiness. About the name of the terrible monk Clément, Sade tells us: '. . . let us paint but his figure. [He] was a man of forty-eight, enormously fat, gigantically tall, with wild, dark eyes, who expressed himself only with harsh words uttered by his gruff voice, a veritable satyr of a man with the appearance of a tyrant.'[43] Rather than being the incarnation of clemency, this person is one of the figures from Sade's 'bestiary' who still awaits an in-depth study. When this is undertaken, it will no doubt have to take account of the animal-like figures associated with 'intemperance' (*distemperanza*), the kind Giovan Battista Della Porta described, and his illustrator drew (illus. 63, 64) to produce the mixed motif of the 'satyr':

> Satyrs are a mixture of men and goats, and symptomatic of lust. They were named 'satyrs' after the Greek, because of the exhibition of the male member and because of the fact that they were licentious and lustful. They have a rasping voice, a mixture of the bleating of the sheep and the whinnying of the horse (. . .) they have flat nostrils and an uneven brow with goats' horns at each end.[44]

A different system was brought into operation when it came to naming the victims. It could be described as a neo-classical onomastic system. The list is long: Hebe, Rose, Zephyr, Adonis, Cupid, Giton, Narcissus, Aglaé, Aurora, etc.[45] Sometimes, however, the levels merge and the desired effects are all the more powerful because they highlight the transgressive inversion. As Justine says: 'The two men who had brought me and whom I could now see more clearly by the light of the candles illuminating the room, were no older than twenty-five to thirty. The first, called La Rose, was a beautiful dark-haired man built like Hercules.'[46]

But Sade's most common method, and the one richest in significance, was probably the one where neo-classical anthroponymy blended with anonymity. Then it is that Adonises, Cupids, the Graces, Hercules, Ganymedes, Venuses, Omphales and a whole host of nudes people orgiastic scenes.

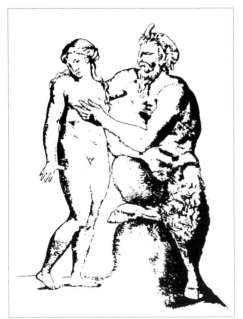 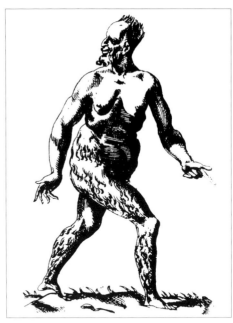

63 *Satyr and Young Woman*, engraving from Giovan Battista Della Porta, *Della fisionomia dell'huomo* (Naples, 1610).

64 *The Lustful Man*, engraving from Della Porta, *Della fisionomia dell'huomo*.

Corresponding to this neo-classical anonymity there is a descriptive formula whose stereotypye has been repeatedly underscored: 'her body was beautiful, very white, the most beautiful arse in the world';[47] 'she was tall, made to be painted';[48] 'beautiful like the very goddess of youth, a very white skin';[49] 'I had never seen such a beautiful body';[50] 'a charming girl, she had the features of Minerva herself, disguised beneath those of Love'[51] – the quotations could go on forever. Sade himself was fully conscious of this descriptive monotony: 'I shall not continue to paint these beauties: they were all so equally superior that my brushes would inevitably become monotonous. I shall content myself with naming them . . .'[52] To name rather than describe is indeed a strange procedure that needs to be examined. It is not difficult to see that there is a paradox in Sade's stroll through the world of perfection: all these monotonous beauties have a narrative function that can be found in the destructive impulses of the libertines. Objects of these libertines' debauchery, they do however, in the majority of cases and as though by a miracle, escape total annihilation.[53] They survive the blows like fleeing fantasies or immovable statues. With 'alabaster whiteness', 'lily-white skin', 'marble-like breasts', Sade's beauties are as attractive and boring as endless collections of neo-classical models (illus. 65) whilst retaining something of the disturbing unfamiliarity of the Roman Carnival masks that so frightened Mme de Staël (see Chapter 1).

We must avoid superficial interpretations. The eroticism with which this stone world is invested does not add a new perversion to a catalogue already rich in Sadeian aberrations. It is, and this is important, the very figure of desire and its failure to satisfy. Sade's approach is distinct in Enlightenment philosophy, which on more than one occasion tackled the metaphor of the animate statue, as we can see, for example, in the justly famous pages of Diderot's *Rêve d'Alambert*:

> 'I should like you to tell me what the differences are, as you see them, between man and statue, between marble and flesh.'
> 'Very little. We make marble with flesh, and flesh with marble.'[54]

The perverse use of this metaphor is, however, new. To the 'divine marquis': 'Women are nothing more than machines of voluptuousness (. . .). The Universe is full of ordered statues that come, that go, that act, that eat and that digest, without ever being aware of anything.'[55] This smooth and perfect world is suddenly brought to life by the 'shocks', 'irritations',

65 Thomas Rowlandson, *The Court of Statues*, *c.* 1800, engraving.

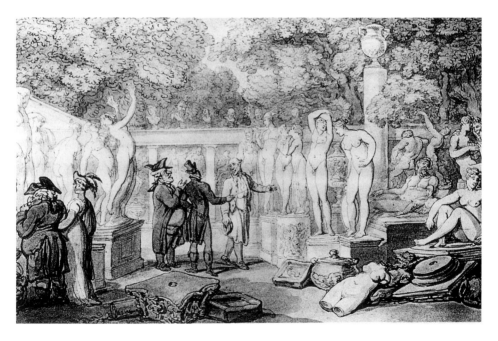

'ticklings', 'violations' and 'pains' of the orgy:[56] 'He looks, he touches, he feels, the air immediately vibrates with a dreadful whistle. All this beautiful flesh changes colour, the brightest shade of carnation mingles with the brilliance of the lily.'[57] Or: '"Come on," he said approaching his victim, "prepare yourself, you must suffer," and the cruel man by striking her twenty-five times soon turned the delicate pink of this fresh skin into vermilion.'[58]

What we have here is a somewhat radical way of 'colouring' the alabaster of perfection. The first process, where Sade brings into play all his imaginative and descriptive talents, involves the ordering of the combinations and permutations that precede voluptuousness. In the same way that neo-classical painters produced paintings of classical statues (illus. 66), so Sade imagined 'paintings' and 'attitudes' (the notions themselves are taken from the language of the studio)[59] whose *dispositio* and *inventio* verged on the unbelievable. We shall spare the reader the more detailed descriptions and limit ourselves to a few examples, in which we are presented with the principles of 'order' and 'composition':

> Saint-Fond woke at five. Everything through the good offices of myself [Juliette is speaking] had been prepared in the drawing room (salon), this is the order in which the persons were arranged: naked apart from a simple garland of roses, we could see, in the right of the tableau the three maids marked out for the orgies; I had grouped them together like the Graces.[60]

We shall see, as we go through these descriptions, that the colour that 'brings' white 'to life' is primarily pink and not the vermilion of orgiastic extremes. We could replace the odd word and write *Salon* with a capital letter so as to give the impression that someone like Bachaumont or Diderot is describing a visit to the Louvre.[61] By way of an example, let us listen to Diderot describing a painting by Jean-Jacques Lagrenée that was shown at the 1767 Salon:

> Hersé is seated on the left. Her left leg is stretched out and rests on Mercury's left knee. She is in profile, Mercury frontal, and seated in front of her, a little lower down and a little more in the background. In the extreme right Aglaure is parting a curtain and glaring angrily and jealously at her

sister's happiness. Artists will perhaps tell you that the principal figures are too heavily delineated and coloured with no tones. I do not know if they are right; but, having recalled nature, I exclaimed despite them and their verdict: 'Oh, the beautiful flesh, the beautiful feet, the beautiful arms, the beautiful hands! The beautiful skin! From which life and the pink of blood exude; Beneath this delicate and sensitive envelope, I trace the imperceptible and bluish course of the veins and arteries. I speak of Hersé and of Mercury. The flesh of art wrestles with the flesh of nature. Take your hand to the canvas and you will see that the imitation is as powerful as reality and that it surpasses it through the beauty of its forms. One never grows tired of perusing the neck, the arms, the breasts, the feet, the hands, the head of Hersé. I take my lips to it and I cover all these charms with kisses. Oh Mercury, what are you doing? What are you waiting for? You allow that thigh to rest on yours, and you do not seize it, do not devour it?[62]

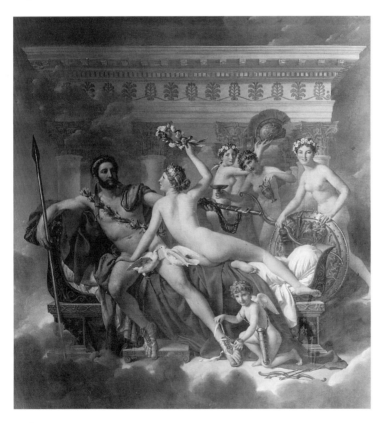

66 Jaques-Louis David, *Mars Disarmed by Venus and the Graces*, 1824, oil on canvas.

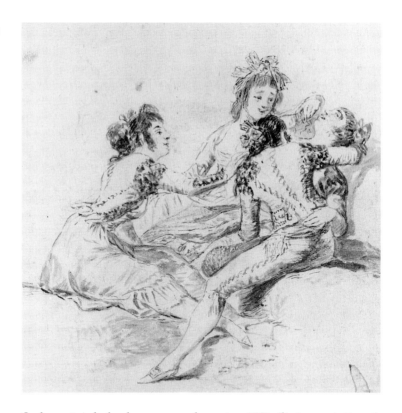

67 Goya, Drawing
B. 7: *The Fainting,*
1796–7, India ink
and wash.

Sade certainly had some good masters! His 'living paintings',
just like many of the paintings of the Salons, are fantasy
machines, representations that display desire instead of con-
suming it. At once alive and static, they follow the silent
rhetoric of the layout and reaction to it: 'All scenes of fucking
are preceded by a moment of calm; it is as though we wish to
savour voluptuousness whole and that we fear it might
escape us should we speak. I had been recommended to
savour it carefully so as to be able to make a comparison; I was
in silent ecstasy . . .'[63]

The road that leads from the 'living painting' of the exhibition to the orgy is sometimes explicitly reversed, and scenes
depicting debauchery then become the 'artistic' model:

Ah! To think that it was necessary to have an engraver
transmit to posterity this voluptuous and divine portrait.
But lust, crowning our actors too quickly was perhaps
unable to give the artist time to capture them. It is not easy
for art, which has no movement, to produce an action
whose movement creates the whole soul; and this is what

127

also makes of engraving the most difficult and most thank-less of arts.[64]

Despite Sade's lamentations (which perhaps primarily con-cerned the difficulty of illustrating his own stories), there is no doubt that the art of 'tableaux' and 'attitudes' developed a language of its own in the second half of the eighteenth and beginning of the next century, a language which, despite its more or less strict links with 'convention', quite openly revealed its true nature to be a *mise-en-scène* of erotic intrigues.[65] The quoted fragment from Diderot's description is a brilliant example of this. Images, whether painted, drawn or engraved, generally sought – essentially for reasons of con-vention – the middle ground between display and censure of Eros. Two examples of this, at one and the same time contrast-ing and similar, are David's *Mars Disarmed by Venus and the Graces* (illus. 66) and Goya's *The Fainting* (illus. 67), where despite a whole battery of decoys and subterfuges (white doves; skilful distortions; functional censures in the first; clothes, ambiguous gestures and torsions in the second) they do not succeed in concealing what cannot be (and should not be) completely concealed, as this would result in the oblitera-tion of the whole image.[66]

We know very little about Sade's familiarity with contempo-rary imagery, but we do have an excellent document on his use of classical art. This is his *Voyage d'Italie* (1775–6) partly re-worked in *Juliette* (1787).[67] When at the end of July 1775, Sade, with charges of sodomy, homo- and heterosexuality, flagella-tion, masturbation on the crucifix and the corruption of young girls hanging over him, fled over the Alps, he was not yet the writer he would become, but he was already the libertine he would remain. His crossing of the Alps, described in detail, instigated a whole series of interconnected transgressive acts. After the Alps it was the Apennines, where in the shade of Pietramala (this toponymy obviously excited Sade's imagina-tion) lay Florence. The city was to inspire his descriptions of the fortified castles[68] that were the arenas for his literary orgies: 'The city is completely surrounded by a great wall and flanked by a few old towers. And inside are ramparts that circumscribe the city.'[69] In the centre is the Palazzo Vecchio: 'This building is like a long rectangular fortress. At the front there is a tower two hundred and sixty feet high and built as an afterthought which

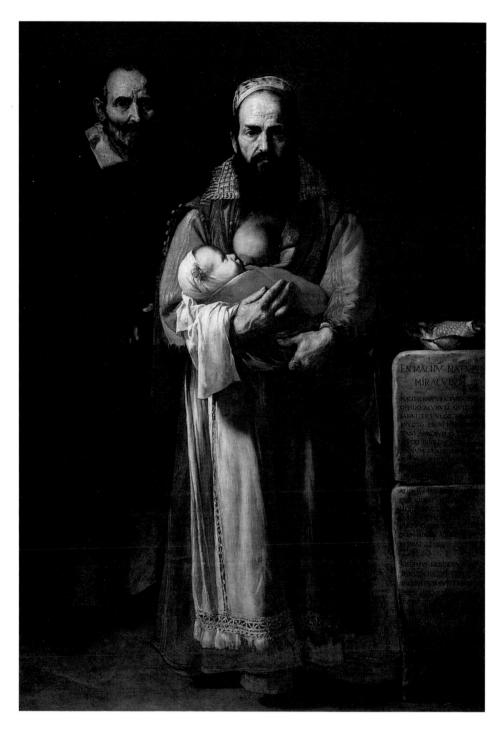

68 Jusepe Ribera, *The Bearded Lady*, 1631, oil on canvas.

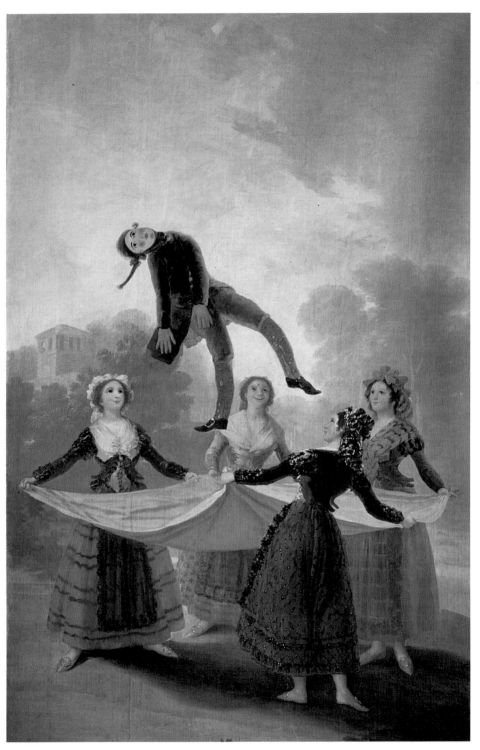

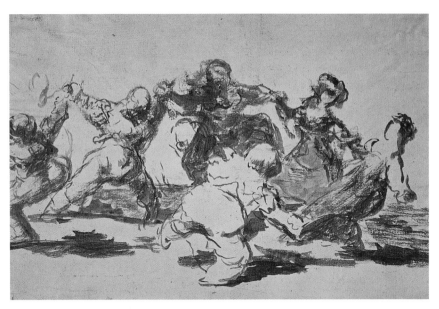

69 Goya, *The Straw Man*, 1791–2, oil on canvas.

70 Goya, Preparatory drawing for *Merry Absurdity*, 1815–24, sepia on paper.

71 Goya, Preparatory drawing for *Capricho* 52, *Fine Feathers Make Fine Birds*, 1797–8, red ink wash.

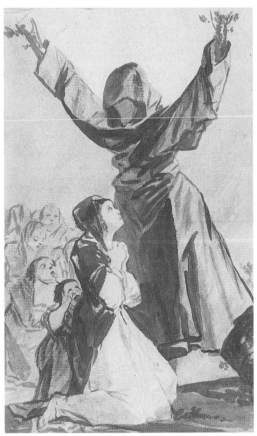

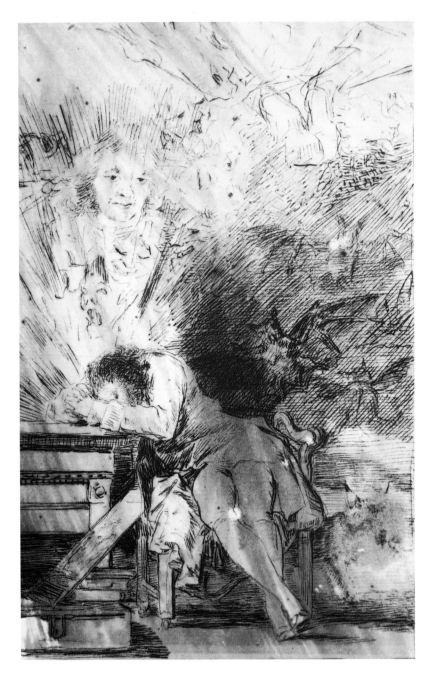

72 Goya, *The Sleep of Reason Brings forth Monsters* (first version), 1797, pen and black ink and sepia over charcoal drawing.

73 Goya, Frontispiece of the *Dreams* series, 1797, pen and and sepia ink over charcoal drawing.

Sueño

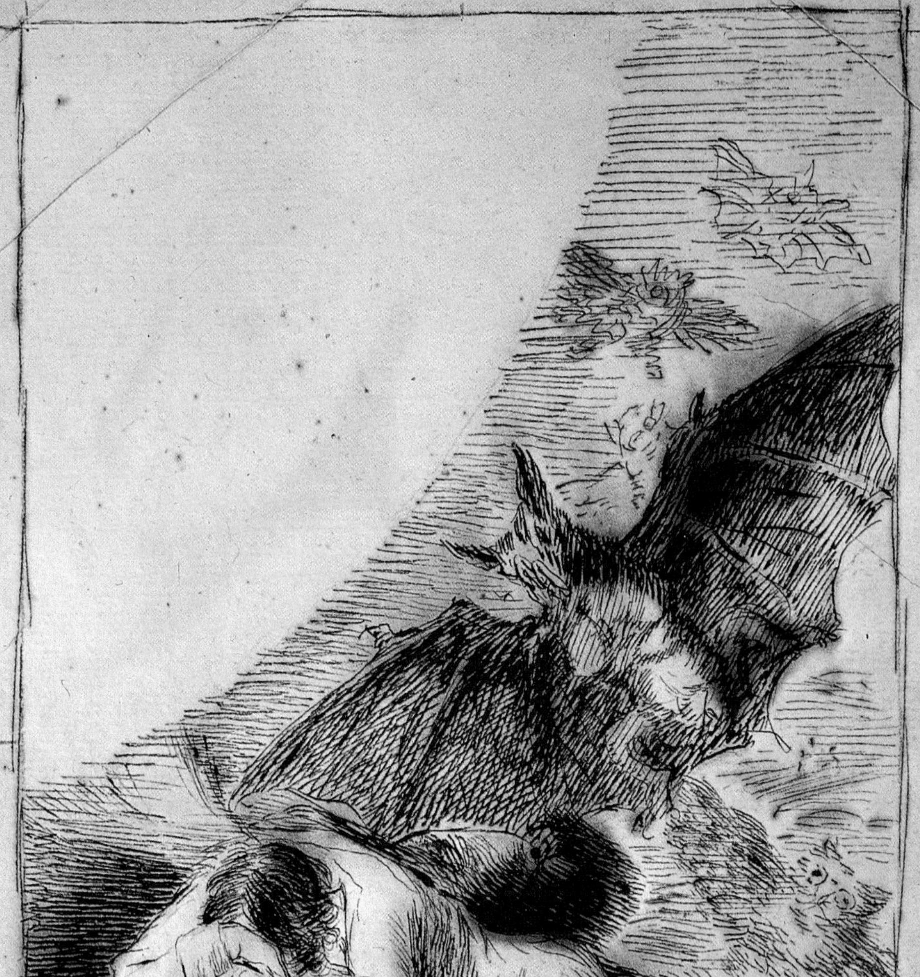

Ydioma univer
sal. Dibujado
y Grabado p.^r
r. d.º Goya
año 1797

El Autor soñando.

Su yntento solo es desterrar bulgaridades
perjudiciales, y perpetuar con esta obra de

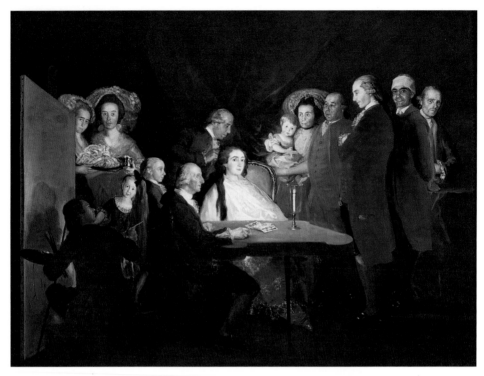

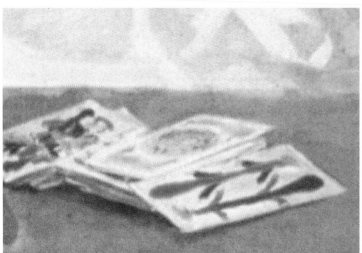

74 Goya, *The Infante Don Luis and His Family*, 1783/4, oil on canvas.

75 Detail of illus. 74.

134

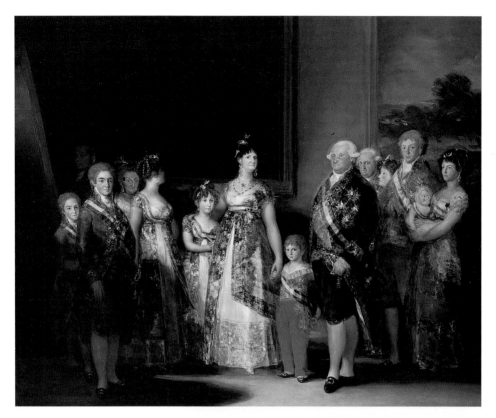

76 Goya, *Charles IV and His Family*, 1800–01, oil on canvas.

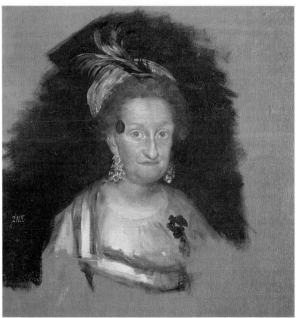

77 Goya, *Study for a Portrait of the Infanta Maria Josefa*, 1799–1800, oil on canvas.

135

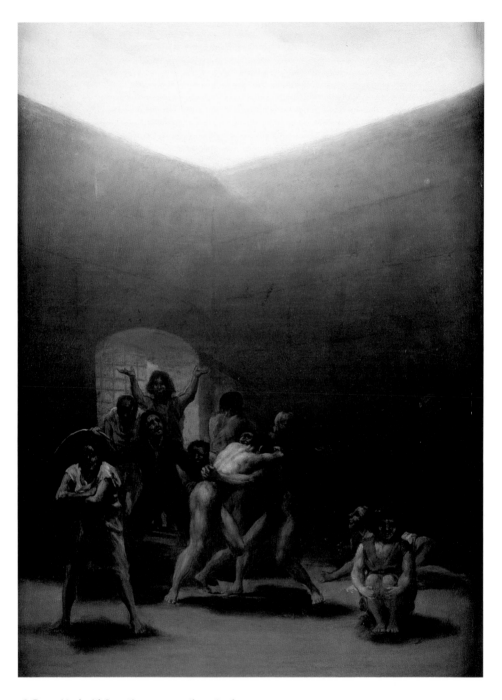

78 Goya, *Yard with Lunatics, c.* 1794, oil on tinplate.

makes its sturdiness all the more extraordinary. The inner courtyard of this palace is dark and gloomy.'[70] The city of Florence, fortress-within-a-fortress, is a transgressive space, to the imagination a perverse and carnivalesque world:

> The women of Florence are very free. The women dress like men, the latter like girls. There are few towns in all Italy where such a strong predilection to betray one's sex can be found, and this idiosyncrasy must surely come from a great need on their part to dishonour both. Popes in days gone by granted the Florentines, devotees of sodomy, plenary indulgences for this vice, within any relationship one might conceive. (. . .) There was once in Florence a very singular law on this subject. On Shrove Thursdays, a woman was not allowed to deny her husband sodomy: if she did not consent and he complained, then she risked becoming the talk of the town. Happy, a thousand times happy the nation wise enough to set its passions up as laws.[71]

But within this system of successive embeddings, there is room to describe the space where the transgression pertains to the symbolic imagination: the Palazzo Vecchio leads directly into the Uffizi, where the famous Tribune takes on the role of a veritable *sancta sanctorum*: 'The shape of this magnificent room is octagonal. The dome is all in mother of pearl and the floor is finished in marble.'[72]

With the help of the huge canvas painted during that same period (1772–8) by the English artist of German-Hungarian extraction Johann Zoffany for Queen Charlotte of England (illus. 79), we can well imagine the impression this already mythical place had on the Marquis.[73] Just like the painting, Sade's text is a *mise-en-scène* of a male gaze encountering a closed world dominated by feminine beauty and the exhibition of naked bodies. A painted orgy that verges on indecency, where 'connoisseurs' mingle with painted or sculpted nudes, the painting did not please Queen Charlotte, who rejected it. Sade's text, which the Queen (fortunately) never had in her hands, is, just like the canvas, full of detailed descriptions of works of art on show in the Tribune, and, as Zoffany does in his painting, Sade highlights two of them: Titian's Urbino Venus and the Medici Venus.[74] Let us read his descriptions:

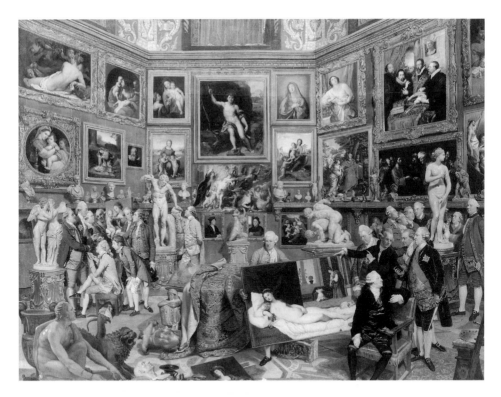

79 Johann Zoffany, *Cognoscenti in the Tribuna of the Uffizi*, 1772 –8, oil on canvas.

Titian's famous *Venus*, who is called his mistress, is a beautiful blond, with the most beautiful eyes in the world, but whose features however are more distinct than delicate. She is stretched out quite naked on a white mattress; with one hand she is scattering roses; with the other she is covering the one nature gave her. Her attitude is voluptuous and one never grows tired of examining the beauty to be found in the details of this sublime painting.[75]

Before going any further, we should point out that Sade is not actually describing a painting but a woman, and that the first quality of this woman-painting is that she is (or was thought to be) Titian's mistress. The phantasmic nature of Sade's reaction could not be more striking.[76] The description of the *Medici Venus*, probably made with the help of Charles-Nicolas Cochin's *Voyage d'Italie* (1758)[77] is significantly different:

The first object to strike one when one enters, is the famous *Venus*. She is located at the back of the room, next to an *Apollo* who is her counterpart and no less beautiful. Opinion varies greatly as to the author and antiquity of this

Venus. Whatever the case might be, it is the most beautiful piece I have ever seen in my life. I felt a stab of sweet and holy emotion as I admired it; and on examining her beauty closely, I was not surprised that tradition claims that the author used five hundred different models to achieve this beautiful work which, as a result, is the product of all the beautiful women in Greece. The proportions of this sublime statue, the gracefulness of the breasts and buttocks, are masterpieces that today could rival nature. And I doubt that had double the models been used, selected from all the beauties of Asia and Europe, it would not have been possible to find one single creature that would not lose out in a comparison. The statue measures around five feet high; it stands on a pedestal three feet high. (. . .) The most beautiful marble has been used for this masterpiece. Age has given her a slightly yellowish gaze, which, together with the delicacy and beauty of the grain, makes her look almost like alabaster.[78]

This time, Sade is describing a work of art, laying heavy emphasis on her specific reality. We are reminded of the ancient painting versus sculpture debate, so alive during the Renaissance and still in operation in the *mise-en-scène* of the two Venuses in Zoffany's painting.[79] This *paragone* can be summarized as follows: in an evaluation that focuses on mimetic criteria, the advantage the painting has is that, through the use of colours and the freedom of body language, the effect it creates can look very real. The advantage of sculpture in the round, on the other hand, is that multiple views create volume. It is in this light that the emphasis on a certain 'gracefulness' of the body must be understood in Sade's description, as well as in the *mise-en-scène* of Zoffany's *cognoscenti* examining the works of art. One of the 'dilettantes' who is inspecting the Medici Venus 'closely' has no hesitation in using his lorgnette in order to appreciate 'certain parts' better (illus. 80). (Queen Charlotte's rejection of the canvas, on the one hand, and the unhealthy interest in it displayed by King George, on the other, would both appear to have derived from the presence of this juicy detail.)

In Sade's case, his insistence on the relationship between ideal beauty and the living model anticipates some of the obsessions that were to come out in his writings. In *The Story of Juliette*, this relationship would be inverted:

Do not suspect me here of enthusiasm, or of metaphor, but in truth I do not exaggerate when I assure you that Aglaé could have served alone as a model for the man who did not find, even among the one hundred most beautiful women in Greece, enough beauty to compose from them the sublime Venus that I had admired at the Grand Duke's palace. Never, no, never had I seen such delightful rounded shapes, such a voluptuous ensemble and details so absorbing; nothing as narrow as her pretty little cunt, nothing as plump as her delightful little arse, nothing so fresh, nothing so well moulded as her breasts and I assure you now, speaking in cold blood, that Aglaé was indeed the most divine creature I had ever celebrated in all my life. As soon as I discovered all these charms I devoured them with caresses and, moving swiftly from one attraction to another, I always felt as though I did not sufficiently caress the one I had previously abandoned. The pretty little hussy, endowed with the lewdest of temperaments, soon fell into my arms.[80]

This excerpt, and others like it,[81] can also be regarded as being a continuation, bordering on convention, of the assimilation of one of the great myths in the History of Western Eros, that of Pygmalion. Let us refresh our memories:

Pygmalion, a bachelor, lived alone; no wife had ever shared his bed. However, thanks to his wonderful skill, he carved from ivory as white as snow, the body of a woman so beautiful that nature could not have created the like and he fell in love with his work. She was a virgin who had all the appearance of being real; she looked alive and as though, but for her modesty that held her back, she wished to move; as art is hidden by dint of art. Filled with wonder, Pygmalion became passionate about this image; often he reached out to his masterpiece searching with his fingers to see whether it was flesh or ivory and he still could not believe it was ivory. He kissed his statue and imagined that she returned his kisses; he spoke to her, he held her in his arms; he imagined her flesh yielding to the touch of his fingers and leaving behind a bruise on the limb they had pressed.[82]

The whole of the eighteenth century was beset by a veritable 'Pygmalion-mania',[83] the high points of which were proba-

80 Detail of illus. 79.

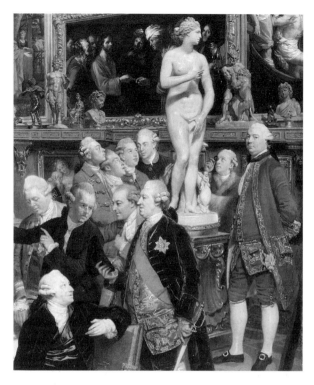

81 Louis Dennel, *Pygmalion and Galatea*, 1775, copper engraving.

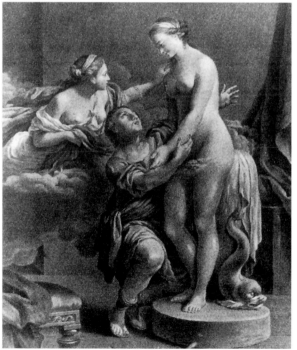

bly Falconet's group of statues (1763), Rousseau's 'lyric scene' (1770) and Herder's essay *Plastik* (1778). Sade did not escape; his transgressive version was performed in the purest spirit of Enlightenment demythification. Ovid was dealt with in a most prosaic manner in Diderot's *Encyclopédie* (1765): 'It would seem that this prince [Pygmalion] found a way of bringing to life a beautiful person who was as cold as a statue.'[84]

In painted, engraved and sculpted figurations, the bringing to life of a phantasm occurred in at least three different ways. It is this very diversity that shows how important the theme and the philosophy attached to it were.[85] Most in keeping with the Ovidian theme is the incorporating of the intervention of the goddess Venus, who, in response to the impassioned pleas of Pygmalion, brings the statue to life. In Dennel's engraving, for example (illus. 81), the beautiful Galatea is still on her pedestal in a contrapose that features the attitudes codified by ancient aesthetics. Touched by the hand of Venus, she comes to life, and the sculptor drops his hammer and chisel so that he can kiss her.

The second way, initiated by eighteenth-century art, and the one that is most in keeping with the general eroticization of the viewer, projects desire and a purely scopic pleasure into the material by bringing the statue to life. This was the solution adopted by Falconet, which Diderot found so pleasing (illus. 82): 'One knee on the ground, the other raised, hands clasped tightly together, Pygmalion is in front of his work and gazing at it. He seeks in the eyes of his statue confirmation of the miracle promised him by the gods.'[86] Finally, the third way is the one closest to Sade's rhetoric of transgression. Here creation, bringing to life, eroticism and destruction merge. Goya has left us the most revealing example of this in one of his later drawings (illus. 84).[87] Here we see Pygmalion in full creative mode, a creation heavy with erotic allusions despite the fact that Galatea is chastely dressed. The statue has already come to life, but, Venus being absent, the miracle would appear to be attributable to the artist himself having got carried away. He does not drop his chisel, as Dennel's Pygmalion does (illus. 81), but is ready to strike again. The focus of this drawing is different from anything else left us by the myth's iconographic tradition. Only by comparing it to the model that is iconographically closest to it but chronologically the furthest

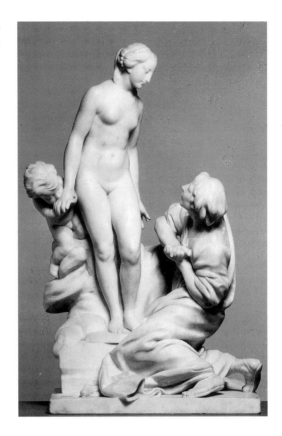

82 Etienne-Maurice Falconet, *Pygmalion and Galatea*, 1761, marble.

away, can we understand it. In the engraving in the 1497 Lyon edition of the *Romaunt of the Rose* (illus. 83), the dynamism of the composition is undeniable as is, in fact, its semi-erotic, semi-artistic character. We are seeing there a rigid statue whose eyes are closed as the blows of the chisel shape and caress her. The permutation (whether direct or indirect does not matter) to be found in Goya is twice as forceful, since the chisel which, with a slight but crucial shift, has left the thigh no longer caresses. But is it still striking?

A MAD(MAN'S) DISCOURSE

Mme de Clairwil, one of Sade's darkest characters has doubts – her very name is indicative of this – as to what she wants and what she is:

> She had never had any children: she loathed them, it was a kind of petty harshness, which, in a woman, is always a

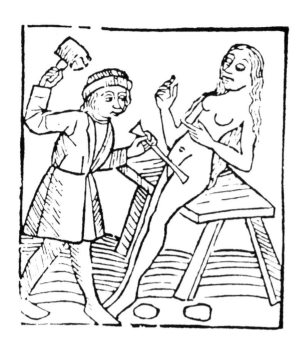

83 *Pygmalion and Galatea,* woodcut
from *Romaunt of the Rose* (Lyon, 1497).

84 Goya, *Pygmalion and Galatea,* from
Album F, 1815–20, brush and sepia
wash.

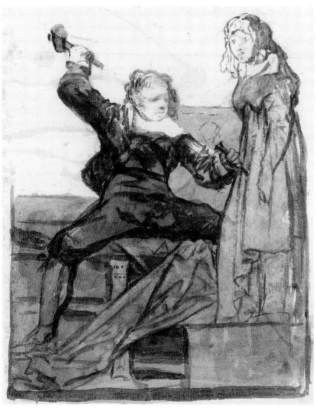

sign of insensibility: moreover we can be assured that Madame de Clairwil's was at its height. She boasted that she had never shed a tear, that she had never been moved by the fate of the unfortunate. 'My soul is impassive,' she used to say; 'I defy any emotion, other than pleasure, to touch it. I am the mistress of the affections of this soul, of its desires, of its reactions; my head controls everything; and that is what is worst, for this head is quite detestable. But I do not complain: I love my vices, I abhor virtue; I am the sworn enemy of all religions, of all gods; I fear neither the evils of life, nor what follows death; and when people are like me, they are happy.[88]

We might consider this declaration of faith to be at the very heart of what has been termed 'the dialectic of the Enlightenment'.[89] The issues involved are enormous since they introduce the supremacy of reason just as it was seen to be collapsing. In the words of Psalm 53: 'The fool has said in his heart, "There is no God!"' (*Dixit insipiens in corde suo: Non est Deus!*). During the Middles Ages and most of modern times, there ensued a whole verbal and logical sequence based on these two lines: the fool is the un-wise man, the *in-sipiens*, the one who disregards God, and madness itself is defined through negation, as a privation of reason: *in-sania, in-sipientia, de-sipientia, a-mentia, de-mentia*.[90]

Clairwil's (Sade's) discourse, by coinciding (up to a certain point) with the Enlightenment discourse, reverses the relationship between reason and madness, and in the absence of Superior Authority marks the actual beginning of the career of a new 'divinity': Reason. Sade's place in this reversal has been underscored time and again. While Horkheimer and Adorno focused on the fact that 'the work of the Marquis de Sade portrays "understanding without the guidance of another person", that is, the bourgeois individual freed from tutelage', (*Das Werk des Marquis de Sade zeigt den 'Verstand ohne Leitung eines anderen', das heisst, das von Bevormundung befreite bürgerliche Subjekt*),[91] Lacan was of the opinion that *The Philosophy of the Boudoir* (1795) 'agreed with', 'completed' and 'gave truth to' Kant's *Critique of Practical Reason* (1788).[92]

This last statement needs to be modified for the simple reason that Kant's second critique is the 'moral' outcome of the proclamation of the absolute supremacy of the new idol created by the *Critique of Pure Reason* (1781), which purports to present as blatantly as possible his first project of a possible profane ethic, whereas *The Philosophy of the Boudoir* only presents – and this is suggested in the title – an anti-ethic. Sade's work should therefore not be seen as following on from Kant but, at the very most, as coinciding with the point where the functioning of Pure Reason had been established but Practical Reason had not yet been born. By referring to this corner of Sade's thinking as the 'Clinic of Pure Reason', we are of course playing with words, but this word game goes beyond its own ludism, for it focuses on the system of a pathology that is produced at the heart of triumphant Reason and that involves the creation of a space to which to retreat, indeed an imaginary course of treatment. Kant in a way anticipated its genesis when he observed that 'Madness and understanding have such ill-defined frontiers that it is difficult to go far into one of these realms without from time to time making a brief incursion into the other.'[93] To subject pure reason to a 'critique' is to determine its limits in order to define it. And yet reason's 'other' is not only 'dogmatism', which certainly remained Kant's selected target, but also 'extravagance', in other words madness. Fortunately, recent studies have drawn attention to the fact that the model of a mad thought is essentially one of the themes that established the *Critique of Pure Reason* as a science of the frontiers of human reason[94] and to the processes that produce, at the actual moment of its apogee, its own irrationality.[95] In the final analysis, when Kant was putting God aside to substitute him for Reason and Moral Law, he was himself a 'fool' or 'madman', an *in-sipiens*, in the meaning given the word by the author of the Psalm. With full knowledge of the facts, before starting on his 'Pure Reason' project (1781), Kant undertook two pre-emptive measures, outlining the two territories – mystical experience and madness – and placed himself in the negative of reason. And so *Essay on the maladies of the mind* (1764) and *Dreams of a Spirit-Seer* (1766) were born. These publication dates reveal how important the discourse on madness was to the project of a critique on understanding: the discourse anticipated by two years the one on mysticism and by fifteen years the one on reason.[96] It is with this in mind that the deliberations of Michel Foucault must be considered, as well as those of others like him who accented the eighteenth century's strange but momentous dialogue with Madness: '. . . the rationality of the Age of Enlightenment uncovered in this kind of blurry mirror, a harmless caricature of sorts (. . .) It was as though classical reason were once more admitting to a proximity, a relationship, a quasi-resemblance between itself and the figures of madness.'[97] Studies on the history of art and of the imagination have also shown the extent to which the iconography of madness was defining the new thematic register that was developing around 1800.[98] What has not yet been done to this day is any kind of research on the 'quasi-resemblance' of the figures of reason and those of madness in the realm of the new visuality of the Enlightenment and the lessons that were to emerge from it. We now propose to give a foretaste of what would be revealed in such a study, which would quite likely, if not almost certainly, go much further than the limits of our study will allow us to do.

Let us return by way of an introduction to Sade, who gives us, in book five of the *Story of Juliette*, the famous description of the Salerne madhouse. More than the actual description, it is the context that is of interest. En route, the group, led by Clairwil (whose head, let us not forget, 'controls everything'), breaks their journey to look at the paintings of Herculanum. This is an opportunity for a short dissertation on aesthetics:

> Generally we find in all his paintings, a luxury of attitudes that are seldom found in nature, and which are proof either of a great suppleness in the muscles of the people who live in the region, or of a great disorder of the imagination. Amongst other things I could quite clearly make out a superb piece depicting a satyr pleasuring himself with a goat: there can be nothing more beautiful, nothing more perfect.[99]

The extract is significant in the way it just slips the themes of the 'great disorder of the imagination' and of perversion into the folds of classical perfection. The description of the visit to the madhouse that is contained in the next few pages does the same thing. Everything takes place on the fringes of the visible. The director of the place, the terrible Vespoli, asks the group if they want to 'see him in action', stressing 'that it pains him to be seen in such a place'. Clairwil's swift response ('we want to see you!') opens the show, which begins when a 'tall young man' appears, 'as naked and beautiful as Hercules,

147

who, the moment he [is] freed, [indulges] in a thousand extravagances'.[100] We shall summarize what we see as the quintessence of the voyeuristic scenario contained in the pages that follow. Madness is a spectacle enjoyed by reason as though it were the living one-upmanship of a painting by Herculanum. The 'Pygmalion complex' is thereby given its most disturbing complement. This is done through the erasing of the boundaries between classical (rational) order and the (irrational) disorder of the madhouse.

In the history of painting, Goya is the one artist to have tackled this theme in a significant way, first in a small 'cabinet painting' produced around 1793–4 (illus. 78) and later in one of his *c.* 1812–19 *borrones* (illus. 87) and the series of drawings made when he was in Bordeaux.[101] A study of all of these has yet to be undertaken. Here we will consciously limit ourselves to considering such aspects as Goya's way of tackling the various elements of madness as a prefatory experience to the classical representation.

His two small paintings of a madhouse are quite different. In the earlier one (illus. 78), he chose a vertical format to facilitate a vaguely pyramidal composition in which he arranged the figures so that they are bathed in unusual lighting, thereby focusing attention on the central action. Structurally, this scenario only just precedes the one we find, a few years later, in Sade's text. It probably reflects, on the one hand, the situation that existed in asylums in Goya's time and, on the other, a genre that already existed in Spanish literature.[102] At the centre of the composition, two internees wrestle, naked in the style of Greek athletes. Another, crouched on all fours, goads them on, while the dressed warden attempts to bring them into line with a whip. Behind him, another internee introduces the scene with a rhetorical gesture to the hypothetical spectator, clearly a powerful authority figure: shielded by the painting's surface, which acts like a protective screen, the spectator is doubly anticipated by each of the two lunatics who, to the left and right of the foreground, stare at him or her wild-eyed.

The later painting (illus. 87) is constructed horizontally. The isolation of the characters and of each of the actions represented is accentuated, while the presence of a beholder is not obligatory, so much so that one of the internees, at the centre of the foreground, has turned away. To echo a well-known distinction introduced into the analysis of eighteenth-century pictorial representation, we could say that in this painting, 'absorption' replaces the 'theatricality' at work in the earlier picture.[103] The theme here is the relationship between insanity and the imagination: at the extreme left, a lunatic (or maybe two) is prostrate before an invisible god. Next to him, another internee, naked, has seized the horns of a bull in an imaginary bullfight. A third wrestles with an imaginary adversary, surrounded by three power-crazed figures: an Indian chief, a king screaming commands that no one heeds, and a naked pope blessing *urbi et orbi*. In the middle ground, at the right, a heaving mass of naked bodies' orgiastic displays have been strategically enveloped in dense shadow.

There is no call to order here as there is in the earlier painting, and if there is any 'order' at all, it derives from the laws of the pictorial *dispositio*, which has not been completely undermined by the madness of the theme. And so we have, despite the absence of a unifying action, people who fall silently into groups or sub-groups, and a central figure (the wrestler with the three-cornered hat) whose paradoxical, dual function is to centralize and decentralize the composition in equal measure. A comparison with one of the drawings from Goya's 'Italian Sketchbook' could be relevant (illus. 86). It depicts a scene that is difficult to identify and that might be an aborted project for a heroic painting[104] or, more probably, a copy from some Roman fresco. The most striking figure, that of the wrestler with the shield is, despite his ungainliness, the fruit of the strivings of a brave student ever mindful of his famous models; it is in fact reminiscent of the anatomical model Goya had just copied (illus. 85). The sub-group resembles the deployment in space of the same model viewed from different angles.

It is remarkable to see in the wrestler with the three-cornered hat (illus. 87) a 'quasi-resemblance' figure emerging in Goya's work. This process is echoed in other figures, such as the 'pope' and the 'king', who have the same unstable dynamic as the fallen warrior at the right in the Italian sketch.

More than 30 years separate the drawing from the painting, and it would be hazardous to jump to the conclusion that there was any 'dialogue' between them. In fact, their relationship is even more significant if we regard it as a pure coincidence, or the result of an accidental or unconscious revival

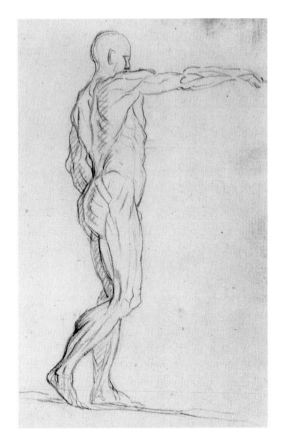

85 Goya, Drawing, fol. 147 from the 'Italian Notebook', 1770–73, pencil and wash.

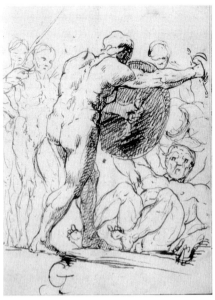

86 Goya, Drawing, fol. 165r from the 'Italian Notebook', 1770–73, India ink.

through which the failure of classical order spills into the counter-order of madness.

We should like to add another example to this extreme case of reversal, also significant because of its programmatic scale and the way signals are mixed at the frontier between madness and the rationality of the ancient. I refer to the *Serment du Jeu de Paume* (*The Tennis Court Oath*) (illus. 88), through which Jacques-Louis David wanted to produce 'the painting of the Revolution'.[105]

It is not possible here to review the complex history of the event depicted or of the work itself, never completed.[106] If we examine the drawings and the preparatory canvas, still in existence today, we can see that the effort David made to construct the work was enormous and almost inversely proportional to the result. The strangeness of the composition is striking because of the way it (literally) discloses the working method of the Neo-classical painter. On the light grey surface of the canvas, dissected by the still visible grid, heroic figures emerge where the white pencil drawing has been highlighted with bistre shading. Only a few of the heads are finished, and the pitiable attitudes of the four characters (the product of an entire tradition of history painting), as well as the co-existence of the heroic nude with the wigs of the *Ancien Régime*, enhance the originality of an attempt which, for us, borders on the

87 Goya,
The Madhouse,
c. 1812–19,
oil on wood.

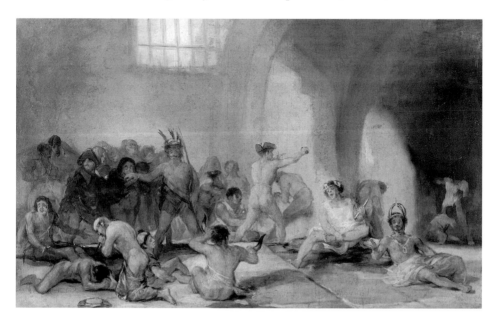

comic. We must be wary of crediting this effect with possible hidden intentions. The fact that David himself placed his work in the purest tradition of history painting, already codified by Alberti at the dawn of modernism, leaves us in little doubt as to his intentions:

> History will touch the souls of the spectators when the men who are painted there visibly manifest the movement of their soul. (. . .) but the movements of the soul are revealed in the movements of the body. (. . .) the quick-tempered and those whose soul swells with anger have a face and eyes that are swollen, they are flushed and the rage of anger makes the movements of all their limbs extremely brisk and agitated (. . .).[107]

And:

> The kind of painting that everyone finds the most agreeable is that which presents a great diversity in the size and movement of bodies. Whether some are standing face on, hands raised, moving their fingers, one foot on the ground, whether others have their heads turned sideways, their arms hanging down by their sides and their feet together, whether each repeatedly gestures and flexes; whether others are seated, resting their elbow on a knee or almost lying down.[108]

The nudity of the figures has inspired several different interpretations, including the hypothesis that David wished the heroes of the Revolution – Mirabeau, Barnave, Prieur, the Abbé Grégoire, Michel Gérard, etc. – to evoke the heroes of Antiquity.[109] Here too, it is Alberti's paradigm that reveals the truth: 'When you create a person who is dressed you must first of all draw a nude, you must first position the bones and muscles and then lightly cover them with flesh and skin so that it is easy to see where the muscles are.'[110] The fact that David followed this classical prescription to the letter clearly reveals his intention, which was to turn a *modern event* into a *historic painting*. The courage and patriotism of the deputies of the French National Assembly taking their vows, on 17 June 1789, to renew the Constitution is glorified and in the guise of Antiquity. In David's painting, therefore, the agents of the Revolution, get into the skins of their Roman doubles and project themselves into an imaginary space, a space where the obsessive importance of

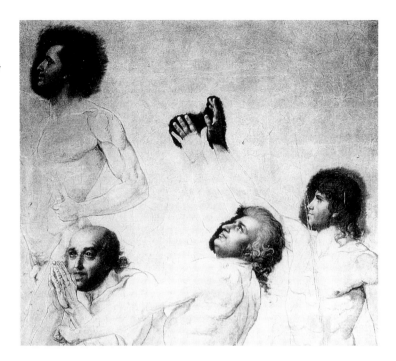

Republican virtues is glorified as an absolute model. In this way, the process of symbolic structuring, initiated by the painter, creates its own negative – at its very apogee – and the composition verges on extravagant irrationality.

We need do no more than glance through the reports of the 1791 Salon, at which a large preparatory drawing for David's composition was hung, to see that reaction to it clashed with precisely those aspects of his great project that contributed to its destructuring:

> . . . let us suppose we have no knowledge of the French Revolution; and let us see what would be the result of the ideas produced in our minds by the different impressions we experience when we examine this beautiful drawing. (. . .) The examination proves to us that the drawing represents the coming together of a great number of persons who are all, with more or less the same energy, taking a common vow. But what is the object of this vow, at what moment was it taken, what risks were being run by taking it: this is what the drawing does not tell us, however, the important thing was to take it.[111]

Or, more explicitly:

> Let us examine this beautiful drawing, and let us ask our-
> selves what it represents, it is a vow being taken by a vast
> multitude of men, in a different state of agitation depend-
> ing on the degree of energy of their character. There are
> those who, fists clenched, threaten . . . who? That is what I
> do not know . . .[112]

And this is how we came to the conclusion that, in the over-
structured representation that follows the models of the perfect prescription, signs – as in the case of madness – lose their
certainty because, by attacking the semantic system to which
they belong from the inside , they become the sign and the
mockery of the sign. Between the supporting structure of
Goya's *Madhouse* (illus. 87) and David's *Oath* (illus. 88), there
is, paradoxically, an abyss and a 'quasi-resemblance'.[113] The
ancient hypothesis according to which David and Goya knew
and appreciated one another is, admittedly, only a legend, but
what a beautiful legend:

> Of all the men he had known in Italy, Goya in his old age
> only ever spoke of the painter David. In a very short time
> they had become close friends. Why? I have no idea and we
> might find this surprising: these two planets did not orbit
> the same world. Although we searched carefully, we could
> only find one point of contact between David and Goya:
> they were both possessed to the same degree with the mad-
> ness of philosophizing.[114]

5 Goya's Pharmacy[1]

CAPRICES, VINEGARS AND OTHER SALTS ('STRONG
WATERS' – FIRST CONJECTURE)

Goya's *Caprichos* or *Caprices* (illus. 13, 59, 62) were put up for
sale on 6 February 1799 in a shop that sold alcohol and per-
fume in the centre of Madrid, near the Puerta del Sol, at 1, calle
del Desengaño (illus. 89, 90). The choice of this shop is intriguing since prints were usually sold through bookshops on a
subscription basis following advertising campaigns.[2] To get a
sense of what was usually on sale in this particular drug-store,
all we need do is look through the newspapers of the time.[3]
For example:

> Desengaño Street, on the corner of Vallesta Street, near
> the barracks of the Invalides, has just taken delivery of
> the following products from France: a variety of differ-
> ent-flavoured lozenges for the mouth called sweets, in spe-
> cially designed boxes with one or more compartments; an
> assortment of vinegars to remove stains from the face and
> for cleaning the teeth; another variety called 'flora' to beau-
> tify the face; phials of vinegar called 'the four thieves' at 14
> reales, very useful when it comes to preventing all manner
> of epidemics and infections; and pots of rouge and white
> powder at 15 reales. Very fine powder from Paris for the
> face and arms: very attractive little cases and cardboard
> boxes with different pieces of glass with subtly changing
> colours to suit all tastes; an assortment of pots of very fine
> ointments in a range of fragrances; packets of different
> scented powders.[4]

Or:

> . . . packets of fine musk- or violet-scented powder, differ-
> ent vinegars for the teeth, different opiates – liquid, fine,
> ultra-fine and in powder, small and very pleasantly per-
> fumed sachets to carry around, plain or embroidered, an

89 Advertisement announcing the sale of Goya's *Caprichos* in the *Diario de Madrid*, 6 February 1799.

Núm. 37   149

DIARIO DE MADRID

DEL MIERCOLES 6 DE FEBRERO DE 1799.

Santa Dorotea Virgen. = *Q. H. en la Iglesia de San Felipe Neri.*

Observacio. meteorolog. de ayer.				Afecciones astronomicas de hoy.
Epocas.	Termom.	Barometro.	Atmosfera.	El 30 de la Luna. Sale el sol á las 7 y 59 m.
7 de la m.	3 s. o.	25 p. 48 l.	O. y Nub.	de la m. y se pone á las
12 del d.	3½ s. o.	25 p. 8½ l	O. y Nub.	5 y un m. de la tarde.
5 de la t.	3 s. o.	25 p. 8½ l	O. y Nub.	

Coleccion de estampas de asuntos caprichosos, inventadas y grabadas al agua fuerte, por Don Francisco Goya. Persuadido el autor de que la censura de los errores y vicios humanos (aunque parece peculiar de la eloqüencia y la poesía) puede tambien ser objeto de la pintura: ha escogido como asuntos proporcionados para su obra, entre la multitud de extravagancias y desaciertos que son comunes en toda sociedad civil, y entre las preocupaciones y embustes vulgares, autorizados por la costumbre, la ignorancia ó el interés, aquellos que ha creido mas aptos á suministrar materia para el ridiculo, y exercitar al mismo tiempo la fantasia del artifice.

Como la mayor parte de los objetos que en esta obra se representan son ideales, no será temeridad creer que sus defectos hallarán, tal vez, mucha disculpa entre los inteligentes: considerando que el autor, ni ha seguido los exemplos de otro, ni ha podido copiar tan poco de la naturaleza. Y si el imitarla es tan difícil, como admirable quando se logra; no dexará de merecer alguna estimacion el que apartandose enteramente de ella, ha tenido que exponer á los ojos formas y actitudes que solo han existido hasta ahora en la mente humana, obscurecida y confusa por la falta de ilustracion ó acalorada con el desenfreno de las pasiones.

Seria suponer demasiada ignorancia en las bellas artes el advertir al público, que en ninguna de las composiciones que forman esta coleccion se ha propuesto el autor, para ridiculizar los defectos particulares á uno ú otro individuo: que seria en verdad, estrechar demasiado los limites al talento y equivocar los medios de que se valen las artes de imitacion para producir obras perfectas.

150
La pintura (como la poesia) escoge en lo universal lo que juzga mas á proposito para sus fines: reune en un solo personage fantástico, circunstancias y caracteres que la naturaleza presenta repartidos en muchos, y de esta convinacion, ingeniosamente dispuesta, resulta aquella feliz imitacion, por la qual adquiere un buen artifice el titulo de inventor y no de copiante servil.

Se vende en la calle del Desengaño n. 1 tienda de perfumes y licores, pagando por cada coleccion de á 80 estampas 320 rs. vn.

assortment of black tablets used to polish shoes and boots, others in the shape of a ball to soften and blacken boots, and a shiny, extremely fine liquid much appreciated by different gentlemen for it is superior to the mixed and invented substances because of their quality and their ease of use, moreover a collection of elegant fans has arrived . . .[5]

Eyewitness accounts of the period help complete the picture. The shop in calle del Desengaño must have resembled the trinket shop portrayed in Luis Paret y Alcazar's famous painting (illus. 91)[6] and the apothecary in one of Goya's own *Caprichos* (illus. 92).

Given that the sale of the *Caprichos* in such a place and such a context was so far removed from the norm, it will come as no great surprise that it was preceded by a long, detailed public notice in the *Diario de Madrid* (illus. 89). The wording of the advertisement (see Appendix)[7] is an obligatory stop on any journey through Goya's world. Though repeatedly quoted and commented upon, its possibilities have not yet been completely exhausted. By reopening this file, we wish to research the transformation of fantasy into market goods.[8] The document in question deals, in fact, with what we would usually refer to as the 'market of symbolic goods';[9] instead of praising the blanching qualities of such and such a toothpaste or the virtues of such and such a miraculous vinegar, it highlights the qualities of 'A collection of Prints of Capricious Subjects, Invented and Etched by Don Francisco Goya' and describes the advantages that could be gained by acquiring them. It uses terms whose intellectualism is clear: 'imitation', 'fantastic', 'individual', 'universal', 'compositions', 'ingeniously arranged', 'Painting', 'Poetry', 'perfect works', etc. Having presented the 'product', the advertisement ends with the

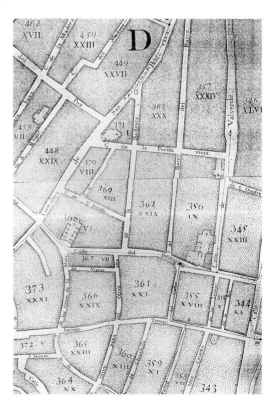

90 Espinosa de los Monteros, Plan of the centre of Madrid in 1769. Servicio Geografico del Ejercito, Madrid.

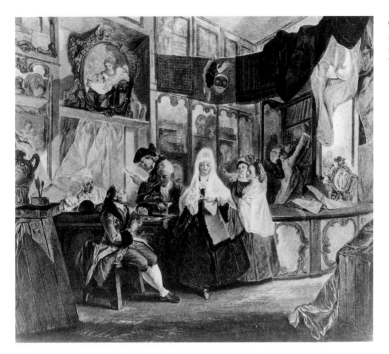

91 Luis Paret y Alcazar, *The Trinket Shop*, 1722, oil on wood.

single and abrupt phrase: *for sale* (*se vende*).

We shall examine the way in which the marriage between 'merchandise' and 'imagination' is brought about in the case of the *Caprichos*. We shall explore the place of the merchandise-image in the creator/public relationship highlighted by the advertisement. We shall also endeavour to see just how closely the *creator/public* binomial tallies with that of the *seller/buyer*. Finally, we shall endeavour to ascertain to what extent the advertisement can be considered to be a *mise-en-scène* of its own dual function (the first being the sale of actual goods, the second being the sale of symbolic goods).

We have focused our research on the double question of 'merchandise'. The first question is 'Who sells to whom?'; the second is 'What is being sold?' Two further questions, apparently marginal, are: 'Where does one sell?' and 'When does one sell?' It is only by tackling all these questions that we can uncover the ramifications of the advertisement, and the great originality of the print series being advertised.

Our objective is not the sociology of the artistic product, but its interpretation. We think that this is an important point of departure, useful for such an interpretation, namely Jacques Derrida's definition of a 'text':

92 Goya, *Capricho 33: At the Count Palatine,* 1797–8, etching and aquatint.

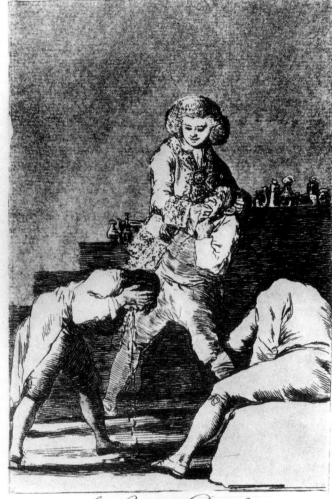

Al Conde Palalino.

A text is only a text if at first glance it hides from the first to come along, the laws of its composition and the rules of its game. In fact a text always remains imperceptible. Laws and rules cannot take refuge in the inaccessibility of a secret, they simply never give themselves up, neither to the present, nor to anything that we could strictly call perception.

And again: 'The concealment of the texture may take centuries to undo its fabric. The fabric enveloping the fabric.

159

Centuries to undo the fabric. Thus reconstituting it as an organism.'[10] The experiment we are offering the reader is that of reconstituting the texture of a text. That the text is a simple advertisement does not simplify things; on the contrary. We find ourselves at the dawn of publicity, and two of its characteristics – still valid in our consumer society – are already evident. As with all publicity material, the text in question contains an obvious message and a secret one. In the case of the commercialization of symbolic goods, the first message is more complex than usual. Indeed, the advertisement in the *Diario de Madrid*, having named the object for sale (the 'collection of prints' / 'by Goya') launches unusually into a dissertation on the intentions of the 'author' (*el autor*), which are said to lie in the 'censure of human errors and vices'. The text goes on to specify that it is society that has provided the themes to the 'artificer's fancy' (*la fantasia del artefice*) as well as 'the matter for ridicule' (*materia para el ridiculo*). In the second paragraph this assertion is partly amended or at least qualified. The 'author' is named yet again, this time in order to draw attention to a need for a pact with the 'connoisseurs' (*los intelligentes*). The latter must understand the innovative nature of an approach that 'stands aloof from' nature, since the artist's work involves the visualization ('putting before the eyes', *exponer a los ojos*) of images, which until then had remained 'obscured and confused' (*obscurecida y confusa*) due to the 'lack of education', or excited due to the 'unruliness of passions'. In this way, the wording of the advertisement introduces a direct allusion to the need for double 'lighting': for bringing into the light (or 'publishing') what was hidden, for clarifying what was unclear (*'obscur'*).

This is probably why the third paragraph widens the pact with the 'author' (*el autor* appears at this point for the third and last time) by naming as its partner not an élite (*los intelligentes*) but the public (*el publico*). The advertisement insists on giving the latter a short lesson in aesthetics (whilst asking to be forgiven for assuming the public to be 'ignorant'). The public must not expect to see in the 'collection of prints' an attack *ad personam*. It must understand that perfect works (*obras perfectas*) have as their object the general, not the particular. The advertisement closes by specifying the address at which the 80 prints can be acquired and their price (320 *reales*).

If experts have found traces of neo-classical aesthetics on

the level of the advertisement's direct message[11] (for which responsibility must fall to Goya's advisers, Moratin or Jovellanos, for example), on the level of the expression, we have found intentions coming from the post-Baroque culture of conceptism – a culture that was familiar with linguistic games and enigmatic images. This can be glimpsed in the statement that this exceptional product – a collection of etched prints – is aimed primarily at an exceptional viewer/reader, someone capable of understanding their most original features. Unfortunately, it is impossible for us to identify this ideal reader. When Goya first alluded to an élitist public of 'connoisseurs', he was placing himself (no matter whether deliberately or not) in the furrow ploughed by Baltasar Gracián (1601–58), his famous Aragon compatriot, who, a century earlier, had described in several key texts the prototype of the 'good listener' or 'judicious and shrewd man':

> He controls objects, and is never controlled by them. The sounding lead goes unrestrained right to the bottom of the deepest depth, he understands perfectly how to anatomize people's talents; he need only see a man to know him fully and completely; he deciphers all his innermost secrets of the heart; he is quick to understand, sharp when it comes to censure, judicious when it comes to drawing conclusions; he discovers everything, notices everything, understands everything.[12]

This ideal portrait to which any interpreter should aspire whilst remaining conscious that he will never achieve it completely, shows us Goya's 'awaiting horizon'.[13] The 'intelligent person/connoisseur' or 'good listener' (*buen entendedor*)[14] will not necessarily be – and this is important – a reader/interpreter of texts, but a decoder of behaviour and decipherer of symbolic systems. He or she will therefore be the most favourite receptor, on the one hand, of the apparently innocuous advertisement published in the *Diario de Madrid* and, on the other, of the complexity of the product to which it refers. In other words, the viewer and most favoured receptor of the *Caprichos*. To get to the heart of the advertisement and enjoy the complexity of the *Caprichos*, we shall have to position ourselves in this person's shadow. If our research is conclusive, the credit should go to him or her. Any errors will of course be due to our own shortcomings and limitations.

The first account of the *Caprichos* to appear in Goya's lifetime, in 1811 (probably during a second sale), confirms the complexity of their reception:

The ordinary run of people who look at them have been of the belief that they represented only the fancies of their author, but the knowledgeable soon realised that they all embraced a certain mystery. Indeed, this collection, comprising eighty prints with more than 400 figures of every kind, is nothing but a book of instruction consisting of eighty engraved moral poems, or a satirical treatise on eighty of those vices and prejudices that most afflict society. From the vices of the most distinguished classes to those of the people of low life, all are nicely ridiculed in this singular work. Misers, lechers, blustering cowards, ignorant physicians, mad old women, the vain and the idle, the old men who ape boys, prostitutes, hypocrites, in fact every kind of stupid, lazy, and roguish person finds himself so sagaciously portrayed that the prints offer much food for meditation. At the same time the subtle conceits hidden in each satire are divined and everyone makes applications, more or less fitting, in his own way and according to his own field of knowledge.[15]

This is a most eloquent text, especially as it expresses, twelve years on and much more clearly, the basic pact that was already discernible in the *Diario de Madrid* advertisement. It underlines the élitist nature of the recipient, making a clear distinction between 'the ordinary run of people' and 'the knowledgeable', and it is careful to describe the moral nature of the product. But the fundamental question concerning the latter is far from having been exhausted.

What, in the final analysis, was the 'author' selling to 'the knowledgeable'? The most satisfactory answer to this question – that of the 'good listener' – must for the sake of clarity, take account of the double quality of the object on sale. Goya's ludic intention (only discernible to the 'connoisseur') was, we believe, to present the *Caprichos* as marketable, and marketed, products (like perfumes, vinegars and miracle salts) and also as 'symbolic goods'. In other words as a product whose metaphorical focus prevailed over its reality as an object. If the *Caprichos* and the publicity notice advertising their sale were primarily destined for an ideal 'good listener' of conceptist descent, then he or she should have been capable of making the connection between 'object' and 'symbol', thus reaching the conclusion that the prints Goya was selling through the calle del Desengaño pharmacy were 'strong waters' of exceptional quality because of their ludic *pluri-semanticism*.

This becomes even more apparent if we read an excerpt from one of the best-known treatises on the methods used in eighteenth-century etching and a page of the first monograph devoted to the Spanish painter.

Here is the excerpt from the treatise entitled *Secrets concernant les Arts et Métiers* (1786):

> You will need to have a well-polished and very clean plate; you heat it on the fire and cover it with dry or liquid varnish, for they are available in both. Then you must blacken this varnish by means of a lighted candle, over which you place the varnished side of the plate. Once this is done, all you need do is copy your drawing onto this plate; which is a much simpler process than engraving. (. . .) It is not enough for the Etcher just to work with the point of his needle or stall, over the whole area of his work, with the strength and gentleness required to bring out the distant and nearest parts. He must also be careful, when it comes to putting the strong water on the plate that it does not eat into the plate equally everywhere; this is done with a mixture of oil and candle soot. (. . .) The strong water, made up of verdegris, vinegar, ordinary salt, sal ammoniac and vitriol, is used to etch the copper by pouring it onto the plates coated with soft or hard varnish, and then exposed according to the drawing you want to etch. When it comes to the refiner's strong water, known as white water, that is only used on soft varnish and it is not poured like the first, which is green water; instead you place the plate flat on a table and after having lined it with wax, you cover it with this white water diluted more or less with ordinary water [illus. 93].[16]

The second quotation comes from Yriarte's monograph entitled *Goya* (1867):

> Goya's method is no easy matter. He needed a method that was subtle, biting, reliable, and that would not fade; a personal method that demanded no translator and that responded well to thought. He wanted his mockery to

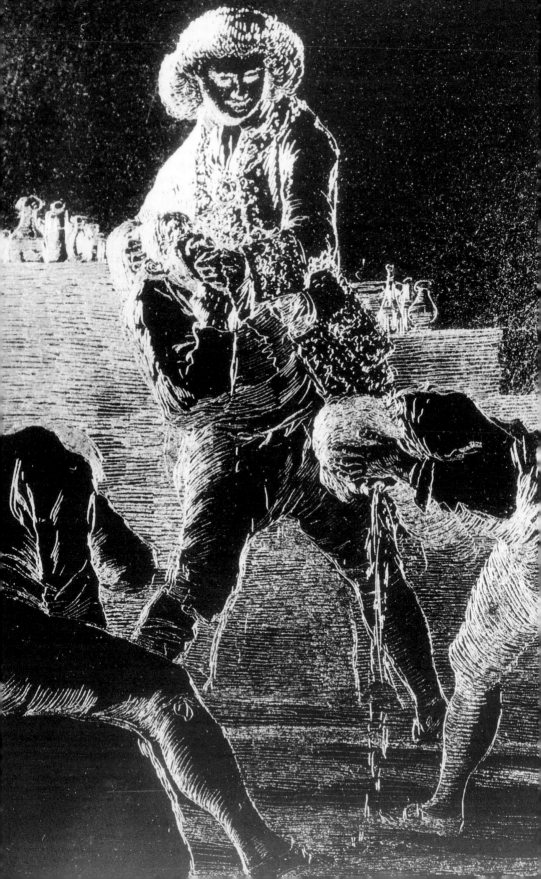

become immortal, and so he used strong water, which to
him was indelible through the very nature of the material,
and which, multiplying itself into infinity, also multiplied
the blows he struck. (. . .) Goya is by no means misunderstood; all those who are involved in art glorify him, and his
works are indelibly etched in their memories, but this must
be extended further; for the study of the arts it is necessary
for his name to become very popular, that a new class of
readers should know who this great artist is, and what a
thinker there is beneath this enthusiastic aquafortist. (. . .)
There is a passionate satirist, who attacks everything and
everyone, always ready to bite, but a bite that is poisoned.
Philosophy, history, religion, decrees, censures, institutions
and constraints, he challenges everything. (. . .) Goya is above
all terrible and his strong water is abundant.[17]

The whole page, especially this last sentence, written in the
still vital spirit of the conceptist 'good listener', shows to what
extent 'the iconology of strong waters'[18] was very much part
of the initial reaction to Goya's *Caprices*.

DREAMS, CAPRICES, HUMOURS ('STRONG WATERS' –
SECOND CONJECTURE)

The analysis of the different versions of the image Goya prepared for the frontispiece of his collection of prints is one of
the *topoi* of Goya-esque exegesis. In order to advance our
understanding of the series within the context of the commer-
cial market, we need to examine it here.

We know of three versions of this image: two of them must
have introduced the old series entitled *Dreams* (illus. 72, 73),
which contained only 72 etchings. The third version (illus. 98)
was integrated into the final series as number 43. The earlier
title was abandoned without giving any clear indication of
what the new one should be (the title of *Los Caprichos* was
established quite quickly and somewhat insistently).

If we compare the first version (illus. 72) with the title page of
the 1699 edition of Quevedo's *Dreams* (illus. 94) (the probable
but not the only source of inspiration), it is easy to spot the similarities as well as the differences.[19] The position of the dreamer
has been changed, as has the means of expression depicted
(ink and paper in Quevedo's image; engraved plate in

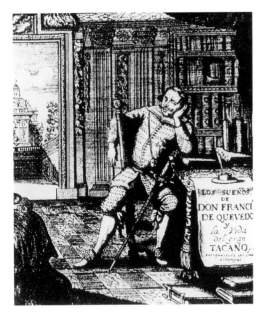

94 Frontispiece of
Francisco de
Quevedo, *Obras*,
vol. I (Antwerp,
1699).

Goya's). Both images contain books, but they are more numerous and tidier in the Quevedo, whereas in the Goya they are used to support the etched plate in the foreground. The most significant difference lies in the thematization of the dream. This is revealed indirectly through the suggestion of a smile on the face of the sleeping poet, whereas in the Goya it is manifested as an explosion of fantasies that physically invade the space. The personal nature of the dreams is reinforced by the fact that the dreamlike world is placed level with the dreamer's head. It is as though, because of a change made to the Quevedo frontispiece, the contents of the dream could no longer be manifested in a fleeting smile, but instead escaped into the space, in a kind of visualization of the 'transparent mind'.[20] This dreamlike world is a confused mixture of disturbing, and for the most part nocturnal, animals and a series of multiple projections of the same face, that of Goya. This first version anticipates one of the major characteristics of the series, which is the split, indeed the multiple self-projection, to which we shall return.

In the second version (illus. 73), the innovations are important. On the one hand, there are fewer animals but, on the other, they are more complicated: the huge bat has been made larger than life and a lynx with enormous staring eyes (erased in the first version) is happily ensconced in the bottom right-hand corner. Important changes have also been made to some of the details of the dreamer's body language. In the first version, his hands are joined, his fingers entwined together, and a long lock of hair falls onto the copper plate. In the second version, the lock is no longer there, while the copper plate and the arms have changed position. Further examination reveals that the dreamer himself has a different hairstyle, indeed that his head is a different shape. In the first drawing (illus. 72) it is not so very different from that seen in Goya's wash self-portrait dating from the same period (illus. 36). The tumbling mane of the frontispiece should probably be placed within the context of an accentuation of the leonine symbolism to be found in the New York drawing that we have already studied (see Chapter 2). Another element probably associated with it is the representation of the dreamer's eye, made prominent in the frontispiece through a section of the brow and face remaining uncovered (illus. 96). There is no doubt that Goya worked at these details, but he did so, as it were, in a regressive way. In the second frontispiece (illus. 73) and in the final etching (illus. 98) the head has sunk lower into the dreamer's crossed arms and his left eye, so conspicuous in the first version, can no longer be seen. Moreover the lynx with its hypnotic gaze has taken over the leonine characteristics. This comparison sheds some light on Goya's experimentation and explorations. In the first version he played with the lion's inherent ability to sleep with his eyes open, which was a real *topos* in bestiaries and books of moral emblems. For example, Diego de Saavedra Fajardo's *Empresas politicas* (1640) contains an *imago* (illus. 95) that Goya could skilfully have used for his frontispiece. The accompanying text specifies that: '. . . the lion is unequivocally acknowledged to be the king of the animals. He sleeps little, and when he does it is with his eyes open. (. . .) This is part of his shrewdness and cunning.'[21]

This emblem has been combined with another motif that was very much part of conceptist culture, that of the split or 'double vision' (*la vista duplicada*) resulting in 'inner sight' (or 'insight') and 'outer sight'.[22] If in the first frontispiece (illus. 72, 96) the leonine dreamer has one eye hidden by his arms and the other quite visible, things are different in the second frontispiece (illus. 73) and in the final etching (illus. 98). What we are seeing is a kind of polarization between the 'inner sight' of the dreamer whose eyes are not completely hidden,

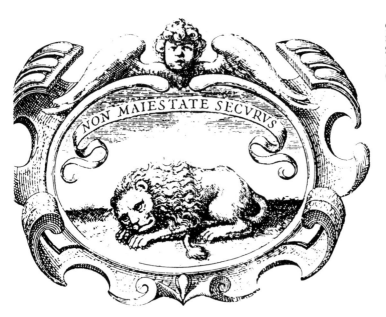

95 'Empresa 45', from Diego de Saavedra Fajardo, *Empresas politicas,* (Milan, 1642).

and the thematization, indeed glorification, of the lynx's 'outer' gaze.

The lynx's sight is an ancient symbolic motif, which was fully codified in Valeriano Bolzani's *Hieroglyphica* (1602)[23] and which became wholly integrated, in Gracián, with the attributes of the 'good listener'.[24] In Goya's second frontispiece, therefore, while the 'author sleeps', his inner sight is at work and the sharp sight of the good listener, the spectator's counterpart, keeps watch.

It is possible that the enigmatic New York self-portrait (illus. 36) contained the early seeds of an idea which was later to develop into polarization. There is not much difference between the size of this drawing and the first frontispiece but the leonine self-portrait should still be viewed as a unique and anticipatory experiment. The wide-open eyes see and do not see, look and do not look, peer into the distance and, at the same time and with the same intensity, turn inwards.

But the comparison between the first and second frontispieces (illus. 72, 73) can and must go very much further. What is so striking is that in the second frontispiece the split within the dreaming person is no longer the dominant theme and the multiple faces have disappeared. The whole of an important section (top left) has been left blank. Several attempts have been made to explain this phenomenon. Werner

96 Detail of illus. 72.

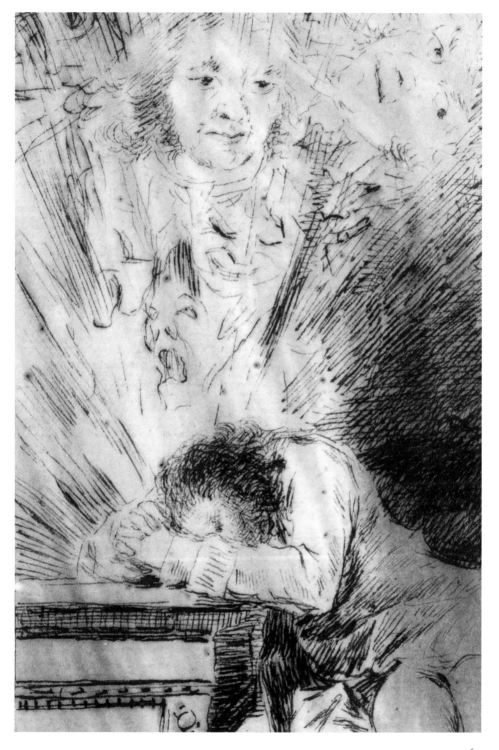

Hofmann suggested that this quarter circle might be connected to the ancient *rotae* through which the medieval system of liberal arts was conceived.[25] Eleanor Sayre, for her part, thought it might have been influenced by one of Saavedra Fajardo's *empresas* that contained a whole moral dissertation on the dialectical relationship between the light of truth and the darkness of lies. It is difficult to choose just one of these interpretations. Instead, we would like to draw attention to what is probably the oldest commentary, an unusual one since it does not come to us in discursive but in figurative form. This is the canvas depicting an *Allegory of the Night* by Zacarias González Velásquez (1763–1834), an artist originally from Aragon who worked in Madrid in circles close to Goya's (illus. 97).[26] There is very little doubt that this painter (who fraternized with Goya and whose brother, the architect Isidro, Goya painted) conducted a dialectic with the drawings of the master, just as there is also very little doubt that his interpretation quite blatantly favoured the classicizing allegories that Goya had long since distanced himself from. In Gonzáles's work, the nightmarish atmosphere has been replaced by intense moonlight. The figure of the dreamer, opium poppy in hand, who combines elements from Goya's first two frontispieces, has become a winged spirit (probably Hypnos himself). Instead of the bat and the owl, Gonzáles has populated his night with cherubs. The great source of light within the painting is the lunar disk against which stands the silhou-

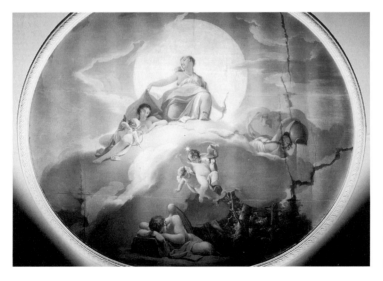

97 Zacarias González Velásquez, *Allegory of the Night*, after 1800, oil on canvas mounted on a wall.

ette of Selene/Diane. It is difficult to establish with any accuracy the precise route that Gonzáles took to reach this classicization of Goya's invention, but what strikes us as important is the fact that its figurative interpretation opens up the possibility of a reverse reading of the 1797 frontispiece as a *mise-en-scène* of a lunary dream.

The theme of the moon's influence on the human imagination is extremely ancient and is found as much in the classical tradition as in popular beliefs.[27] This would not be the first, nor the last time, that Goya was to show himself as sensitive to it.[28] What is important, however, is not that he adopted it here but that he eventually abandoned it. The final version (*Capricho* 43, illus. 98) once again appears to be the fruit of a situational reversal. The dreamer's head has sunk into his crossed arms, and the moonlight has been replaced by the darkest of darks.

Whether or not this is accepted, one thing is for certain. The large quarter circle that fills the upper left-hand corner of the 1797 version (illus. 73) is neither an accident nor the consequence of the image's 'unfinished state'. On the contrary, this drawing, which bears traces of copper and which had therefore been used as an etched impression that no longer exists, shows that a lot of thought was given as to its function as an endpaper to a series of images. With its double frame, its centre has been reserved for the image and its margins for the text(s). In the upper part we can read the title: *Sueño 1°/1ˢᵗ Dream*. In the lower part we have what is a stage direction:

> The artist dreaming.
>
> His only purpose is to banish harmful, vulgar beliefs, and to perpetuate in this work of caprices the solid testimony of truth.

A final caption can be found within the actual pictorial field, on the plinth on which the dreamer rests his head:

> 1st dream.
> Univer
> sal Language. Drawn
> and Etched by F.co de Goya.
> Year 1797

This second version is a very good and extremely important example of the 'paratextual' phenomenon.[29] Title, date and

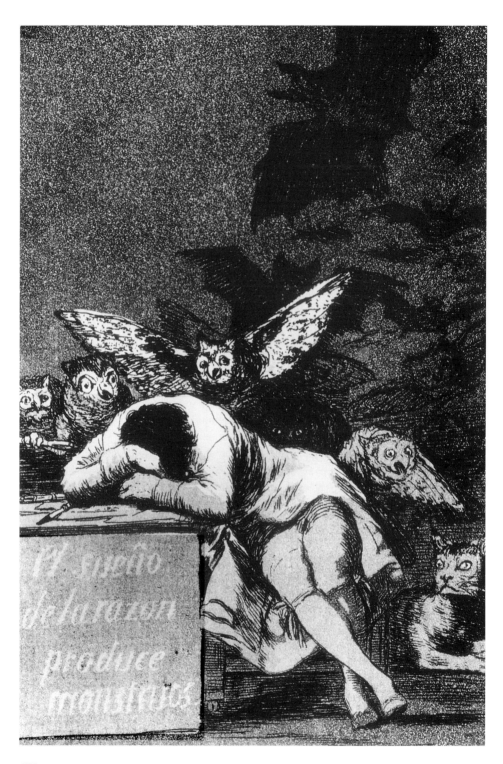

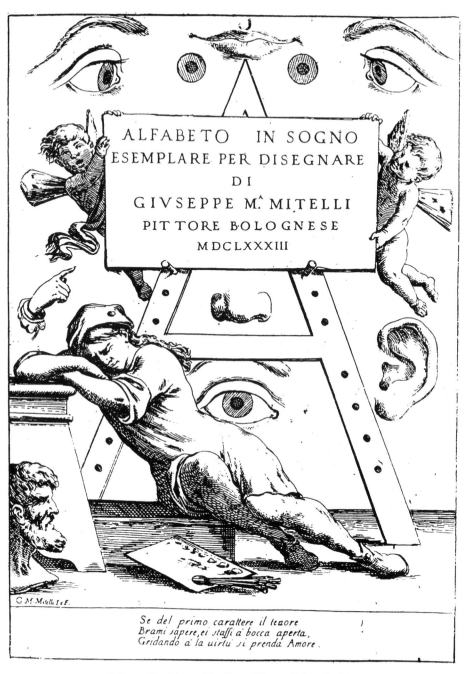

ALFABETO IN SOGNO
ESEMPLARE PER DISEGNARE
DI
GIVSEPPE M.ª MITELLI
PITTORE BOLOGNESE
MDCLXXXIII

Se del primo caraltere il tenore
Brami sapere,ei staffi a'bocca aperta,
Gridando a' la uirtu' si prenda Amore.

98 Goya, *Capricho 43: The Sleep of Reason Brings forth Monsters*, 1797–8,
etching and aquatint.

99 Frontispiece of Guiseppe Maria Mitelli, *L'Alfabeto in sogno*
(Bologna, 1683).

author's name are all there. In this triad, the author is probably the most privileged, for he appears three times: in the image, as the dreamer; in explanatory form ('the artist dreaming') and, finally, in the nominal form which takes the place of the signature: 'F.co de Goya'. What we have here is a phenomenon absolutely central to Goya's art: subjective, personal, self-reflective. In the first version (illus. 72) this idea first manifested itself as a split in the person dreaming. In the final version (illus. 98) we are being confronted by a multiple highlighting of the 'person' of the creator: dreamer-author-signatory. In the advertisement that appeared in the 1799 *Diario de Madrid*, the same idea re-surfaced in response to the insistent call of auctorial authority. For Goya, as for so many eighteenth-century creators, the 'auctorial experience' is also (and particularly) the 'experience of me'.[30] The rest of the text(s) that appears in the 'first dream' requires particular attention because of the two syntagms that are to be found there: 'work of caprices' (*obras de caprichos*) and 'Universal Language' (*Ydioma universal*). This last syntagm is inserted, not into the actual paratextual space, but into the image itself. It has been repeatedly subjected to in-depth analyses[31] that generally favour the ancient myth of the 'universal language', as resuscitated and revivified by eighteenth-century grammarians and philosophers (illus. 99).[32] It was also at around this time that cultured Spaniards became aware of the myth, by way of experiences such as hypnosis, mesmeric telepathy, teaching and entertainment.[33] These were probably the same people who attended demonstrations of magic lanterns and fantascopes. An article from the 1799 *Diario de Madrid* reveals that among the participants were the Duke and Duchess of Osuna, who were members of the most progressive intelligentsia in Madrid.[34] Because there are so few visual records of these events, it is difficult to draw any conclusion as to their exact role in the evolution of Goya's figurative language. We can, however, presume that they did have a role. The *Diario* reveals that these experiments were meant to demonstrate the pre-eminence of images in inter-human communication and it is easy to imagine just how appealing this concept would have proved to the artist: 'This mute and purely ocular language can easily be converted into a spoken language destined to the hearing since it presents the true prototype of a universal language.'[35] We now need to examine briefly the syntagm

obras de capricho that is part of the inscription and that anticipates the change that was to come two years later, when the
title *Sueños* was finally abandoned for good. It could be called
a *para-* or *pre-title*.

In 1799 when the series of 72 etchings was expanded to 80,
and the new title of *Los Caprichos*[36] began to replace the old
title of *Sueños*, what is being seen is not just a change of title
but also (and above all) a variation in the system of entitling
books. The fact can never be over-stressed that the title, *Los
Caprichos*, appears neither on the endpage of the series nor
anywhere else. The 1797 premonitory inscription refers to *obra
caprichosa*, the advertisement in the 1799 *Diario de Madrid* to a
'collection of Prints and Capricious subjects' (*colección de
estampas de asuntos caprichosos*) and one of the earliest critics,
as we have already seen, uses the expression 'a book of
witches and satyrs'. The first documentary evidence to come
from the artist himself, the receipt for the four series pur-
chased by the Osuna family, uses a more precise expression
but one that is not without ambiguity: 'quatro libros de caprichos y grabados'.[37]

The frontispiece to the series, in its definitive format, contains
neither title, nor date, but only the portrait of Goya with his
signature-name (illus. 100). This was not totally unusual, as
his English colleagues had already produced similar authorial frontispieces.[38] Several details are worth emphasizing. For
example, Goya has abandoned all allegorizing allusions in
order to demonstrate his modernity and the topicality of his
vision. The French-style clothes, especially the top hat, present him as a liberal if not as a 'free' intellectual (illus. 7).[39]
Some time later, this costume was to become the symbol of
those who used the reversing of the world as an anti-world
(illus. 3, 103). But one particularly important aspect is that the
self-portrait is numbered and that it is therefore the *first capricho* of the series of 80.

This first 'caprice', then, is not a narrative scene (unlike the
next one) but an unusual self-portrait, since it is in profile. It is
not difficult to ascertain why this kind of self-portrait is so rare:
no-one can see and reproduce their own profile without the
help of a whole complicated system of objectivation. Once he
had abandoned the idea of an allegorical frontispiece (*el autor
soñando*; illus. 72, 73), Goya even toyed with the idea of a full-
frontal self-portrait,[40] an idea that he soon abandoned. By por-

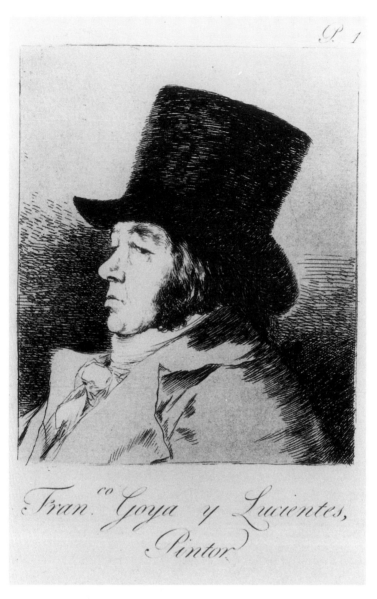

100 Goya, 'Franciso Goya y Lucientes, Painter', frontispiece of the *Caprichos*, 1797–8, etching and aquatint.

traying himself in profile, he was opting for a solution that was not completely unfamiliar to him since he had tackled it before in the integrated self-portraits produced in the 1780s (illus. 141, 142). By returning to it at this point, he was drawing attention to certain details, the first being the self-objectivation. The symbolic shape of the profile (unlike the frontal image) is 'in the form of the third person'. It always represents a 'he', a 'him'. It corresponds in effect to Goya's repeated efforts to

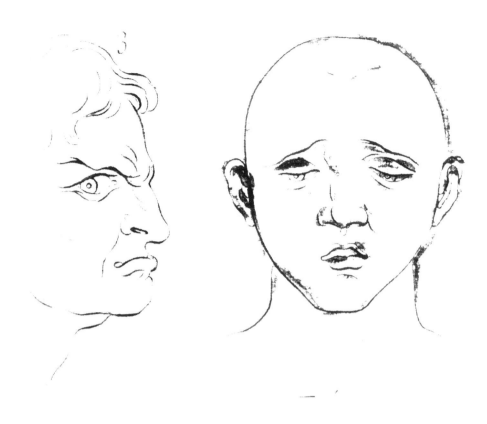

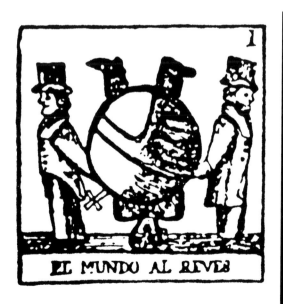

101 Franciso de Paula Martì Mora, *Disprecio* (Contempt), engraving from Fermin Eduardo Zeglirscosac, *Ensayo sobre el origen y naturaleza de las pasiones* (Madrid, 1800).

102 Martì Mora, *Tristeza* (Sadness), engraving from Zeglirscosac, *Ensayo sobre el origen y naturaleza de las pasiones*.

103 Catalan, '*The World Upside Down*', early 19th century, print.

EL MUNDO AL RIVES

name himself in a neutral fashion (*el autor*, *el pintor*, etc.). It also involves the idea of the 'person' becoming the 'object of observation'. In other words, whereas frontality establishes a *me/you* dialogue, the contemplation of the profile will always be the contemplation of '*the other*'.[41] But Goya's trick will no doubt have been spotted: he avoids a full profile by twisting the head slightly. The result is no doubt significant: he is the person who is allowing himself to be both observed and observer, both object and subject of the representation. Instead of the 'dreaming author' of the first frontispiece (illus. 72), we have an 'observed/observing author'. Something of the early split of the thematized gaze remains, but in a different form. The artist's left eye, half-covered by the heavy eyelid, and the oblique gaze with which he looks at the world are probably the key to the whole series.

Eleanor Sayre has drawn attention to the possibility that Goya might have been inspired by the print and description associated with 'Contempt' from Charles Le Brun's treatise on 'expressions of passion'.[42] This is an interesting hypothesis but needs to be modified. It seems likely that Goya's direct source was not Le Brun but rather his Spanish interpreter Fermin Eduardo Zeglirscosac, who in 1800 published an illustrated *Essay on the Origin and Nature of the Passions*.[43] If Goya was familiar with this essay shortly before its publication, as we assume he was, he chose not to copy a single one of its expressions but instead to produce an interesting and quite remarkable pair of illustrations representing Contempt (*Disprecio*) and Sadness (*Tristeza*) (illus. 101, 102). The profile view he used for Contempt is not only that of one of the figures that appeared in Zeglirscosac's essay but also corresponds to the particular attention paid to the shape of the profile as an 'objective' form of the person. It was Lavater in particular who saw the profile as the perfect method by which to analyze personalities (see Chapter 7). It should come as no surprise, therefore, to find that the earliest commentary on the self-portrait-frontispiece of the *Caprichos* uncovered *this* very unequivocal aspect, interpreting the first page of the *Caprichos* as a self-portrait *and* at the same time as a physiognomical essay. Let us consider the three main manuscript explanations:

> *Ayala Manuscript*: True portrait of oneself, in satirical attitude (*Verdadero retrato suyo, de gesto satirico*).

Stirling Manuscript: True portrait of oneself, in malicious attitude (*Verdadero retrato suyo, de gesto maligno*).

Manuscript from the National Library of Madrid: True portrait of oneself, in a bad humour and in a satirical attitude (*Verdadero retrato suyo, de mal humor, y gesto satirico*).

All the commentators have used the same syntagm to express the notion of self-portrait (*Verdadero retrato suyo*/true portrait of oneself), but differ when it comes to defining the physiognomy (*el gesto*). This was referred to as 'satirical' the first time, as 'malicious' the second and as 'satirical and in a bad humour' the third. This last description places the definition of the self-portrait (and therefore the account of the whole vision governing the *Caprichos*) on a complex symbolic level.

El mal humor, the 'bad humour', to which the explanatory manuscript from the National Library of Madrid refers, is a notion that comes from the medico-philosophical tradition. *El mal humor*, before being a 'state' or a 'emotion of the soul', originally referred to a 'character' or more precisely to a 'temperament'. It was the new name given to the ancient *black bile* (the *atrabile, la mélainè cholè*), or more precisely, to its harmful variant since an 'excessive' or 'corrupt humour' could, in extreme cases, lead either to genius or madness.[44] Black bile, or more precisely the 'bad humour' referred to by physiognomists, is a concentrated substance that is acrid, irritating and bitter. The most complete phenomenology we have, is the one left us by Galen:

> . . . it resembles the most mordant vinegar . . . It causes ulcers by eating away all the areas of the body it comes into contact with if it is not diluted. Vinegar, because it is deceiving, escapes easily, whereas the density of the black bile, by procuring itself a stable location, is the cause of the corrosion.[45]

In Spain the most revealing description can be found in Huarte de San Juan's huge tome, *Examen de ingenios para las ciencias* (1594), a great classic in the literature on melancholy:

> It is necessary to know that among doctors and philosophers there is a great discussion around the nature and qualities of vinegar, dry bile and ash. (. . .) We are therefore able to verify that vinegar and dry melancholy open up and make earth ferment because of the heat and do not close it

up, even when the majority of these humours is cold. It follows therefore that dry melancholics marry great intelligence with much imagination.[46]

We find ourselves once again confronted with a description of a corrosive liquid substance, which reacts as a result of a shift from substantial register to metaphoric register. As scholars have demonstrated,[47] in the seventeenth but more especially in the eighteenth century, the Latin word *humor* resurfaced in English as *humour* and spread to almost all European languages. It was sometimes defined as 'the ability to depict things that cause gaiety and laughter, whilst pretending to be solemn and serious'.[48] *Humour* very soon became associated with *wit* and was accepted as a syntagm, as for example in Shaftesbury's *Essay on the Freedom of Wit and Humour* (1709). In this text, the author makes a clear distinction between 'humour' and 'humours', the 'humours' being by antonomasia 'bad humours'.[49]

The expression used in the explanatory manuscript from the National Library of Madrid – 'true portrait of oneself, in a bad humour and in a satirical attitude' – belongs to the tradition that combines *humour* with *wit* ('mal humor' with 'gesto satirico'). The only difference is that, by qualifying 'humour' and stressing that it is a 'bad humour', the traditional atrabilious origins of the term are recalled. All the ancient philosophers, from Galen on, have underlined its pathological as well as prophylactic nature. An excess of humour, dangerous since it could cause madness, was treated in one of two ways: either by 'drying' or 'purging' the humours.[50] A seventeenth-century engraving (illus. 104) illustrates both these methods, but in a comic way which demonstrates how people distanced themselves from the medicine of the ancient 'humorists'. The engraving shows the inside of an *apotheca*, where people came to be cured, as the inscription indicates, of fantasy or purged of madness. On the right, the apothecary is introducing the head of a patient into a hot oven which, by 'drying the humours', releases into the atmosphere the fantasies they had created. In the background of the shop the purgative substances are lined up on shelves and labelled 'Virtue', 'Reason', 'Good Spirit', etc. The doctor on the left is forcing a sick man to swallow a good dose of 'Wisdom', which instantly makes him expel, through a hole in the chair, three lumps of waste

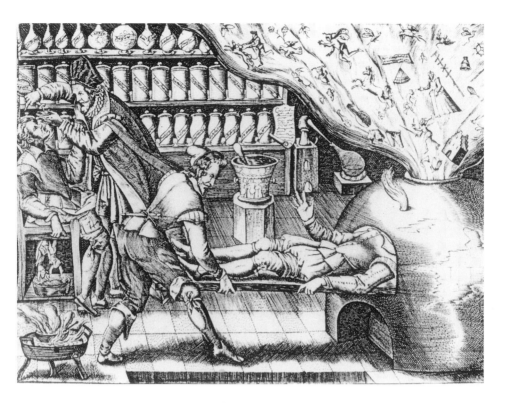

104 German, *The Doctor Curing Fantasy, also Purging Madness with the Use of Drugs, c.* 1630, copper engraving.

material in the form of lunatics.[51] Goya mocks this kind of practice on more than one occasion. In the *Caprichos*, for example, he tackles the theme of enforced purgation within a satirical context aimed at the clergy and doctors. *Capricho* 58 (illus. 105) shows a monk armed with a giant syringe with which he intends to purge a crowd of sinners who do not appear to be too pleased at the prospect. The *mise-en-scène* is carnivalesque and works through reversal, since it is 'bad humour' that is struggling against 'good humour'. The print is reminiscent of the ancient processions of 'madmen' at whom people used to squirt mud through giant syringes.[52] In the carnivalesque world, purification and foulness were dialectically connected.[53]

Capricho 33 (illus. 92, 93) attacked false apothecaries who used false purges. There are no direct allusions to ancient humoral medicine, but the context is that of a fairground where the charlatan had an established place.[54]

A third reference is found not in an image, but in an undated letter written by Goya to his soul-mate Martin Zapater, which experts usually place around the end of 1792,

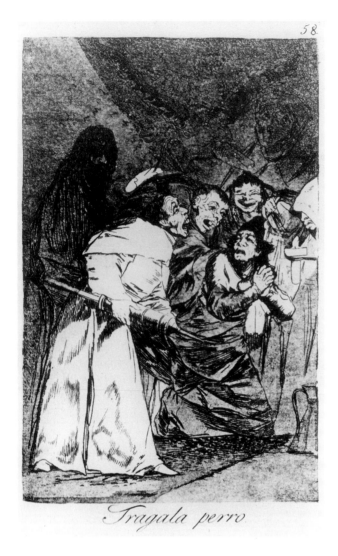

58.

Tragala perro

105 Goya, *Capricho 58: Swallow That, You Dog*, 1797–8, etching and aquatint.

that is to say at the time of the onset of the illness that was to have a profound effect on him:

> I cannot live like that, with these problems always on my mind, it puts me in a bad humour until I put my hand below my navel – you laugh but do the same, do the same and you will see the beneficial effect this has and you really do need to for the time for bad thoughts bad words and bad deeds has come and my thanks to my Aunt Lorenza who taught me this thing.

To be frank, at first all that made me absent-minded, but

now I fear neither witches, nor spirits, nor ghosts, nor swaggering giants, nor cowards nor brigands nor any kind of body, I fear nothing and no one save humans . . .[55]

This letter, one of the most famous Goya ever wrote, is difficult to understand because of all its twists and turns, especially as the style is so personal – and probably at times in code (for information on Goya's codes, see Chapter 6). Some commentators have detected allusions to masturbation, while others have seen allusions to the imagery of the future *Caprichos*. There is another possible interpretation. It seems possible that Goya is complaining to his friend of his 'bad humour' and of its effects (*brujas, duendes, fantasmas*, etc.). He describes, in a mocking tone, his own cynical method of purgation. The problem is fairly obvious: bad humour (*el mal humor*) is eliminated through bad thoughts, bad words, bad deeds (*malos pensamientos, palabras, obras*).

The year is probably 1792. The following year, having recovered from his terrible illness, Goya began the long period of reflection that would lead to the creation of the drawings and plates populated with the spirits and humans that had so terrified him during the crises of 'bad humour' described to his friend. It would appear that Goya was fortunate enough to find another, more appropriate way of freeing himself from his 'black bile'.

1, DISENCHANTMENT STREET, MOONLESS NIGHT ('STRONG WATERS' – THIRD CONJECTURE)

Goya probably bought the house in the calle del Desengaño in 1779[56] and it seems likely that he found the name of this old Madrid street appealing.[57] When, a few years later, in 1799, he decided to sell the *Caprichos* himself through the drug-store on the ground floor of the house, by specifying in the *Diario de Madrid* announcement that the sale would be held at calle del Desengaño no. 1 (1, Disenchantment Street), he was creating a poetic space in the heart of reality. It was not to be the last time he would undertake such a venture. He did so again, at least once more, when, alone and ill, he left Madrid and bought himself a house on the outskirts of the city. This house bore the beautiful name of *Quinta del Sordo*/the House of the Deaf Man. There is little doubt but that this name (and house itself) met the old painter's requirements. The way he gave symbolic shape to this space with paintings inspired by his fantasies is too well known to be investigated here.

Just as the décor of the *Quinta del Sordo* is unavoidably linked to its name, so the sale of the *Caprichos* in the calle del Desengaño no. 1 cannot be unrelated to the cultural and symbolic content of this toponymic. Goya's participation in the game may have been inspired by the playful experiments that were very much in vogue in the literary and intellectual circles he frequented. José Cadalso, for instance, in his *Cartas Marruecas* (1789), by tackling the figure of the charlatan-apothecary, provides an example of the burlesque publicity that surrounded miracle products: '... we have not seen products so honourable to the human spirit, so useful to society and so marvellous in their effects as the extraordinary salts invented by Mr Frivoletti in the rue saint Honoré in Paris.'[58] There is a remnant of this kind of self-reflective publicity in the advertisement that appeared in the *Diario de Madrid*. *Mutatis mutandis*, we could say that the 'caprices' on sale at the 'pharmacy' in Disenchantment Street were to Goya what the 'miracle' salts on offer in the rue saint Honoré were to Mr Frivoletti. With Goya, however, the irony (evident in Cadalso) turned to seriousness.

In order to ascertain just how wide-ranging this new form of play was, the semantic realm of the word *Desengaño* should be examined.[59] The word is virtually untranslatable today, due to its complexity. It is the opposite of the word *engaño* (error, illusion, charm, deception, hoax, trickery, pretence) and covers a vast territory that ranges from 'discovery' (as in 'discover a deception'), 'disillusion' or 'disenchantment' to nuances such as 'disappointment' and 'sadness'. The eighteenth-century Spanish dictionary gave the word three principal meanings, all related:

<Desengaño. s. m.
Luz de la verdad, conocimiento del error con que se sale del engaño. Lat. *Erroris cognitio.*
[The light of truth, the exposing of the error that helps dispel the charm.]

Desengaño. Se llama tambien el objeto que exercita al desengaño. Lat. *Quod erroris cognitionem excitat.*
[It is also the means by which we discover a deception.]

Desengaño. Vale assimismo claridad que se dice a otro, echandole la falta en la cara. Lat. *Proprum libere dicterum*. [Can also be used to mean a truth we have told another by throwing an error in his face][60]

It was as part of this relative polysemantism that eighteenth-century moral literature used the word. An eloquent testimony to this is Father Feyjoo's collected essays entitled 'Universal critical theatre or diverse discourses of all kinds to be used for the exposing of common errors' (*Teatro critico universal o discursos varios de todo genero de materias para el desengaño comunes errores*, 1725–8). Goya's etchings also work in the same way. Thus in the inscription on the frontispiece to the 'Dreams' (illus. 73) the author specifies that their aim is to 'banish (*desterrar*) harmful, vulgar beliefs and to perpetuate in this work of caprices the solid testimony of truth'. The advertisement in the *Diario de Madrid*, on the other hand, speaks of 'the censure of human errors and vices' (*censura de los errores y vicios humanos*).[61] In the self-portrait-frontispiece to the final series (illus. 100) Goya includes additional elements from his own authorial *mise-en-scène*. He places himself, as we have seen, in a dual position: on the one hand, he is a *desengañado* (a disappointed, disenchanted person), 'sad' and 'contemptuous', and, on the other, a *desengañador* (he who disenchants, who discovers a deception).

There is a degree of shrewdness and, at the same time, a degree of violence in the very act of disenchantment. The literary figure of the *Desengañado/Desengañador*, as invented by someone like Quevedo or Gracián, is a dual and duplicitous creation. The *Desengañado/Desengañador* – the disenchanted person who disenchants – knows in this instance that all is lies and illusions. Even the word 'world' (*mundus*), which originally meant 'clean', is a lie. The world, explains Gracián, is dirty and foul: '*mundus imundus*'.[62] Everything is back to front, and the *Desengañado/Desengañador* is the one who *knows it* and who *reveals it*. He always has one eye open, adds Quevedo, and is therefore capable of seeing the inside of things (*mirar por dentro*),[63] seeing through appearances, recognizing deceptions, scanning the world in reverse (*mirar al rebes*).[64] The *Desengañado/Desengañador* is the one who can see, and who reveals that the world is representation, spectacle, appearance and deception. Goya gets into the skin of this dual person, as his self-portrait and the structure of the *Caprichos* demonstrate. The product of an examination (free of illusions) of the world, these images, in order to fulfil their destiny, had in their turn to return to the world, not to 'enchant' it but to 'disenchant' it. No. 1, Discovering, Disillusion, Disenchantment and Sadness Street was probably the most appropriate place for this to happen.

Goya probably first began to think about this series after his illness in 1793. In the biographical account written by his son Xavier in 1831, the date given for the completion of the etchings was 'around 1796–7'.[65] Xavier might have been being a little optimistic, but the drawings for the 'Madrid Sketchbook' do in effect indicate that by 1797 Goya's ideas were already at an advanced stage and Valentin Carderera, in a very important article, refers to an early sale of the smaller series (*The Dreams*) during that same period.[66] In any case, and the experts are unanimous on this, by 1798 the final version, with its 80 plates, was finished. Goya took his time creating the series, and was certainly in no hurry to distribute it. By the beginning of 1799, the prints were in circulation (the Osuna family having acquired four copies in January),[67] but they did not go on public sale until February, due to a delay that we now need to examine.

Above the famous publicity notice, the first page of the *Diario de Madrid* (illus. 89) publishes some significant facts. Below the title of the newspaper, we see the day and the date ('Wednesday, 6th February 1799'). It was common practice to insert, after the date, the saint whose name day it was (Saint Dorothy) and the name of the church where a special mass would be held (the 'Iglesia de San Felipe Neri'). As was the custom in all newspapers at the time (a leftover from the early almanacs),[68] this was followed by the meteorological information for the day and, in the very last section, details pertaining to the sun and moon. On 6 February 1799 the sun rose at 7.59 and set at 5.01 in the evening. The moon was in its thirtieth day. This last, and apparently banal detail, has until now gone unnoticed. And this is unfortunate. The 'thirtieth day' of the moon, is the day (or night) of the 'new moon'. In classical astrology and later in popular astrology, the expression 'new moon' (*nova luna*) meant that the planet was between two lunar months.[69] At the end of this period, during which the moon was completely invisible, or, according to ancient

186

beliefs, 'hidden' so as to be reborn,[70] a thin crescent appeared in the sky, and this was the *prima luna*, marking the moon's 'renaissance'. According to tradition, when the moon was in its 'thirtieth day' it was in its most dangerous phase, poised at the uncertain boundary between disappearance and appearance. This stage was also referred to as the 'dry moon' (*luna sitiente* or *luna sicca*) because it was thought that the planet, finding itself unable to inhale the humid exaltations it usually fed on, 'was turning its back' on the earth.[71]

In the preliminary stages that took Goya from the early studies for the *Dreams* frontispiece (illus. 73) to the final version of his famous *Capricho* 43 (illus. 98), he appears to have modified, or rather reversed his earlier intentions. Having originally focused on the influence of the nocturnal planet on dreams, he preferred, in the end, to reflect on the relationship between the imagination and the state of the 'dry moon' that dominates the world of the *Caprichos*. As well as the 'nocturnalism' in the series, repeatedly and quite rightly underscored by the various interpreters,[72] the conspicuous absence of moonlight should also be noted. Its significance is even greater since it was so skilfully exploited in other nocturnal pieces.

To all these observations we must add another crucial factor. In the month of February (the month chosen by Goya to put his *Caprichos* on the market) the two, or three 'moonless' days (nights) were different from all the other moonless nights of the year since they coincided with the climax and therefore the end of the Carnival.[73] By announcing that the moon, on Wednesday, 6 February, was in its 'thirtieth day', the *Diario de Madrid* was pointing out that this Wednesday was in fact Ash Wednesday. Goya's project – the *Caprichos* – was therefore even more ambitious and of much greater significance than has been recognized until now. It should be considered as the most important *mise-en-scène* of the preface to the dying century.

Goya's decision to publish his great series on Ash Wednesday 1799 is undoubtedly important and is directly related to the ancient rites of passage.[74] These had already been graphically illustrated in the sixteenth century, as we can see from an engraving after Pieter Bruegel the Elder (illus. 101). This depicts a carnivalized sublunary world, dominated by madness, lust and avarice at the very moment when astronomers, measuring the first crescent of the February

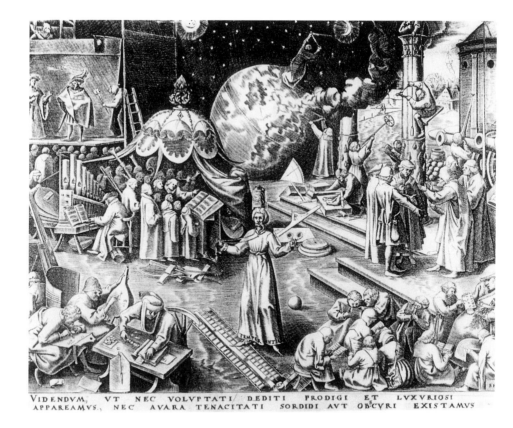

VIDENDVM, VT NEC VOLVPTATI/ DEDITI PRODIGI ET LVXVRIOSI
APPAREAMVS., NEC AVARA TENACITATI SORDIDI AVT OBSCVRI EXISTAMVS

moon, are heralding the end of one time (the Time of Vices) and the beginning of another (the Time of Temperance).

By the end of the eighteenth century, the significance of the Carnival/Lent relationship had changed, and Goya obviously intended to provide it with a more allusive and indirect *mise-en-scène*. Instead of presenting us with a didactic image as Bruegel had done (and as was still being done in the first half of the eighteenth century [illus. 107]), he used the daily press and a publicity notice to introduce his own transgressive imagery into the actual temporality of the last Carnival of the century. A reading of the newspapers published on the days concerned gives the impression that the ancient Carnival/Lent conflict has been remodelled. Signs of this change can be found in the *Diario de Madrid* of Wednesday, 6 February. Apart from the (obligatory) insertion of the moon's phase, there appears to be no reference to the Carnival finishing or to Lent beginning. The only references to a change of temporal order are indirect, although fairly obvious. For example, the paper announces the

106 Philip Galle after Pieter Brueghel, *Allegory of Temperance*, c. 1600, etching.

188

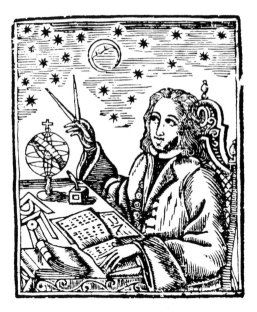

107 Frontispiece of Diego Torres Villarroel, *Nueva folla astrologica* (Madrid, 1761).

NUEVA FOLLA ASTROLOGICA.

PISCATOR

PARA EL AÑO DE 1-61.

beginning of Lent customs, such as the 'novenas for the souls in purgatory', or refers to the arrival of a special delivery of cod, or again, mentions the baker, who, worried that he might lose customers during the days of fasting, points out that his products contain no pork fat.[75]

However, the significance of Goya's choice of Lent as a context continues to intrigue. The most important question is raised by the timing of this choice. In other words, why was the series not on sale to the public during Sunday, Monday and Tuesday of the Carnival (especially since it could have been, given that it was completed in January)? Why wait until the day of the great farewell, that is, until Ash Wednesday? Once again, a comparison with tradition is enlightening.

If there is a symbolic product, which, through its structure and import, anticipates Goya's *Caprichos*, then it must be *The Ship of Fools* (*Das Narrenschiff*) (illus. 58). Attributed to Sebastian Brant, this famous book was published in Basel in 1494, 1495 and then finally in a revised and enlarged version in 1499. An account of its reception in Spain at the end of the Middle Ages and the beginning of modern times has not yet been written.[76] But this is not what concerns us here.[77] Instead, let us examine the symbolic import of the publication dates. Scholars have pointed out that all three editions of *The Ship of Fools* were published on Shrove Tuesday and that, in the case of the 1499 edition, it was a special Shrove Tuesday since it was the last of the century, or, more importantly, 1499 preceded the great Jubilee marking the holy year of 1500.[77] The same scholars have repeatedly stressed how carnivalesque thinking was echoed in the structure of the texts and images of the *Narrenschiff*. In other words, these texts are reminders of the texts and images distributed to the people during the Sunday, Monday and Tuesday prior to Ash Wednesday in anticipation, and as mementoes, of the forthcoming days of abstinence. Carnivalesque madness was seen as temporary, as a necessarily limited time of excess, and Sebastian Brant uses every means available to remind his audience of this. The 1499 edition actually carries a clear warning, directed at those who try to prolong the carnival into the days of abstinence:

> I know of many carnival fools
> Who continue to wear hats
> Even during Holy Lent
> One goes around smeared in soot
> Another masked and in disguise,
> Parades in Shrovetide
> His intentions most lewd. (. . .)
> Only fools could have invented
> Celebrations in Lent
> When thoughts should be on Salvation.
> A right black night <zu Recht Fast-Nacht>!
> And in the streets they constantly run
> Filthy and mad.[78]

If, on Shrove Tuesday 1499, Sebastian Brant anathematized those who dared prolong the Carnival, on Ash Wednesday 1799, at the end of the eighteenth century, Goya was to produce the greatest shock in the history of the ancient closing ceremony. His action – selling the imagery of licence on the first day of Lent – can best be understood in the light of carnivalesque ludism rather than Lenten gloom. The whole *mise-en-scène* of the distribution of the *Caprichos* can be interpreted as an enormous farce that prolongs the Festival beyond its boundaries. There is a possibility that selling 'strong waters' from a pharmacy on the first day of Lent might have had moralizing and 'purgative' ramifications. Whilst emphasizing the quality of the strong waters and their ability to 'censure human errors and vices', the advertisement does not say whether they were designed as a remedy or a poison. Remedy or poison (or perhaps more precisely remedy *and* poison), Goya's strong waters, on sale at a symbolic price (320 *reales* was equivalent to one ounce of gold) are the product of a double carnivalization of the time to repent, since in this act, as in the particular prints that deal with this theme (illus. 85, 86, 100), purification and foulness stand side by side.

In conclusion, on Ash Wednesday 1799 (the day of the funeral of the last Carnival of the Century), Goya, a painter in a bad humour (*desengañado/desengañador*), launched, from the drug-store in Disenchantment Street, for the price of one ounce of gold, strong waters that embodied the transgressive and licentious imagination. In so doing he was performing an actual inversion in the calendar. His symbolic gesture, instead of restricting his imagination to those days specially reserved for madness and licence, projected it into time. Rather than surrounding it, he liberated it; instead of circumscribing it, he released it. By putting his *Caprichos* on the market at the very moment that the last Carnival of the century breathed its last, he was establishing another: this time one that was imaginary, unlimited and perpetual. In the black night of the dying carnival, waves of images (strong waters) established the permanence of a new Carnival. The modern world was born.

6 The Carnival of Language

THE CHALLENGES OF REPRESENTATION

There are two preoccupations that run through all the critical literature on Goya's *Caprichos*. The first is their order, the second their meaning. Of course, these are not two separate issues but simply facets of the same immense hermeneutic challenge thrown up by this work. Any attempt, ambition or claim to have answered all the questions is based on a misunderstanding of the principle. Trying to find a 'clear and definitive order' in the *Caprichos* is tantamount to insanely endeavouring to force the freedom of the Carnival into the corset of the norm; in the same way that providing a sequence for the 80 etchings or giving each image an absolute meaning is as crazy as claiming to have found an infallible 'key to the interpretation of dreams'. And yet, neither order nor meaning are completely irretrievable since the artist numbered his plates (thus indicating their order) and inserted a caption under each picture (thus hinting at their interpretation). However, despite the importance of these notes, they are of limited use and tend rather to add to the questions than provide the answers. What emerges from this is the idea that Goya's *Caprichos* is an infinitely interpretable object, a work in which the relationship between the presence and absence of order, and the presence and absence of meaning is in a state of perpetual flux.

The oldest known (1811) critical analysis, that of Gregorio González Azaola, identified this characteristic when it highlighted the intentionality of an 'enigmatic significance' (*cierto misterio*) in the author's apparent extravagance (*rarezas de su autor*) and in the conclusions it drew about the individual, free, open and subjective nature of the interpretation.[1] The fact that the actual structure of the *Caprichos* instigated, indeed produced such an interpretation and that it has always remained unstable and indefinite is also corroborated by the phenomenon, unique in the history of art, of the many 'hand-written commentaries' the series engendered soon after its creation and whose actual validity is difficult to define, once and for all. Although their content may be questionable and of doubtful accuracy, the commentaries remain important since they indicate the speed with which the interpretative reflex was triggered by Goya's work.

Very early in its career, and as soon as the series of etchings began to circulate beyond Spain's borders, the question of the interpretation of the *Caprichos* re-emerged, stronger than ever. It was to soar to dramatic heights. Thus, when Grandville published three of the etchings in the *Magasin pittoresque* in 1834, barely six years after Goya's death, the baffled Paris editor was forced to confess, 'Greetings to the good listener: we have to admit to having understood nothing'.[2] The world had to wait for Baudelaire's brilliant mind to recognize Goya's modernity, presented in the etchings' 'love of the imperceptible'.[3]

However, it would be a mistake to give up all hermeneutic concerns and to turn the underlying structure of the *Caprichos* into something vague and absurd. The error would be all the more serious if the texts reporting the early reactions to the etchings did no more than emphasize the tradition behind the interpretation, which is – as González Azaola suggests – that of a glorious rhetoric of the eminently Spanish *conceit* (as an embodiment of wit) that makes them inherently difficult to understand. González Azaola's text is all the more significant as it draws attention to the fact that the pleasure to be had from the satirical content of the *Caprichos* is only one aspect of their enormous appeal. The other aspect is the way in which the satire is created as it is directed to the spectator's mind. We are, therefore, being given an invaluable clue that confirms the message already detected in the text announcing the sale:

> . . . the subtle conceits hidden in each satire are divined and everyone makes applications, more or less fitting, in his own way and according to his own field of knowledge.

> . . . entre tanto que se van adivinando los finos conceptos envueltos en cada satira, y hace cada qual a su modo y segun la esfera de sus conocimientos, mas o menos felices aplicaciones.[4]

The thinking surrounding conceits (*conceptos*) is probably part of a second, though no less important, level of reaction to the etchings. Without an examination of the form, the actual interpretation of the content is seriously unsound. It is worth pausing at this stage to outline this problem, especially since the translation and interpretation of Gonzáles Azaola's text has come into conflict with a particular, understandable but pernicious, terminological timidity. Enriquetta Harris, to whom fell the credit of having discovered and published Gonzáles Azaola's text, used (to us) excessive caution when she translated *finos conceptos* as 'subtle notions'.[5] Nigel Glendinning preferred *'subtle ideas'*.[6] And yet it strikes us that when Gonzáles Azaola drew attention to the need to enjoy the subtle conceits underlying each satire (*finos conceptos envueltos en cada satira*), what he was in fact giving was a clue to their form and not to their content, by implicitly linking Goya's *Caprichos* to the conceptist tradition of Gracián or Quevedo.[7]

Two questions arise at this point that must be addressed. How are we to understand what 'conceptism' meant to Goya, an artist working at the end of the eighteenth century, if the rhetoric of conceit/wit had reached its peak in the seventeenth century? Moreover: how are we to define 'conceptism' within the sphere of figurative expression when the rhetoric of conceit/wit had emerged and evolved within the sphere of verbal, indeed textual expression? We believe that this double shift was in operation inasmuch as it is precisely this that reveals the workings of Goya's imagination and the means by which it was expressed. Before tackling it, however, it is absolutely necessary to define the terms. Let us listen to what Gracián says: 'Conceit is an act of understanding that expresses the correspondence between objects. The artistically created expression of this same consonance or correlation is objective subtlety.'[8] This last observation focuses on the effect of meaning that can suddenly emerge from any verbal arrangement, and on the fact that the real meaning of conceit or wit is to be found in the reaction engendered in an individual who must find something to decipher beneath the immediate surface of the discourse or thing. And in effect, Gracián and his Italian colleagues (and competitors) produced a valuable catalogue of conceptual figures, *agudezas* or *argutezze*[9] to help with the deciphering and creation of conceptist texts. Their aim was to communicate the pleasure of discovering (and indeed of creating) wit.

However, by the eighteenth century conceptism had run its course and increasingly fierce reactions against its excesses were being voiced more or less everywhere. Even in the Latin countries, generally considered to be the strongholds of verbal wit, the new classicist poetics had banished affectation and cultism in favour of the clarity and rationalism of enlightenment.[10] It is in this context that a phenomenon, whose importance has not been sufficiently stressed, was produced: in the eighteenth century conceptism survived only inasmuch as it provided a combinatory freedom forbidden by the Academy, and insofar as it acknowledged the validity of a verbal wit that was a wholly rational attack on language. It could be said that, far from being affected and highly cultured, as had been the case in previous centuries, conceptism offered, within the context of eighteenth-century rationalism, a kind of para-language, or – to be more flexible without being less precise – that it proclaimed its validity, its viability and its vitality only insofar as it was set up as the 'carnival of language'.[11] This is why, from being exclusive and élitist, conceptism became popular; and also why, out of the whole catalogue of *concetti* established a century earlier, only a small part survived, in the form of the popular conceptism of 'word games', 'allusions' and 'double meanings'.

TO SPEAK OR NOT TO SPEAK

In his conceptist book, *Agudeza y arte del ingenio* (1647), Baltasar Gracián devoted a whole chapter to 'wit through paronomasia, puns and word games' (*De la agudeza por paronomasia, retruécano y jugar del vocablo*) from which he quite openly distanced himself:

> This kind of conceit is considered to be the most popular form of wit, against which each himself rubs and all prick themselves, more by facility than by subtlety. Many use it unsuccessfully as a common thing like a reserve of wit, without ever achieving ever-higher artistic conceits. (. . .) The ingenuity of these conceits lies in changing a letter or syllable of the word or name in order to give it a different significance, either satirical or complimentary. The meaning is transformed by transforming a letter. When this is done with great aptness and in harmony with the subject, the

conceit is sublime. (. . .) If the pun has a moral relationship with the subject, it attains a *proportional correspondence*, which is a remarkable skill. There is also correspondence and proportion between words and their signified, the one corresponding to the other (. . .). The variety of this wit is as great as the licence to shuffle and mix the syllable of the noun, of the verb and vice-versa. (. . .) One can sometimes cut a word in two and the parts retain their significance. To the word one can either add a syllable, or another word. The change of syllables is not always necessary, sometimes an accent removed or added is enough to invite the establishing of a beautiful witticism. (. . .) The composition of anagrams comes under this type of creation: the syllables are changed into praise or satire.[12]

It is interesting to see how Gracián's own opinion fluctuates between praise and criticism of popular wit. Goya himself tackled wit with resolve, adapting it to suit his own ends and means. We have already had occasion to see this in one of the drawings from the *Sketchbook-Journal* (illus. 15) where he revealed, by using an artificially created name, 'an enamoured' (*enamorado/onamorado*). The satirical impact of this drawing comes from both text and caption. Another form of wit from the same family (this time probably complimentary) is to be found in the Metropolitan Museum self-portrait (illus. 36).[13] Here, the painter makes himself conspicuous not only, as we have already suggested, through his *facies leonina*, but also through the detail of the piece of jewellery that he wears on his chest and which bears his signature (appearing upside down to the spectator). It is difficult to ascertain with any certainty the significance of this strange nominal insertion but we think it should be sought through the paronomasia *Goya/Joya* (Goya/Jewel) that the painter also attempted in other contexts. The fact that the name is upside down would suggest to the spectator that its true meaning is to be found through an act of reversal, and it is edifying at this point to see how Gracián dealt with nominal acuity in one of the chapters of his book (*Discourse XXXI*):

The name occasions observations and mysterious ponderations. A word is like a vocal hydra for, as well as its own and direct significance, if we cut or reverse it, from each syllable subtle wit is reborn and from each accent conceit. (. . .) The name then corresponds to the thing designated as well as to its adjuncts (. . .) by transforming it or by reading it upside down, by making of it then a pleasant retortion (. . .) Ordinarily, we underline the harmony that exists between the mysterious name and the subject, or its adjuncts that are the causes, effects, properties, circumstances, etc. and when we discover this ingenious correspondence, we express it with delicate subtlety. There is no less subtlety in discovering a delicate lack of correspondence or contradiction between the name and the effects or circumstances of the subject designated; even better, we then raise the witty objection, we show the difficulty of the contradiction between the extremes of the comparison and we give it an appropriate exit by way of a brilliant fall.[14]

In each of these two examples the wordplay relies on a ludic interpretation and comparison of caption and image. We can (and must) ask ourselves just how far the conceptist poetics of word games could survive in an artistic expression in which figurative games outstripped word and caption games. In other words: we must ask ourselves just how autonomous the *Caprichos* are when they make use of such textual techniques as paronomasia, puns and word games.

By way of an example, let us turn to *Caprice* 79 (illus. 108). It shows a group of monks in a wine cellar secretly indulging in a bout of drinking. In the preparatory drawing, there was a skylight in the top right-hand corner of the image, thus emphasizing that the event was taking place underground. In the final print, on the other hand, the skylight has disappeared and the only object to indicate where we are is the large barrel in the right of the foreground. The caption – *Nadie nos ha visto* / *No-one saw us* – further accents the clandestine nature of the meeting, thus reflecting on the indiscreet if not denunciatory nature of the image. All three of the hand-written explanations conclude that it is indeed the vice of drunkenness that is being mocked in the image. In his classical study on the *Caprichos*, López-Rey suggested that, because the etching was the last but one and therefore at the end of the series, it could be taking on the role of a conclusion to the anti-religious criticism that permeates the whole cycle.[15] We could take this a step further and ask ourselves whether the caption ('no-one saw us') was not in this case of even greater pro-

197

108 Goya, *Capricho 79, No-one Saw Us*, 1797–8, etching and aquatint.

¿Nadie nos ha visto.

grammatic significance: for it is in effect the *Caprichos* that bring to light what no-one usually sees, that is to say the hidden vices.

The presentational mechanism used in the etching is extremely simple and ingenious since it reveals the transition from the particular situation ('five monks drinking wine in secret') to a more general message. However, this is only accessible to those who are 'able to see' (and decipher) not only the content of the representation but also the form. Goya comes to our assistance for he places in the foreground an object that is, as it were, 'glaringly obvious' and that the spectator cannot fail to see in all its aggressive presence: the barrel. The satire is born of the incompatibility of seeing monks gathered around (or next to) a barrel. The roots of this satire are to be found in the punning techniques of carnivalesque origin, which had been around for some time. Rabelais had already written glosses on the worship of the 'Divine Bottle' and had played with the paronomasia *du vin/divin*.[16] By changing just one letter, he produced an effect of comic and denunciatory reversal on the 'upside down worship' of which the monks were guilty. However, Goya opted for a different expression, one that was specifically Spanish and that came from a conceptist culture that was not around in Rabelais's time.[17] By putting the barrel (in Spanish *bota*) in the foreground and the 'devotees' (*devotos*) in the centre of the representation, he is introducing a paronomasia that is only possible in Spanish (where the *v* and *b* have the same phonetic weight) and which presents to the eye of the ideal 'ingenious reader' the key to the print, which is the mockery of the 'devotees of the barrel' (*devotos de la bota*).

In so doing, Goya reveals his double face: that of the 'popular' and that of the 'cultured' artist, since the pun in question was well-established in literary tradition and had been used in different contexts by Cervantes, Calderón de la Barca, Góngora and Gracián.[18] In Gracián, paronomasia was used within the context of a social critique, very similar to the one used by Goya: 'Look at that one, the more bloated he is the emptier he is, whereas the others seem to have taken their vows (*siendo de voto*) with the order of the barrel (*son de bota*).'[19] Goya, like Gracián, uses paronomasia to establish an antithesis and to produce a situational reversal, which, once it has been deciphered, results in the pleasure of discovery and understanding. Ideally, the spectator's culture and acuity correspond to the culture and acuity of the creator and the deciphering of the wit is equivalent to its creation.

There is, however, in the case of the *Caprichos* an added difficulty in relation to Gracián's *Criticón* that springs from the fact that the medium of the *word game* is not a text but an *image*. In order to be fully aware of the joke, the spectator must not only *see* the barrel in the foreground (an action the artist does his best to facilitate) but he must also *pronounce* it, translating the image into its phonetic equivalent; without this, the

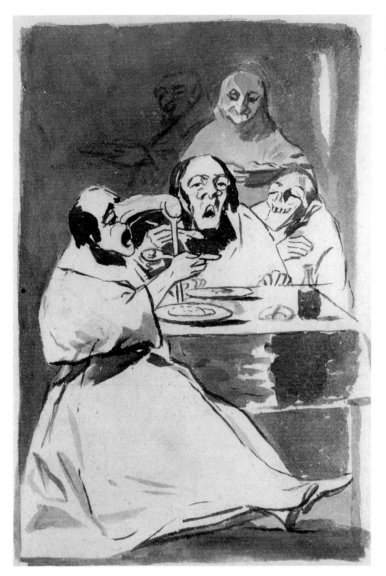

witticism will remain undetected. However, this does not
mean that the *Caprichos* will remain impenetrable to the eye
blind to all these mechanisms. On the contrary, as Goya
announced in 1799 and Azaola reiterated in his 1811 article,
the series can be interpreted on a number of different levels,
depending on the abilities and interpretative skills of the spectator. And yet, there are instances where the artist himself leaves
the ambiguity in a state of maximal indecision. *Capricho* 13 (illus.
110), which also satirizes the clergy, is a good example, since it

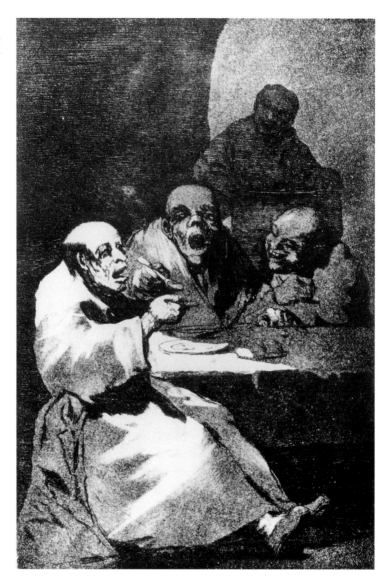

lacks any reading instruction such as the one Goya gave plate 86
(the barrel in the foreground). The relationship between the
caption (*estan calientes*/'it's hot') and the image remains
ambiguous and even the famous hand-written commentaries
shed no light on how it should be interpreted. The interpretation only begins to take shape when we compare (as has been
done time and again in studies on the history of art)[20] the final
version with the original idea, as it appears in a drawing in the
Madrid Sketchbook (illus. 109). This comparison provides evi-

201

dence for the self-censure Goya subjected himself to. In the drawing, the nose of one of the monks is shaped like a grotesque phallus and seems to suggest fairly clearly that the sin of greed (highlighted by the main action of the image) was a counterpart to the sin of lechery. In the transition from drawing to print (a slow process that would have had intermediary stages),[21] self-censure purged the image of its obscenity, an

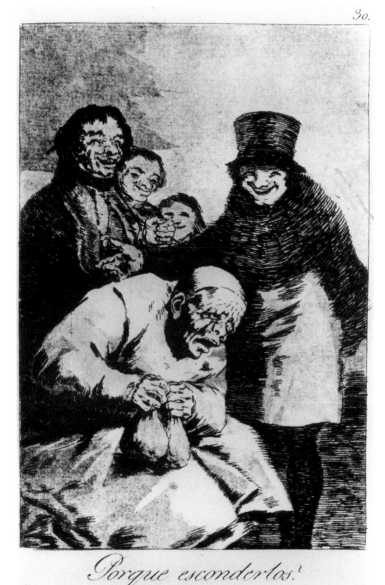

111 Goya, *Capricho* 30: *Why Hide It?*, 1797–8, etching and aquatint.

Porque esconderlas?

action partly offset by the allusive textual insertion. Just how far the insertion ('it's hot') is really empowered to replace the censured detail (the phallic nose) is a question that remains unanswered.

There are other examples that remain permanently and constantly ambiguous. In *Capricho* 30 (illus. 111), for example, it will probably always be impossible to determine with any certainty whether the satire of avarice also contains sexual undertones, as the two purses featured in the foreground and certain ambiguous gestures in the middle distance might lead us to believe. However, any attempt to interpret *Capricho* 42, entitled *You Who Cannot Do It, Carry Me on Your Shoulders* (*Tu que no puedes*) (illus. 112) in this context, proves to be much more complex. We immediately recognize one of the favourite motifs of the 'world upside down' (illus. 2, 3), in this case animals mounting humans.[22] By focusing on the aspects of social criticism embodied in this image, the hand-written commentaries in fact draw attention to the true meaning of the reversal: 'The useful classes of society shoulder all its weight, or real donkeys on their backs. (*Ayala Manuscript, no. 42*).' There is an additional allusion, however, that opens up the possibility of a double interplay in which social metaphor and sexual metaphor unite. The title '*Tu que no puedes*' (You who cannot do it) is taken from a popular proverb whose double meaning had already been commented on by writers of the Golden Age. Lope de Vega, for example, playfully invited two different readings of the syntagm; the first he called 'serious', the second 'vulgar', since it alluded to impotence:

> otra es termino vulgar
> que dice que cuando llega
> un ombre a no poder mas
> que con su mujer se acuesta[23]

We know that Goya chose the actual title of the print somewhat late in the day and we suspect that he did so in full knowledge of the facts. Some of the details in the image would lead us to believe that he wanted to create an ambiguous effect, not only on the level of the caption but also on the even more delicate level of the image. The most important detail is the way in which one of the donkey's legs sticks out between the legs of one of the humans, giving the impression that the latter is as 'well-endowed as a donkey'. The ludic effect is reinforced through the contrast with the drooping tail of the donkey in the foreground.

The principle behind these conjectures is as follows. Firstly, both the self-censure and the obscure ambiguity only emerge when erotic and sexual taboos are being targeted. Obscene ambiguity had, in fact, long been a traditional part of the Western culture of the Carnival,[24] and conceptist poetics only took it on against its better judgement. It is significant that Gracián attempted to salvage ambiguity's decency by primarily giving it a 'befitting' definition: 'Delicate ambiguity is like a double-edged word and a double-lit significance. Its ingenuity involves using a word that has two meanings in such a way as to cast doubt on what one had meant to say.'[25] But it is all the more significant that he feels the need to conclude, after a long detour, and rather more drastically: 'Ambiguous conceits are not very serious, and consequently, more suited to satirical and burlesque subjects than to serious or moral subjects.'[26] Thus the role played by the *Caprichos* in the double culture of the carnivalesque and conceptism stands out more clearly. However, we should not overlook the fact that the prints, unlike the drawings that had heralded or prepared them, were destined for the public domain. The way they were put up for sale reveals that the carnivalesque intent had to be reconciled with the predilections and taboos of an eclectic public, in which women were probably in the majority. This last fact is not a problem, however, since reliable sources testify to a fondness, among the women of Madrid, for all kinds of double meanings. Jean-François Bourgoing, French Consul to Spain, was outraged when he recorded certain characteristics of Spanish women that made them different from his own countrywomen: 'Ambiguities, paintings made with a not very fine brush, obscenities even, easily exonerate all the witticisms, all the indiscretions of the language.'[27] However, we should add to Bourgoing's observations that, in line with the conceptist culture of the pun, in order to be perfect an ambiguous word game should preserve – and the ladies of Madrid must have known this – its constant ambiguity. This is precisely what makes it attractive and, in the case of Goya's prints, difficult.

Sexualization is spoken to be silenced, and silenced in order to be spoken. In other words, it is impossible to find, whether on the erotic level of conceptist literature, or in witti-

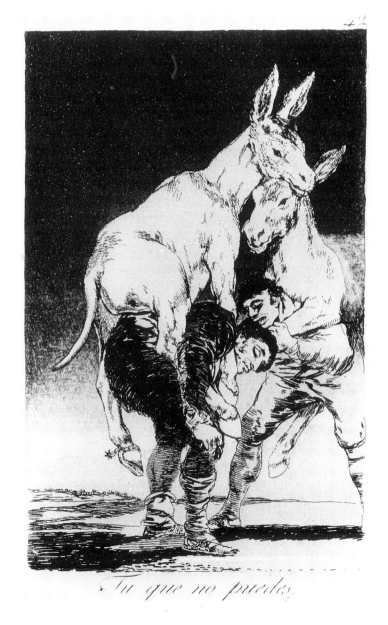

112 Goya, *Capricho 42: You Who Cannot Do It, Carry Me on Your Shoulders*, 1797–8, etching and aquatint.

Tu que no puedes.

cisms acceptable in society, or in Goya's sexual imagination, any clear and linear paronomasia of the kind featured in *Capricho* 79. There, the overt linguistic game was possible because the taboo it targeted was fairly straightforward. The moment the taboo became serious, then self-censure intervened or the coding was intensified. This is why *Capricho* 13

205

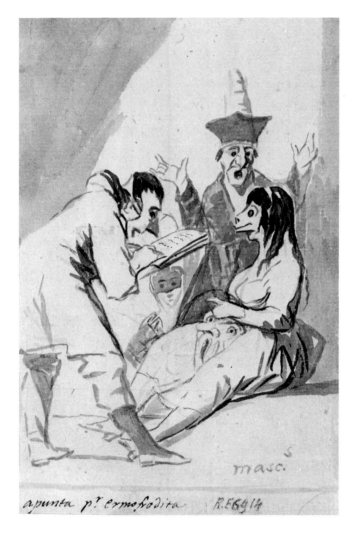

(illus. 110) strays so far from Goya's original intention (illus.
109) and why *Capricho* 42 (illus. 112) cannot say more than it
suggests.

TO REVEAL OR NOT TO REVEAL / TO SEE OR
NOT TO SEE

There are in Goya several instances when the transition from
drawing to print reveals – through the experiments, uncertainties, twists and turns and tricks – how an allusive mechanism
that brings together conceptist culture and carnivalesque
tradition, by using figurative art, is instigated. We now propose

206

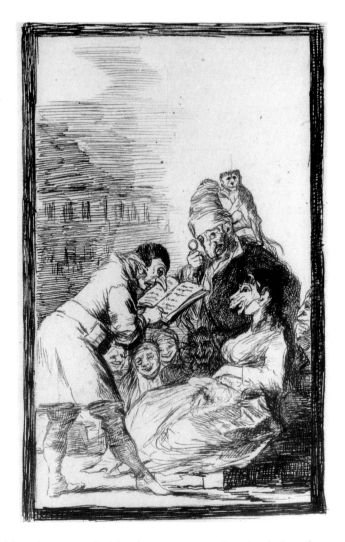

to tackle what is probably the most complex (and therefore
most significant) *mise-en-scène* of the combined interplay of
words and images in Goya's work. This is *Capricho* 57, entitled
The Lineage (illus. 116).

It took several years and several versions to produce this
print. The earliest version, documented in the *Madrid Sketchbook*,
varies in date from 1793 to 1797 (illus. 113).[28] The last version
was probably the print put on sale in 1799 (illus. 116).
Between the two were the drawings that not only signalled
a development but also a reduction of the earlier allusive
techniques (illus. 114, 115).

The hand-written commentaries generally agree that the

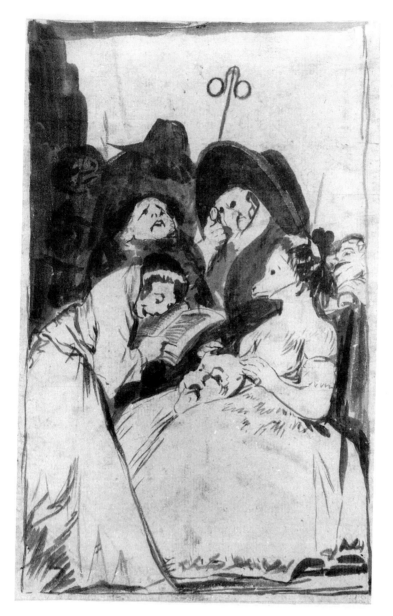

115 Goya,
Preparatory draw-
ing for *Capricho* 57,
The Lineage,
c. 1797–8, red ink
wash.

theme of *Capricho* 57 (illus. 116) is deception. A young man is
being introduced to his future wife, whose true identity
remains hidden: 'The purpose is to wheedle the bridegroom
by showing him the pedigree, and who the parents, grandparents, great grandparents, and great-great-grandparents of
the young lady were. But, who is she? He will find it out later.
(*Prado Commentary*)' In the light of these early commentaries,

116 Goya,
Capricho 57,
The Lineage,
c. 1797–8, etching
and aquatint.

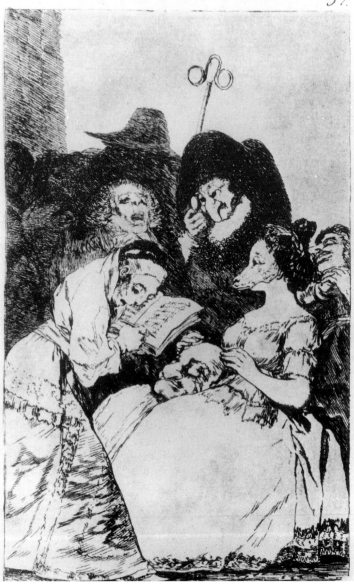

certain modern interpretations have tried to see the print (and
the preparatory drawings) as a satire on fashionable marriages,[29] while others have preferred to stress the carnivalesque nature of the *mise-en-scène.*[30] We favour this second
hermeneutic approach and would like to develop it further by
adding some thoughts on the techniques of allusion and word
game that are part of Goya's artistic arsenal.

In a recent study, Reva Wolf quite rightly drew attention to the way in which the phenomenon of self-censorship worked in the sequencing of the four versions of the same image. The conclusions drawn by Wolf, which focus on the intensity of the final version as opposed to the freedom of the earlier ones, seem absolutely valid and can be re-examined from another, complementary point of view.

The first drawing, from the *Madrid Sketchbook* (illus. 113), is also the simplest because of the number of characters involved. There is a man bending over his register on the left, a seated woman with a mask on the right, and between the two another man with a strange hairstyle. Emerging from the background is a (woman's?) veiled head. None of these people can be identified as a deceived bridegroom, especially since the caption at the bottom of the page is 'He puts her down as an Hermaphrodite' (*Le apunta p.r ermafrodita*). Inside the rectangular frame, outlined with a light brushstroke, there is another caption (*masc.s*), generally interpreted to be an abbreviation of the word 'masks' (*masc<ara>s*) or 'masquerades' (*masc<arada>s*). This may be intended as a polysemy, alluding to the '*mask*ed *masc*ulinity' of the seated woman who is one of the focal points of the representation. Moreover, this person is doubly disguised. One mask covers her face, the other her sex. This second mask has a gaping mouth and a giant nose, and is a complex figure of ambiguity: it masks and unmasks, covers and uncovers, although it has, at one and the same time, the characteristics of both sexes in a caricatural and allusive way. The person behind, whose attitude conveys both surprise and the codified apotropaic body language (his left hand is, in effect, making the well-known gesture that signifies 'cuckold'),[31] together with the veiled woman in the background, focuses attention on the 'surprising' nature of the action.

This whole *mise-en-scène*, and probably the significance of the title, convinces us that the representation should be integrated into the context of the carnivalesque customs still popular at the end of the eighteenth century, when cross-dressing, burlesque scenes and symbolic births were very much defining features. Goya's drawing is the nearest graphic description of this we have, just as Goethe's literary description is the most suggestive:

A troupe of men dressed in the Sunday clothes of the lower

classes (. . .) are taking a stroll with some men disguised as women. One of these appears to be in a state of advanced pregnancy; they come and go peacefully. Suddenly discord breaks out among the men and a lively altercation ensues, (. . .). At that moment, having had a fright, the pregnant woman feels unwell; a chair is brought, the other women see to her, she thrashes about pathetically, and, to the delight of her assistants, unexpectedly gives birth to a non-descript, shapeless being. Having given their performance, the troupe sets off to play the same farce, or another fellow-creature, in another venue.[32]

This is neither the time nor the place to stress the symbolic role of male or hermaphroditic pregnancy and giving birth (see Chapter 2), but the obvious conclusion is that the subject of the drawing – as identified by the title – is not so much the registration of the person who gives birth but that of the newly-born in the pseudo-registers of births, marriages and deaths of the world upside down.[33]

The way Goya plays with ambiguities is even more striking when the drawing is integrated into the context of the *Madrid Sketchbook*, a book full of erotic allusions and permeated with a sensuality that borders on licence (illus. 20, 67, 117). We should point out, however, that for those *Sketchbook* scenes of daily life with erotic undertones, Goya devised a strategy of concealments so extensive that his everyday scenes, although highly sexualized, are (sometimes literally) veiled in decency (illus. 117). On the other hand, in the most important carnivalesque scene from the same collection, indecency, indeed obscenity, dominates the picture, and if the euphemistic technique is still at work, then this time it comes from the carnivalesque arsenal of licence and transgression. Goya was obviously not altogether satisfied with this experi-ment since he amended it in another drawing, which should have served as the basis for one of the prints in the earlier *Dreams* series (illus. 114). Numerous changes have been intro-duced into this sepia drawing with its traces of sanguine. The man in the middle distance, for example, is wearing a differ-ent hat and has changed position. He appears to be accompa-nied by a monkey, and through his monocle casts sidelong glances at the act of registration. Several laughing faces appear in the space left vacant between the main characters, and the seated woman's two masks have been changed. The one that covers her face has become fox- and horse-like, whereas the one that hides her sex emphasizes more boldly than before the anatomical details. The polysemy of the drawing is more significant and the caption at the bottom of the page would seem to want to tell us so. *Mascaras de caricaturas / q.e apuntaron p.r su significado* has generally been translated as 'Masquerades of caricatures that are famous for what they represent'.[34] However, we believe that, by using a multiplicity of disguises, Goya was trying to point to a heightened significance. The targeted, indeed marked (*apuntado*) signified, is precisely sexual ambiguity. Here, more than in the first drawing, it is the mask over the sex that forms the focus of attention. All eyes converge on it, including those of the hypothetical spectator. The aim of the simultaneous presence of the instrument of optical magnification (which points as much to the register as it does to

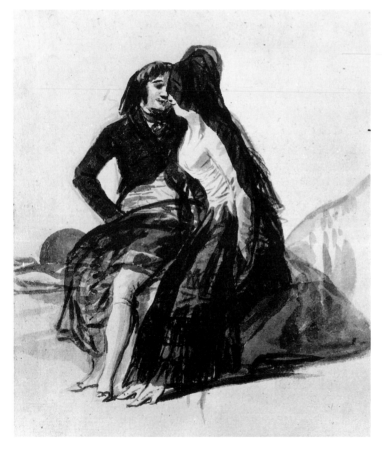

117 Goya, Drawing B. 24: *Lovers Seated on a Rock*, 1796–7, India ink wash.

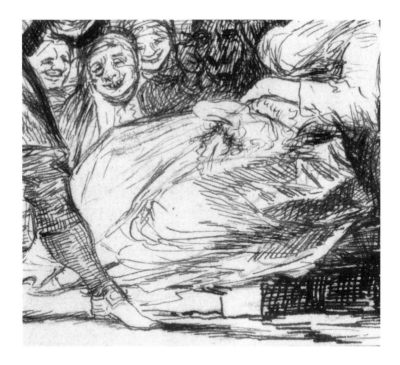

the double sex displayed in the foreground) and the laughing, jeering faces placed around this focus would appear to be to highlight the scandalous detail (illus. 118). The stomach-face is an ancient figure in orgiastic rites, which, in the form of Baubô the vulva-goddess, provoked beneficial and regenerative laughter,[35] and which survived in carnivalesque processions until the end of the eighteenth century. Goethe, for example, noted that it was still there in the famous Roman Carnival of 1788.[36] Not so common, but there all the same,[37] was the double presentation of Baubô (the mythical vulva) and Baubon (the symbolic phallus). Goya includes this motif in his drawings, combining both sexes in one and the same person. The process by which Goya does this is worthy of our full attention since it reveals the fondness of the artist (whose conceptist origins surface once again) for giving the same signifier to one or more signifieds. Thus the monocle is probably an object that draws attention to the *mise-en-scène* of the scopic impulse and to the problem of the magnification of the detail.[38] It should be borne in mind that the monocle as an instrument appeared frequently in eighteenth-century art, and that it was used to highlight a voyeuristic pleasure that bordered on indecency (illus. 55, 80). However, in Goya it takes on a

213

second signification resulting from phonic similarity. The
Spanish for 'monocle' is *monoculo* and the simplicity of the
spelling focuses on its somewhat risqué connotations, since
'culo' (arse) is the first and most transparent euphemism for
the sexual organs. The bisexuality of the seated person is thus
highlighted not only by the instrument of magnification (the
monocle) but also by its name (*mono-culo*) that tells us quite
clearly that this being is both 'double' and 'single'. Goya's
propensity for word games, rebus and anagrams is well
known. His correspondence (which was also not immune
from erotic undertones)[39] with his lifelong friend Martin
Zapater is peppered with encoded games in which image and
phonetic backup collaborate to construct (or conceal) the
meaning (illus. 119).[40] However, it is quite legitimate to raise
questions as to the function and functioning of word games in
the case of the drawings and prints.

There is something else that can help us make a more complete interpretation of Goya's strategies. This is the appearance
in the second drawing of the monkey who was nowhere to be
seen in the first. Like the monocle, the monkey is a new signifier and the two join forces to help bring to light an allusive
meaning. The first element of their collaboration is on the
level of their phonetic value since 'monkey' in Spanish is
mono. On this level, therefore, the monkey (*mono*) accentuates
the allusive quality of the monocle (*mono-culo*). This new combination of several signifiers into a 'wise union' (*sagaz junta*)
was a feature highly praised in conceptist poetics[41] and Goya
appears to have had a particular talent for it. He depended,
we believe, on the pluri-semy of the term '*mono*' which in
Spanish means 'unique' (and 'only'), 'monkey' and 'pretty'
(or 'cute').

In satirical literature every possible expressive ambiguity

has been used to exploit the complexity of the term, particularly its sexual ambiguity. By way of an example, here is the portrait of a homosexual from a seventeenth-century ditty with a double meaning:

De gatilla tiene el tono
cuando mas alto se entona;
de la cinta abajo es mona,
de la cinta arriba es mono

Roughly translated, this means:

He has the voice of a cat
when he speaks up and loud;
from the belt down, he's cute (*mona*)
from the belt up, he's a monkey (*mono*)[42]

Mindful of tradition, Goya was to return to this motif on at least one more occasion. In the *Sketchbook-Journal*, he depicted a hybrid creature with ape-like features accompanied by an

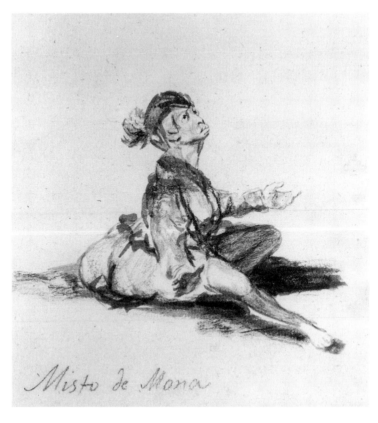

120 Goya, Drawing
C. 36, 1803–24,
India ink wash.

215

ambiguous caption (illus. 120). This caption – *Misto de Mona* – read in conjunction with particular figurative signs, such as the creature's hairy legs and ample bosom, reveals that we are probably looking at a representation of a hermaphrodite that mirrors the position of the central character in *Capricho* 57 (illus. 116) as well as the monkey's in one of the drawings (illus. 114).[43]

In this context, it is interesting to note that the monkey (and consequently all the phonic and symbolic connotations that accompany it) were no longer there in the last known drawing (illus. 115), that is to say the sanguine on which the final version of *Capricho* 57 was based (illus. 116). This disappearance is counterbalanced by the appearance of a new object: the spectacles. Do the spectacles, so important in the final version, where they are projected against an empty space, really 'replace' the monkey or are they not instead part of, with other elements of the composition, another network of more complex conceptist allusions? A closer examination of both drawing and print reveals that a head whose mouth and eyes are closed has replaced the bisexual mask of the earlier drawings and that the nose is abnormally proportioned. Goya opted for this solution rather late in the day and in all probability because the print was destined to be circulated to the public at large. The ostentatious nature of the hermaphroditic mask of the first drawings is moderated, indeed eliminated. It is into this void, we believe, that the spectacles come. The 'binocle' forms a structure with the 'monocle' and unveils, although in an extremely encoded way, the allusion and ambiguity on which the print is based.[44] What we have here is a true process of displacement (*Verschiebung*), in the sense given to it by Freud in his theory on the interpretation of dreams and of Witz.[45] Set on top of a long stick, the spectacles are like a constant call, stimulating the interpretative process. The care with which Goya prepared his phallic allusion becomes especially clear when the print is compared to the preparatory drawing. Only one element has been added, at the junction between the stick and the spectacles, but it is this extra feature that uncovers the ambiguity. The licentious implications of eyeglasses in tradition had already been tackled in a context that was not so far removed from that of Goya's print. The Flemish print that dates from the beginning of the seventeenth century (illus. 121) plays on the double function of eye-

121 Claes Janz.
Clock, *The Glasses
Vendor*, 1602,
copperplate
engraving.

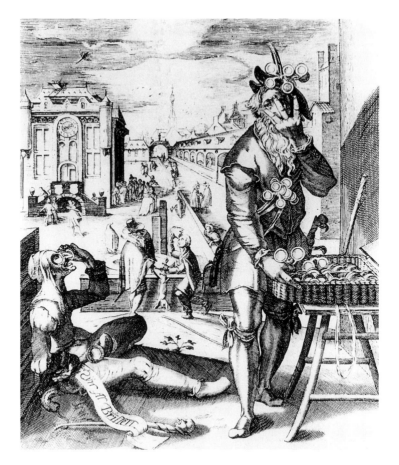

glasses. They were firstly an instrument of magnification and then a substitute or manifestation of masculine attributes.[46] It is not impossible that Goya's found the spectacles useful when he was looking for a suitable solution for his final print. What is certain is that the system of connections that has been instigated here is so elaborate, the title selected so elliptical, that the spectator finds it almost impossible to interpret all of the image's many and complex implications. The *bi-/mono-*interaction on which the structure is based is only revealed to he who understands the road Goya travelled, or to he who has glasses strong enough to help him penetrate the impenetrable conceptist darkness. The difficulty of this image is, in effect, an almost perfect illustration of the difficulty of allusion as a stylistic feature, which is why Gracián had already given it a prefatory position:

Allusion has as its basis what other forms of wit have as ornament. Its very name of allusion would appear to be a censure rather than a definition, for, deriving from the word ludo, which means 'to play', it seems to cast doubt, indeed to deny, all seriousness, all gravity, all that is sublime to the form that is being founded. Its formal ingenuity consists in establishing a relationship with some term, some history or circumstance, without expressing it, but by mysteriously suggesting it. Encoded subtlety so that we cannot understand the key unless we are highly cultured or have such wit that sometimes knows how to play the seer. (. . .) The extreme delicacy of the art of making allusions: denied here, endorsed there, in the other term. So much so that we more or less disguise the relationship between the two poles of the allusion, but always in the manner of an enigma, which is the appeal of this conceit. One does not say absolutely, one does not silence completely what one wants to say. It is ordinarily used in satire and malicious insinuations. (. . .) There are those who maintain, by forcing the argument, that allusion, in itself, is not a conceit, unless it includes other kinds of conceits that raise it, such as correspondence between correlations, mis-entry, comparison or parity and others. But the fact remains that, even alone, allusion can be classed as a conceit (. . .). With the result that the ingenuity of allusion, like comparisons, involves an insinuation that does not entirely explain, but which is enough to occasion surprise, to awaken the curiosity of he who does not hear it and the pleasure of he who penetrates it.[47]

We have one final observation to make. We believe that a conceptist interpretation of Goya's art still remains to be done. These preceding, cursory considerations have no other aim than to give a foretaste of a possible debate and a possible study likely to lead much further. But we also believe that it is no coincidence that the most complex of Goya's series of drawings, with their ambiguous and allusive decoys (illus. 113–16), should have bisexuality as their theme; because these very tropes – ambiguity and allusion – are, in the great catalogue of *concetti*, uncertain and ambivalent figures. Hermaphrodites then, on the level of their verbal essence.

7 Royal Games

In 1783, when Goya was still at the beginning of his career as a portrait-painter, he painted the large canvas representing *The Infante Don Luis and His Family* (illus. 74). Having made his name as a religious painter in his native Aragon, and then in Madrid, as the creator of models for the Royal Tapestry Factory, the art of the portrait was far from his favourite sphere of activity. The challenge of a commission of this type must have been great, not to mention the effort involved in demonstrating his knowledge. The success of the enterprise is quite evident in a letter he wrote to his friend Zapater, dated 20 September 1783:

> I have just returned from Arenas, very tired. His Majesty has lavished upon me one thousand marks of honour; I painted his portrait, that of his wife, his boy and small daughter with unexpected success, for other painters had tried but were not successful in this enterprise. (. . .) I spent a whole month with them: they are angels, they gave me a present of a thousand duros and a dressing gown for my wife, all embroidered in silver and gold, worth thirty thousand reales . . .[1]

The issues involved in this painting, which drew Spanish high society's attention to the young portraitist, were no doubt considerable. Nevertheless, art historians often treat it with restraint and an apparent lack of enthusiasm, considering it at times 'a veritable failure' and full of 'quite absurd' details,[2] or else, from slightly more indulgent pens, a simple 'extravagance'.[3] If the painting is regarded as an experiment and a demonstration, it can be seen to contain secrets that need to be unlocked. In the first part of this chapter, the strategies of the representation implemented by Goya in this youthful, experimental work of art will be analyzed. In the second part, we shall concentrate on the strategies used in the second major group portrait painted by Goya, the one created at the height of his career, that is to say *Charles IV and His Family* (1800; illus. 76). The aim is to bring together the 'popular' and 'secret Goya' of the tapestry cartoons, *Caprichos* and drawings with the 'Aulic', indeed the 'official' and 'public Goya'. A second but no less important aim is to set the debate surrounding this figure of a creator who lived between two worlds – that is to say, Goya – into the context of the dialogue between 'the high' and 'the low', at a time when history was permeated by inverted hierarchies.

However, we should ask ourselves just how far and in what way subliminal aims or messages can be attributed to these aristocratic images (and their author). If the portrait of *The Infante and His Family* really does contain a 'low' element, then it is not apparent in the way Don Luis de Bourbon, the King's brother, and the members of his family are portrayed, but rather in the position of the portraitist himself. Seated on a stool in the corner of the painting, he has placed himself within the area of the image, in an obvious position of hierarchical inferiority. His body is quite startlingly reduced in size and the strange, somewhat unnatural torsion of his neck and head means that his eyes move upwards along one of the central diagonals of the painting. The humbling self-representation, which can in fact be found in other paintings from the same period (illus. 142), is even more striking when we compare it with the painting's most obvious model of authorial integration. This is Velázquez's *Las Meninas* (1656), a painting Goya was passionate about and which he had translated into an etching some years earlier (illus. 122).[4] Whereas in *Las Meninas* Velázquez depicts himself as a strong, self-confident person (thus attracting some sharp criticism),[5] Goya, even though he also places himself in the position of the painter at work, humbles his status and thus endows himself with something akin to the function of the merry company who can be found on the extreme right of *Las Meninas*.

This almost mandatory comparison with Velázquez's work also uncovers other similarities and other differences, of a more general nature. The most important similarity is that Goya's painting, in the wake of *Las Meninas*, is more than a simple group portrait; it is a work that has as its theme the art of portraiture and the performative *mise-en-scène*. As to the major differences, these are the product of an historic back-

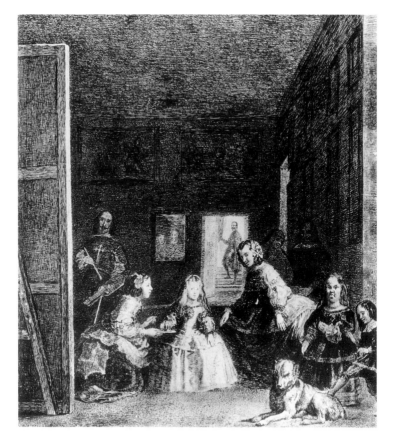

wards step that Goya would appear to have taken consciously, not only in the way he discourses (in a manner befitting his era) on the art of portraiture and the issues involved, but also in the innovative way he captures the sub-genre of the 'group portrait'. Thus, despite its apparent spontaneity, *Las Meninas* still bears traces of the etiquette in force at the court of the Spanish Habsburgs.[6] The painting of *The Infante Don Luis and His Family*, on the other hand, by taking us into the intimacy of the small, brightly lit court of Arenas de San Pedro, is more like a homely, almost bourgeois scene.

Let us examine the painting (illus. 74) more closely. The Infante and his morganatic wife, Maria-Teresa de Vallabriga, are seated at a green table on which he has spread a pack of cards in the candlelight, while the hairdresser is attending to her hair. The couple's three children are present: Luis Maria behind his father, the little Maria Teresa de Bourbon, accompanied by her two ladies-in-waiting, and the very young

221

Maria Luisa in the arms of her nurse. The four men on the right have been identified as the Infante's secretary, Manuel Moreno, corpulent and solemn and closest to the table, the former court painter, Alejandro de la Cruz, who gazes sadly at the spectator from the edge of the painting, the smiling Francisco del Campo, and finally next to him Luigi Boccherini, musician to the court of Arena, seen in profile.[7] Two elements require explanation. The first is that, of the fourteen people depicted, only five are actual members of the Infante's family. The other nine belong to it only in the broader sense of the term. Velázquez's large painting (illus. 122), which was at the time referred to as *el cuadro de la familia*,[8] probably represented a similar situation. The second element is that Goya's picture is a mixture of genre scene and group portrait. This too was anticipated by *Las Meninas* but, as experts have been quick to point out, Goya's work also shows signs of having been influenced by contemporary art from the other side of the Channel, where *conversation pieces* had for some time been recognized as a pictorial genre in their own right.[9]

This last observation, however, raises a fairly important question, since there is no evidence that a large group portrait of the *conversation piece* genre was ever known in Spain in Goya's time. Yet it is still possible that Goya was familiar with this art, not through having viewed English paintings (which would have been very difficult for him to do), but through seeing other works of art which, due to the smallness of their size and the lightness and mobility of their support, were easy to circulate. The prints[10] or much-loved 'silhouettes' that were all the rage at the time throughout Europe[11] (illus. 123) may well have acted as catalysts. The artificial lighting and the portrayal of several people in strict profile could be evidence of this. Goya's version, however, is far from indistinct or gratuitous. The experimental feel that permeates the whole painting, probably attributable to the author's desire to illustrate in an exemplary manner a new way of envisioning portraiture through a group portrait, is revealing. In his letter to Zapater, Goya describes, though not in any great detail, the innovation and its 'unexpected success'. *The Infante Don Luis and His Family* can be analyzed as an experimental *mise-en-scène* of a new aesthetic of the portrait. In this context, many of the work's 'extravagances' can be understood, beginning with one of the most original elements, the artificial lighting.

Artificial lighting was, of course, and on more than one occasion, used in 'conversation pieces' to create special effects.[12] The way Goya uses it, however, is somewhat special, for his painting does not only show some 'conversation piece' or other unfolding in the candlelight, it also establishes a relationship, at the very heart of a single representation, between artificial lighting, projected shadows and pictorial discourse with, on the one hand, profile portraiture and, on the other, full-face portraiture. In other words, Goya's painting works with the most important elements to be found within the specific mechanisms used to produce portraits and silhouettes (illus. 124).[13] These factors, however, appear as though deconstructed and their logic is problematic. We could, of course, always consider *The Infante Don Luis and His Family* to be a somewhat disjointed 'conversation piece' that introduces us into the intimacy of an evening at home where the various members of the family are playing cards, trying out a new hairstyle and in which a painter has taken on the role of a shadow-tamer.[14] Alternatively, we could take a step forward and endeavour to understand Goya's 'extravagances' by asking ourselves if these elements, which today appear to lack coherence, could not at the time have been part of a logic that now escapes us.

Let us begin with the clue Goya gives us, in the unusual way he has portrayed himself in front of the canvas, which is transformed into a projection screen. Some have seen this as an allusion to the ancient myth of the origins of painting, as Goya's

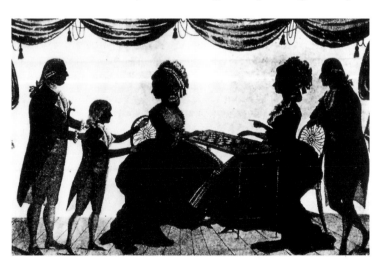

123 William Wellings, *The Austen-Knight Family*, 1783, silhouette painting on paper.

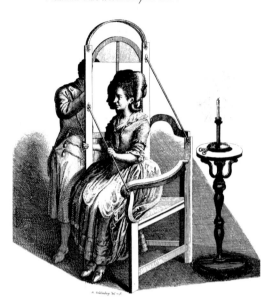

way of reminding the spectator.[15] Whilst this is a possibility, Goya may also be giving us a much simpler and more obvious clue, one more closely linked to the *mise-en-scène* of a discourse on the 'modern' elements of portraiture. By tackling the relationship between portraiture, physiognomical analysis and silhouette-making, his first aim was to show the spectator – but primarily his aristocratic patrons who were, after all, the recipients and heroes of his pictorial experiments – that he saw his own approach as a pictorial replica of what contemporary thinking had already presented in a discursive form. The champion of the most advanced experiments to be done in this field was unquestionably the Swiss pastor Johann Lavater. The French translation of his major work, entitled *Essai sur la physiognomie* (*Essays on Physiognomy*), was published just before Goya began his own 'essay on portraiture', that is to say *The Infante Don Luis and His Family*. It seems highly possible that the text and prints of this edition – which, now that Lavater was more accessible, made him once again fashionable among the European intelligentsia – were a major contributing factor to Goya's experiment.[16]

That Lavater's writings are of interest to all those who are interested in the art of the portrait is undeniable. In volume two, published in 1783, the author, amongst other things, gave a summary of the most advanced theories on the portrait the era was to see.[17] Here are a few extracts:

> The Art of the portrait is the most natural, the most noble, and the most useful of all the Arts – it is also the most diffi-cult, however easy it might appear to be (. . .) What is the *Art of the Portrait*? It is the representation of a real individual or of part of his body; it is the reproduction of our image; it is the art of showing at first glance the shape of man, depicted in a way that cannot be done with words. (. . .) The philo-sophical study of man, that is to say, the particular and at the same time general knowledge of his being, this is what is missing from the majority of portraits of Painters, and it is also the great defect that shocks me so in almost all their works (. . .). The soul is painted on the face; it must be per-ceived in order to be translated onto the canvas; and he who is not capable of grasping this expression has never been a Painter of portraits.[18]

It is a well-known fact that Lavater thought that the most direct way of reading (or representing) a person's soul was by studying his profile and that it was this sinuous line, with its rich semiology, that spoke with the greatest clarity in the 'sil-houette', that is to say in the contour of the shadow:

> Is the silhouette here not more expressive than the shaded part of the face! The one announces the other, it is true, an admirable man through his goodness, his honesty and his eagerness to please; but the Physiognomist is more attached to the silhouette because it shows him more nobil-ity in the lower part of the profile, more poetic feeling in the nose . . .[19]

The art of interpreting silhouettes spread through Europe quickly and, by the end of the eighteenth century, it had become a favourite high society party-game.[20] The modern reader would find it difficult to see from the print accompa-nying Lavater's deliberations (illus. 125) exactly where the expressive superiority of the outlined shadow lay, and it seems likely that even someone like Goya must have had to explain to his noble patron and model why, rather than paint-ing an elegant portrait of his face, he had forced him into a rigid pose that was unexpected and uncomfortable, and that would capture for all eternity not his face, but his profile.

Goya could have responded to the fairly understandable zeal of Don Luis, fond – we know – of all the artistic and scientific innovations that were around at the time, by quoting one of the above extracts from Lavater. He could have gone on to elaborate, beginning for example with Lavater's exemplary analysis of a princely profile:

> Casting my eye for the first time over this profile [illus. 126], I would say: here is the face of a *Prince*; and I would judge him as such by the silhouette only, although it might not be absolutely right. There is nothing here to announce a bourgeois air; and if I am to believe my own personal feeling, this physiognomy is one of those that can be referred to as *marked by the finger of God*. In it I discern nobility, dignity and courage; much resolution; a great talent for locking away deep inside himself all that must be hidden and unreservedly communicating what must be known: a talent that is so difficult to combine and so necessary however to those of elevated rank. Moreover I perceive total prudence, exempt from defiance and anxiety; and without having seen the eye, I read in just the contour of the brow and nose, a sure, firm, imposing gaze that perceives the hidden man, unmasks the deceitful person, makes the traitor tremble, but which also inspires confidence in the good man. The contour of the brow is most extraordinary; it augurs the greatest and the most beautiful of enterprises. The outline of the mouth is a little too hard; but it nevertheless has an air of candour, of goodness and of courage.[21]

There is no suggestion that Goya in any way painstakingly reproduced what he had read in Lavater, but rather that his experimental style was formed by incorporating certain analytical procedures from the physiognomical discourse into the art of the portrait. Goya put flesh on the silhouettes and gave his whole attention to analyzing his models' individual characteristics, yet without abandoning the road travelled by the Swiss physiognomist. And so, it seems that when painting the portrait of Don Luis, the painter combined his model's physiognomical and psychological disposition with his vision of the prince's exemplary image. He blends the individual features (inevitably different from the example Lavater analyzed and illustrated) with some of the characteristics of princely dignity, as postulated in the *Essai sur la physiogno-*

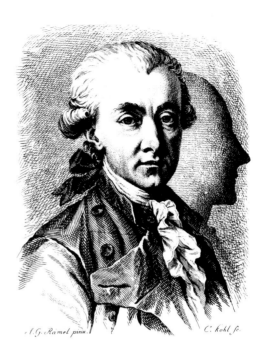

125 A. G. Rämel, *Portrait and Profile of Shadow*, from Lavater, *Essai sur la physiognomie*, vol. II.

mie. What is so striking is that both Lavater's text and print and Goya's portrait highlight the 'extraordinary' prominent brow, auguring – if we are to believe Lavater – the 'greatest and the most beautiful of enterprises'.

This feature is repeated in the silhouette of the young Luis Maria, which is so strikingly similar to his father's. Goya depicts the Infante's son as being his father's miniature double. He does this by replacing the lack of any physical similarity with a fairly obvious body language: the movement of the child's arm and leg extends or reproduces the position of the father's arm and the movement of his leg. The son's silhouette therefore appears to have been 'caste' in the same mould as the father's, despite the fact that the young prince's physiognomy is so very different (illus. 127). Like his name – Luis Maria – the features of the Infante's son combine those of his mother, the beautiful Maria Teresa, and his father, Don Luis. His father's features are less obvious, but they correspond to Lavater's physiognomical theory, according to which, 'We find in the son, feature by feature, the character, the temperament, and the majority of the moral qualities of the father.'[22] If we were wanting to be (a little, but not overtly) ironic, we could say that the young Luis Maria had inherited

227

T.

Au premier coup d'œil jetté fur ce profil, je dirois : voilà le vifage d'un *Prince* ; & je le jugerois tel fur la fimple filhouette, quoique peut-être elle ne foit pas tout à fait exacte. Rien n'annonce ici l'air *bourgeois* ; & fi j'en crois mon fentiment individuel, cette phyfionomie eft une de celles qu'on peut appeller *marquées du doigt de Dieu*. J'y découvre de la nobleffe, de la dignité & du courage ; beaucoup de réfolution ; le grand talent de renfermer profondé- ment ce qui doit être caché, & de communiquer fans referve ce qui peut être fû : talent fi difficile à combiner, & fi néceffaire pourtant dans un rang élevé. J'apperçois de plus une prudence confommée, exempte de défiance & d'inquiétude ; & fans avoir vu l'œil, je lis dans le feul contour du front & du nez, un regard fûr, ferme, impofant, qui pénètre l'homme caché, démafque le fourbe, fait trembler le traître, mais qui infpire auffi la confiance à l'homme de bien. Le contour du front eft des plus extraordinaires ; il préfage les plus grandes & les plus belles entreprifes. Le deffin de la bouche eft un peu trop dur ; mais elle n'en conferve pas moins une expreffion de candeur, de bonté & de courage.

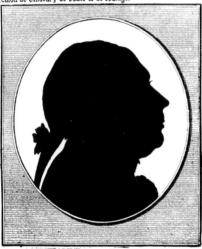

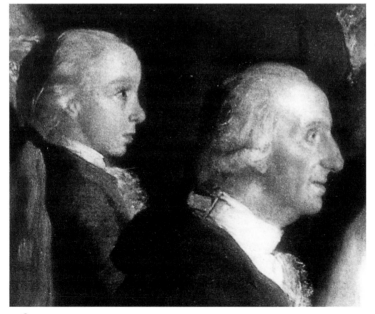

126 *A Prince,* from Lavater, *Essai sur la physiognomie,* vol. II.

127 Detail of illus. 74.

his mother's pretty nose, but his father's prominent brow. Consequently he is not far removed from the ideal of the prince, as imagined by Lavater (illus. 126).

If – as we believe – Goya retained something of the divinatory nature of physiognomical practice (a very controversial aspect in the debate surrounding the silhouette method and its aims),[23] he did so in full knowledge of the facts. Moreover, he integrated it into the thematic context, a feature we must pay particular attention to, for in his painting, the exhibition of the silhouettes and the practice of telling the cards correspond to one another.

Even today opinion differs as to what activity Don Luis de Bourbon is engaged in, but it seems highly unlikely that he is playing a card game or 'patience' (experts tell us that this pastime was not invented until much later). Cartomancy was one of the most popular activities in the eighteenth century and the cards Don Luis has spread in front of him are so clearly visible that they suggest that they hold messages for the wise spectator (illus. 75). They are double-headed cards (and thus stamped with the symbolism of reversal) whose 'modernity' leaves us in no doubt: the oldest-known Spanish playing cards to have had reversed figures dated from 1791,[24] which would suggest that Don Luis's cards were a great novelty.

Today it would probably be somewhat risky to attempt a definitive interpretation of the game the prince was playing. But we could presume that he must have seen some reference in the cards to his position as prince-in-exile, for the mysteries of the dynastic succession were indeed more complicated than ever in 1783. Charles, the heir to the throne, whose wife Maria Luisa had just lost both her twins, had no male heir. This situation could have led to power being transferred to the family of the Infante Don Luis. The *terzetto* formed by the *Jack* of clubs (also referred to as the Infante) and the *Two* from the same suit that flanks the golden *Ace* (the royal card par excellence) probably contains allusions similar to those presented by the physiognomical discourse of the portraits and also maybe – who knows? – a good omen for the future.

Let us now imagine that, prompted by the conversation between Goya and his aristocratic patron regarding certain aspects of pose and attitude, other members of the Infante's court, depicted in the painting, were in turn to voice their curiosity. If, let us say, Luigi Boccherini (illus. 126) (if we are to accept that the young man seen in profile on the right is indeed him, as some interpreters have maintained)[25] had questioned him as to the significance of his own profiled representation, Goya could have shown him the second volume of Lavater's *Essai*, which contains a comparative analysis of a head (illus. 128), viewed from three different angles (three-quarter, left and right profile):

> Reserve, resolve, self-assurance, such are the distinctive characteristics of these three drawings of the same head. You risk nothing by predicting that this man will always choose with prudence, and that his activity will not embrace a great number of objects. He is thoughtful without being profound and without having clearly developed ideas. When in love, his love will be faithful, deep, strong, but his affection, like his activity, will not extend to many objects. The brow and eyebrows in these three faces, especially in *a* and *c*, are indicative of genius (the print we are examining is the imperfect image of a great Musician), that is to say, an ability to receive certain impressions, and the talent to communicate them; and we can also see that his ability in this instance is unique. It enthusiastically seizes its object, enjoys it, delights in it, and identifies with it.

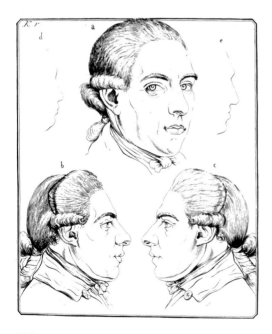

128 Physiognomy of a musician, from Lavater, *Essai sur la physiognomie*, vol. II.

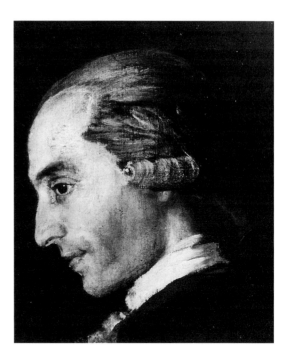

The lips in *b* & *c* express a poetic talent that cannot be subjected to the constraints of rules. In *d* and *e* there are no contrasts, only extremes: the first relishes, the second vanishes; one gives, the other forces you to accept its gifts.[26]

Had Goya wanted to give similar 'Lavaterian' replies to Santos Garcia (he too is portrayed in profile in the centre of the canvas, where he is seeing to Maria Teresa de Vallabriga's magnificent hair [illus. 130]), he might have found this difficult, for in no volume of the *Essai sur la physiognomie* does Lavater deal with the physiognomy of hairdressers. But it is quite possible that Garcia would not have troubled him with such questions, understanding at once or recognizing early on the allusions in his portrait. For example, he could have seen Goya's *mise-en-scène* of himself and his activity, as a tribute to one of his most glorious ancestors, the 'patron saint' almost of all eighteenth-century hairdressers. This was J. H. Marchand, known as Monsieur Beaumont, author of the *Encyclopédie perruquière. Ouvrage curieux à l'usage de toutes sortes de têtes*, which was published in Paris in 1762. The title page featured an emblematic image that was somewhere between an author's stamp and the perfect model of the wigmaker's art (illus. 131). He might also have read another great book, *L'Art du*

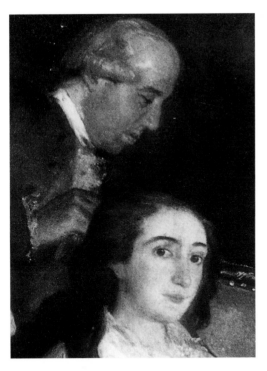

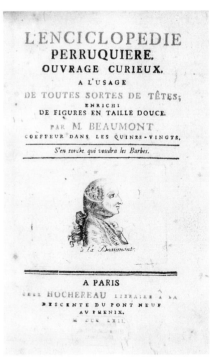

L'ENCICLOPEDIE
PERRUQUIERE.
OUVRAGE CURIEUX.
A L'USAGE
DE TOUTES SORTES DE TÊTES;
ENRICHI
DE FIGURES EN TAILLE DOUCE.
PAR M. BEAUMONT
COEFFEUR DANS LES QUINZE-VINGTS.

S'en torche qui voudra les Barbes.

à la Beaumont

A PARIS
CHEZ HOCHEREAU LIBRAIRE A LA
DESCENTE DU PONT NEUF
AU PHENIX.
M DCC LXII.

perruquier by M. de Garsault (Paris, 1767), that drew up certain fundamental principles, concerning not only the status of the profession in the second half of the eighteenth century but also the programmatic integration presented in Goya's painting:

> The cutting of hair is a science that gives natural hair a regular shape, by removing any irregularities and by layering it so that it is gracefully arranged to complement the face. (. . .) It would seem that a little practice only is required to achieve this, however some wigmakers are much better than others when it comes to doing this. As there are no precise rules governing this operation, it is therefore a matter of genius, for which a certain flair, taste and eye are all that is required.[27]

From this excerpt we see that, during this era, the art of 'haute coiffure' was perceived and defined through the double relationship of physiognomical practice and artistic 'genius'.[28] Beaumont himself emphasizes this in the postscript where he presents the same idea in a language peppered with puns inherited from the conceptist, indeed affected literary tradition:

130 Detail of illus. 74.

131 M. Beaumont [J. H. Marchand], Title page of *L'Encyclopédie perruquière* (Paris, 1762).

232

Never will a book be more deserving of a Preface or a Postface, than a book on the presentation and ornamentation of faces. To work on this beautiful subject is to deliver oneself to the care of the most beautiful part of nature. Man is almost the only one to possess a face; other animals have a beak, a snout, a jowl and for the majority of them as for us, it is an asset to have well-groomed hair. While some have wine, love, ambition go to their heads, others fill theirs with wild dreams, and others are born with a caul, but fortunately these different hairstyles do not prevent them from wearing a Wig. And it is to this physical headwear only that I have limited myself with no intention of representing moral hairstyles.[29]

To give his own art a more substantial image, Beaumont provides several plates that illustrate some extremely ingenious models of men's wigs (illus. 132). But he insisted on adding:

In this first edition I have used only faces with no likeness or character, and such as it pleased the Engraver to picture them at random, but if someone is then anxious to have his graces and taste admired by the Public, he can send me his portrait and I shall have care to have him engraved with the most elegant of accuracy.[30]

In his painting, Goya portrays the activity of the 'artist'/'physiognomist' hairdresser, as though he is following the principles of someone like Beaumont. Santos Garcia is depicted in the process of dressing the hair of the Infante's wife, but some of the others look as if they have already passed through his hands or are awaiting their turn. Among them is Francisco del Campo, standing on the right of the canvas, whose head has already been bandaged while he waits to be fitted with his new wig.

The famous hairdresser would probably not have dared present himself at the Infante's court and would not have been able to get anywhere near the head of the prince's beautiful but pretentious wife, had he not already discovered and armed himself with the most attractive and modern techniques of his art. But he could, doubtless, have declared, quoting Beaumont: 'For this purpose I studied all the physiognomies and the relationship they should have with the kind of Hairstyle that was appropriate to them.'[31] A study of the *Essai sur la physiognomie* would only have been of limited assistance to him here, the main problem being that for Lavater, the hair (like everything else that was fashionable) was as a rule something that masked rather than unmasked the soul.[32] Thus, commenting on a plate in his first volume (illus. 133), Lavater explained:

> Some People would say at first glance, that from the hair-style alone, the four profiles resembled one another. It is a fact that if they were distributed on four different pages of this Work, and if the hair was arranged in the same way, many people would be sure to say: 'here is a face I have already seen two or three times.' The four faces that we have in front of us present reality with nothing that is heterogeneous; but their characteristics are sufficiently different however for a real Observer to feel revolted if they were to be confused.[33]

This would lead us to conclude that at the end of a good physiognomical analysis, the hairstyle in Lavater's opinion was a confusing rather than an enlightening factor.

It is for this reason that we believe that the physiognomy-hairstyle relationship, as portrayed at the heart of the *Infante and His Family*, transcended the *Essai sur la physiognomie* and, in the light of this, was bringing in the most advanced thinking of the period that was attempting to correct Lavater. We are thinking primarily of Alexander Cozens's *Principles of Beauty relative to the Human Head*. Published a few years earlier in London in a bilingual (English–French) edition, Cozens's book, with its numerous loose plates, was aimed at the upper echelons of contemporary European society. Its publication had in fact been part-funded by personal subscriptions from such high-ranking individuals as the King of England himself, the Duchess of Cumberland, and also artists such as Joshua Reynolds, John Flaxman and Joseph Wright of Derby. It was a combination of neo-classical aesthetics, physiognomy and party games, dedicated to constituting sixteen (sensitive, melancholic, resolute, languid, majestic, etc.) types of 'composite' feminine beauty based on 'simple beauty'. Cozens's point of departure was the codification of a 'line of beauty' that in fact coincided with Lavater's profile; the only difference being that Cozens could (and had to) combine, indeed become symbiotic with, the hairstyle, now considered to be a counterbalance at the centre of an equilibrium that was constantly moving and always expressive:

> I was convinced also, that the expressions in the faces might be considerably augmented by suitable dresses of the hair. I have therefore composed as many of them as there are faces, interleaving them where I presumed they

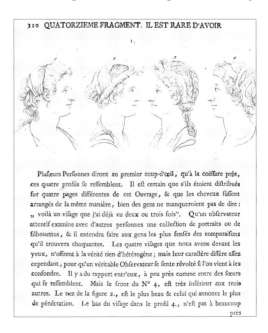

110 QUATORZIEME FRAGMENT. IL EST RARE D'AVOIR

1.

Plufieurs Perfonnes diront au premier coup-d'œil, qu'à la coëffure près, ces quatre profils fe reffemblent. Il eft certain que s'ils étoient diftribués fur quatre pages différentes de cet Ouvrage, & que les cheveux fûffent arrangés de la même manière, bien des gens ne manqueroient pas de dire : „ voilà un vifage que j'ai déjà vu deux ou trois fois". Qu'un obfervateur attentif examine avec d'autres perfonnes une collection de portraits ou de filhouettes, & il entendra faire aux gens les plus fenfés des comparaifons qu'il trouvera choquantes. Les quatre vifages que nous avons devant les yeux, n'offrent à la vérité rien d'hétérogène ; mais leur caractère diffère affez cependant, pour qu'un véritable Obfervateur fe fente révolté fi l'on vient à les confondre. Il y a du rapport entr'eux, à peu près comme entre des fœurs qui fe reffemblent. Mais le front du N° 4, eft très inférieur aux trois autres. Le nez de la figure 2., eft le plus beau & celui qui annonce le plus de pénétration. Le bas du vifage dans le profil 4., n'eft pas à beaucoup près

133 *Four Profiles of Women*, from Lavater, *Essai sur la physiognomie*, vol. i.

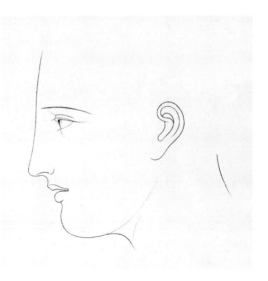

134 Alexander Cozens and Francesco Bartolozzi, *Simple Beauty* (profile), engraving from *Principles of Beauty Relative to the Human Head* (London, 1778).

were best adapted, proposing that they should be applied to or laid over the faces so as to produce the most proper effect. For this purpose they are printed on transparent paper, and intended not to be bounded in the book, in order to give an opportunity of moving them at pleasure on any one face, and likewise of applying them to any of the rest of the faces. (. . .) I am conscious much more may be said upon the subject of the beauty of the human face, but I have presumed only to give a hint of a new practical scheme to the public, referring the ultimate decision of principles to the feelings and experience of mankind; and I shall rest extremely pleased, if this undertaking shall promote a discussion of the subject among the curious.[34]

It is precisely in the furrow ploughed by this imperative that we can place Goya's painting, at the heart of which the painter depicts a scene that has at times either perplexed or been misunderstood by interpreters because of its singularity, especially when compared to the more usual *'conversation pieces'*. Furthermore, it seems very likely that we are not witnessing any old 'conversation', and even less a 'getting-ready-to-go-to-bed' scene, as has been assumed time and again. This last hypothesis ignores the other elements of the painting: why, for example, would the artist begin painting a canvas if his subjects were about to go to bed, why would the Infante be telling the cards, why would the smiling young man be waiting for

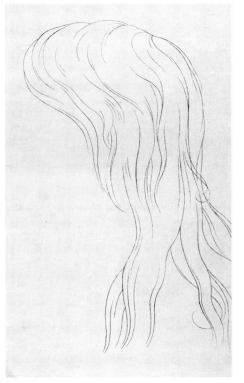

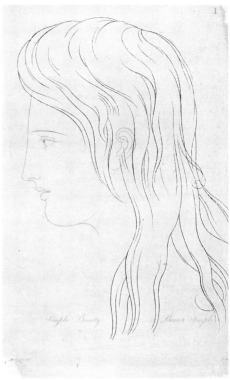

135 Cozens and Bartolozzi, *Simple Beauty* (hair), engraving from *Principles of Beauty Relative to the Human Head*.

136 Cozens and Bartolozzi, *Simple Beauty* (profile and hair), engraving from *Principles of Beauty Relative to the Human Head*.

his wig? We would like to venture the hypothesis that the central scene does not depict the Infanta's hairdresser 'unmaking' her hair. On the contrary, he is 'making' her hair,[35] that is to say endeavouring to find the most suitable hairstyle, the one that would best suit her physiognomy. We would also like to suggest that the candle, which has pride of place on the green table, might, together with the large green curtain in the background and the screen of the prepared canvas on the extreme left, correspond to a structure inspired by Lavater's device: his 'machine for drawing silhouettes' (illus. 124). Moreover, far from being an indication that the events are taking place in the evening or at night, the candle points to the fact that we are witnessing several experiments being carried out 'in camera', probably during the day. The primary aim of artificial lighting is to delineate the profiles more clearly and to provide an opportunity for a part-aesthetic, part-divinatory discourse to take place around them.

It is within the context of these deliberations that the assimilation of the theory expounded by Cozens in his treatise

237

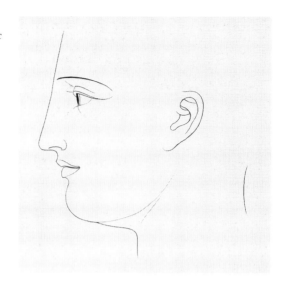

137 Cozens and Bartolozzi, *Majestic Beauty* (profile), engraving from *Principles of Beauty Relative to the Human Head*.

shows its true range. With the help of the hairdressing scene, placed at the centre of his canvas, Goya is presenting us with a complex but precise discourse around the beauty of Maria Teresa Vallabriga. The hairdressing session that unfolds in front of the spectator (illus. 74 , 130) is a *mise-en-scène* reminiscent of the 'simple beauty' theorems postulated in Cozens's treatise (illus. 134–6). The loose, flowing hair is that of an – as it were – pre-formal state of an ideal beauty, one that is still waiting for its true qualities to be fully realized.

Maria Teresa's portrait has one particularly intriguing feature: the profiled representation, of Lavaterian origin and still crucial to Cozens, appears only indirectly and requires a certain effort on the part of the spectator to reconstruct it. The spectator's position is privileged as he is able to look at the Infante's wife from the front. However, the reconstruction is not too difficult since all the spectator has to do is put himself in the painter's position, at the extreme left of the canvas. Goya was obviously determined to suggest the possibility and nature of this second viewpoint through the awkward twist of his body and by using the ambiguous and shapeless shadow projected onto the canvas. In this way he was endeavouring to capture, on the level of pictorial scenarios,[36] Lavater's discourse on the relationship between 'silhouette' and 'shaded part of the face' (illus. 125), while at the same time continuing Cozens's discourse. However, it was not in *The Infante and His Family* that Goya carried this initiative

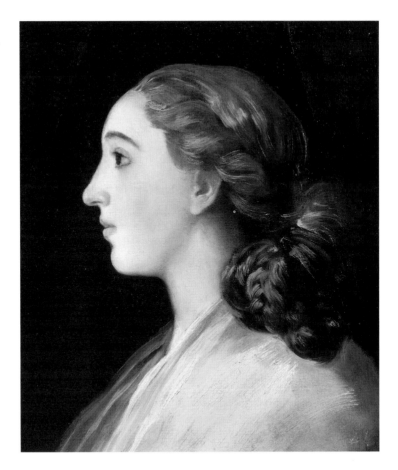

through but in another work, which is one of the most beautiful portraits he ever painted. It shows Maria Teresa de Vallabriga and is held by the Prado (illus. 138). This canvas can quite justifiably be considered to represent a coming together of the Lavaterian discourse, the thinking inspired by Cozens's *Principles of Beauty* and, last but not least, the work of an artist whose talent and knowledge is unparalleled.

The portrait can also be regarded as the second act or epilogue to the central theme of the *Family*. A label stuck on the back, of uncertain authorship, originally accompanied it. The writing on the label is quite relevant:

PORTRAIT OF DOÑA MARIA TERESA DE VALLABRIGA
WIFE OF HIS HIGHNESS THE INFANTE
OF SPAIN LUIS ANTONIO
JAIME DE BORBÓN

239

THAT FROM 11 TO 12 IN THE MORNING THE DAY
OF 27 AUGUST 1783
DON FRANCISCO DE GOYA WAS MAKING

(RETRATO DE DOÑA MARIA TERESEA DE VALLABRIGA
EPOSA DEL SERMO SEÑOR YNFANTE
DE ESPAÑA D.ᴺ LUIS ANTONIO
JAIME DE BORBON
QUE DE 11 A 12 DE MAÑANA EL DIA
27 DE AGOSTO EL AÑO DE 1783 HACIA
D.ᴺ FRANCISO DE GOYA)[37]

There are two remarkable elements in this inscription. The first
is the choice of the imperfect tense (*hacia*) of the verb 'to make',
a form which in Spanish contains a particular nuance. This
inscription therefore appears to want to unveil 'the picture
Goya was in the process of making' at 11 o'clock on a particular day in August. The second factor, which is also atypical for
a painting label, is that the precise time at which the painting

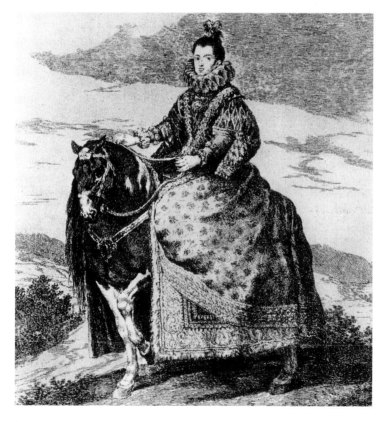

139 Goya,
*Equestrian Portrait
of Margarite of
Austria* (after
Velázquez), 1778,
etching and dry-
point engraving.

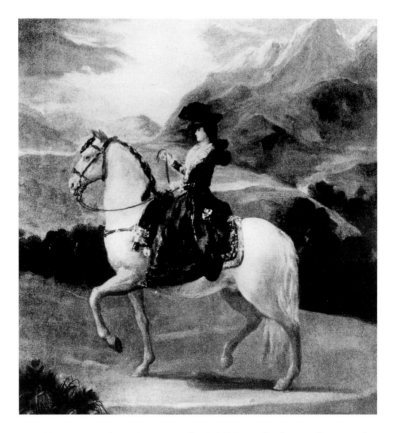

140 Goya, *Portrait of Maria Teresa of Vallabriga on Horseback*, 1783, oil on canvas.

was being produced is specified (although the verb is in the imperfect tense, rather than in the simple past). This highlights the diurnal nature of a sitting that might, at first sight, appear nocturnal (given the dark background and some aspects of the lighting), but which produced the actual silhouette-portrait the spectator is looking at. Let us examine it more closely. It is not only a study in profile but also a study of hair.

We could search in vain for Maria Teresa's simple, yet complicated, hairstyle among those displayed in Cozens's book. The year is 1783 and a hairstyle that was fashionable in 1778 would hardly have pleased the wife of the Infante. Although Santos Garcia's art speaks for itself, he still reflects the thinking of Cozens since, if we understand correctly, the beautiful hairstyle is not being applied to the anonymous head of a 'simple beauty' (illus. 134), but forms the counterbalance to a profile that follows (while taking account of Maria Teresa's individual features) the codified lines of Cozens's *Majestic Beauty* (illus. 137).

The final portrait can therefore be seen as the extension of a divinatory, secret and silent game begun in the large canvas of the *Family* and which now marks the (no doubt imaginary) triumph of the 'majestic' morganatic wife of a prince who would – alas – never be king.

Goya's, in truth somewhat flattering intentions, are also reflected in a second portrait of Maria Teresa, in which she is on horseback against a background of mountains outside Avila (illus. 140). The issues involved in this painting are immense, since, within the framework of an ancient tradition, the equestrian portrait in general, and the female portrait in particular, was a symbolic form, reserved for the chosen few. Goya was well aware of this, for he had transformed Velázquez's huge equestrian paintings into etchings (illus. 139), and he added a clear dynastic message, not only through the subject's pose but also through the background landscape, which combines royal dignity with dominion over terrain. A subtle interaction justifies (and conceals) the subliminal message of this portrait of Maria Teresa Vallabriga: once again, the profiled view has been chosen, apparently unexpectedly.

This particular view was generally avoided in large equestrian portraits because it was seen as an infringement of a monarch's most important quality – his 'majesty'. The *in maiestas* position implies a full-frontal representation in hierarchical attitude, and it is interesting to see how Velázquez resorted to fairly complicated solutions in his attempts to incorporate the lateral view of the horse as well as the 'in majesty' view. If Goya, though still alluding to the Velázquez models he knew so well, presented Maria Teresa, wife of Don Luis, in profile, this was because the new code manifested in the specially modulated and subtle 'line of beauty' had made it possible.

A final word needs to be said on the portrait of *The Infante Don Luis and His Family* and especially on the role Goya gave himself in this complex scenario. His own, humbled almost to the point of ostentation, position is in part justified by the references within the representation to the 'majesty' of the principal characters. However, it remains a difficult issue, especially when we take into account the level of the speculative knowledge he was testing. If we examine the details of this self-portrait more closely (illus. 141), we see that it is very close to the earlier self-portrait in which he depicts himself, but so reduced in size that he almost looks like a dwarf, in the company of the Prime Minister Floridablanca (illus. 142). The

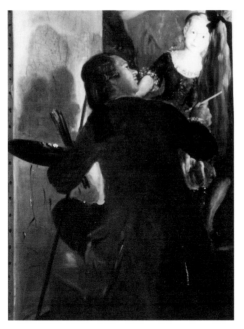

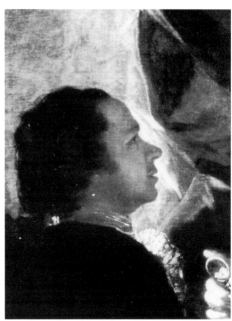

La vignette qui termine cette Introduction eſt l'image imparfaite d'un homme prudent , actif & entreprenant. L'expreſſion de ſon mérite eſt moins viſible dans le front que dans le ſeul contour angulaire & coupé de la pointe du nez. Cette remarque fera rire encore ; à la bonne heure. Mais j'en appelle aux Connoiſſeurs ſi elle eſt fondée ou non.

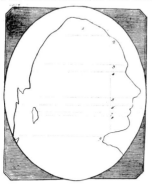

141 Detail of illus. 74.

142 Detail of Goya, *Portrait of Count Floridablanca*, 1783, oil on canvas.

143 *Profile of a Prudent Man*, from Lavater, *Essai sur la physiognomie*, vol. II.

two portraits are in profile, a particularly problematic form for self-portraits because of the difficulty of self-contemplation. What is the justification then for these portraits against the light, particularly when they show a person who is part of a representation that has discoursed on every level of the subject with such obvious sophistication (illus. 74, 142)? Is this a last reference to Lavater? And if the answer is yes, how should it be interpreted? The answer is once again to be found in *Essai sur la physiognomie*. The 'eleventh fragment', entitled 'Silhouettes', closes with a print (illus. 143) that constitutes the secret image on which Goya based his portrait and which is accompanied by the following tract:

> The vignette that ends this introduction is the imperfect image of a prudent, active and enterprising man. The expression of his worth is less visible in the brow than in the simple angular and truncated contour of the end of his nose. This remark will soon enough provoke laughter again. So I call upon the connoisseurs to say whether it is founded or not.[38]

THE KING'S FAMILY

Over fifteen years separate *Charles IV and His Family* (illus. 76), begun in the spring of 1800, from *The Infante Don Luis and His Family*. Although they are almost identical in size, these two group portraits could not have been designed more differently. Whereas the 1783/4 painting, inspired by the modern 'conversation pieces' (illus. 74), shows us the members of an alternative court in a relaxed mood, the characters in the 1800 painting are limited to the members of the royal family. Their poses and positions are subtly calculated and based on the conventions surrounding royal representations, the constraints of etiquette and secret hierarchical relationships. Whereas, through its subtleties, *The Infante Don Luis and His Family* was targeted at a select audience, made up of friends and initiates, the primarily official message of *Charles IV and His Family* is aimed at the 'public domain'.[39] Unlike the first painting with its freedom of composition and the 'modernity' of its immediate sources, *The Royal Family* belongs to the tradition of the large state portraits,[40] a genre that was really over, particularly since the monarchy as an institution had been in crisis all over Europe in the aftermath of the French Revolution. Finally, whereas *The Infante and His Family*, by developing its spontaneous and improvised side, marked a return to the great model of Spanish art, *Las Meninas*, *The King's Family* is a very official and highly codified version of the same mythical painting.

The most important element common to both canvases is, without a doubt, the artist's insertion into the composition and into the final message of each of these works of his own portrait and a representation of the act of painting. Such an insertion was not too difficult to achieve in the 1783/4 painting because of its semi-personal nature and because its general theme was what we could call 'the making of the princely image', depicted by the painter in a ludic and performative way. However, in the case of *The Royal Family*, the presence of the self-portrait could only be justified by reference to the hugely prestigious *Las Meninas* (illus. 122). If the authorial insertion is only possible because of its famous predecessor, the changes that occur, due principally to the aulic and official nature of the representation, must be taken into account. In other words, whereas in *Las Meninas*, and, later (but in a different way) in *The Infante and His Family*, the painter puts himself in the foreground of the representation, in *The Royal Family* he is virtually hidden at the back of the canvas and hidden so well that it would take only a minor visual defect (or a reproduction where the contrast was poor) for him to disappear completely into the surrounding shadows. This does not, however, diminish the importance of the fact that the painter wanted (and managed) to draw attention to his own work and to the relationship of this work to the painting we have before us. When comparing this relationship to the one in *The Infante and His Family*, we find there are differences that cannot be ignored. They arise from the fact that 'the making of the princely image' has now been replaced by a more difficult, more demanding and more delicate activity. Let us call this 'the making of the royal image'.[41]

In neither painting is the creative act represented *ipso facto*, but rather symbolically. This means that in *The Infante and His Family* the painter does not depict the actual production of the scene we have before us, but instead he 'represents' it symbolically, in the form (that, to him, best defines its essence) of shadow games. In *The Royal Family* – and this has been noted on several occasions – the removal of the painter into the background of his painting gives rise to a whole series of questions about the strict logic of the representation that remain unresolved to this day. We can (and must) examine the possibility of a symbolic interpretation, but in this case (as with *The Infante and His Family*) the solution does not present itself straightaway. Only by analyzing *The Royal Family* as an official group portrait, originating from monarchic ideology and, *at the same time*, as a symbolic *mise-en-scène* of the 'making of the royal image' can a valid answer be found.

Théophile Gautier's famous witticism, according to which the painting could easily have passed as that of 'the corner baker and his wife, proud they'd won the jackpot'[42] is based on a misunderstanding, although it is no less significant, since it captures, beneath the veil of the witticism, several of the work's essential characteristics: the ostentatious atmosphere of the sitting, the relative unimportance of some of the people and their affected pomposity at their high position. From there, to asking ourselves whether the representation does not verge on caricature – as has been done on more than one occasion – is but one step away. This question, however, must be avoided at all costs. All we need do is examine the other portraits of the king and queen, produced during the same period,[43] to realize that, far from attacking their features with a malicious brush, Goya has treated them with a realism that is tinged with unequivocal forbearance. Returning to Gautier's sally, it could be said that the aura of having won the 'jackpot' that hovers over this self-satisfied family could be attributed to the king's luck in the great lottery of history. Indeed, when Charles IV ascended the Spanish throne in 1789, his cousin was embarking on his unavoidable journey to the scaffold (illus. 4–6) and his English contemporary George III (1760–1820) was sinking into madness. In fact, we need do no more than compare Goya's painting with the last of the (symbolic and posthumous) 'group portraits' of the French royal family (illus. 144) to understand indirectly the enormity of the issues involved.

The year Goya produced this painting, 1800, was a wonderful opportunity for a symbolic assessment. The Spanish royal family emerged triumphant. We do not know how far this triumph contributed to the birth and *mise-en-scène* of the great portrait, but we do know that, on the level of the dissemination of the royal image to the public, a comparison between the new century (that in Spain dawned under the sign of stability and continuity) and the upheavals taking place on the other side of the Pyrenees was on the agenda. By way of an example this is the publicity notice from the 1800 almanac, published in the *Diario de Madrid* on 14 January of the same year:

> Synopsis for the year 1800, composed of a frontispiece and seven pages in which you will find all that you need to know about the forthcoming year, comparing the French year with the era that is flourishing here, in a copper-plate engraving and illustrated with fine allusive prints, that deal with each table and with the portraits of Kings, our Lord. These make up a small book the size of a card so that it can be easily carried in the pocket.

In the light of these deliberations, the portrait can be seen as an example of a symbolic, ostentatious and propitiatory structuring of an institution – the king's family – during a time of crisis. Charles IV is in full evening regalia, standing with one foot forward. He is, in the etymological and symbolic sense of the word, *prominent*. On his bulging chest we see the highest decorations of the land, blinding in their brightness. A mea-

144 Jean Duplessi-Bertaux after François-Louis Prieur, *Last Meeting of Louis XVI and His Family,* beginning of the 18th century, copper engraving.

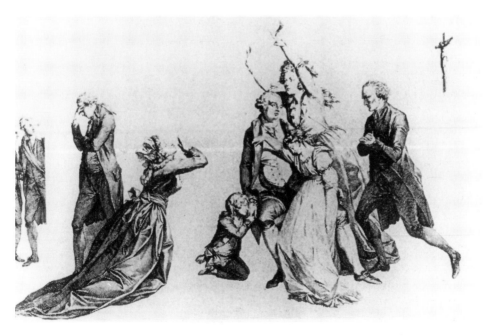

surement of the lighting in this canvas would reveal that the King marks the point of maximum intensity, just as, on the other side of the canvas, the point of minimum intensity is where Goya finds himself, the observer in the shadow of the royal representation.

A hierarchical analysis of this painting would show that the subtlety of the *mise-en-scène* is remarkable and its equilibrium has been well calculated. In this context, however, Queen Maria Luisa is a difficult figure whose positioning has obviously been very carefully thought out: although she stands at quite a distance from the foreground, she is in fact the real centre – of the 'painting' and of the 'family'. From the point of view of the *prominentia*, she is not actually the one who is closest to the King. This position of honour is given to her son, the Prince of the Asturias, the future Ferdinand VII, in the foreground on the left. Half in the shadows, he thrusts one foot forward like his father, thus indicating that he holds second place in this complicated dance of etiquette and dynastic succession that is the painting's *mise-en-scène*.[44] Behind him is the twelve-year-old Infante Don Carlos Maria Isidro, who, it would appear, is the only one not to like his portrait.[45] Perhaps he would have preferred to be in the place of the young Francisco de Paula (aged six), who stands between his father and his mother, on display as dynastic 'reserve' should the need arise. However, Don Carlos's displeasure may well be attributable to other causes and history was to prove his fears justified. Alienated from the throne just as he was about to succeed his heirless brother, he threw himself into a succession of civil wars that were to dominate the course of Spanish history throughout the nineteenth century (*las guerras carlistas*). In the painting, Goya depicts him as being the 'third' link in a tight line of succession (after the King, and after the Prince of Asturias) but gives him an ambiguous position, very similar to that given to the Infante Don Antonio Pasqual (the King's brother), whose head can be seen looming over the monarch's shoulder. We might therefore surmise that, in relation to the future King Ferdinand, he would only ever be what the Infante Don Antonio Pasqual was in relation to the present king; that is to say, his miserable and ridiculous double. If, as we believe, this was indeed what he was thinking, in the first place he was mistaken and in the second he was imagining it. He was wrong insofar as his place was far more 'prominent'

248

than that of Antonio Pasqual, who is in the back row of the picture next to the King's other relatives (the Prince of Parma and his family; old Maria Josefa is on the left); but he was correct inasmuch as, in a *mise-en-scène* whose rationale has yet to be examined, Goya gave the King's brother, whose congenital simple-mindedness was no closely kept secret,[46] a special place – as can be seen in the way their two heads come close together – which is further reinforced by their disconcerting likeness (illus. 146).

We have now arrived at a tricky point in a 'family romance'[47] to which we must pay particular attention, without dwelling too much on its impact on the *mise-en-scène* executed by Goya in his great portrait. This is the personality of Charles IV and essentially his abilities as a monarch. It is well known that this Bourbon was a weak king. It is also no secret that Maria Luisa was the mistress of Prime Minister Godoy, who was in fact suspected of being the father of her youngest sons. The whole situation (drastically abbreviated here) became an extremely thorny issue within the context of the fundamental destabilization of the institution of the monarchy that was taking place on the European stage. As a rule, a king's loss of charisma (a loss that could manifest itself in a multitude of ways) was the first sign of a possible collapse of the ancient order. However, it would be a complete distortion of the facts to claim that Goya, who had been appointed 'first court painter' in 1799, was working covertly and in *this* actual painting, to undermine the royal image. On the contrary, his task and his aim were to present the public at large with an image of a strong family structure, a monolithic organism and a sound administration, whose poisons were being eliminated, wherever they existed, by a perfect internal metabolism.

Through the apparent ludism imparted by the close similarities between the King and his brother, the painting reinforces the importance of one man, whilst making the other look absurd. The King, chest covered in decorations, one foot forward, well and truly visible, is portrayed as a real 'royal body'[48] whereas his brother, who stares vacantly into space, drowning in the abyss of his own mental emptiness, is nothing more, as it were, than a hilarious double, an absurd head placed on an invisible body. The implications of this contrast, which Goya obviously worked very hard to produce, are many, but it should be noted that, despite the apparent originality of the painting, Goya's work is not totally innovatory. In a way he is doing no more than adopting and adapting, in the context of the 'modern' monarchic imagery, the mechanisms that glorify power and conceal weaknesses, which had been so long at work in court art. Goya's version is, however, extremely ingenious and its implications are so wide that they cannot be over-emphasized.

The emblematic figure who traditionally personified all the functions of derision and ritual humiliation in the context of absolutist courts was the 'court jester' or 'king's fool' (illus. 146, 147). Those who have looked into his origins and history[49] have demonstrated, with a profusion of details and arguments, the complexity of his role. The fool brought gaiety to the life of the court and made people laugh because of his intrinsic otherness and because of the liberties he was allowed to take, the first and most important of which was aping the king. The fool was nothing other than the 'king upside down', his double, and his antithetical relative. It is no coincidence that King Lear's fool sometimes addressed him as 'nuncle', at others as 'sirrah',[50] or that one of the most famous fools of Philip IV of Spain, immortalized by Velázquez, was known as *El Primo* ('the cousin').[51] The art of the court portrait had integrated this figure of the reversed relative into its imagination and the *cuadro de la familia*, according to *Las Meninas* (illus. 122), where the dwarf Mari Barbola is the Infanta Marguerite's counter-figure, is another paradigmatic example of this. An examination of other examples might prove useful at this point. *The Portrait of Philip IV and the Dwarf Soplillo* (illus. 146) depicts the young monarch in the company of his miniature double. The clothes and pose make the fool into a *mimus regis*[52] and we can (and must) ask ourselves what the function and deeper significance of this kind of painting was. The obvious conclusion is that the antithesis around which Rodrigo Villandrando constructed his painting did not necessarily intend to mock the dwarf, but rather to glorify the king. Commenting on this painting, Barry Wind[53] drew attention to the importance of the rhetorical discourse on the greatness of the king, initiated by this kind of representation, and also to the fact that Gracián used it in a programmatic way, when, in the 'sixth crisis' in the second part of his *El Criticón* (1651), he has a dwarf in conversation with a giant around the *topos* of Fortune and her avatars.[54] Fernando Bouza, on the other hand, stressed how in all double portraits depicting prince and fool together, another figure was at work, once again theorized by Gracián as *agudeza de improporcion y disonancia* ('wit through disproportion and dissonance').[55] Thus a stylistic of the double court portrait was established at a time when its popularity was at its greatest. It has been traced back to its earliest origins. These involved the same notion of freakish 'dissimilarity' (*dissimilitudo*), which, in Western philosophy, was devised by Aristotle and later developed by Augustine.[56] The *similitudo–dissimilitudo* relationship allowed for the establishment of a brief link between the king and his fool. The monarch is a divine being and his *similitudo* pleases God, whereas the fool can only be king during the 'reign of dissimilarity' (*regio dissimilitudinis*).

Let us turn to another example. In critical works on Velázquez, there has been much debate surrounding the date, function and message of the double portrait of *Prince Baltazar Carlos with a Dwarf* (illus. 147). Experts are generally agreed that this is the painting the great artist made of the heir to the throne at the moment when, in 1632, and not quite three years old, he had to swear allegiance to the Cortes of Castille. This was tantamount to his being officially recognized as the heir to the throne.[57] If we accept this hypothesis, then the presence of the dwarf is all the more disturbing and needs to be carefully re-examined. It has quite rightly been stated that the dwarf forms an antithetical image in relation to the young prince, whose qualities as a future monarch are highlighted by a whole arsenal of signs pertaining to the court etiquette surrounding royal appearances and presentations. As for the dwarf, he is the negative replica of the future monarch. He is a reversed king, a playful king, a 'mock king' who enjoys himself by aping sovereignty and by displaying, in the form of the rattle and apple, the simulacra of monarchic authority: the orb and sceptre.

If we accept the date and ritual nature of the painting, there is one question that still remains unanswered: why, rather than producing a simple portrait of the Infante in all the splendour of his appearance, did Velázquez choose (or was asked) to tackle a *mise-en-scène* that focused on the interaction of dualities? Neither a 'realistic' ('the Prince is depicted with his playmate') nor a moralistic explanation ('the Prince is turning his back on childhood in favour of his new royal dignity') is particularly satisfying. It seems likely that the most appropriate answer might be found by analyzing, on the one hand, the issue of the public appearance (and of the painting that celebrates it) and, on the other, the major function of the fool as the prince's companion and double. Credit for this analysis must go to anthropological studies, since art history has failed to provide an answer.

In a key book,[58] Enid Welsford put forward a theory providing one of the principal reasons behind the adoption and use of dwarves and fools in the courts of kings. Her explanation was the fear of the evil eye, a rather vague notion[59] that probably covered a very broad spectrum ranging from 'cosmic jealousy' (feared in primitive societies) to malignant optical effluvia, a belief which survived in Europe until the Age of Enlightenment. It would be interesting at this point to see how a first attempt in 1787 to write about the evil eye, from an enlightened point of view, defined the phenomenon:

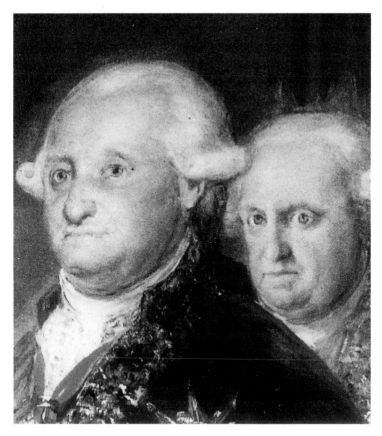

145 Detail of illus. 76.

146 Rodrigo Villandrando, *Philippe IV and the Dwarf Soplillo*, c. 1621, oil on canvas.

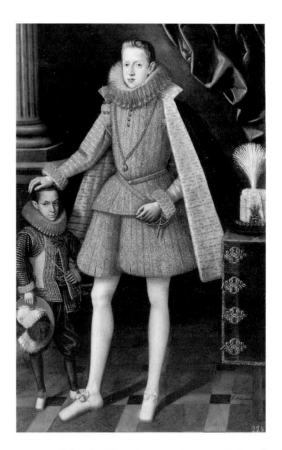

147 Diego Velázquez, *Don Baltasar Carlos with a Dwarf*, 1632, oil on canvas.

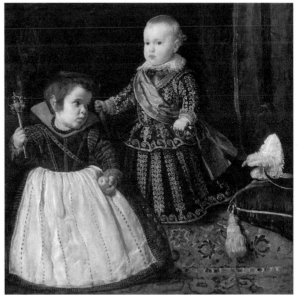

What is an evil eye? An evil comes from the eyes of other men, from their effluvia or from the Chain of Being (. . .). The evil eye is cast by men or women like a war shell, which, more often than not, we do not see from where it comes and which we only perceive when it has already exploded and caused losses (. . .). It is a lesion that we bring to others, and which is often born of hate, love, envy of the beautiful and which is transmitted by means of the eyes, the tongue, the touch, or generally speaking by the noxious body.[60]

According to tradition the sovereign, because of his unique position, was the favourite target of this kind of occult attack. Welsford explained the significance and simplicity of warding off the (conscious or unconscious) evil, with the help of an object of deflection. The fool was such an object. He also took on the role of 'a permanent scapegoat, whose official duty it is to jeer continually at his superiors in order to bear their ill-luck on his own unimportant shoulders'. The same author goes on to say:

Moreover a fool or dwarf was naturally lucky and might transfer his good luck to you while you transferred your bad luck to him. Now, this lucky-unlucky creature would be valuable as a permanent inmate of a household, and particularly in request as a safeguard for the King.[61]

It is within this context that the institution of the fool at the Habsburg court must be understood, as well as his appearance and importance within the framework of the royal portrait. In the case of the latter, the fool's function is crucial since the royal portrait itself (illus. 146, 147) is an ambiguous object.[62] On the one hand, the fool's presence celebrates royalty by making it *visible* (the purple curtain that opens the representation symbolizes the privilege of *seeing* the king)[63] and, on the other hand, it protects the image of the king, while it is being exhibited, from hostile eyes. When the prince was a child (illus. 147) and whenever he fell ill (which was often the case with Baltasar Carlos, who never made it to the throne), the role of the fool in royal presentations became crucial.

We can now recognize the subtlety with which Velázquez executed the *mise-en-scène* and the way it takes into account this metaphysic of transfers and reversals.[64] If the dwarf is in the foreground of the painting, contravening court etiquette, it is so that he can block and absorb any hostile looks and so that the prince, relegated to the middle distance, though in a position that is no less elevated, can enjoy his *maiestas* in peace.

The time has come, after this long detour, to return to Goya's painting (illus. 76). The work is ambiguous and, in the main, difficult because its aim is to combine elements from earlier royal representations (illus. 122, 146, 147) with the imperatives of a 'modern' presentation, originating from an enlightened monarchy. This concern for modernity can be detected in many of the details, such as the women's fashions or the way motherhood is portrayed, a virtue constantly stressed in Enlightenment philosophy.[65] In this context, it is not the absence of the traditional figure of the fool that is troubling, but its oblique, allusive, transferred and integrated presentation. In order to understand this in its proper context, we need to remind ourselves of a few facts. The most important one is that in Spain the institution of the royal fool came to an end when the Bourbons came to power in 1700.[66] This forsaking of the figure of the 'professional scapegoat', which was happening all over Europe, originated in an enlightened idea and culminated, towards the end of the eighteenth century, in the first systematic and scientific analysis of the role of the fool. In his *Geschichte der Hofnarren* (symbolically published in 1789), the author, Karl Friedrich Flögel, underlined the unworthy role of the fool as being typical of an absolutist mentality.[67]

In the eighteenth century the institution of the fool was, without a shadow of a doubt, relegated to history. However, this manoeuvre, designed to give the institution of the monarchy a more rational structure, purged of ancient rites and myths, coincided (primarily in Spain, but to a certain extent all over Europe) with the reappearance of an old, and alas not unfounded, fear of the growing threat of 'real madness' that had begun to invade the larger European courts. The first two Spanish Bourbons, Philip V (1700–47) and Ferdinand VI (1747–59) died mad, and when Goya was celebrating the Spanish royal family with his great portrait, the English monarchy was in crisis because of the sovereign's madness (George III). This is why the last chapter of one of the most important nineteenth-century books to be written on the history of the court fool is devoted to the new theme of 'princes who have been their own fools'. Its pages are haunted by the spectre of the madness of King George but, interestingly, this madness is seen as belonging to a much broader picture. The following lines refer to the royal madness in Spain:

> The Spanish royal family of the last century affords us an instance of the Heir to the Throne not only being his own fool, but of his raising his friends to the dignity of folly, by conferring on them its insignia. Lord Ligonier was English Ambassador at the court of Madrid during a portion of the reign of Charles III, which lasted from 1759 to 1788. After Lord Ligonier's introduction to the King, he was conducted to the apartments of the Heir to the Crown, the Prince of Asturias. The latter was, subsequently, that Charles IV who was his own Queen's especial fool throughout the term of their married lives. As Lord Ligonier approached the Prince's chamber, he saw issuing therefrom a number of grandees, each wearing with proud gravity, a fantastic fool's cap. On inquiring the meaning of such a pageant, he was informed that his Royal Highness possessed the fancy of distinguishing his most cherished friends as his 'fools'. The Prince, too, was often pleased to confer this mark of his favour on celebrated foreigners. Lord Ligonier was alarmed. (. . .) Ultimately, and after many messages and counter-messages had passed between the Prince in his room, and the English Envoy in the antechamber, announcement was made that the Prince of Asturias would not attempt to clap the fool's-cap on the head of Lord Ligonier.[68]

A careful reading of this passage reveals that the author's real, but never acknowledged, intention was to show that the English King's madness was not just a one-off affair but should be seen within the context of the much wider (but differently manifested) madness that was sweeping through the courts of Europe. The young Prince of Asturias (the future Charles IV) was, in the sub-text of this anecdote, no more than a figure moving from an old symbolic madness to a new and more disturbing one. To the fear, which is so conspicuous in the above excerpt, we should add another, even greater fear that came along in 1789. This was the fear of the desacralization of the person of the sovereign (illus. 5), indeed of his annihilation (illus. 6), and it resulted from the Monarchy being challenged by both the Philosophers and the Revolution.[69] The road taken by the King of France to the scaffold took on the significance of an inverted rite, a long and painful ceremony, whose ad hoc imagery was in itself confirmation of the issues being symbolized. An examination of this imagery of desacralization and mockery[70] will provide us with a clearer picture, through a reversed reflex, of the symbolic world from which Goya was operating. Two examples will suffice.[71] Both deal with different forms of the *topos* of the king's double.

The first is the motif of the 'king's mask', as it first began to appear in the revolutionary press in 1791 and as it appeared in caricature in 1792 (illus. 148). By removing his mask (to show that his head is nothing but a simulacrum), Louis Capet is revealing his real face, his real head, a mere 'jug' with a halo. The precise meaning of the reading is not important: empty (a symbol of stupidity) or full of wine (an allusion to Louis XVI's legendary drunkenness), the jug is one of the richest counter-figures of the head and this caricature has a symbolic importance. In a way that is very striking, it indicates that Louis's execution in January 1793 was anticipated by a symbolic 'loss of head', by a decapitation *in effigy*.

A second, more complex example shows Louis XVI with the dual features of king and fool (illus. 149). It is thought, and probably quite rightly, that this print was circulated at the beginning of July 1792 in anticipation of the declaration of the Republic. It would appear that it was preceded by a lengthy and dogged campaign of skilfully orchestrated rumours claiming that the King had suddenly gone mad.[72] The incident is interesting on the level of the symbolic split it produced that highlighted the pluri-semantic nature of madness. In other words, the rumours claimed that the King's madness was bordering on the pathological, and that the loss of his mental faculties therefore justified his abdication. In the image, on the other hand, what we see is not only a lunatic from an asylum captured in a fit of anger, but also a court fool who has taken the King's place. In this way, the print, modest on the level of its formal achievement, carries out an extremely valuable symbolic transition. This *'roi fou'* ('mad king') (again the inscription plays with the possibility of this interpretation) is at the same time a *'roi fool'* ('king fool'). In his agitation, brandishing a fool's bauble instead of a sceptre, he has knocked over the throne. Time is standing still. 'Capet the Elder' is now

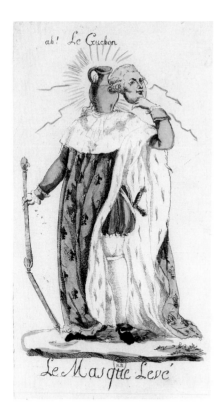

ah! Le Cruchon

Le Masque Levé

148 French, *The Mask Removed*, June 1791, etching.

the upside-down king, the '*mad*' royal, the royal '*fool*'. The spectator's gaze is drawn through the purple curtain on the left to a private area; on the right, next to the fireplace, obscene graffiti suggest that the deposition of the cuckold-king should begin even earlier. But the most valuable symbolic object is without a doubt the broken mirror above the fireplace. It has been broken by the desacralized sceptre – the fool's bauble. Having subjected this print to a careful analysis, Annie Duprat came to some interesting conclusions:

> The caricature is duplicated through the effect produced by the mirror; broken by the king's bauble the shards bear traces or not, as the case may be, of the shattered and seemingly multiplied face of the king: a technical examination of the different copies held in the National Library in Paris, show that the same copper plate has been reworked in order to create the most striking visual effect: the king's shattered face is coloured bright pink, he is reflected as much in the mirror as he is in the fragments on the ground.[73]

258

However, the point that has never been highlighted until now is that, through this interaction, the print forms an important epilogue to a motif that was fundamental to the history of the notion of kingship, that of the dual nature of the king. The motif of the broken mirror, already exploited by Shakespeare in *Richard II*, and examined by Kantorowicz in his seminal study *The King's Two Bodies*, signals the end of all catoptromancy, the end of any likelihood of there being a second – subtle, virtual and sacred – king's body.[74] The only possible reflective interplay takes place beyond the mirror: the king is his own fool.

Let us now return, after this final detour, to Goya's portrait (illus. 76). The French Revolution is over and done with. It is now 1800, a new century has just begun and the Spanish Bourbons are (still) *there*. Moreover, they are making their presence felt. The operation is complex and the painting is proof of permanence. It is the family – and this is the essential message of the painting – which guarantees the permanence of the king's body. It is a family that has crossed important thresholds: in 1789 it put on the throne the monarch who is now, in 1800, affirming his 'prominence'. It is a family that has been able to renew itself: at the beginning of this new century, it has created a new image for itself. For example, it has readily adopted the clothes from beyond the Pyrenees, fashionable in the entourage of the First Consul, who was about to become the Great Usurper. And finally, it is the family that is present-

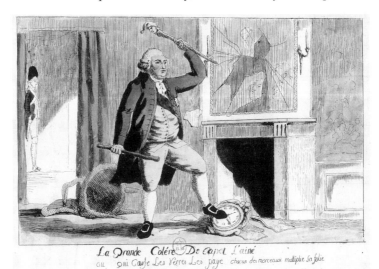

149 French, *The Great Anger of Capet the Elder,* June 1791, etching.

ing the – sacred – body of the king, exorcising it by making itself the double sacrifice. This sacrifice is then 'em-bodied' into the large monarchic body, which is what the family above all else is, in the form of the king's counter-figure. We might well ask ourselves if this idea is not manifested – probably in a particular form – in one or two other cases as well. Don Carlos Maria Isidro might well be one of these counter-figures (and the Prince in all probability feels that he is), while Doña Maria Josefa, the old lady with the wild eyes on the left, could be another. If Doña Maria Josefa does have an expiatory function in the economics of the representation, as seems likely, this is brought about in a more encoded way than with the royal double. The intensity of her presence, however, which also comes out in the magnificent preparatory portrait Goya made at the time (illus. 77), draws attention to this sister of the King (a spinster 'not very tall, but a little deformed and having an unpleasant face' [*no muy alta, aunque algo contrahecha y de cara desagradabe*]).[75] She could, in fact, quite easily have remained hidden in one of the dark corners of the Royal Palace since she is the only person in the whole composition to have no place in the hierarchy of the dynastic succession. The Infanta 'Pepa', as Goya portrays her in the painting, is a counter-figure of feminine majesty, and therefore the Queen's counterpart.

One seemingly unimportant detail, resulting from the way in which her body is presented, reveals the allusive way in which this quality came to be implied. This is the large black stain on her temple. The history of this not insignificant feature goes back a long way. The black patch (usually referred to as a *lunar* in Spain and as a *mouche* in France, which also means 'a fly') is the descendant of the 'beauty spot' or 'mole' that decorated the faces of beautiful ladies in the eighteenth century.[76] The 'cosmetic' function of the '*lunar*' was to bring out the whiteness (and thereby the beauty) of the face on which it was placed. In the course of the century, the manufacturing process was refined and the 'spot' could be stuck in different places on the face depending on its wearer's outfit. However, the beauty spot was also the descendant of the wart, which, according to the divinatory art of metaposcopy, could reveal a person's destiny. To interpret these signs, real astral cards of the face were laid out.[77]

The 'beauty spot' was, therefore, at the crossroads where

two traditions met. One originated in the ancient stylistic of contrasts, which we have already had occasion to look at, and the other came from the custom of distinctive and propitiatory symbols. In eighteenth-century Spain, the *lunar* went through an extraordinary process of hyperbolization and the huge, increasingly large spots that decorated the left temple of Maria Luisa in so many of Goya's independent portraits[78] demonstrate this. This enormous stain (the only one to compare with it was the one worn by the beautiful Duchess of Alba in the 1790s) was endowed, because of its aesthetic and symbolic importance, with the characteristics of a genuine 'talisman of supremacy'.[79]

And yet, for the first time, the Queen does not wear it in the portrait of *The Family*. Maybe Goya no longer considered it to be fashionable, or maybe she did not need it any more. But there are other elements which appear to suggest a subtle shift in function. Goya has strategically turned the Queen's head slightly to the left, thus concealing the temple where all eyes might have looked for the famous symbol. At the same time, the *lunar* re-appears at the opposite end of the canvas, but reversed, on the Infanta Pepa's right temple. If this patch was no longer fashionable, as would appear to be the case (it never appeared again in subsequent portraits of the Queen), its transfer, in the Goya painting, to the face of the poor Infanta, takes on the significance of an exorcism. In the preparatory portrait (illus. 77), Goya presented the stain as a black-paste mark that floats on the Infanta's temple like the black insignia that decorates her chest. Moreover, both these features have been produced in the same pictorial manner as the shaded background against which Goya has placed his model's head. Projection and background are therefore consubstantial and interchangeable. Maria Josefa's brightness is deepset: it is the brightness of the shadow, the shadow of a brightness. And it is in this way therefore that, within the scenography of the painting, she takes on a symbolic typology (to which the beauty spot belongs) as the 'survivor of a century gone-by' (illus. 150). Within the framework of the monarchic body, she *is,* as it were, *la mouche* through whom distinction and brilliance are glorified.

At the dawn of a new century, it is the glitter of the royal body that defies time. The Queen has transferred the old symbols and is presenting herself radiant at the heart of *The*

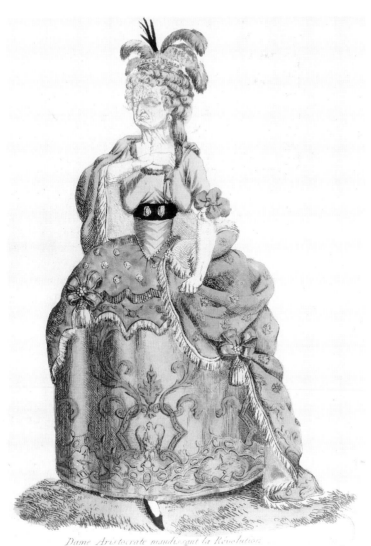

150 French,
*Aristocratic Lady
Cursing the
Revolution*,
1792, coloured
engraving.

Dame Aristocrate maudissant la Révolution

Family: the Queen never grows old!

Goya's clever game of transference and doubling (illus. 76) was the only way he could unite the ideological realism of the Enlightenment with the expiatory function of the ancient figures of reversal (illus. 42, 44, 147, 148). His painting, in which the painter himself participates, thematizes the making of the monarchic body. This body is the Family, of which the King is the head. The personality of Charles IV, who, as far as the public was concerned, was the very incarnation of a 'mock king', shines through in the best possible light in the painting. So does that of the Queen. In the actual game of likenesses, the representation confirms that the evil has been relegated, indeed pushed back into the background of a dynastic body that is declaring its regenerative ability, its vitality and its viability.[80]

One last word on the possibility of Goya's approach being given a rhetorical interpretation. If the notions of 'disproportion' and 'dissonance' – as others have suggested – played an important part in defining the burlesque eighteenth-century imagination, they were no longer operating when 'similarity' had replaced 'dissimilarity' as a form of rhetorical wit (illus. 26–9). But the 'prudent' Goya would have had no great difficulty in bringing this transformation about, and Gracián could once again have been his guide, since he stressed as no other had done before or has done since, that: 'Similarity is an inexhaustible source of wit.'[81] Standing at the back of the canvas, the painter who, in his turn, was able to manipulate, transform and turn similarities upside down as no other had done before or has done since, could have subscribed to Gracián's discourse: 'All similarity is not necessarily subtle and only becomes a conceit (some think) when it includes some other form such as mystery, contrariety and correspondence . . .'[82] Why then did he have to place himself, in order to get a better view of all this, there, where he is – 'in the shadows' and 'behind things'? But that is another story.

8 Ha-ha, Ho-ho, Hu-hu, He-he!

GOYA'S EYEGLASSES

There are two Goya self-portraits, both difficult to date, that are closely linked to the background of *Charles IV and His Family* (illus. 76). One is in the Musée de Castres (illus. 152), the other in the Musée de Bayonne. Originally dated by experts as having been produced between 1788–92, they were subsequently post-dated to 1796–7 by Xavier de Sales because of their most significant feature – the eyeglasses – which, according to the Spanish scholar, alluded to the meticulous work of etching the painter was engaged in at the time.[1] There are some question marks over whether these portraits should be linked to the creation of *Los Caprichos*. We believe that, if a relationship does exist, it is not of a technical order but rather of a symbolic order. In other words, we believe that the glasses Goya displays in these self-portraits do not primarily or nec-essarily pertain to the technical acuity of sight but rather to its symbolic *mise-en-scène*.

There are several elements to support this hypothesis. The first can be found in a whole series of self-portraits produced by such notable artists as Reynolds (1789) and Chardin (1771, 1775, 1779). In these pictures the wearing of magnifying lenses was considered to be a symbol of the painter-intellec-tual in general, and, though not in any restrictive way, as the symbol of the painter-etcher in particular.[2] The integration of Goya's self-portraits into this wider European context does, however, also highlight their specific difference. This is to be found in the way the Spanish artist accentuates what could be referred to as the characteristic feature of his 'vision', which is, in this instance, the disassociation of the gaze. Here again, a comparison with his contemporaries could prove useful. Chardin, for example, was not completely unaware of this practice, for in one of his paintings he depicts himself peering at the spectator through thick lenses (1775) and in the other two he is glancing at him over spectacles that have slipped down his nose (1771, 1779). Never, however, does the French artist look 'through' and 'over' at one and the same time. And this is precisely what Goya does. A careful comparison between the Castres and Bayonne self-portraits, and a comparison between these two and the self-portrait in the background of *Charles IV and His Family* might suggest that they all date from around 1799–1800, that is to say from an important but also 'disassociated' period of Goya's life. This was a period of extreme contrasts, represented by the distribution of the *Caprichos* on the one hand, and the creation of the large state painting of *Charles IV and His Family* on the other.

In all three self-portraits, the artist focuses on – but in different ways – the thematization of sight. The Castres *Self-Portrait* reproduced here (illus. 152) clearly reveals (more so than the Bayonne painting) that the painter's right eye is looking at the world through the lens whereas his left is looking directly at the world without an intermediary. In the *Charles IV and His Family* (illus. 151), Goya has the same pose, the same clothes, and, we could even go so far as to say, the same gaze, the only difference being that in this case the eyeglasses have disappeared. That we are in fact dealing with a 'disappearance' and not simply an 'absence' is confirmed by the alterations to the face visible through the paint, especially around the eyes. It is clear that there was originally a large pair of spectacles, painted over for the final version of the painting.

All this experimentation could probably be attributed to pure coincidence. However, the way Goya doggedly approaches, corrects, caricatures and changes his self-portraits tempts us to initiate a debate as to the – possible – deep significance. This chapter, therefore, will present a first hermeneutic and plausible approach to subsequent developments. Those aspects that seem the most important will be tackled, such as the complex symbolism of the instruments of optical magnification, the motif of the double sight, and finally, the significance of the relationship between the 'presence' of this motif and its 'effacing'.

A letter written by Goya, probably in 1793, is often quoted whenever the Castres and Bayonne self-portraits are examined. As with most of his correspondence with Zapater, the contents are difficult to understand and to translate as they are probably partially encoded: 'Well, you demon. How could I rejoice if I do not see the other? Do not be long in coming, and

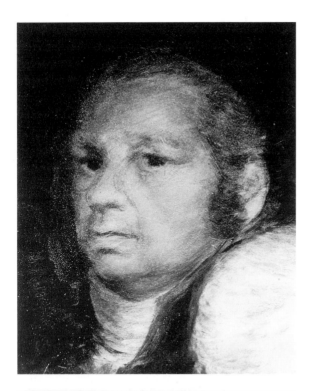

151 Detail of illus. 76.

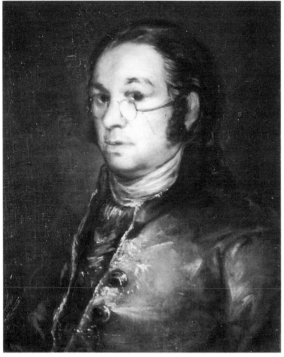

152 Goya, *Self-portrait*, *c.* 1797–1800, oil on canvas.

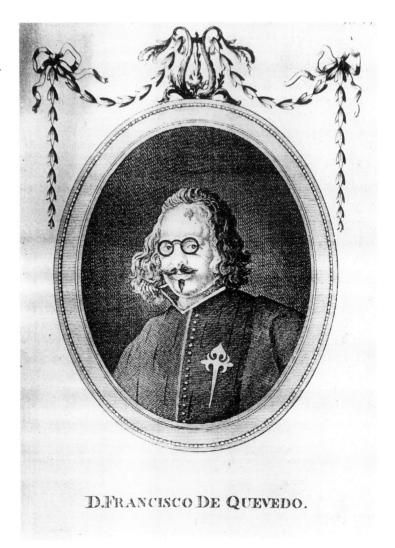

D.FRANCISCO DE QUEVEDO.

bring your good mood (*buen humor*), and do not forget my
monocle (*mi antiojo*), since with the one I have I cannot see any
"serapia", and I need it for making the crucutria.'[3]
Interpretations of this letter usually focus on the eye problems
Goya was experiencing in 1792, which explains why he is
asking his friend to bring him new glasses, so crucial when
working on 'caricatures' (the usual translation of the enigmatic word *crucuturia*). However, it seems more likely that
this is one of the many double-meanings that pepper Goya's
correspondence. In our opinion, a close examination of the
whole context is essential, for, in effect, what Goya is asking

267

Zapater is not only that he should join him and bring him new glasses (or a new monocle) but that he should also bring his 'good mood' (*humor*/humour/mood). This might have been seen as just a chance remark, had the *eyeglasses/good mood* (indeed *burlesque*, indeed *practical joke*) dyad not belonged to the long tradition that has already been mentioned and which had already inspired some important creations (illus. 121). We shall stay with the spirit of the letter and conclude that, despite those expressions that remain unintelligible, it confirms a double desire: for 'magnified sight' and for 'entertainment'. For this reason we would place it within the context of the ancient 'satires of the partially-sighted', a tradition stretching back to at least the fifteenth century.[4]

In an excellent article on the fool and humanist irony, Robert Klein drew attention to the farcical, indeed diabolical, element that was always associated with glasses.[5] Since Klein, others have studied the motif and have seen it as being part of an arsenal of tricks and deceptions. In this context, however, the main function of glasses lies in their ability to decipher the hidden meaning of things, the ideal eyeglasses being veritable magic instruments capable of discovering the truth behind the codified madness of the world.[6] The fact that Goya was aware of this tradition is revealed in the way he uses it in *Capricho* 57 and his preparatory drawings (illus. 114–16). As has been demonstrated, this was a special case, extremely complicated and subtle because of the appeal of word games of conceptist origin. It would probably be somewhat hasty to link, without some caution, Goya's self-portraits where he is wearing glasses, to this tradition alone. One important factor, however, comes to our assistance. This is the special importance that Spanish culture bestowed on the symbolism of magnifying lenses, a symbolism that Goya would have found difficult to ignore. Just two examples from Goya's own national tradition serve to outline the conceptual basis on which the Spanish painter probably integrated the topos of the 'intellectual gaze' (to be found, as we have seen, in other European eighteenth-century self-portraits) into a more specific and wider context. The first example is one of the best known 'portraits of an author' handed down by tradition, that of the poet Francisco de Quevedo (illus. 153). The author of *Dreams*, whose spiritual links with Goya have been repeatedly underlined,[7] Quevedo was the beneficiary of a famous and celebrated portrait (no longer in existence) attributed to Velázquez. The many etched portraits that served as frontispieces to the poet's works were probably related to Velázquez's famous prototype. In almost all of these etchings, the writer, the insignia of the Knight of the Order of Santiago on his chest, is scrutinizing the spectator through spectacles. However, what is of interest to us, is not that Francisco de Quevedo wore glasses (other men of letters before and since have done so),[8] but the fact that the glasses became part of his public image, and that moreover it was precisely this detail that early commentators specifically focused on. Antonio Palomino's description of the prototype-portrait is therefore highly significant:

> Velázquez made another portrait of Don Francisco de Quevedo Villegas, Knight of the Order of Santiago and Lord of the town of Torre de Juan Abad. His printed works bear witness to his rare talent, for he was a divine Martial of Spanish poetry and a second Lucian of prose. (. . .) He painted Quevedo with spectacles, which he usually wore, so that the Duke of Lerma said in a ballad he wrote in reply to a sonnet sent him by Don Francisco de Quevedo (. . .):

> Lisura en verso, y en prosa,
> Don Francisco, conservad.
> ya que vuestros ojos son
> tan claros como un cristal.[9]

According to Palomino, two elements characterize Quevedo's personality, both of which come out in Velázquez's portrait of him. The first is his *ingenio* (talent), leading to comparisons with Martial (the author of caustic epigrams) and with Lucian (the author of merciless satires). The second is his spectacles. This characteristic is the external sign of his inner quality (*ingenio*) and draws attention to its lucid and penetrating nature. The lines Palomino quotes are pluri-semantic since they consciously play with the term *lisura* that refers to the finish, elegance and perfection of the style, as well as to the candid, sincere and direct nature of Quevedo's verse. We understand from the outset that it is the poet's actual gaze that is clear, lucid and all-seeing. The conceptist opening towards a 'nominal point' not mentioned by Palomino, but present between the lines of his text, is almost inevitable since eyeglasses open the way to a paronomasia of the name *Quevedo*. 'What do I see?' (*Que veo?*) is in fact a question that permeates the work of the poet and especially his *Dreams*.[10]

To this conceptist question – 'What do I see'/*Que veo?* – we can give the obvious reply: what the *ingenio* perceives (the eyeglasses are, let us not forget, only an external sign) is the world 'such as it is' monstrously magnified, its proportions and appearance turned upside down.

This is, in fact, the reply given in the most important book on the Spanish literature of the Golden Age, in regard to the symbolism of glasses. In the allegorical tale *Los Anteojos de Mejor Vista* (*Eyeglasses for Better Sight*) by Rodrigo Fernández de Ribera (written between 1625–30) a strange character, armed with terrible spectacles, shows the author the city of Seville from the top of La Giralda. The key scene is the one in which the mysterious character passes his instruments of magnification over to the author:

> Eagerly I took the eyeglasses in order to try them, giving as an excuse that they would tell me the truth. I put them on, as one does normally, but I think, hardly had I done so, that despite myself I uttered a cry. And this was in no way inappropriate, since what I saw was so strange, new and wonderful that even the tower where I was standing would have been scandalised and would have backed away in surprise, if it had had my eyes.
>
> 'And what is that, Master,' I asked, 'Where am I?'
>
> 'You are in all your senses,' he replied.
>
> 'I thought so,' I replied.
>
> 'And what do you see now?' he asked.
>
> 'I see uncommon things,' I replied.
>
> 'What do you see?' he asked.
>
> 'The same place as before,' said I, 'but full of vultures and crows, kites, eagles and doves, all mixed together.'
>
> 'You therefore see that before you did not in truth see,' said he then, 'for before you thought that there you saw court clerks; there, prosecutors; there the Minister of Justice, and supplicants – those doves there – flapping around them for

fear of leaving their feathers behind.'[11]

It should be pointed out that the whole fauna uncovered by the 'eyeglasses for better sight' was not without its donkey-doctors and men-women, thus anticipating somewhat uncannily the world of the *Caprichos*. This seems to confirm the permanence in Goya's work of the motif of 'second sight', capable of discovering hidden truths with the assistance of such symbolic instruments as magnifying lenses and magic mirrors (illus. 26–9). However, the relationship between the glasses and the creating of the *Caprichos* should not be sought solely in the technical status of glasses as instruments of magnification but also (or maybe even first and foremost) in their status as symbolic pointers to the deep and hidden aspects of things and the world. In Rodrigo Fernández de Ribera's short story, the mystery owner of the magic glasses does not reveal his identity until the end: his name is Master Disenchantment (*Maestro Desengaño*), his eyeglasses were constructed by 'experience' and the lenses are made of 'pure truth' ('*Estos anteojos los labrò la experiencia, el vidrio es de la misma verdad*').[12] Given the intellectual and symbolic context in which the *Caprichos* were created and which we have already attempted to outline (see Chapter 5), Goya's 'Quevedo-style' self-portrayal, with its characteristics of a modern *Maestro Desengaño* (illus. 152), should come as no surprise. And yet what must be underlined is the fact that we are also witnessing a process of 'modernization' of this ancient figure. A close examination of his self-portraits reveals that Goya is wearing a variation of the 'liberty clothes' imported from France (illus. 7), easily identifiable from the unbuttoned jacket and the large white scarf around his neck. Whereas in the frontispiece to the *Caprichos* (illus. 100) the allusions to French fashions were completed by a top hat, in the Bayonne and Castres *Self-Portraits* the glasses are the distinguishing feature. The adoption of this symbol-object, far from challenging the coherence of the 'liberty clothes', reinforces it, for, as recent studies have suggested, the ancient motif of the magic spectacles experienced a new lease of life during the French Revolution. The proof of this can be found, for example, in the pamphlet entitled *The Eyeglasses of the Zealous Citizen* (April 1789) and the short-lived Paris newspaper *The Enchanter Merlin's Lorgnette Found Under the Ruins of the Bastille* (1790).[13]

We would go so far as to maintain that – much like the *Disenchanted Master* and the *Zealous Citizen* – the synthesis Goya carried out when producing his self-portrait is conspicuous because of the innovative nature of the dissociated gaze, and this should be included in the backdrop to 'bifocality', which Werner Hofmann saw to be the most striking feature of the art produced around 1800 and, even of modern art in general. [14] Goya had already manifested his interest in bifocality in the first frontispiece to the *Dreams* (illus. 72, 96), in which one of the 'author's' eyes is dreaming while the other keeps watch, thereby pointing out to the spectator that the 'key to dreams' is to be found in the complementary relationship between 'in-sight' and 'sight'. Bifocality is perhaps also present in the very original self-portrait with top hat in the final version of the *Caprichos* (illus. 100), in which the artist's left eye is looking obliquely at the spectator and the world, while the right eye remains invisible.

In the case of the painted self-portraits dating from the same era (illus. 152), Goya's fondness for bifocality, affirmed by the adoption of the double gaze, appeared to be a perpetual swinging or perfect simultaneity between observation and introspection, vision and snapshot, realism and distortion. Thus, if, by adopting eyeglasses, Goya was portraying himself as both an 'all-seeing disenchanted man' (*desengañado vedor de todo*) and a lucid observer (*hombre judicioso y notante*), conscious of the fact that the world is a cipher whose inner core must be penetrated[15] through the adoption of 'double sight' (*vista duplicada*),[16] he is stressing the duality of his person and of his personality, on the one hand, and the double focus of his art, on the other.

The duality of Goya's personality and work is manifested on several levels, one of the most important being the transition, apparently devoid of tension, that took place in 1799/1800 between his activity as a satirical etcher and as the king's official court painter. His new role in the theatre of the royal court from the end of 1799 forced him to make some significant revisions when it came to his symbolic self-portrait. Thus, when portraying himself as the artist at work in *Charles IV and His Family* (illus. 76, 151), he depicted himself partially withdrawn into the shadows at the back of the stage, as all 'prudent' men should be in similar circumstances. It was probably also his 'prudence', a quality he had already glossed on another occasion (illus. 141–3) (and a subject Gracián had tackled in one of his most famous books)[17] that drove him to remove the eyeglasses that he had originally painted from Master Disenchantment and Citizen Zealous. If, however, he retained a trace of fondness for conceptist ciphers, then it is to be found in the way he approached another motif dear to Gracián and the authors of the Golden Age, that of the inside-out view (*mirar al rebes*): 'To see the world inside out compared to what others do, implies seeing it from the other side of its appearances. He who looks the wrong way round in reality looks the right way round.'[18]

Whereas in *The Infante Don Luis and His Family* (illus. 74) Goya depicted himself in a painful twisted position so as to communicate his idea better, in *Charles IV and His Family* (illus. 76) he adopted a more comfortable position, which, for all that, is devoid of difficulties on the level of the logic of the representation. In an attempt to explain the other difficulties, Fred Licht suggested that the whole of the royal family must have posed in front of an enormous mirror, and that it is this reflection that the artist is painting on the large canvas in front of him.[19] This interesting (but as yet unproved) hypothesis could be a way of explaining the artist's otherwise illogical viewpoint, at the back of the canvas. However, it does not explain why, once he had decided to use the mirror, Goya *necessarily* had to position himself behind his *models*. He could have painted them (and at the same time *himself*), in the hypothetical mirror, but from closer up, especially as Velázquez's famous model was inviting him to do just this (illus. 122). His withdrawal into the shadows and right into the background of his painting may be explained by, on the one hand , his wish to highlight the 'prudence' needed by a member of the court and, on the other, his desire to reformulate the theme of 'inside-out sight'. To Goya, as with his conceptist predecessors, the inside-out view (*mirar al rebes*) or the view from the inside of things (*mirar por dentro*) gave access to the truth. By placing himself in the background of his painting (illus. 76, 151), Goya was displaying a sui-generis conceptist form of self-portrayal, capable of thematizing 'true sight', even in the absence of the traditional instruments of optical magnification or symbolic penetration of appearances. Their effacing is strategic, since the magic eyeglasses could have blasphemously transformed the royal court into a giant henhouse as was (doubtless and partly) the case in *Los Caprichos*. 'In-sight' or 'inside-out sight', on the other hand, presents it purely and simply 'such as it is'.

GOYA'S LAUGHTER

The fact that 'in-sight' is also one of the *topoi* of the *Caprichos* is significant. Often linked to the theme of laughter that unmasks (illus. 86, 114, 118), the *mirar por dentro* would also

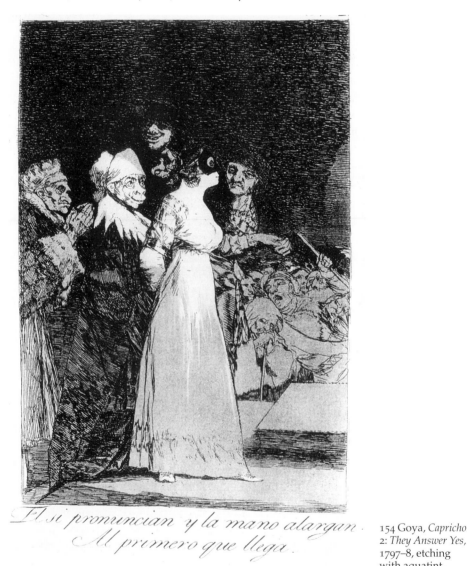

El si pronuncian y la mano alargan Al primero que llega.

154 Goya, *Capricho 2: They Answer Yes*, 1797–8, etching with aquatint.

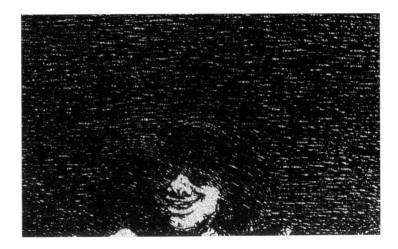

appear to have been on more than one occasion a fairly obvious form of auctorial self-projection. An inventory of these
appearance-projections in Goya's pictorial corpus could one
day prove very useful. For the present, however, we shall
limit ourselves to focusing on the cases that have the widest
implications. One of them – and this strikes home immediately – is to be found in the first narrative print, *Capricho* 2
(illus. 154), which follows immediately after the frontispiece-
self-portrait depicting the author 'in a bad humour and in a
satirical attitude' (illus. 100). In the background to this social
satire, a face bisected by a huge smile emerges from the spot
where the darkness is almost total (illus. 155). There is something both enigmatic and dynamic about this figure which
gives the impression that at any moment it will be engulfed by
the night from which it has just emerged. Its origins are evident since it duplicates the features of the caricatured self-portrait Goya made during what appeared to be a social
gathering with friends (illus. 35). We can also see that the great
nocturnal smile of *Capricho* 2 (illus. 155) is not unlike the enormous black laughing moon that the artist was to chose for his
undulating Ash Wednesday banner (illus. 1, 8).

Within the various contexts of the *Caprichos* cycle, the auctorial projection endows the person of the artist with a new
significance. It is a self-portrait hidden 'inside' (and 'behind')
the world of the representation, a self-portrait on the unstable
boundary between appearance and disappearance. It establishes a kind of inner dialogue not only with the social masquerade to which it belongs but also with its alter ego of the

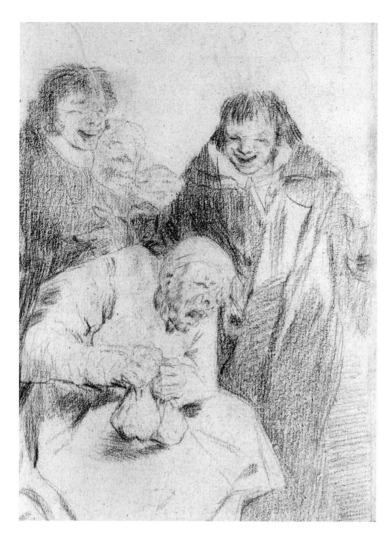

frontispiece. Taken at face value, we could be led to believe
that if in the frontispiece (illus. 100) – which is also the first
Capricho of the series – Goya was depicting himself in, as we
have seen, 'a satirical attitude and in a bad humour', in the
next *Capricho* (illus. 154, 155), his intention was to present
himself as the (hidden) author 'in a satirical attitude and in a
good humour'. Whilst this first impression is not altogether
wrong, it becomes more plausible through subsequent
amendments. What we instantly discover is a programmatic
approach, reinforced by a clear repetition throughout the
whole series of the 'hidden' and 'laughing' self-portrait. The
most important example of this is in *Capricho* 30 (illus. 111),

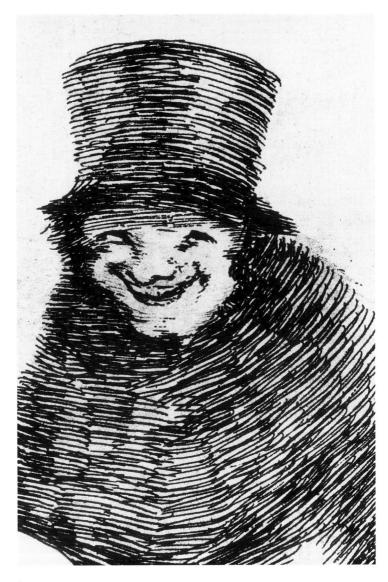

which is particularly revealing because it focuses, with a clarity that is unusual in Goya, on the alternation between the
revelation and the concealment of sources and motives. In this
Capricho the representation is polarized between the object of
ridicule (the miserly monk in the foreground) and the laughing people in the middle distance. The page setting and cut-
ting endow the figures with a uniform hugeness. One figure
in particular stands out, for he has taken a step towards the
spectator to present the object of general derision, a strange

being in fancy-dress.[20] His bisected mouth (illus. 157) is reminiscent of that in the concealed self-portrait in *Capricho* 2 (illus. 155); his headgear, though handled with almost ludic spontaneity, mimics the top hat of the frontispiece (illus. 100). The figure's expression should be read dialectically and within a double context: in the context of the scene to which it belongs, the laughing face presents the painfully grimacing features of the mocked miser, while in the context of the series as a whole, it suggests a split in the auctorial personality – the first, distant and in a bad mood, the second integrated and in a cheerful mood. That this creature is the product of a painstaking and deep reflection on the part of Goya, is reflected in the preparatory drawing housed in the Prado (illus. 156). Any changes made by Goya for the final version are to be found in the body language, the physiognomy and the symbolism of the clothes; the most significant detail being the top hat, an accessory that puts the 'laughing person' of the *Capricho* on a subtle (and delayed) equal footing with his sullen twin of the frontispiece.

On the level of the physiognomical experiment that can be detected below the surface, the frontal representation of the 'cheerful author', unlike the gloominess of the first self-portrait, facilitates the presentation of a planimetry of the face distorted by laughter. Both the physiology and phenomenology of laughter have had a long and rich tradition, and Goya might have been familiar with some of it. If, however, Goya's laugh has an obvious parallel, this is, in our opinion, the print (illus. 158) and its accompanying text found in Fermin Zeglirscosac's *Ensayo sobre el origen y naturaleza de las pasiones* (composed in the same year as Goya's *Caprichos* and published in Madrid in 1800), the best-known Spanish treatise. It was written in the wake of the trail blazed by Charles Le Brun and focused on the question of expressions:

> This movement (laughter) is expressed by raising the eyebrows towards their middle whereas the eyes become oblique and almost closed and look slightly towards the nose. The mouth parts to reveal the teeth and pushes up towards the ears. The oblique corners of the mouth form wrinkles in the cheeks, which bulge and make the eyes look deep-set. The skin tone turns pink, the nostrils flare,

the eyes become damp to the point where they release a few tears. These do not have the same origin as those caused by sadness and consequently do not alter the features of the face in the same way that sadness does.[21]

The comparison between laughter and tears, sadness and cheerfulness, seen as extreme expressions that are at the same time both opposite and similar, had enjoyed a long tradition.[22] It would appear that Goya wanted to develop much further the suggestions made in the treatises on expressions with which he came into contact. His approach transcends a simple gloss on the representation of the 'passions of the soul' and in fact targets, through the double authorial projection, two complementary attitudes to the world. The tradition of this motif, so dear to moral philosophy, goes back to the very origins of satire as a genre, and it was in fact Juvenal who gave this genre – as tutelary figures – the contrasting and diametrically opposed figures of Heraclitus in tears and Democritus roaring with laughter.[23] Between the Renaissance, when Marsilio Ficino updated the famous philosophical couple, and the eighteenth century, the sadness/derision dialectic was periodically adapted and revised[24] but it was Goya who carried it to an extreme. A rich iconography was elaborated

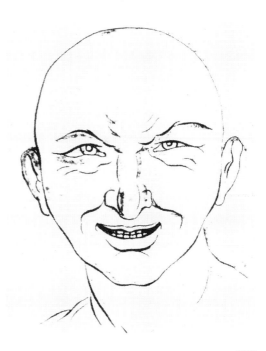

158 Francisco de Paula Martì Mora, *Risa* (The laugh), engraving from Fermin Eduardo Zeglirscosac, *Ensayo sobre el origen y naturaleza de las pasiones* (Madrid, 1800).

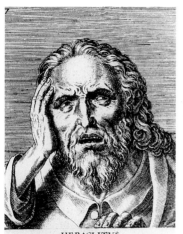

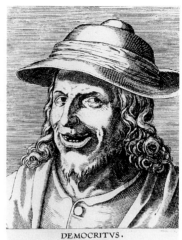

HERACLITVS.

Flens HERACLITVS miseræ ludibria vitæ
Conspicit, atq hominum perdolet ysq vicem.

DEMOCRITVS.

DEMOCRITVS quidquid nugali cernit et audit
In mundo, vanum ridiculumq putat.

159 Philips Galle, *Heraclitus*, engraving from the series *Variae comarum et barbarum formae*, c. 1600.

160 Philips Galle, *Democritus*, engraving from the series *Variae comarum et barbarum formae*.

during the sixteenth and seventeenth centuries (illus. 159–60)[25] but more particularly during the eighteenth century when self-portraits 'in the style of Democritus' or 'Heraclitus' abounded.[26] Each century has re-updated this symbolic couple and it is essential that we examine how Goya used them.

One quotation, taken from a multitude of possible examples, illustrates the permanence of the motif, at the same time as it throws light on the cultural environment in which Goya was able to develop his own ideas:

At this miserable century
Heraclitus fittingly wept
While Democritus, prudently,
At this very same century mocked.
Two contrary effects produced
By the same cause in two different men
Of which one wept and the other guffawed
At the sight of the same events

And thus in our present century
Reasons to weep there are many
As are the reasons to laugh.[27]

There are in the subject-matter (and vocabulary) of this poem, despite its somewhat clumsy form, several significant factors worth highlighting. The first is the fact that this time the object

280

of the tears and laughter is not simply 'the world', as tradition would have it be, nor is it 'human life', as postulated in later developments,[28] but it is something that belongs to both, without actually being either one or the other. The object of the tears and laughter is *'the century'*, a complex notion, that is superimposed, as a temporality whose surrounding sacred aura has been destroyed, on the 'world' as a profane space. It is therefore 'the century' and all that that involves, which forms the object of the sadness and derision of the philosophers. A second factor is the symbol of 'prudence' that the verses attribute to Democritus. The presence of this symbol, whose significance to the moral philosophy of the Golden Age does not need further elaboration here,[29] is highly significant in more than one respect. In the first place, it give Democritus a certain advantage over Heraclitus, who, in this poem, has no particular symbol. The Spanish author was therefore able to identify with a tradition that wanted to see in the laughing Democritus's attitude, the wisest option (in this instance, the most 'prudent' one). It was Montaigne who provided the exemplary wording for this option; he was even able to invert the usual order in which the story of the two philosophers was told:

> Democritus and Heraclitus were two philosophers, the first of whom, finding the human condition vain and ridiculous, only ever went out in public with a mocking and laughing face; Heraclitus, feeling pity and compassion for this same condition of ours, wore a face that was continually sad, and eyes that were full of tears (. . .).

> I prefer the first humour, not because it is more pleasing to laugh than to cry, but because it is more disdainful, and because it condemns us more than the other.[30]

A second connotation of 'prudence', a quality with which Democritus is invested in the Spanish text quoted above, can only be understood against the backdrop of the laughing philosopher's original story. This character was initially suspected, or so the sources tell us, of being quite the opposite of a wise man. Democritus's reputed madness, which was manifested by his incessant and insane laughter, was the theme of the famous 'Romance of Hippocrates', in which the great doctor, urgently summoned by the Abderites, eventually diagnosed the laughing person as having an 'excess of black bile' – and therefore 'melancholia' – thus inspiring his 'superlative philosophy' (his *hiperphilosopheîn*).[31] In the light of this, laughter is at one and the same time both the symptom and the remedy of melancholia. Anti-depressant therapy, achieved through 'good humour', was a motif known to ancient medicine, and was considered to be a way of physiologically purging black humour.[32] Melancholic laughter is, however, controlled laughter, and therefore a long way from the vital and cosmic outbursts to be found, for example, in Gargantua's guffaws. The differences are significant and soon codified. Prospero Aldoriso, in his *Gelotoscopia* published in Naples in 1611, had already produced a grid for reading the different forms of laughter, based on varying vocal tones. Father Mersenne, in his book *Harmonie Universelle* (1636), subsequently developed the motif of laughter as an outer manifestation of the real 'complexion'. He refers to the work done by Aldoriso, according to which different vowels correspond to each of the humours:

> *A* indicates humidity and the ease with which the tongue opens, and consequently proves that one is sanguine, but *E*, *O*, and *I* demonstrate dryness, those who form these letters while laughing reveal a temperament that is cold and dry; just as the vowel *U* denotes that one is cold and humid; the vowels *I* and *O* show that one is hot, dry and bilious; *E* denotes melancholy, and *U* denotes phlegm.[33]

This interpretation, based on the theory of the humours, survived until the Age of Enlightenment. It is mentioned, though in a slightly modified form, in the most important eighteenth-century book to be written on laughter, Louis Poinsinet de Sivry's *Traité des causes physiques et morales du rire* (Amsterdam, 1768) but only so that the author could berate 'a certain book' that 'distinguished the temperaments (sic) of men by the way they laughed. The *hi-hi-hi* according to this burlesque treatise, identify the melancholic person; the *he-he-he*, the phlegmatic; the *ho-ho-ho*, the sanguine.'[34] And he goes on to say, '[the author of the book] fails to mention the laughter of fools: it would seem that either he applied it to all these categories of laughter, or that he had never analysed his own properly.'[35] Goya, however, was not intimidated by the process of disenchantment to which the ancient physiology of laughter was subjected in his own time, preferring to use the theory of correspondences and analogies to highlight the atra-biliousness of his laughter. This could never be mistaken for the sanguine *ho-ho-ho* of Gargantua, who marked the essential triumph of the carnivalesque principle that periodically renews the world.[36] Goya's laughter is shown, through unmistakable visual signs – the narrow slit of the mouth, the hunched shoulders, the black clothes and hat (illus. 157) – to be a 'melancholic laugh' sounding like an incessant *he-he-he* that floats above the Carnival as though to establish itself in the world, as though to find a permanent country of its choice.

Seen in this light, Goya's double authorial projection (illus. 100, 157) is shown to be the product of a profound reflection born from a rich tradition. By capturing the complementary nature of the two philosophical attitudes – laughter and tears – Rabelais had already postulated the existence of a 'heraclis-ing Democritus and a democrising Heraclitus'.[37] Just as Heraclitus and Democritus are in the final analysis but two facets of the same person, so the author of *Los Caprichos* has two faces. The sad mask is external, while laughter is internal. And yet the similarities do not conceal the differences, for the (inner) laughing-person-portrait is both the product of a process of abstraction and of an allegorization of the fron-tispiece-portrait. Viewed against the backdrop of conceptist tradition, the triumph of laughter over tears is justified by the fact that it is in dark laughter that disenchantment is fully expressed. Antonio Lopez de Vega, in his philosophical dia-logue *Heraclito y Democrito de nuestro siglo* (Madrid, 1641), therefore declared, 'By giving victory to the Laughter of Democritus, I follow the opinion of the best authors, Ancient as well as Modern. I make him Victorious because he is the most Disenchanted (*el más Desengañado*) and I put all truths in his mouth.'[38] In Quevedo's *El mundo por dentro* (1627), the ven-erable old man, much reduced and in rags, who shows the narrator the world 'from the inside' and 'such as it is', is, as has been repeatedly stressed, a hypostasis of the Abderite Democritus,[39] and, at the same time, as he himself admits, between toothless guffaws (*carcajadas sin dientes*), the incarna-tion of the ancient principle of Disenchantment:

> My clothes indicate that I am an honest man, but their impoverished and ragged state shows that I am also a

161 Goya, *Old Man on a Swing*, 1824–8, black chalk on paper.

friend to truths that must be spoken at all costs. I am Disenchantment and the tears in my clothes are the symbols of the great love the world bears me, and the bruises you see on my face come from the blows I receive instead of welcomes, for everyone claims to want to see Disenchantment, but once this happens, it is despair, curses and disbelief that are born in the minds of men.[40]

Traces of this eloquent portrait of Quevedo's can be seen in what we believe to be one of the very last self-portraits produced by Goya, painted in exile, towards the end of his life. The *Old Man on a Swing* from the 'Bordeaux Sketchbook' (illus. 161), displays both the unmistakable Goya-type smile (illus.

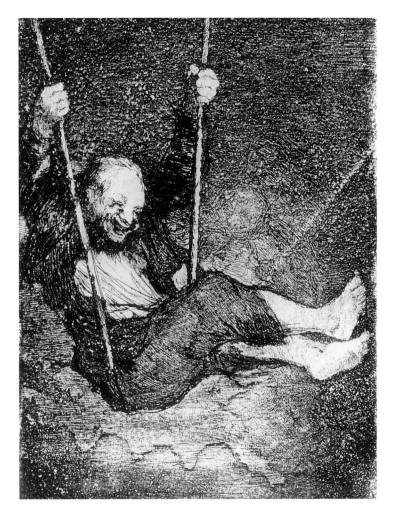

162 Goya, *Old Man on a Swing*, 1825–7, etching and aquatint.

35, 155, 157) and the rags of a last 'Master Disenchantment'.

This was not the first time that Goya tackled the theme of the swing, as beloved of eighteenth-century French art. He also used it in that first happy period in his career when he was producing cartoons for the Royal Tapestry Factory.[41] And yet this was the first time that Goya gave the theme autobiographical connotations that transcended the rococo triteness of rural flirtations in order to once again re-establish his close ties to a particular baroque sensitivity. In the most important treatise on the significance of games to come down to us from seventeenth-century Spain, written by Rodrigo Caro, the habit of swinging, in relation to the regular festivals of rebirth, was considered to be a metaphor for a perpetual 'oscillation' between heaven and earth, and also an allegory of the vanity of the things of this world: 'Swings were invented so that through their instability we might contemplate the fickleness of things human that go up and rise, so that, a moment later they can come down swiftly and without fail.'[42] The fact that Goya undertook an autobiographical interpretation based on this concept of the symbolic motif of the swing was brilliantly captured in Pierre Gassier's commentary: 'The rope is attached to nothing and the old man is swinging above nothing, as though projected into oblivion, without beginning and without end.'[43]

In a later print, not produced until after the artist's death (illus. 162), the swing's trajectory is projected against a dark sky populated by fantastic spirits. Below is an indeterminate shape, the outline maybe of a continent seen from the sky. The changes made to the gaze and the movement are interesting. In the drawing (illus. 161), the ropes cross the white page diagonally and impart a strong dynamism to the whole image that presents us with an 'interval', as brief as the blink of an eye. The disappearance of this hilarious old man beyond the boundaries of the representation is depicted as imminent. In the print, the swing's momentum is relatively moderate, and the old man, clutching the ropes that hang from nowhere, directs his gaze (and his smile) towards the world stretched out at his feet. In the drawing, on the other hand, it is we who are being looked at, we who are being laughed at.

The laughter, despite this slight but significant change of direction, is the same. It is the atrabilious *he-he-he* traditionally attributed to Democritus. This was the last time that Goya was to tackle it. And in so doing, he – maybe – also discovered the importance of swinging as a magical rite[44] or at least its symbolic importance. The perpetual oscillation between high and low, between here and there, between heaven and earth, transforms the children's game of swinging into a symbol of existence in general and of Goya's existence in particular. In this way the ludic investment of this last self-portrait is not only reminiscent of Democritus, but also of his twin, Heraclitus, for whom the game represented the underlying structure of the world, with the eternal child as it emblem.

A constant capacity to depict opposites dialoguing is thereby brought into play. The old man – but is he not rather, at least in the drawing, an indeterminate and asexual character?[45]

– swings between being and non-being. He flies, he plays 'like a crafty kid of a hundred', as an ancient author could quite well have described him.[46] *Puer senex* or *puer senilis*, the game to him is above all else serious and, by definition, funny.[47] It is difficult to judge whether the grimace he hurls at the world does not also hold a tear mingled with that last burst of laughter that shakes him, before he leaves us, dying of laughter.

Appendix: Publicity Notice from the *Diario de Madrid*, 6 February 1799

A collection of Prints of Capricious Subjects, Invented and Etched by Don Francisco Goya. Since the artist is convinced that the censure of human errors and vices (though they may seem to be the province of Eloquence and Poetry) may also be the object of Painting, he has chosen as subjects adequate for his work, from the multitude of follies and blunders common in every civil society, as well as from the vulgar prejudices and lies authorised by custom, ignorance or interest, those that he has thought most suitable matter for ridicule as well as for exercising the artificer's fancy.

Since the majority of the objects represented in this work are ideal, it may not be too daring to expect that their defects will perhaps meet with forgiveness on the part of the connoisseurs as they will realize that the artist has neither followed the examples of others, nor been able to copy from nature. And if imitating Nature is as difficult as it is admirable when one succeeds in doing so, some esteem must be shown toward him who, holding aloof from her, has had to put before the eyes forms and attitudes that so far have existed only in the human mind, obscured and confused by lack of illustration, or excited by the unruliness of passions.

One would be assuming too much ignorance of the fine arts, if one were to warn the public that in none of the compositions which form this series has the artist had in mind any one individual, in order to ridicule particular defects. For truly, to say so would mean narrowing overmuch the boundaries of talent, and mistaking the methods used by the arts of imitation in producing perfect works.

Painting (like Poetry) chooses from the universal what it considers suitable to its own ends: it reunites in a single fantastic personage circumstances and characteristics that nature has divided among many. From such a combination, ingeniously arranged, results the kind of successful imitation for which a good artificer deserves the title of inventor and not that of servile copyist.

TRANSLATED BY J. LOPEZ-REY, 1953

288

References

PREFACE AND ACKNOWLEDGEMENTS

1 M. Bakhtin, PhD thesis (in Russian), 1940 (English trans.: *Rabelais and his World* [Cambridge, MA, 1968]). Quotations are taken from the French translation *L'oeuvre de François Rabelais et la culture populaire au moyen âge et sous la Renaissance* (Paris, 1970).
2 M. Bakhtin, *Problems of Dostoevsky's Poetics* (1929; Ann Arbor, 1973).
3 Bakhtin, *L'oeuvre de François Rabelais*, p. 43.
4 There is no single work on this theme, but we would point to the exemplary study by T. Castle, *Masquerade and Civilisation: The Carnivalesque in Eighteenth-Century English Culture and Fiction* (London, 1986). Other books will be quoted in the course of this book.

1 THE TURN OF THE CENTURY AS A SYMBOLIC FORM

1 Madame de Staël, *Corinne ou l'Italie* (1807; Paris, 1985), p. 239.
2 *Ibid.*, pp. 239–40.
3 All our quotations have been taken from J. W. Goethe, *Italienische Reise*, ed. A. Beyer and N. Miller (Munich, 1992), p. 572. The Roman Carnival episode was originally the subject of a separate publication (*Das Römische Karneval* [Berlin, 1789]). We should point out that Goethe's view illustrates only one aspect, albeit an extremely significant one, of a process subjecting the Carnival and the carnivalesque to a hermeneutic approach spanning the eighteenth century. See also the following essential works: Du Tilliot, *Mémoires pour servir à l'histoire de la Fête des Fous* (Lausanne and Geneva, 1741); K. F. Flögel, *Geschichte des Grotesk-Komischen* (1788; reprinted as Fr. W. Ebeling, *Flögels Geschichte des Grotesk-Komischen* [Leipzig, 1862]). See also E. Nährlich-Slatewa, 'Das groteske Leben und seine edle Einfassung. "Das Römische Karneval" Goethes und das Karnevalkonzept von Michail M. Bachtin', *Goethe-Jahrbuch*, 106 (1989), pp. 181–202; H. A. Glaser, 'Karneval und Karnevalstheorien – anlässich Goethes *Das römische Karneval*' in K. Manger (ed.), *Italienbeziehungen des klassischen Weimar* (Tübingen, 1997), pp. 101–12.
4 Goethe, *Italienische Reise*, p. 607.
5 See F. Clementi, *Il Carnevale romano nelle cronache contemporanee*, vol. II (Città di Castello, 1938), pp. 223–4; A. Ademolo, *Il carnevale di Roma nei secoli XVII e XVIII* (Rome, 1883), pp. 126–33.
6 Madame de Staël, *Corinne*, pp. 240–41.
7 A. van Gennep, *Les Rites de passage* (Paris, 1909; English trans.: M. B. Vizedom and G. L. Caffe, *The Rites of Passage* [Chicago, 1960]).
8 J. Caro Baroja, *El Carnaval (Analisis historico-cultural)* (1965; Madrid, 1979).
9 C. Merlo, 'I nomi romanzi del carnevale' (1911), reproduced in *Studi Glottologici di Clemente Merlo* (Pisa, 1934), pp. 97–137.
10 H. Bénichou, *Fêtes et calendriers: Les Rhythmes du temps* (Paris, 1992), pp. 193–203; C. Gaignebet and M.-C. Florentin, *Le Carnaval: Essai de mythologie populaire* (Paris, 1974), pp. 18–23.
11 J. G. Frazer, *The Golden Bough* (1923; New York, 1940); Caro Baroja, *El Carnaval*, pp. 161–78, 298–304.

12 M. Grinberg and S. Kinser, 'Les Combats de Carnaval et de Carême: Trajets d'une métaphore', *Annales: Economies, Sociétés, Civilisations*, 38 (January–February 1983), pp. 65–98; N. Schindler, 'Karneval, Kirche und die verkehrte Welt: Zur Funktion der Lachkultur im 16. Jahrhundert', *Jahrbuch für Volkskunde*, n.s. 7 (1984), pp. 9–57; G. Ciappelli, *Carnevale e Quaresma: Comportamenti sociali e cultura a Firenze nel Rinascimento* (Rome, 1997). The issue has inspired lengthy debates among German anthropologists. An excellent summary of these can be found in W. Mezger, *Narrenidee und Fastnachtbrauch* (Konstanz, 1989), pp. 9–30.

13 V. W. Turner, *The Ritual Process: Structure and Anti-Structure* (Chicago, 1966), pp. 94–130.

14 The indispensable introduction to the history of this notion is J. Delumeau, *La Peur en Occident (XIVᵉ–XVIIIᵉ siècles)* (Paris, 1978).

15 Goethe, *Italienische Reise*, p. 572.

16 Madame de Staël, *Corinne*, pp. 244–5.

17 Goethe, *Italienische Reise*, p. 578. (For women disguised as men, see p. 581).

18 Madame de Staël, *Corinne*, pp. 241–2.

19 Refer especially to G. Cocchiara, *Il Mondo alla rovescia* (1963; Turin, 1981); R. Chartier and D. Julia, 'Le Monde à l'envers', *L'Arc*, 65 (1976), pp. 43–53; D. Kunzle, 'World Upside Down: The Iconography of a European Broadsheet Type', in B. B. Babcock, ed., *The Reversible World: Symbolic Inversion in Art and Society* (Ithaca and London, 1978), pp. 39–96; P. Wescher, 'Die verkehrte Welt im Bild. Ihre Geschichte und Bedeutung' in *Gesammelte Aufsätze zur Kunst* (Cologne and Vienna, 1979), pp. 3–33; F. Tristan and M. Lever, *Le Monde à l'envers* (Paris, 1980); C. A. Mihailescu, 'Le Monde renversé', in E. Kushner and P. Chavy, *Histoire comparée des littératures de langues européennes, Vol. 4, Crises et essors nouveaux (1560–1610)* (The Hague and Philadelphia, forthcoming).

20 K. Thomas, 'Work and Leisure in Pre-Industrial Society', *Past and Present*, 29 (December 1964), pp. 53–4; N. Zemon Davis, *Society and Culture in Early Modern France: Eight Essays* (Stanford, 1975), chap. 4.

21 E. Le Roy Ladurie, *Le Carnaval des Romans: De la Chandeleur au mercredi des Cendres 1579–1580* (Paris, 1979).

22 See P. Weidkuhn, 'Fastnacht-Revolte-Revolution', *Zeitschrift für Religions- und Geistesgeschichte*, XXI (1969), pp. 289–306; B. Scribner, 'Reformation, Carnival and World Turned Upside-down', *Social History*, 3 (January 1978), pp. 303–29; M. Egli, 'Mundus inversus: Das Thema der "verkehrten Welt" in den reformationszeitlichen Einblattdrucken und Flugblättern'', *Georges-Bloch-Jahrbuch des Kunstgeschichtlichen Seminars der Universität Zürich*, 4 (1997), pp. 41–59.

23 Y.-M. Bercé, *Fête et révolte: Des mentalités populaires du XVIᵉ au XVIIIᵉ siècle* (1976; Paris, 1994), p. 55ff.

24 A. de Baecque, *Le Corps de l'histoire: Métaphores et politique (1770–1800)* (Paris, 1993), pp. 195–225; A. de Baecque, *La Caricature révolutionnaire* (Paris, 1988); A. Duprat, *Le Roi décapité: Essai sur les imaginaires politiques* (Paris, 1992), pp. 75–88.

25 Bakhtin, *L'oeuvre de François Rabelais*, p. 241.

26 See K. Herding, 'Kunst und Revolution', in R. Reichardt, ed., *Die Französische Revolution* (Fribourg, 1988), pp. 200–40; K. Herding, *Im Zeichen der Aufklärung: Studien zur Moderne* (Frankfurt am Main, 1988), pp. 95–126.

27 On this subject, see N. Hertz, *The End of the Line: Essays on Psychoanalytical Sublime* (New York, 1985), pp. 161–215; D. Outram, *The Body and the French Revolution* (New Haven and London, 1989), pp. 110–23; D. Arasse, *La Guillotine et l'imaginaire de la Terreur* (Paris, 1987); D. Bindman, *The Shadow of the Guillotine* (London, 1989).

28 Madame de Staël, *Corinne*, p. 242.

29 A. Rey, *'Révolution': Histoire d'un mot* (Paris, 1989), esp. pp. 21–53.

30 A. Furetière, *Dictionnaire Universel* (The Hague and Rotterdam, 1690), under 'Révolution'.

31 R. Koselleck, 'Der neuzeitliche Revolutionsbegriff als geschichtliche Kategorie', *Studium Generale,* 22 (1969), pp. 825–38; R. Reichardt and H.-J. Lüsebrink, 'Révolution à la fin du 18e siècle. Pour une relecture d'un concept-clé du siècle des Lumières', in *Mots*, 16 (1988), pp. 35–68.

32 P.-H. Th. d'Holbach, *Système de la nature*, vol. II, chap. II (1770; Hildesheim, 1966), p. 39ff.

33 *Ibid.*, vol. I, chap. IV, pp. 61–2.

34 J.-J. Rousseau, *Emile ou de l'éducation*, book III (1762; Paris, 1966), p. 252.

35 W. Krauss, 'Der Jahrhundertbegriff im 18. Jahrhundert', *in idem, Studien zur deutschen und französischen Aufklärung* (Berlin, 1963), pp. 9–40; J. Schlobach, 'Fin de siècle et philosophie de l'histoire au siècle des Lumières', in H. Chudak, ed., *Les Fins de siècle dans les littératures européennes* (Warsaw, 1996), pp. 11–19; W. Lepenies, *Das Ende der Naturgeschichte* (Frankfurt am Main, 1978), pp. 9–15; R. Koselleck, 'Das achtzehnte Jahrhundert als Beginn der Neuzeit', in R. Herzog and R. Koselleck, *Epochenschwelle und Epochenbewusstsein* (= Poetik und Hermeneutik XII) (Munich, 1987), pp. 269–82. In the same volume, see also the studies by Manfred Frank, Reinhard Herzog, Niklas Luhmann and Karlheinz Stierle.

36 Abbé du Bos, *Réflexions critiques sur la poésie et sur la peinture* (1719; Paris, 1993), p. 213.

37 B. Baczko, 'Le Temps ouvre un nouveau livre à l'histoire: L'Utopie et le calendrier révolutionnaire', in *Pour une histoire qualitative: Etudes offertes à Sven Stelling-Michaud* (Geneva, 1975), pp. 179–94; S. Bianchi, *La Révolution culturelle de l'an II* (Paris, 1982), pp. 198–235; M. Meinzer, 'Der französische Revolutionskalender und die "Neue Zeit"', in R. Koselleck and R. Reichardt, eds, *Die französische Revolution als Bruch des gesellschaftlichen Bewusstseins* (Munich, 1988), p. 23ff. (In the same volume, see also pp. 61–7.)

38 M. Ozouf, *La Fête révolutionnaire 1789–1799* (Paris, 1976).

39 De Baecque, *Le Corps de l'histoire*, pp. 303–41, contains the best synopsis of this notion. See also L. Hunt, *Politics, Culture and Class in the French Revolution* (Berkeley, Los Angeles and London, 1984), pp. 53–83.

40 Marat in *L'Ami du peuple*, 21 December 1789 (quoted in De Baecque, *Le Corps de l'histoire*, p. 330).

41 De Baecque, *Le Corps de l'histoire*, p. 330.

42 See Hunt, *Politics, Culture and Class*, p. 82. For an excellent overview of this problem, see D. Roche, *La Culture des apparences* (Paris, 1989).

43 See O. Elyada, 'La Presse populaire parisienne et le temps de Carnaval: 1788–1791', in M. Vovelle, ed., *L'Image de la Revolution française*, vol. I (Paris, Oxford and New York, 1989), pp. 108–17.

44 'Le Carnaval jacobite ou bal, banquet et mascarade patriotique' (1790), in De Baecque, *Le Corps de l'histoire*, p. 336.

45 *Le Carnaval politique de 1790 ou l'exil de Mardi gras à l'Assemblée nationale* (1790), quoted in De Baecque, *Le Corps de l'histoire*, p. 335.

46 *L'Ombre de Mardi gras, ou les mascarades de la cour réunies à celles du corps législatif, de la municipalité et de quelques femmes titrées* (1791), in De Baecque, *Le Corps de l'histoire*, p. 338.

2 THE CARNIVAL IS DEAD, LONG LIVE THE CARNIVAL!

1 See esp. N. Glendinning, 'Some Versions of Carnival: Goya and Alas', in N. Glendinning, ed., *Studies in Modern Spanish Literature and Art Presented*

to Helen F. Grant (London, 1972), pp. 65–78; *idem*, 'La problemática histórica de los Disparates y su interpretación carnavalesca', in *Francisco de Goya grabador: Instantáneas* (Madrid, 1992), pp. 11–32; *idem*, 'Recuerdos y angustias en las pinturas de Goya, 1793–1794', in *Goya*, exh. cat. (Seville, 1992), p. 141ff.; T. Lorenzo de Márquez, 'Tradiciones carnavalescas en el lenguaje icónico de Goya', in *Goya y el espíritu de la ilustración*, exh. cat. (Madrid, 1989), pp. 99–110. For Goya and popular culture, see V. Bozal, *Imagen de Goya* (Barcelona, 1983); J. Held, 'Goyas Bildwelt zwischen bürgerlicher Aufklärung und Volkskultur', *Idea*, IV (1985), pp. 107–31.

2 We should mention here the pioneering role played by the exhibition catalogue *Goya: Das Zeitalter der Revolutionen 1789–1830* (Hamburg, 1981), edited by W. Hofmann.

3 The most thorough texts we followed, but only so far, are J. A. Tomlinson, *Goya in the Twilight of Enlightenment* (New Haven and London, 1992), pp. 181–5; J. Tomlinson, *Francisco Goya y Lucientes, 1746–1828* (London, 1994), pp. 233–4.

4 The catalogue by P. Gassier and J. Wilson-Bareau, *Vie et oeuvre de Francisco Goya* (Fribourg, 1970), mentions (under no. 970) a possible dating between 1812 and 1819.

5 Marques de Valmar, *Cuadros selectos de la Real Academia de Bellas Artes de San Fernando* (Madrid, 1885); E. Pardo Canalis, 'Una carta de Mesonero Romanos y un articulo del Marques de Valmar sobre "El Entierro de la Sardina"', *Goya*, 252 (1996), pp. 324–5; C. Buezo, *El Carnaval y otras procesiones burlescas del viejo Madrid* (Madrid, 1992), pp. 77–90.

6 J. Caro Baroja, *El Carnaval (Analisis historico-cultural)* (1965; Madrid, 1979), p. 117.

7 *Ibid.*, pp. 117–19.

8 See, for example, J. Blanco White's account, *Cartas de España* (1822; Madrid, 1986), pp. 209–12.

9 See X. de Salas, 'Precisiones sobre pinturas de Goya: *El Entierro de la Sardina*, la serie de obras de Gabinete de 1783–1784 y otras notas', *Archivo Español de Arte*, 41 (1968), pp. 1–16.

10 See A. van Genepp, *Manuel de folklore français contemporain*. Vol III: *Les Cérémonies périodiques et saisonnières, 1. Carnaval-Carême-Pâques* (Paris, 1947), pp. 933–9.

11 R. de Mesonero Romanos, 'El Entierro de la Sardina' (1839), in *Escenas y tipos matritenses* (Madrid, 1993), pp. 395–403.

12 See Pardo Canalis, 'Una carta de Mesonero Romanos', p. 324.

13 F. Bertran, 'Nona carta pastoral sobre los desordenes del Carnaval', in *Coleccion de las cartas pastorales y edictos del Excmo: Señor Don Felipe Bertran*, vol. I (Madrid, 1783), p. 408.

14 *Ibid.*, p. 410.

15 It is interesting to note that, apart from Goya's undertaking, the most noteworthy attempts at representing crowds in paintings are to be found in works of art that have revolution as their theme. On this subject, refer to W. Kemp, 'The Theater of Revolution: A New Interpretation of Jacques-Louis David's *Tennis Court Oath*', in N. Bryson, M. A. Holly and K. Moxey, eds, *Images, Visual and Culture. Interpretations* (Hanover and London, 1994), pp. 202–27.

16 We should not forget that the *borrón* as a concept had enjoyed a long tradition in both the technical and critical language of Spanish painting. See M. Socrate, 'Borrón e pittura "di macchia" nella cultura letteraria del Siglo de Oro', in *idem, Studi di letteratura spagnuola: Facoltà di magistero: Università di Roma* (Rome, 1966), pp. 25–70. The term can be found in inventories drawn up in the early nineteenth century (we are of course thinking of the famous '*Catorce Borrones en tabla . . .*' in several Madrid collections).

17 See, recently, J. Wilson-Bareau, in J. Wilson-Bareau and M. B. Mena
    Marques, eds, *Goya: El Capricho y la invencion: Cuadros de gabinete, bocetos y
    miniaturas* (Madrid, London and Chicago, 1994), p. 154; R. Lopez Torrijos,
    'Goya y la fabula burlesca', *Boletin del Museo del Prado*, 1997, pp. 21–8.
18 Apollodorus, *Bibliotheca*, 2, 6, 3; Diodorus of Sicily, *Bibliotheca*, IV. 31, 6–8.
19 For information on this subject, see H. Kenner, *Das Phänomen der
    verkehrten Welt in der griechisch-römischen Antike* (Klagenfurt and Bonn,
    1979), pp. 134–41.
20 M. J. Friedländer and J. Rosenberg, *The Paintings of Lucas Cranach* (New
    York, 1978), nos 272–5.
21 J. Rosenberg, *Die Zeichnungen Lucas Cranachs des Älteren* (Berlin, 1960), no.
    57.
22 For the 'women on top' *topos*, see N. Zemon Davis, *Society and Culture in
    Early Modern France: Eight Essays* (Stanford, 1975), chap. 5.
23 Abbé Coyer, *L'Année merveilleuse ou les Hommes-femmes: Bagatelles morales*
    (Paris, 1754), pp. 1–2. For details, see P. Perrot, *Le Travail des apparences: Le
    Corps féminin, XVIII–XIXe siècles* (Paris, 1984), pp. 33–60; C. Jacot Grapa,
    L'Homme dissonant au XVIIIe siècle, *Studies on Voltaire* 354 (Oxford, 1997),
    pp. 303–51. For the broader picture, see M. Garber, *Vested Interests: Cross-
    Dressing & Cultural Anxiety* (New York and London, 1992); R. Haidt,
    *Embodying Enlightenment. Knowing the Body in Eighteenth-Century Spanish
    Literature and Culture* (New York, 1998).
24 See P. Gassier, *Les Dessins de Goya: Les Albums* (Fribourg, 1973), pp.
    223–384. The drawing discussed here can be found under cat. nos 21, 38
    and 64.
25 J. López-Rey, *A Cycle of Goya's Drawings* (London, 1956), p. 90.
26 M. Bakhtin, *L'oeuvre de François Rabelais*, p. 326ff.; Caro Baroja, *El Carnaval*,
    p. 110ff.
27 Gassier, *Les Dessins de Goya*, p. 567.
28 J. W. Goethe, *Italienische Reise* (Munich, 1992), pp. 593–4.
29 See F. Delpech, 'La Patraña del Hombre preñado: Algunas versiones
    hispanicas', *Nueva Revista de Filologia Hispanica*, 2 (1985–6), pp. 548–98.
30 R. Zapperi, *L'Homme enceint: L'Homme, la femme et le pouvoir* (Paris, 1983).
31 See R. Stephan-Maaser, *Mythos und Lebenswelt: Studien zum 'Trunkenden
    Silen' von Peter Paul Rubens* (Münster and Hamburg, 1993); S. Alpers, *The
    Making of Rubens* (New Haven and London, 1996), p. 110.
32 Alpers, *The Making of Rubens*, p. 136.
33 Zapperi, *L'Homme enceint*, pp. 162–71. See also J. A. Brundage, 'Let Me
    Count the Ways: Canonists and Theologians Contemplate Coital
    Positions', *Journal of Medieval History*, 10 (1984), pp. 81–93.
34 T. Sánchez, *De sancto matrimonio sacramento*, IX, XIV, 1, in Zapperi, *L'Homme
    enceint*, p. 171.
35 See J. Sawday, *The Body Emblazoned: Dissection and the Human Body in
    Renaissance Culture* (London and New York, 1995); A. Carlino, '"Knowe
    thyself": Anatomical Figures in Early Modern Europe', *Res: Anthropology
    and Aesthetics*, 27 (1995), pp. 51–70.
36 Gassier, *Les Dessins de Goya*, p. 130.
37 L. S. Mercier, *Le Tableau de Paris* (Paris, 1781), quoted in Perrot, *Le Travail
    des apparences*, p. 86.
38 Coyer, *L'Année merveilleuse ou les Hommes-femmes*, p. 72, quoted in Jacot
    Grapa, *L'Homme dissonant*, p. 331.
39 This is suggested by its similarity to drawing E. 23 (Musée du Louvre,
    Paris), which depicts a mother showing two women a child-freak (see
    Gassier, *Les Dessins de Goya*, p. 214).
40 What we have here is a real *topos*, repeated in countless texts, which
    alludes to the fact that one of the most remarkable women thinkers of the
    eighteenth century was called Mme Barbapiccola.

41 See, more recently, A. E. Pérez Sánchez, in *idem* and N. Spinosa, eds, *Ribera: 1591–1652* (Madrid, 1992), pp. 228–30 ; B. Wind, *A Foul and Pestilent Congregation: Images of 'Freaks' in Baroque Art* (Aldershot and Brookfield, 1997), pp. 49–65.

42 L. Konecny, 'Una pintura de Juan Sánchez Cotán, emblematizada por Sebastian de Covarrubias', in *Actas del I Simposio Internacional de Emblematica, Teruel, 1 y 2 de Octubre de 1991* (Teruel, 1994), pp. 823–34.

43 A. de Sandoval, *Un tratado sobre la esclavitud (De instauranda Aethiopum salute, 1647)* (Madrid, 1987), p. 209.

44 We were unable to consult the work of J. Rof Carvallo (*Enigmas de la mujer barbuda de Ribera* [Madrid, 1975]), who, according to C. Felton and W. B. Jordan, *Jusepe de Ribera, lo Spagnoletto, 1591–1652* (Fort Worth, 1982), p. 131, studied this idea.

45 T. Lorenzo de Márquez had already drawn attention to this (*Goya y el espíritu de la Ilustración*, pp. 379–81**).**

46 See below, pp. 85ff.

47 R. Lionetti, *Latte di Padre: Vitalità, contesti, livelli di lettura di un motivo folklorico* (Brescia, 1984), p. 55ff. See also H. Baumann, *Das doppelte Geschlecht: Ethnologische Studien zur Bisexualität in Ritus und Mythos* (Berlin, 1955); S. Breton, *La Mascarade des sexes: Fétichisme, inversion et travestissement rituels* (Paris, 1989); M. Bettini, ed., *Maschile/Femminile. Genere e ruoli nelle culture antiche* (Rome and Bari, 1993).

48 M. Horkheimer and T. W. Adorno, *Dialektik der Aufklärung: Philosophische Fragmente* (1944; Frankfurt am Main, 1995), pp. 262–71 (English trans.: *Dialectic of Enlightenment*, trans. John Cumming [London, 1997], p. 245ff).

49 See P. Gassier, *Les Dessins de Goya*, vol. II (Fribourg, 1975), pp. 489–97.

50 It was J. López-Rey who identified this character as a student; see *Goya's Caprichos: Beauty, Reason, & Caricature*, vol. I (1953; Westport, CT, 1970), p. 71.

51 López-Rey, *Goya's Caprichos*, pp. 57–72.

52 F. Nordström, *Goya, Saturn and Melancholy* (Stockholm, 1962), pp. 76–94.

53 R. Andioc, 'Goya y el temperamento currutáquico', *Bulletin of Hispanic Studies*, LXVII (January 1991), pp. 67–89.

54 Document published in V. de Sambricio, *Tapices de Goya* (Madrid, 1946), nos 62–4.

55 Nordström, *Goya, Saturn and Melancholy*, p. 37.

56 J. A. Tomlinson, *Francisco Goya: The Tapestry Cartoons and Early Career at the Court of Madrid* (New York, 1989), pp. 101–2.

57 G. B. Della Porta, *Della Fisionomia dell'uomo* (1610; Parma, 1988), p. 145; Morel d'Arleux, *Dissertation sur un traité de Charles Le Brun concernant les rapports de la physiognomie humaine avec celle des animaux* (Paris, 1806). On this subject, see T. Kirchner, 'Physiognomonie als Zeichen: Die Rezeption von Charles Le Bruns Mensch-Tier-Vergleich um 1800', in G. Gersmann and H. Kohle, *Frankreich 1800* (Stuttgart, 1990), pp. 34–48; J. Montagu, *The Expression of the Passions: The Origin and Influence of Charles Le Brun's Conférence sur l'expression générale et particulière* (New Haven and London, 1994), pp. 18–30. For an overview, see J. Baltrusaitis, *Aberrations* (Paris, 1957), pp. 7–46; O. Baur, 'Der Mensch-Tier-Vergleich und die Mensch-Tier-Karikatur: Eine ikonographische Studie zur bildenden Kunst des neunzehnten Jahrhunderts' (PhD thesis, Cologne, 1973).

58 On this subject, see the excellent study by H. Grabes, *Speculum, Mirror and Looking-Glass* (Tübingen, 1973), esp. pp. 119–69.

59 G. B. Della Porta, *Della Magia naturale* (1558; Naples, 1687), IV, 14, pp. 473–4.

60 J. C. Lavater, *Physiognomische Fragmente, zur Beförderung der Menschenkenntnis und Menschenliebe*, 4 vols (Leipzig and Winterthur, 1775–8). Goya probably consulted J. C. Lavater, *Essai sur la physiognomie*, 3

vols (The Hague, 1781–6). In the third volume of the French edition, on p. 30ff., Lavater writes about animal physiognomy. For physiognomical studies in Spain, see J. Caro Baroja, *Historia de la Fisionomica: El Rostro y el Carácter* (Madrid, 1988).

61 There is a second ramification to the confrontation between 'student' and frog that derives from the former's amphibious nature. Amphibiousness was a sign of 'double nature' and therefore of bisexuality. Goya's drawings that follow on from 'the student and the frog' suggest that this is what he had in mind, although he never developed the idea. See Gassier, *Les Dessins de Goya*, vol. II, pp. 497–9.

62 In Andioc, 'Goya y el temperamento currutáquico', p. 77.

63 See J. Quicherat, *Histoire du costume en France depuis les plus reculés temps jusqu'à la fin du XVIIIe siècle* (Paris, 1975), pp. 621–47; N. Pellegrin, *Les Vêtements de la Liberté: Abécédaire des pratiques vestimentaires françaises de 1780 à 1800* (Aix-en-Provence, 1989).

64 D. Roche, *La Culture des apparences: Une Histoire du vêtement (XVIIe–XVIIIe siècles)* (Paris, 1989), pp. 437–40, reminds us that Directoire clothing was notoriously uncomfortable.

65 Gassier, *Les Dessins de Goya*, vol. II, p. 492.

66 F. Boix, *Los Dibujos de Goya* (Madrid, 1922), no. 179.

67 See J. J. Ciofalo, 'Goya's Enlightenment Protagonist – A Quixotic Dreamer of Reason', *Eighteenth-Century Studies*, (1997), pp. 421–36.

68 Della Porta, *Della Fisionomia dell'uomo*, p. 539. For the characteristics traditionally attributed to the lion, see N. J. Zaganiaris, 'Le Roi des animaux dans la tradition classique' *Platon*, 29 (1977), pp. 26–48. As for the tradition of the *facies leonina* in Renaissance art, see P. Meller, 'Physiognomical Theory in Renaissance Heroic Portraits', in *Studies in Western Art: Acts of the Twentieth International Congress of the History of Art*, vol. II (Princeton, 1963), pp. 53–69; E. Rebel, *Die Modellierung der Person: Studien zu Dürers Bildnis des Hans Kleberger* (Stuttgart, 1990), pp. 42–61 (with bibliography).

3 VERTIGO

1 J. Offray de La Mettrie, *Traité sur le vertige* (1737), in *Oeuvres Philosophiques*, vol. II (Paris, 1987), p. 15.

2 See also M. Herz, *Versuch über den Schwindel* (Berlin, 1786). For vertigo in eighteenth-century art and philosophy, see E. Jollet, *Figures de la pesanteur: Fragonard, Newton et les plaisirs de l'escarpolette* (Nîmes, 1998). For vertigo as a symbol of modernity, see J. Simmen, *Vertigo: Schwindel der modernen Kunst* (Munich, 1990).

3 E. de Condillac, *Traité des animaux* (Paris, 1787), p. 376.

4 J.-J. Rousseau, *Oeuvres complètes*, vol. I (Paris, 1959), p. 999.

5 J. Cadalso, 'Cartas marruecas', *Diario de Madrid*, 13 January 1795, in E. Helman, *Trasmundo de Goya* (Madrid, 1986), p. 126.

6 De La Mettrie, *Traité sur le vertige*, p. 27.

7 See J. Starobinski, *1789: Les Emblèmes de la raison* (Paris, 1979), p. 128.

8 See V. de Sambricio, *Tapices de Goya* (Madrid, 1946), doc. no. 129. For iconographical sources, see J. Held, *Die Genrebilder der Madrider Teppichmanufaktur und die Anfänge Goyas* (Berlin, 1971).

9 C. E. Kany, *Life and Manners in Madrid 1750–1800* (Berkeley, 1932), p. 282ff.

10 Another interpretation of this painting which refers to the symbolism of the time is included in S. Dittberner, *Traum und Trauma vom Schlaf der Vernunft: Spanien zwischen Tradition und Moderne und die Gegenwelt Francisco Goyas* (Stuttgart and Weimar, 1995), pp. 171–9. See also J. Milam, 'Fragonard and the Blindman's Game: Interpreting Representations of Blindman's Buff', *Art History*, 21 (1998), pp. 1–25.

11 F. Colonna, *Hypnerotomachia Poliphili* (1499); G. Pozzi and L. A. Ciapponi, eds, vol. I (Padua, 1980), p. 26.

12 For details, see J. Caro Baroja, *La estación de amor (Fiestas populares de Mayo a San Juan)* (Madrid, 1979), esp. p. 119ff.; J. Caro Baroja, *El estió festivo (Fiestas populares del verano)* (Madrid, 1984), p. 103ff.

13 For the broader picture, see R. Caillois, 'Temps circulaire, temps rectiligne', *Diogène*, 42 (1963), pp. 3–14; S. J. Gould, *Time's Arrow, Time's Cycle: Myth and Metaphor in the Discovery of Geological Time* (Cambridge, MA, and London, 1987).

14 R. Girard, *La Violence et le sacré* (Paris, 1972), p. 454; see also H. P. Duerr, *Obszönität und Gewalt* (Frankfurt am Main, 1993).

15 H. Bergson, *Le Rire* (1899), in *Oeuvres* (Paris, 1970), p. 391.

16 C. Baudelaire, 'De l'essence du rire et généralement du comique dans les arts plastiques' (1855), in *Ecrits sur l'art*, vol. I (Paris, 1971), p. 301.

17 We borrowed this expression from L. Jenny's beautiful book, *L'Expérience de la chute de Montaigne à Michaux* (Paris, 1997), pp. 66–71. An indispensable book on the poetic phenomenology of the motif of the fall is G. Bachelard, *L'Air et les songes: Essai sur l'imagination du mouvement* (Paris, 1943), pp. 107–28. For the emblematic manifestation of the same motif, see C. Ginzburg, *Miti Embleme Spie: Morfologia e Storia* (Turin, 1986), pp. 107–32 and E. Bourguinat, *Le Siècle du persiflage 1734–1789* (Paris, 1998), pp. 135–42.

18 Other examples: drawings D. 13, and D.c (109) in the Gassier catalogue.

19 For the portrayal of the sky in Goya's works and, more generally, the problems linked to the *topos* of inversion, see T. Hölscher, *Bild und Exzess: Näherungen zu Goya* (Munich, 1988).

20 For the eighteenth-century context, see G. Gusdorf, *Dieu, la nature, l'homme au Siècle des Lumières* (Paris, 1972); for Goya, see esp. Hölscher, *Bild und Exzess*, pp. 121–9.

21 H. Holländer, *Goya: Los Disparates* (Tübingen, 1968). See also the contributions of Holländer and Hofmann, in W. Hofmann, ed., *Goya: Das Zeitalter der Revolutionen 1789–1830* (Hamburg, 1981).

22 Horkheimer and Adorno, *Dialektik der Aufklärung: Philosophische Fragmente*, pp. 9, 11, 35; M. Gauchet, *Le Désenchantement du monde: Une Histoire politique de la religion* (Paris, 1985).

23 J. Held, 'Goyas Akademiekritik', *Münchner Jahrbuch der bildenden Kunst*, 17 (1966), pp. 214–24.

24 S. Bianchi, *La Révolution culturelle de l'an II* (Paris, 1982). For the Spanish context, see C. Bédat, *L'Académie des Beaux-Arts de Madrid 1744–1808* (Toulouse, 1973).

25 Held, 'Goyas Akademiekritik', p. 214.

26 There are important deliberations around this subject in A. Boime, 'The Sketch and Caricature as Metaphors for the French Revolution', *Zeitschrift für Kunstgeschichte*, 55 (1992), pp. 256–67.

27 Fr. Calvo Serraller, M. B. Mena Marqués and J. Urrea, *El Cuaderno Italiano 1770–1786: Los origenes del arte de Goya* (Madrid, 1994).

28 Details and bibliography in V. I. Stoichita, *Visionary Experience in the Golden Age of Spanish Art* (London, 1995).

29 See J. Wilson-Bareau, 'Pinturas de tema religioso: 1780–1788', in Wilson-Bareau and Mena Marqués, eds, *Goya: El Capricho y la Invención*, p. 132.

30 The manuscript in the Prado was published in J. Sánchez Cantón. *Los 'Caprichos' de Goya y sus dibujos preparatorios* (Barcelona, 1949).

31 J. Wilson-Bareau, *Goya: La Década de los Caprichos: Dibujos y aguafuertes* (Madrid, 1992), p. 87.

32 See I. Jucker-Scherrer, *Der Gestus des Aposkopein: Ein Beitrag zur Gebärdensprache in der antiken Kunst* (Zurich, 1956); Stoichita, *Visionary Experience*, pp. 162–96.

33 For details, see J. Vega, 'The Modernity of *Los Desastres de la Guerra* in the Mid Nineteenth-Century Context', in J. Held, ed., *Goya: Neue Forschungen: Das internationale Symposium 1991 in Osnabrück* (Berlin, 1994), pp. 113–16.

34 D.-F. de Merveilleux, *Mémoires instructifs pour un voyageur in les différents Etats de l'Europe* (Amsterdam, 1738). This quotation is from B. and L. Bennassar, *Le Voyage en Espagne: Anthologie des voyageurs français et francophones du XVIe au XIX siècle* (Paris, 1998), pp. 600–3.

35 L. Réau, *Histoire du vandalisme: Les Monuments détruits de l'art français* (1958; Paris, 1994), pp. 233–549; F. Souchal, *Le Vandalisme de la Révolution* (Paris, 1993); E. Pommier, *L'Art et la Liberté: Doctrines et débats de la Révolution Française* (Paris, 1991), pp. 93–165; and, for the broader picture, D. Gamboni, *The Destruction of Art: Iconoclasm and Vandalism since the French Revolution* (London, 1997), pp. 9–50.

36 Hofmann, *Goya: Das Zeitalter der Revolutionen*, p. 111. See also N. Glendinning, 'El asno cargado de reliquias en los *Desastres de le guerra*', *Archivo Español de Arte*, xxxv (1962), pp. 221–30; J. Vega, 'The Modernity of *Los Desastres de la Guerra*', in J. Held, ed., *Goya: Neue Forschungen*, pp. 113–23 (here p. 116).

37 Held, 'Goyas Akademiekritik', p. 214.

38 See the pioneering study by T. Hetzer, 'Goya und die Krise der Kunst um 1800' (1932), in *Aufsätze und Vorträge* (Leipzig, 1957), pp. 177–98; F. Licht, *Goya and the Modern Temper in Art* (New York, 1978); V. Bozal, *Goya y el gusto moderno* (Madrid, 1994).

39 J. J. Winckelmann, *Geschichte der Kunst des Altertums* (1764; Darmstadt, 1972), pp. 345–7. For his famous description, refer to C. Justi, *Winckelmann und seine Zeitgenossen* (1866–72; Leipzig, 1932), vol. II, p. 41ff.; A. Potts, *Flesh and the Ideal: Winckelmann and the Origins of Art History* (New Haven and London, 1994), pp. 174–80. On the critical fortunes of the *Torso*, see F. Haskell and N. Penny, *Taste and the Antique: The Lure of Classical Sculpture 1500–1900* (New Haven and London, 1981), pp. 311–14.

40 For information on this subject, see A. Potts, in E. Pommier, ed., *Winckelmann et la naissance de l'histoire de l'art à l'époque des Lumières* (Paris, 1991), p. 29.

41 It is, amongst other things, the undisputed model for the aquatint portraying the *Giant* (c. 1818) and for *Capricho* 37. For the latter version, refer to J. Tomlinson, *Francisco Goya y Lucientes, 1746–1828* (London, 1994), p. 193.

42 M. Bakhtin, *L'oeuvre de François Rabelais*, p. 177ff.

43 For the phenomenology of torture, we referred to M. Foucault's classic study, *Surveiller et punir: Naissance de la prison* (Paris, 1975), pp. 7–72; E. Scarry, *The Body in Pain: The Making and Unmaking of the World* (New York and Oxford, 1985); E. Peters, *Torture* (New York, 1985).

44 P. Gassier, *Les Dessins de Goya* (Fribourg, 1975), p. 41 (drawing A.b).

45 L. B. Alberti, *De Pictura/De la peinture* (1435) (French trans.: J. L. Schefer [Paris, 1992], pp. 183–5).

46 The first to establish this was J. López-Rey, *Goya's Caprichos: Beauty, Reason, & Caricature*, vol. 1 (1953; Westport, CT, 1970), p. 16.

47 V. Cartari, *Le Imagini dei Dei de gli Antichi* (Venice, 1556; Vicenza, 1996), pp. 469–70. For details concerning the statue, its variants and critical fortunes, see Haskell and Penny, *Taste and the Antique*, pp. 316–18; G. Säflund, *Aphrodite Kallipygos* (Stockholm, Göteborg and Uppsala, 1963).

48 Säflund, *Aphrodite Kallipygos*, p. 45.

49 Alberti, *De Pictura/De la peinture*, p. 185.

50 See F. J. Sánchez Cantón, *Los dibujos del viaje a Sanlœcar* (Madrid, 1928), p. 13; Gassier, *Les Dessins de Goya*, p. 41.

51 V. Mertens, *Mi-parti als zeichen. Zur Bedeutung von geteilter Gestalt in der Ständetracht, in literarischen und bildnerischen Quellen sowie im*

Fastnachtbrauch vom Mittelalter bis zur Gegenwart (Remscheid, 1983).

52 For information on context, see Calderón de la Barca, *Las Carnetolendas*, in *Comedias de Don Pedro Calderón de la Barca*, vol. IV (Madrid, 1945), p. 654.

53 M. Eliade, *Méphistophélès et l'androgyne* (Paris, 1962), p. 164.

54 Regarding this subject, see W. Busch, *Nachahmung als bürgerliches Kunstprinzip: Ikonographische Zitate bei Hogarth und in seiner Nachfolge* (Hildesheim and New York, 1977); W. Busch, *Das sentimentalische Bild: Die Krise der Kunst im 18. Jahrhundert und die Geburt der Moderne* (Munich, 1993); K. Herding, 'Inversionen: Antikenkritik in der Karikatur des 19. Jahrhunderts', in *idem* and G. Otto, eds, *Karikaturen. Nervöse Auffangsorgane des inneren und äusseren Lebens* (Giessen, 1980), pp. 131–71.

55 J. Grego, *Rowlandson the Caricaturist* (London, 1880), vol. II, p. 217; R. Paulson, *Rowlandson: A New Interpretation* (Oxford and New York, 1972), pp. 26–37.

56 Details in B. Fort, 'Voice of the Public: The Carnivalization of Salon Art in Prerevolutionary Pamphlets', *Eighteenth-Century Studies*, 22 (1989), pp. 368–94.

57 W. Hogarth, *The Analysis of Beauty, written with a view of fixing the fluctuating Ideas of Taste* (1753); J. Burke, ed., *William Hogarth, The Analysis of Beauty, with the rejected passages from the manuscript drafts and autobiographical notes* (Oxford, 1955), chaps IX, X; for allusions to Hogarth's aesthetics contained in Rowlandson's print, see R. Paulson, *The Beautiful, Novel, and Strange: Aesthetics and Heterodoxy* (Baltimore and London, 1996), pp. 235–6. See also M. Podro, *Depiction* (New Haven and London, 1998), p. 109ff.

4 CLINIC OF PURE REASON

1 Details in G. Lély, *Vie du Marquis de Sade écrite sur des données nouvelles et accompagnée de nombreux documents, le plus souvent inédits*, vol. I (Paris, 1952), p. 182ff.

2 'L'an mil sept cent soixante huit, le trois avril (. . .) je soussigné Pierre Paul Le Comte M^tre chirurgien. Correspondant de Lacadémie Royale de chirurgie Demeurant à Arcueil. Me suis transporter au chateau d'Arcueil a l'effet de visiter une femme qui venoit d'estre maltraité que j'ai apris se nommer Rose Kailair, que j'ai trouvé souffrante de plusieurs partie de son corps, que j'ai examiné et reconnus toute l'estendu des fesses et une partie des lombes vergette et excorié avec coupure et contusion forte et longue sur l'épine du dos, et en outre une contusion echimosé et dechirure sur le dessu de la main gauche, que tout ma paru estre fait par quelque instrument contundant et tranchant, ay aussi remarqué de la cire fondu sur quelqu'une des playes. Fait a Arcueil ce trois avril mil sept cent soixante huit.' This extract, from Lély, *Vie du Marquis de Sade,* p. 205, is quoted with the original spelling.

3 Lély, *Vie du Marquis de Sade*, vol. I, pp. 230–31.

4 Suggested parallel reading: R. von Kraft-Ebing, *Psychopathologia Sexualis: Etude médico-légale à l'usage des médecins et des juristes* (1923; Paris, 1963).

5 Lély, *Vie du Marquis de Sade*, vol. I, p. 216.

6 A. van Genepp, *Manuel de folklore français contemporain*, vol. III. *Les Cérémonies périodiques et saisonnières, 1. Carnaval-Carême-Pâques* (Paris, 1947), p. 1146ff.

7 *Ibid.*, p. 1376.

8 Ovid, *Fasti*, II, 30–35; see also C. Gaignebet and M.-C. Florentin, *Le Carnaval: Essai de mythologie populaire* (Paris, 1974), p. 22ff.

9 J. K. Huysmans came up with the expression 'bastard of Catholicism' in reference to sadism; see *A Rebours* (1884; Paris, 1975), p. 254. For a reading of 'Catholic Sade', see P. Klossowski's classical study, *Sade, mon prochain*

(Paris, 1983).

10 For the 'humour' of Sade, see P. Roger, *Sade: La Philosophie dans le pressoir* (Paris, 1976), p. 209ff.

11 M. Blanchot, *Lautréamont et Sade* (Paris, 1963), p. 19.

12 Lély, *Vie du Marquis de Sade*, vol. I, p. 28.

13 Blanchot, *Lautréamont et Sade*, p. 24.

14 *Ibid.*, p. 18.

15 T. Airaksinen, *The Philosophy of the Marquis de Sade* (London and New York, 1995), p. 13.

16 D. A. F. de Sade, *Les Cent Vingt Journées de Sodome* (= *Oeuvres*, M. Delon, ed., vol. I [Paris, 1990]), p. 69.

17 D. A. F. de Sade, *Les Infortunes de la vertu* (Paris, 1970), p. 125.

18 *Ibid.*, p. 114.

19 The expression is Juliette's in D. A. F. de Sade, *Histoire de Juliette ou Les Prospérités du vice* (Paris, 1969), p. 69.

20 See Sade, *Oeuvres*, vol. I, p. LXXVIII.

21 J. Bergman, ed., *Aurelii Prudentii Clementis carmina* (Vienna and Leipzig, 1926), p. 165ff.

22 Sade, *Les Infortunes de la vertu*, p. 224.

23 Boethius, *Philosophiae Consolatio*, II, 1–16. H. R. Patch's study, *The Goddess Fortuna in Mediaeval Literature* (1927; New York, 1967) is essential reading. See also L. Galactéros de Boissier, 'Images emblématiques de la Fortune: Eléments d'une typologie', in Y. Giraud, ed., *L'Emblème à la Renaissance* (Paris, 1982), pp. 79–125.

24 Details in A. Katzenellenbogen, *Allegories of the Virtues and Vices in Medieval Art: From Early Christian Times to the Thirteenth Century* (1939; Toronto, Buffalo and London, 1989).

25 S. Brant, *Das Narrenschiff* (Strasbourg, 1494; Frankfurt am Main, 1986), song 37.

26 See J. Heers, *Fêtes des Fous et Carnavals* (Paris, 1983), p. 243.

27 This is the so-called Ayala manuscript and ms. 20558 n. 23 in the National Library of Madrid, published in Helman, *Trasmundo de Goya*, p. 212. Appendix II of Helman's book provided us with a useful opportunity to read the three hand-written explanations of the *Caprichos*. On the question of the hand-written commentaries, see esp. R. Andioc, 'Al margen de los Caprichos: Las "explicaciones" manuscritas', *Nueva Revista de Filologia Hispanica*, XXXIII (1984), pp. 257–84.

28 Sade, *Les Infortunes de la vertu*, p. 228.

29 *Ibid.*, p. 203.

30 *Ibid.*, pp. 253–4.

31 Sade, *Histoire de Juliette*, p. 16.

32 R. Barthes, *Sade, Fourier, Loyola* (Paris, 1971), p. 127ff.

33 I. Kant, *Logik, Werke*, vol. VIII (Berlin, 1923), p. 343. For the Kant/Sade binomial, see Horkheimer and Adorno, *Dialektik der Aufklärung: Philosophische Fragmente*, pp. 88–127; J. Lacan, *Ecrits 2* (Paris, 1971), pp. 119–50.

34 Sade, *Histoire de Juliette*, p. 124.

35 *Ibid.*, p. 42.

36 *Ibid.*, p. 44.

37 *Ibid.*, p. 158.

38 See M. Hénaff, *Sade: L'Invention du corps libertin* (Paris, 1978), esp. p. 219ff.

39 Bakhtin, *L'oeuvre de François Rabelais*, pp. 302–65.

40 D. A. F. de Sade, *La Philosophie dans le boudoir ou Les Instituteurs immoraux* (Paris, 1976), p. 60.

41 Sade, *Histoire de Juliette*, p. 111. Lély, in *Vie du Marquis de Sade*, vol. II (Paris, 1957), p. 226, states that the Marquis possessed at least one replica in his bedroom before 24 June 1783, 'the day on which the jailer,

inadvertently dropped her when he was doing the cleaning, and (. . .) her head was broken by the fall'.

42 Sade, *La Philosophie dans le boudoir*, p. 161.

43 D. A. F. de Sade, *Justine, ou Les Malheurs de la vertu* (Paris, 1973), p. 152.

44 Della Porta, *Della Fisionomia dell'uomo*, pp. 556–60.

45 On this subject, see J. Molino, 'Sade devant la beauté', in *Le Marquis de Sade (Actes du Colloque d'Aix-en-Provence)* (Paris, 1968), pp. 144–5.

46 Sade, *Justine*, p. 341.

47 Sade, *Histoire de Juliette*, p. 76.

48 *Ibid.*, p. 108.

49 D. A. F. Sade, *Les Crimes de l'amour* (Paris, 1987), p. 53.

50 Sade, *Histoire de Juliette*, p. 271.

51 Sade, *Les Crimes de l'amour*, p. 96.

52 Sade, *Les Cent Vingt Journées de Sodome*, p. 46.

53 See Lacan, *Ecrits 2*, p. 131; T. Dipiero, 'Disfiguring the Victim's Body in Sade's 'Justine', in V. Kelly and D. von Mücke, *Body & Text in the Eighteenth Century* (Stanford, 1994), pp. 247–65.

54 D. Diderot, *Le Rêve d'Alembert*, ed. J. Varloot (Paris, 1987), p. 90ff.

55 Sade, *Justine*, p. 203–4.

56 For the context to which Sade belonged, see S. Bruhm, *Gothic Bodies: The Politics of Pain in Romantic Fiction* (Philadelphia, 1994).

57 Sade, *Les Infortunes de la vertu*, p. 194.

58 Sade, *Justine*, p. 124.

59 On this subject, see K. G. Holmström, *Monodrama, Attitudes, Tableaux vivants: Studies on Some Trends of Theatrical Fashion 1770–1815* (Stockholm, 1967); P. Frantz, *L'Esthétique du tableau dans le théâtre du XVIIIe siècle* (Paris, 1998); B. Joos, *Lebende Bilder. Körperliche Nachamungen von Kunstwerken in der Goethezeit* (Berlin, 1999); S. Michalski, *Tableau und Pantomime: Historienmalerei und Theater in Frankreich zwischen Poussin und David* (Hildesheim, Zurich and New York, forthcoming).

60 *Histoire de Juliette*, p. 162.

61 For Diderot's descriptive techniques, see J. Starobinski's classical study, 'Diderot descripteur: Diderot rêve et raconte la passion de Corésus', *Cahiers du Musée National d'Art Moderne*, 24 (1988), pp. 83–96.

62 D. Diderot, *Oeuvres*, Vol. *IV. Esthétique-Théatre* (Paris, 1996), p. 563.

63 Sade, *Histoire de Juliette*, p. 43.

64 *Ibid.*, p. 78.

65 For an excellent synopsis of the erotic engraving, see P. Stewart, *Engraving Desire: Eros, Image & Text in the French Eighteenth Century* (Durham and London, 1992). See also P. Wagner's observations in *Reading Icontexts: From Swift to the French Revolution* (London, 1995), esp. pp. 139–60.

66 It is extremely interesting to note how the most authoritative commentaries on this drawing desist out of a sense of decency: 'This is a representation of a woman fainting, assisted by a *majo* and two women companions. The blank background is so limpid that it is difficult to decide whether the drawing represents an interior or exterior even though the shadow behind the fainting woman falls on the back of what seems to be a sofa. The group centers the composition about itself with almost no indication of its surroundings. However, there is an important difference between this drawing and most from the smaller sketchbook. The figures are now related to each other, not what they express: fainting, helping, smiling. Thus, the theme is no longer the uniqueness of the human figure but the variety of human feelings and interactions, which in this particular drawing appear coloured by sensuality.' (López-Rey, *Goya's Caprichos*, p. 28); or 'This drawing is not just a sketch of people, it depicts a *fait divers*: the maja fainting during a pleasure party. The majo

assisted by his two companions, carries her to a sort of sofa and supports her head. (. . .) The characters' feelings are clearly expressed through their gestures and attitudes. (Gassier, *Les Dessins*, p. 124). In our opinion, this drawing, together with others from the *Madrid Sketchbook*, has to be seen within the context of an erotic series verging on impropriety (Gassier: B. 4; B. 13; B. 15; B. 16; B. 18; B. 24; B. 26; B. 85.).

67 Esp. in books IV, V and VI of *Juliette*.

68 J. de Jean, *Literary Fortifications: Rousseau, Laclos, Sade* (Princeton, 1984), esp. pp. 263–315.

69 D. A. F. Marquis de Sade, *Voyage d'Italie*, ed. M. Lever (Paris, 1995), p. 56.

70 *Ibid.*, p. 62.

71 Sade, *Histoire de Juliette*, vol. II (Paris, 1977), pp. 24–25 should be compared to Sade, *Voyage d'Italie*, pp. 70–73.

72 Sade, *Voyage d'Italie*, p. 65.

73 For all details, refer to O. Millar, *Zoffany and His Tribuna* (London, 1966).

74 Sade, *Voyage d'Italie*, p. 63 points out that he discovered the famous Venus of Urbino when he visited the 'painter's room', where 'a somewhat mediocre painter was busy copying it'.

75 Sade, *Voyage d'Italie*, p. 63.

76 This phenomenon is explained in M. Hobson's book, *The Object of Art: The Theory of Illusion in Eighteenth-Century France* (Cambridge, 1982), esp. pp. 47–83, 194–226. See also N. Bryson, *Tradition and Desire: From David to Delacroix* (Cambridge, 1984); R. Démoris, 'Peintures et Belles Antiques dans la première moitié du Siècle. Les statues vivent aussi.' *Dix-huitième siècle*, 27 (1995), pp. 129-42; recently, B. Hinz, *Aphrodite. Geschichte einer abendländischen Passion* (Munich, 1998).

77 C.-N. Cochin, *Voyage d'Italie, ou recueil de notes sur les ouvrages de peinture de sculpture, qu'on voit dans les principales villes d'Italie* (1758; 3 vols, Paris, 1769).

78 Sade, *Voyage d'Italie*, p. 64.

79 L. O. Larsson, *Von allen Seiten gleich schön: Studien zum Begriff der Vielansichtigkeit in der europäischen Plastik von der Renaissance bis zum Klassizismus* (Stockholm, 1974); L. Mendelsohn, *Paragoni: Benedetto Varchi's 'Due Lezioni' and Cinquecento Art Theory* (Ann Arbor, 1982).

80 Sade, *Histoire de Juliette*, vol. II, pp. 48-9. The English version is based on M. Crossland, ed., *The Passionate Philosopher: A Marquis de Sade Reader* (1991), pp. 128-9.

81 The most notable, which we chose to spare our readers, can be found in 'Eugénie de Farval, nouvelle tragique', in Sade, *Les Crimes de l'amour*, pp. 302, 348-9.

82 Ovid, *Metamorphoses*, x, 245-59. We have used the French translation contained in the bilingual edition by G. Lafaye (Paris, 1985), vol. II, p. 130.

83 See esp. J. L. Carr, 'Pygmalion and the *Philosophes*: The Animated Statue in Eighteenth-Century France', *Journal of the Warburg and Courtauld Institutes*, XXIII (1960), pp. 239–55; I. Mülder-Bach, *Im Zeichen Pygmalions: Das Modell der Statue und die Entdeckung der Darstellung im 18. Jahrhundert* (Munich, 1998); Michalski, *Tableau und Pantomime*, chap. IV.

84 Diderot and D'Alembert, eds, *Encyclopédie*, under 'Pygmalion'.

85 See A. Blühm, *Pygmalion: Die Ikonographie eines Künstlermythos zwischen 1500 und 1900* (Frankfurt am Main, Bern, New York and Paris, 1988).

86 Diderot, *Oeuvres*, vol. IV, p. 186 (*Salon de 1763*). See also O. Bätschmann, 'Pygmalion als Betrachter: Die Rezeption von Plastik und Malerei in der zweiten Hälfte des 18. Jahrhunderts', in W. Kemp, ed., *Der Betrachter ist im Bild: Kunstwissenschaft und Rezeptionsästhetik* (Cologne, 1985), pp. 183–224.

87 See E. A. Sayre, 'Pygmalion y Galatea', in *Goya y el espíritu de la ilustración*, exh. cat. (Madrid, 1989), pp. 428–31; J. J. Ciofalo, 'Unveiling Goya's Rape

of Galatea', *Art History*, 18 (1995), pp. 477–98.

88 Sade, *Histoire de Juliette*, vol. II, p. 109.

89 Horkheimer and Adorno, *Dialektik der Aufklärung*.

90 J.-M. Fritz, *Le Discours du fou au Moyen Age* (Paris, 1992), p. 7ff.

91 Horkheimer and Adorno, *Dialektik der Aufklärung*, p. 93.

92 Lacan, 'Kant avec Sade', in *Ecrits II*, p. 120. See also H. Böhme, *Natur und Subjekt* (Frankfurt am Main, 1988), pp. 274–307.

93 I. Kant, *Träume eines Geistersehers*, in *Werke II: Vorkritische Schriften bis 1678*, vol. 2 (Frankfurt am Main and Wiesbaden, 1960), p. 969.

94 M. David-Ménard, *La Folie dans la raison pure* (Paris, 1990).

95 H. Böhme and G. Böhme, *Das Andere der Vernunft: Zur Entwicklung von Rationalitätsstrukturen am Beispiel Kants* (Frankfurt am Main, 1985), esp. p. 271ff.

96 See M. David-Ménard, 'Présentation', in I. Kant, *Essai sur les maladies de la tête* (Paris, 1990), pp. 7–44.

97 M. Foucault, *Histoire de la folie à l'Age Classique* (Paris, 1961), p. 204. See also W. Promies, *Die Bürger und der Narr oder das Risiko der Phantasie* (Munich, 1966); K. Dörner, *Bürger und Irre: Zur Sozialgeschichte und Wissenschaftssoziologie der Psychiatrie* (1969; Hamburg, 1995); W. Lepenies, *Melancholie und Gesellschaft* (1969; Frankfurt am Main, 1998); H.-J. Schings, *Melancholie und Aufklärung: Melancholiker und ihre Kritiker in Erfahrungsseelenkunde und Literatur des 18. Jahrhunderts* (Stuttgart, 1977); E. Moser-Rath, *'Lustige Gesellschaft'. Schwank und Witz des 17. und 18. Jahrhunderts in kultur- und sozialgeschichtlichem Kontext* (Stuttgart, 1984).

98 S. L. Gilman, *Seeing the Insane* (New York, 1982), pp. 129–40; J. E. Kromm, *Studies in the Iconography of Madness, 1600–1900* (Ann Arbor, 1984), pp. 90–183; W. Busch, *Die notwendige Arabeske: Wirklichkeitsaneignung und Stilisierung in der deutschen Kunst des 19. Jahrhunderts* (Berlin, 1985), p. 30ff.; T. Bhattacharya-Settler, *Nox Mentis: Die Darstellung von Wahnsinn in der Kunst des 19. Jahrhunderts* (Bern, 1989) pp. 14–30.

99 Sade, *Histoire de Juliette*, vol. II, p. 378.

100 *Ibid.*, vol. II, p. 380.

101 For information on the 1793–4 painting and its context, see P. K. Klein, '"La fantasia abandonada de la razón": Zur Darstellung des Wahnsinns in Goyas "Hof der Irren"', in J. Held, *Goya: Neue Forschungen: Das internationale Symposium in Osnabrück* (Berlin, 1994), pp. 161–94. For the Bordeaux drawings, see B. Antoniol, 'Goya, peintre de la folie', in F. Ribemont and F. Garcia, eds, *Goya: Hommage* (Bordeaux, 1998), pp. 101–16.

102 See esp. J. de Mondragón, *Censura de la locura humana y excelencia d'Ella* (Lérida, 1598); P. de Medina, *Hospital de incurables* (Madrid, 1667).

103 M. Fried, *Absorption and Theatricality: Painting and Beholder in the Age of Diderot* (Chicago, 1980).

104 Serraller, Marqués and Urrea, *El Cuaderno Italiano*, p. 72; Wilson-Bareau, in *Goya: El Capricho y la Invencion*, p. 97.

105 The expression comes from a letter Girodet wrote to Gérard, dated 11 August 1790, and quoted by P. Bordes, *Le Serment du Jeu de Paume de Jacques-Louis David* (Paris, 1983), p. 39.

106 See Bordes, *Le Serment du Jeu de Paume*; A. Schnapper, in *Jacques-Louis David 1748–1825*, exh. cat. (Paris, 1989–90), pp. 242–75; W. Kemp, 'The Theater of Revolution.

107 Alberti, *De Pictura/De la Peinture*, II, 41; Schefer, ed., p. 175.

108 *Ibid.*, II, 40, p. 173.

109 H. W. Janson, 'Observations on Nudity in Neoclassical Art', in *Akten des Internationalen Kongresses für Kunstgeschichte in Bonn 1964* (Berlin 1967), vol. II, pp. 198–207.

110 Alberti, *De Pictura/De la Peinture*, II, 36, p. 163.

111 *Essai sur la méthode à employer pour juger les ouvrages des beaux-arts du*

dessin, et principalement ceux qui sont exposés au salon du Louvre, par une société d'artistes (Paris, 1790), pp. 7–8.

112 *Lettres analytiques, critiques et philosophiques sur les tableaux du Salon* (Paris, 1791), pp. 48–9.

113 In this context, see also B. M. Stafford, *Body Criticism* (Cambridge, MA., 1991), p. 15ff.; W. Hofmann, 'El Naufragio permanente', in *Goya: El capricho y la invención*, pp. 48–9.

114 L. Matheron, *Goya* (1858; Madrid, 1996), p. 202.

5 GOYA'S PHARMACY

1 We borrowed this title (and more) from J. Derrida's essay, 'La Pharmacie de Platon', in *La Dissémination* (Paris, 1972), pp. 69–197.

2 Details in N. Gramaccini, *Theorie der französischen Druckgraphik im 18. Jahrhundert: Eine Quellenanthologie* (Bern *et al.*, 1997), p. 299ff. It would appear that this was Goya's original intention since he had already prepared the announcement of the subscription in 1797. See V. Carderera, 'François Goya', *Gazette des Beaux-Arts*, 15 (1863), pp. 241–2.

3 The press was inundated with announcements advertising the products on sale at the 'Millot Drugstore', whose address was usually quoted as being Calle del Desengaño on the corner of Calle Balesta (see, for example, *Diario de Madrid* of 13 March 1799, 23 April 1799, 20 September 1799, etc.). The number of the house appears only once, in the advertisement of 6 February 1799 that mentions Goya's prints. The topographical and toponymical fluctuations in this area of Madrid, however, imply that there might be a weakness in the hypothesis that Millot's shop and Goya's house were both at 1. See M. Molina Campuzano, *Planos de Madrid de los siglos XVII y XVIII* (Madrid, 1960).

4 *Gaceta de Madrid*, 11 June 1799, p. 789.

5 *Diario de Madrid*, 20 September 1799, p. 1171.

6 For details, see J. Luis Morales y Marín, *Luis Paret: Vida y obra* (Saragossa, 1997).

7 The advertisement in the *Diario de Madrid* was published in A. de Beruete, *Goya grabador* (Madrid, 1918), p. 183.

8 This problem was tackled with exceptional success by W. Hofmann, in 'Goyas negative Morphologie', in *idem et al.*, *Goya: 'Alle werden fallen'* (Frankfurt am Main, 1987), p. 17ff.

9 For the notion of a 'market of symbolic goods', see P. Bourdieu, *Les Règles de l'art: Genèse et structure du champ littéraire* (Paris, 1992).

10 Derrida, 'La Pharmacie de Platon', p. 71.

11 V. Bozal, 'Los Caprichos: El Mundo de la noche', in *Francisco de Goya: Grabador: Instantaneas: Caprichos* (Madrid, 1992), p. 19.

12 B. Gracián, *Oraculo Manual y arte de prudencia* (1647), in B. Gracián, *El Heroe, El Discreto, Oraculo manual y arte de prudencia* (Madrid, 1984), p. 49.

13 We have used, but not in the same context, the notion of *Erwartungshorizont* ('waiting horizon') (coined by representatives of the *Rezeptionsästhetik* from the Constance School). See esp. H. R. Jauss, *Literaturgeschichte als Provokation* (Frankfurt am Main, 1979), pp. 168–206.

14 Gracián, *El Heroe*, p. 220.

15 G. González-Azaola, 'Satiras de Goya', *Semanario Patriótico* (Cadiz, 27 March 1811). The text (and its English translation reproduced here) was published in E. Harris, 'A Contemporary Review of Goya's "Caprichos"', *Burlington Magazine*, CVI (1964), pp. 38–3. See also N. Glendinning, *Goya and His Critics* (New Haven and London), pp. 59–60.

16 *Secrets concernant les Arts et Métiers*, 2 vols (Caen, 1786), vol. I, pp. 2–6; the extract is from Gramaccini, *Theorie der französischen Druckgraphik im 18. Jahrhundert*, pp. 28-31. For information regarding the situation in Spain,

see M. Rueda, *Instruccion para gravar en cobre, y perfeccionarse en el gravado a buril, al agua fuerte, y al humo . . .* (Madrid, 1761). Regarding Goya's technique, T. Harris's two volumes, *Goya: Engravings and Lithographs* (Oxford, 1964), give the most complete synopsis. For other information, we referred to J. Blas, ed., *Goya grabador y litografo: Repertorio bibliografico* (Madrid, n.d.). Also useful is the more recent work by J. Carrete Parrondo, 'Los cobres grabados por Goya, reproducidos por primera vez', in *Francisco de Goya grabador: Instantaneas: Caprichos*, pp. 11–16; J. Vega, 'Imaginación a la realidad: Dibujar y grabar el capricho', in *Caprichos de Francisco de Goya: Una aproximación y tres estudios* (Madrid, 1996), pp. 113–31.

17 C. Yriarte, *Goya: Sa Biographie, les fresques, les toiles, les tapisseries, les eaux-fortes et le catalogue de l'oeuvre* (Paris, 1867), pp. 102–3.

18 See G. Bandmann, 'Bemerkungen zu einer Ikonologie des Materials', *Städel Jahrbuch*, n. s., 2 (1969), pp. 75–100. For other works connected with the 'techno-iconology' of eighteenth-century engraving, see Stafford, *Body Criticism*, p. 70ff.

19 See G. Levitine, 'Some Emblematic Sources of Goya', *Journal of the Warburg and Courtauld Institutes*, 22 (1959), p. 114, in E. Sayre, 'Pygmalion y Galatea', in *Goya y el espíritu de la ilustración*, exh. cat. (Madrid, 1989), pp. 227–9. For the Goya–Quevedo relationship, see López-Rey, *Goya's Caprichos*, p. 99ff. We have already developed this interpretation in our article, 'Goyas Apotheke', in A. Nova and K. Krüger, eds, *Imagination und Wirklichkeit. Zum Verhältnis von mentalen und realen Bildern in der Kunst der frühen Neuzeit* (Mainz, forthcoming).

20 See M. Friedman, *Stream of Consciousness: A Study in Literary Method* (New Haven and London, 1955); W. C. Booth, *The Rhetorics of Fiction* (Chicago, 1961).

21 D. de Saavedra Fajardo, *Empresas politicas* (Milan, 1642), F. J. Diez de Revenga, ed. (Madrid, 1988), no. 45, pp. 287–9. The motif of the perpetually open lion's eye also appears in Gracián, *El Criticón*, ed. E. Corea Calderón (Madrid, 1971), vol. II, 342, 345.

22 Gracián, *El Criticón*, vol. I, p. 136ff.

23 V. Bolzani, *Hieroglyphica* (Lyon, 1602), p. 105.

24 Gracián, *El Oraculo manual*, no. 25, p. 115.

25 W. Hofmann, 'Der Traum der Vernunft, oder: Täter und Opfer', in *idem*, *Goya: Das Zeitalter der Revolutionen*, pp. 58–9.

26 On Zacarías González, see Y. Bottineau, *L'Art de cour dans l'Espagne des Lumières 1746–1808* (Paris, 1986), pp. 367–77; J. A. Tomlinson, 'Goya in Context: Painting at the Court of Carlos IV', in J. Held, *Goya: Neue Forschungen: Das internationale Symposium in Osnabrück* (Berlin, 1994), pp. 43–64.

27 See P. Saintyves, *L'Astrologie populaire étudiée spécialement dans la doctrine et les traditions relatives à l'influence de la lune* (Paris, 1937).

28 See J. Bialostocki, *Stil und Ikonographie: Studien zur Kunstwissenschaft* (Cologne, 1981), pp. 148–9; F. Nordström, *Goya, Saturn and Melancholy* (Stockholm, 1962). Goya's treatment of the lunar theme awaits interpretation.

29 For the notion of 'paratext', see G. Gennette, *Seuils* (Paris, 1987).

30 See G. Poulet, *Entre moi et moi* (Paris, 1977), pp. 9–37; Jacot Grapa, *L'Homme dissonant au dix-huitième siècle*, p. 144ff.

31 See H. Hohl, 'Giuseppe Maria Mitellis "Alfabeto in sogno" und Francisco de Goyas "Sueño de la razón"', in H. W. Grohn and W. Stubbe, eds, *Museum und Kunst: Beiträge für Alfred Henzen* (Hamburg, 1970), pp. 107–18; B. Growe, '"Ydioma universal": Goya und die Sprachlichkeit der Kunst', *Giessener Beiträge zur Kunstgeschichte*, VII (1985), pp. 33–56; Sayre, in *Goya y el espíritu de la Ilustración*, pp. 227–32; B. Kornmeier, '"Ydioma

universal"': Goyas Taubstummenalphabet im Kontext seines
Geniekonzepts', *Zeitschrift für Kunstgeschichte*, 61 (1998), pp. 1–17.

32 M. V. David, *Le Débat sur les écritures et l'hiéroglyphe au XVIIe et XVIIIe siècles et l'application de la notion de déchiffrement aux écritures mortes* (Paris, 1965); M. Duchet and M. Jalley, eds, *Langues et langages de Leibniz à l'Encyclopédie* (Paris, 1977); U. Eco, *La ricerca della lingua perfetta nella cultura europea* (Bari, 1993), pp. 289–341.

33 R. Darnton, *Mesmerism and the End of Enlightenment in France* (Cambridge, MA, 1968); Stafford, *Body Criticism*, pp. 401–63.

34 *Diario de Madrid*, 8 September 1799, p. 1114. In this context, it would be useful to consult J. M. Serrera's article, 'Goya, los Caprichos y el teatro de sombras chinescas', in *Caprichos de Francisco de Goya: Una aproximación y tres estudios* (Madrid, 1996), pp. 83–111; J. Caro Baroja, *Teatro popular y magia* (Madrid, 1974), esp. pp. 225–55; J. E. Varey, *Cartelera de los titeres y otras diversiones populares de Madrid: 1758–1840: Estudio y documentos* (Madrid, 1995), esp. p. 160ff. For the European context, see R. M. Isherwood, *Farce and Fantasy: Popular Entertainment in Eighteenth-Century Paris* (New York and Oxford, 1986); T. Castle, 'Phantasmagoria: Spectral Technology and the Metaphorics of Modern Reverie', *Critical Inquiry*, 15 (Autumn 1988), pp. 26–61; and, more especially, B. M. Stafford, *Artful Science: Enlightenment, Entertainment and the Eclipse of Visual Education* (Cambridge, MA, and London, 1994).

35 *Diario de Madrid*, 7 September 1799, p. 1110.

36 On the origins and fortunes of the words *capriccio/capricho*, see L. Hartmann, 'Capriccio' — Bild und Begriff', PhD thesis, Zurich, 1970; Nürnberg, 1973; E. Mai and J. Rees, eds, *Das Capriccio als Kunstprinzip* (Milan, 1996); R. Kanz and W. Busch, in E. Mai and J. Rees, eds, *Kunstform Capriccio. Von der Groteske zur Spieltheorie der Moderne* (Cologne, 1998).

37 Gassier and Wilson, *Vie et oeuvre de Francisco Goya*, p. 384.

38 For information on Goya's contacts with the art of English engravers, see R. Wolf, *Goya and the Satirical Print in England and on the Continent 1730 to 1830* (Boston, 1991).

39 See A. Stoll, 'Goyas Zylinder: Der ästhetische Geniesbericht der "Caprichos" und das Medienpublikum', in *Merkur*, 516 (1992), pp. 219–36.

40 Sayre, in *Goya y el espíritu de la Ilustración*, pp. 205–7.

41 Details in V. I. Stoichita, *A Short History of the Shadow* (London, 1997), pp. 29–41.

42 Sayre, in *Goya y el espíritu de la Ilustración*, p. 206. For the relationship between Goya and the tradition of physiognomy and body language, see also R. Alcalá Flecha, 'Expresión y gesto en la obra de Goya', *Goya*, 252 (1996), pp. 341–52.

43 F. E. Zeglirscosac, *Ensayo sobre el origen y naturaleza de las pasiones* (Madrid, 1800), p. 9ff.

44 Aristotle, *Problemata*, xxx, 1. An excellent edition now exists by J. Pigeaud: *L'Homme de génie et la Mélancolie: Problem XXX, 1* (Paris, 1988).

45 Galien, *De la bile noire*, V. Barras, T. Birchler and A.-F. Morand, eds (Paris, 1998), pp. 40–43.

46 Huarte de San Juan, *Examen de ingenios para las ciencias* (1594; Madrid, 1989), p. 458.

47 R. Boyle, 'Humor und Humore', *Zeitschrift für vergleichende Literaturgeschichte*, 1895, p. 1ff.; F. Baldensperger, 'Les Définitions de l'Humour' in *Etudes d'Histoire Littéraire*, I (Geneva, 1973), pp. 176–222; J. Bremmer and H. Roodenburg, eds, *A Cultural History of Humour. From Antiquity to the Present Day* (Cambridge, 1997), pp. 1–4.

48 See B. Croce, 'L'Umorismo', *Journal of Comparative Literature*, 1903, p. 223ff.

49 Earl of Shaftesbury, *Characteristics of Men, Manners and Opinions, Times*,

vol. I (London, 1732), p. 134.

50 J. Starobinski, *Histoire du traitement de la mélancolie des origines à 1900* (Basel, 1960), pp. 9–22; R. Klibansky, E. Panofsky and F. Saxl, *Saturn and Melancholy. Studies in the History of Natural Philosophy, Religion and Art* (London, 1964). For a more up-to-date approach, see H. Tellenbach, *La Mélancholie* (1961; Berlin, 1983).

51 See W. Harms, M. Schilling, B. Bauer and C. Kemp, eds, *Die Sammlung der Herzog August Bibliothek in Wolfenbüttel. Kommentierte Ausgabe.* Vol. I: *Ethica. Physica* (Tübingen, 1985), pp. 122–3.

52 See M. Bakhtin, *L'oeuvre de François Rabelais*, pp. 150–52; Bercé, *Fête et Révolte*, p. 33.

53 The classic study by M. Douglas, *Purity and Danger. An Analysis of Concepts of Pollution and Taboo* (London, 1966) is essential reading on the mythological context of this problem.

54 P. Burke, *Popular Culture in Early Modern Europe* (1978; Aldershot, 1994), p. 92ff.

55 F. de Goya, *Cartas a Martin Zapater*, M. Agueda and X. de Salas, eds (Madrid, 1982), No. 123, p. 210.

56 See E. Lafuente Ferrari, *Antecedentes, coincidencias e influencias del arte de Goya* (1947; Madrid, 1987), pp. 288–9.

57 See esp. W. Hofmann, 'Goyas negative Morphologie', p. 22. The expression 'surrealistische Koinzidenz' is from S. Dittberner, *Traum und Trauma vom Schlaf der Vernunft*, p. 319.

58 J. Cadalso, *Cartas Marruecas* (1789/1793; J. M. Caso González, ed., Madrid, 1989), p. 55.

59 We are basing ourselves here on H. Schulte, *El Desengaño. Wort und Thema in der spanischen Literatur des Goldenen Zeitalter* (Munich, 1969).

60 *Diccionario de autoridades*, vol. II (Madrid, 1732). See under 'desengaño'. [Translator's note: The English translations are from French translations of the original Spanish, which I felt was essential to reach an understanding of the use of the word in Goya's time. *The Oxford English Dictionary* defines 'disenchantment' as 1) The act of disenchantment or fact of being disenchanted. 2) To be freed from enchantment, magic spell or illusion. 3) To be delivered from a charm.]

61 See Dittberner, *Traum and Trauma vom Schlaf der Vernunft*, p. 127.

62 B. Gracián, *El Criticón*, vol. I, chap. VI (Madrid, 1971), p. 91.

63 F. Quevedo, *Los Sueños*, vol. II (Madrid, 1954), pp. 1–57.

64 Details in Schulte, *El Desengaño*, p. 117.

65 Text published for the first time by P. Beroqui in *Archivo Espagñol de Arte*, 3 (1927), pp. 99–100. This can now be found in Tomlinson, *Francisco Goya y Lucientes 1746–1828*, p. 306.

66 V. Cardera, 'François Goya', pp. 241–2.

67 Gassier and Wilson, *Vie et oeuvre de Francisco Goya*, p. 384.

68 See G. Bollème, *Les Almanachs populaires aux XVIIe et XVIIIe siècles. Essai d'histoire sociale* (Paris and The Hague, 1969).

69 F. Link, *La Lune* (Paris, 1970).

70 P. Saintyves, *L'Astrologie populaire étudiée spécialement dans la doctrine et les traditions relatives à l'influence de la lune*, p. 38ff.

71 S. Lunais, *Recherches sur la lune*. Vol. I: *Les Auteurs latins de la fin des Guerres Puniques à la fin du règne des Antonins* (Leyden, 1979), pp. 207ff, 329ff.

72 See esp. Hofmann, *Goya. Das Zeitalter der Revolutionen*, p. 62ff.; Bozal, 'Los Caprichos: El Mundo de la noche'.

73 See Gaignebet and Florentin, *Le Carnaval. Essai de mythologie populaire*, p. 19ff. and C. Gaignebet, *Au Plus haut sens. L'Esotérisme spirituel et charnel de Rabelais*, vol. I (Paris, 1986), p. 154ff.

74 Bakhtin, *L'oeuvre de François Rabelais*. See R. Wolf's interesting observations in 'Sexual Identity, Mask, and Disguise in Goya's "Los

Caprichos"', in Held, ed., *Goya, Neue Forschungen*, p. 100.

75 *Diario de Madrid*, 6 February 1799, p. 152 and 8 February, p. 160.

76 However, see F. Márquez Villanueva, 'Literatura bufonesca o del "Loco"', *Nueva Revista de Filologia Hispanica*, 34/2 (1985–6), pp. 501–28; E. Gonzáles Duro, *Historia de la locura en España*, vol. 1 (Madrid, 1994), p. 219ff.

77 See details in K. Manger, *Das Narrenschiff. Entstehung, Wirkung, Deutung* (Darmstadt, 1983) and S. Mausolf-Kiralp, *Die 'traditio' der Ausgaben des Narrenschiffs von Sebastian Brant mit besonderer Berücksichtigung der Strassburger Editionen* (Aachen, 1997).

78 From the modern German edition, S. Brant, *Das Narrenschiff. Text und Holzschnitte der Erstausgabe 1494. Zusätze der Ausgaben 1495 und 1499* (Frankfurt am Main, 1986), p. 351ff. See Harris, *Goya: Engravings and Lithographs*, vol. I, p. 105.

6 THE CARNIVAL OF LANGUAGE

1 González Azaola, 'Satiras de Goya'.

2 See I. Hempel Lipschutz, *La Pintura española y los romanticos franceses* (1972; Madrid, 1988), p. 89.

3 C. Baudelaire, 'Quelques caricaturistes étrangers' (1857), in *Ecrits sur l'art*, vol. I (Paris, 1971), p. 363. For more general reactions to the *Caprichos*, see Glendinning, *Goya and His Critics*, p. 58ff.

4 González Azaola, 'Satiras de Goya'. [Translator's note: '*los finos conceptos*', here translated as 'subtle conceits' (also as 'subtle notions', Harris, note 5; 'subtle ideas', Glendinning, note 6) can also be translated as 'subtle wit' and both expressions will be used in the pages that follow. For further information on the problems of rhetorical terminology, and especially the concept of 'wit', see A. Zárate Ruiz, *Gracián, Wit, and the Baroque Age* (New York, Bern, Frankfurt am Main, 1996); M. J. Woods, *Gracián meets Gógora*, (Warminster, 1995).]

5 Harris, 'A Contemporary Review of Goya's "Caprichos"', pp. 38–43.

6 Glendinning, *Goya and His Critics*, p. 60.

7 E. Hidalgo-Serna, *Das ingeniöse Denken bei Baltasar Gracián* (Munich, 1985); M. Blanco, *Les Rhétoriques de la Pointe. Baltasar Gracián et le Conceptisme en Europe* (Paris, 1992); M. Chevalier, *Quevedo y su tiempo: la agudeza verbal* (Barcelona, 1992); Z. Ruiz, *Gracián, Wit and the Baroque Age*.

8 B. Gracián, *Agudeza y arte del ingenio*, vol. 1 (1647; Madrid, 1969), Discourse II, p. 55. On this subject, see M. Blanco, 'Qu'est-ce qu'un concepto?', in *Les Langues néo-latines*, 254 (1986), pp. 5–20.

9 For the relationship between *concepto* and *agudeza* see M. Blanco, *Les Rhétoriques de la Pointe*, pp. 55–7.

10 L. Muratori, *Della perfetta poesia italiana* (Modena, 1706); I. de Luzán, *La poetica o reglas de la poesia en general y de sus principales especies* (1737, 1789; Madrid, 1974). For the fortunes of Gracián in the eighteenth century, see also E. Lavadena y Calero, 'Anotaciones al Oraculo Manual: Los atisbos ilustrados de Gracián', in *Gracián y su epoca. Actas, Ponencias y comunicaciones* (Saragossa, 1986), pp. 173–80.

11 We borrowed the expression from J. Toscan, *Le Carnaval du langage. Le lexique érotique des poètes de l'équivoque de Burchiello à Marino (XVe–XVIIe siècles)*, 2 vols (Lille, 1981).

12 Gracián, *Agudeza y arte del ingenio*, vol.II, Discourse XXXII, pp. 45–51; *Art et figures de l'esprit*, pp. 215–17.

13 See the famous portrait of the Duchess of Alba in the Hispanic Society of New York and that of Narcisa Barañana de Goicochea in the Metropolitan Museum, New York.

14 Gracián, *Agudeza y arte del ingenio*, vol. II, Discourse XXXIII, pp. 36–45.

15 López- Rey, *Goya's Caprichos. Beauty, Reason, & Caricature*, p. 102.

16 On this subject, see G. Demerson, *Humanisme et Facétie. Onze études sur Rabelais* (Orleans, 1994) pp. 171–89.

17 However, it is not impossible that Goya's original idea came from Rabelaisian tradition (on this subject, see drawing B. 67 of the *Madrid Sketchbook*, in Gassier, *Les Dessins de Goya, Les Albums*, pp. 99 and 132).

18 Details in Chevalier, *Quevedo y su tiempo*, p. 52.

19 Gracián, *El Criticón*, vol. ii, crisis 5, p. 125.

20 See the more recent J. Wilson-Bareau, *Goya. La decada de los Caprichos. Dibujos y aguafuertes* (Madrid, 1992), pp. 303–5.

21 On this subject, see J. Vega, 'El Sueño Dibujado', in *Realidad y sueño en los viajes de Goya* (Saragossa and Fuendetodos, 1996), pp. 41–60.

22 L. de Márquez, 'Tradiciones carnavalescas en el lenguaje icónico de Goya', p. 107. See also Wilson-Bareau, *Goya. La Decada de los Caprichos*, pp. 211–36.

23 L. de Vega, *Quien más no puede*, ii, 140b–141a. We are indebted to Chevalier for this example, *Quevedo y su tiempo*, p. 118.

24 See Bakhtin, *L'oeuvre de François Rabelais*, pp. 148–97; Toscan, *Le Carnaval du langage*; G. Ferroni, 'Il doppio senso erotico nei canti carnascialeschi fiorentini', *Sigma*, n. s. xi, 1 (1978), pp. 233-50.

25 Gracián, *Agudeza y arte del ingenio*, vol.ii, xxxiii, p. 53; Gracián, *Art et figures de l'esprit*, p. 218.

26 Gracián, *Agudeza y arte del ingenio*, vol. ii, xxxiii, p. 61; Gracián, *Art et figures de l'esprit*, pp. 220–1.

27 J.-F. Bourgoing, *Tableau de l'Espagne moderne*, vol. ii (Paris, 1797), p. 518.

28 On this subject, see Vega, 'El Sueño Dibujado', p. 45ff.

29 R. Alcalá Flecha, *Literatura e ideologia en el arte de Goya* (Saragossa, 1988), pp. 245–53.

30 See J. Held, 'Groteske Erotik. Zu Goyas frühen Karikaturen', *Idea*, 9 (1990), p. 141; L. de Márquez, 'Tradiciones carnavalescas en el lenguaje icónico de Goya', p. 105 and, more especially, Wolf, 'Sexual Identity, Mask and Disguise'.

31 Details in A. DeJorio, *La mimica degli antichi* (Naples, 1837), pp. 89–120; J. Engemann, 'Der "corna" Gestus, ein antiker und frühchristlicher Abwehr-und Spottgestus', in *Pietas. Festschrift für Bernhard Kötting, Jahrbuch für Antike und Christentum, Ergänzungsband*, 8 (1981), pp. 483–98.

32 Goethe, *Italienische Reise*, pp. 593–4.

33 On this subject, see the deliberations of E. Lafuente Ferrari, *Los Caprichos de Goya* (Barcelona, 1978), p. 150.

34 Gassier, *Les Dessins de Goya*, vol. ii, no. 50, p. 87.

35 C. Picard, 'L'épisode de Baubô dans les mystères d'Eleusis', *Revue de l'Histoire des Religions*, 91 (1927), pp. 220–55; M. P. Nilson, *Geschichte der Griechischen Religion*, vol. i (Munich, 1976), pp. 656–67; G. Devereux, *Baubô. La Vulve mythique* (Paris, 1983).

36 Goethe, *Italienische Reise*, pp. 606–8.

37 Devereux, *Baubô. La Vulve mythique*, p. 170ff.

38 For the wider picture, see Stafford, *Body Criticism*, pp. 341–400; G. Schröder, *Logos und List. Zur Entwicklung der Ästhetik in der frühen Neuzeit* (Königstein, 1985), pp. 41–9.

39 Goya's homo-eroticism is still a taboo subject in historical studies of art. However, see J. Hara's introduction to her English translation of the Goya-Zapater correspondence, *Francisco Goya (1746–1828). Letters of Love and Friendship in Translation* (New York, 1997), pp. 1–14.

40 For the tradition and context to which this predilection belongs, see E.-M. Schenck, *Das Bilderrätsel* (Hildesheim/New York, 1973); J. Céard and J.-C. Margolin, *Rébus de la Renaissance. Des images qui parlent* (Paris, 1986); M. V.-David, *Le Débat sur les écritures et l'hiéroglyphe aux xviie et xviiie siècles et l'application de la notion de déchiffrement aux écritures mortes* (Paris, 1965); J.

Derrida, *De la Grammatologie* (Paris, 1967), esp. p. 131ff. For the situation in Spain, see *Verso e Imagen. Del Barroco al siglo de las Luces* (Madrid, 1993).

41 Blanco, *Les Rhétoriques de la Pointe*, p. 54.

42 We are indebted to Chevalier, *Quevedo y su tiempo*, p. 39, for this example.

43 See Gassier, *Les dessins de Goya. Les Albums*, no. C.36, p. 362; López-Rey, *A Cycle of Goya Drawings*, p. 90.

44 In this context, see also Wolf's observations in 'Sexual Identity, Mask and Disguise', p. 92.

45 S. Freud, *Die Traumdeutung* (1900; Frankfurt am Main, 1972), pp. 280–309; S. Freud, *Der Witz und seine Beziehung zum Unbewussten* (Leipzig and Vienna, 1905). See also Blanco, *Les Rhétoriques de la Pointe*, pp. 142–9.

46 For information on this engraving, refer to Harms, Schilling, Bauer, Kemp, eds, *Die Sammlung der Herzog August-Bibliothek in Wolfenbüttel*, p. 122. For information on the symbolism of the eyeglasses, see J.-C. Margolin, 'Des lunettes et des hommes ou la satire des mal-voyants au XVIe siècle', *Annales*, 30 (March–June 1975), pp. 375–93; H. H. Mann, *Augenglas und Perspektive. Studien zur Ikonographie zweier Bildmotive* (Berlin, 1992), pp. 87–120.

47 Gracián, *Agudeza y arte del ingenio*, II, Discourse XLIX, p. 151ff; Gracián, *Art et figures de l'esprit*, pp. 264–7.

7 ROYAL GAMES

1 Goya, *Cartas a Martin Zapater*, pp. 107–8; A. Camellas López, *Diplomatario* (Saragossa, 1981), p. 250. The exact date on which the paintings of Don Luis de Bourbon were produced and whether Goya is here referring to the group portrait (illus. 76) or to individual portraits have been the subject of much debate amongst experts. In our opinion, the questions surrounding the interpretation of all these paintings – which is the aim of this chapter – form a whole, and in this context the exact date is no more than a detail. For all these problems, see D. Angulo Iñiguez, 'La familia del Infante Don Luis pintada por Goya', *Archivo Español de Arte*, 41 (1941), pp. 49–58; P. Gassier, 'Les Portraits peints par Goya pour l'Infant Don Luis de Borbón à Arenas de San Pedro', *Revue de l'Art*, 43 (1979), pp. 9–22; A. E. Pérez Sánchez, *Goya y el Espíritu de la Ilustración*, pp. 146–9; J. M. Arnaíz, 'Goya y el Infante Don Luis', in *Goya y el Infante Don Luis de Borbón. Homenaje a la 'infanta' Doña María Teresa de Vallabriga* (Saragossa, 1996), exh. cat., pp. 19–35.

2 A. de Beruete, *Goya pintor de retratos* (Madrid, 1916), p. 22.

3 F. J. Sánchez Cantón, *Vida y obras de Goya* (Madrid, 1951), p. 28.

4 See the more recent E. A. Sayre, *The Changing Image: Prints by Francisco Goya* (Boston, 1974), pp. 49–51.

5 See, for example, F. da Costa, *Antiguidade da Arte da Pintura* (1685–88; 1696; G. Kubler, ed. [New Haven and London, 1967]), p. 258.

6 On this subject, see J. A. Emmens, 'Les Ménines de Velázquez. Miroir des Princes pour Philippe IV', *Nederlands Kunsthistorisch Jaarboek*, 12 (1961), pp. 51–79; V. I. Stoichita '*Imago Regis*. Kunsttheorie und königliches Porträt in den *Meninas* von Velázquez', *Zeitschrift für Kunstgeschichte*, 49 (1986), pp. 165–89; M. Mena Marqués, 'El encaje de la manga de la enana Mari-Barbola en *Las Meninas* de Velázquez, in *El Museo del Prado. Fragmentos y detalles* (Madrid, 1997), pp. 135–63.

7 For the problems surrounding the identity of the characters, see above, n. 1.

8 On this subject, see F. J. Sánchez Cantón, *Las Meninas y sus personajes* (Barcelona, 1952), pp. 9–10.

9 See the more recent Tomlinson, *Francisco Goya y Lucientes*, p. 63. See also: Mario Praz, *Conversation Pieces. A Survey of the Informal Group Portrait in Europe and America* (Rome and London, 1971).

10 Lafuente Ferrari, *Antecedentes, coincidencias e infulencias del arte de Goya*, pp. 120–21, justifiably draws attention to Daniel Chodowiecki's engravings.

11 Amongst others, see P. Hickman, *Silhouettes* (New York, 1968) and S. McKechnie, *British Silhouette Artists and their Work, 1760–1860* (London, 1978).

12 Chodowiecki and Wright of Derby, for example, are artists to whom A. E. Pérez Sánchez drew attention in *Goya y el espíritu de la Ilustración*, exh. cat., p. 147.

13 See M. Dumont, 'Le succès mondain d'une fausse science', *Actes de la Recherche en Sciences Sociales*, 54 (September 1984), pp. 1–30 and, for the broader view, Stafford, *Body Criticism*, pp. 84–103.

14 This interpretation was put forward by the late Juan Miguel Serrera, though unfortunately it was never developed as it deserved to be. See Serrera, 'Goya, los Caprichos y el teatro de sombras chinescas', pp. 87–8.

15 Tomlinson, *Francisco Goya y Lucientes*, p. 63.

16 The four volumes of *Physiognomische Fragmente zur Beförderung der Menschenkenntnis und Menschenliebe* were published by J. C. Lavater (Leipzig and Winterthur, 1775–8). A French translation/adaptation (the first of many) was published over a period of time in The Hague, also in four volumes, under the title *Essai sur la physiognomie* (1781–1803). We think Goya, who had rudimentary French, must have consulted this edition and that he was familiar with the illustrations. His great interest in physiognomy, which probably started at the beginning of the 1780s, and which resurfaced following the publication of Volume IV of the *Essai* in 1803, produced a whole series of drawings (see Gassier, *Les Dessins de Goya*, nos 354–7).

17 As Lavater openly admitted, his thoughts on the portrait were an extension of those expressed by Johann Georg Sulzer in his *Allgemeine Theorie der schönen Künste*, 2 vols (Leipzig, 1771 and 1774). For an excellent synopsis of the whole issue, see R. Kanz, *Dichter und Denker im Portrait* (Munich, 1993), pp. 61–119.

18 Lavater, *Essai sur la physignomie*, vol. II, pp. 214–17.

19 *Ibid.* p. 240.

20 An interesting document, now in the Prado, on the fortunes of silhouette games in the Spanish court circles includes the decorations of semi-precious stone tables, that were part of Charles III's furniture. See the beautiful colour reproductions in A. Gonzalez-Palacios, 'Piedras duras del Prado', *F.M.R.*, 1 (1993), pp. 89–102. Originally limited to an élite, silhouette portraits had, by the end of the century, become more of a form of middle-class entertainment. An advertisement in the *Diario de Madrid* on 1 December 1798 quoted the price of 120 reales for the production of 'profile portraits etched in the style of India ink drawings, with the help of a machine' (*retratos de perfil grabados al estilo de tinta china, por medio de una maquina*), stating that they 'resembled the physiognomy of the person whose portrait was being done' (*parecidos, segun la fisonomia de la persona que se retrata*) and that portraits of women would be a little more expensive 'because of their adornments and hairstyles' (*los retratos de señora, por causa de los adornos y peinados no se deben entender al mismo precio*).

21 Lavater, *Essai sur la physignomie*, vol. II, p. 192.

22 *Ibid.*, p. 22.

23 We have in mind the particular stand taken by G. C. Lichtenberg, *über Physiognomik, wider die Physiognomen* (Göttingen, 1778). There are an enormous number of books on with this subject. For a short list, see V. I. Stoichita, *A Short History of the Shadow*, pp. 153–67.

24 We are indebted to Thierry Depaulis and Walter Haas for the information

they passed on to us and for their thoughtfulness and willingness to answer our questions on the history of playing cards and cartomancy. On this subject, see J.-P. Etienvre, *Figures du Jeu. Etudes lexico-sémantiques sur le jeu de cartes en Espagne (XVIe–XVIIIe siècle)* (Madrid, 1987); A. Pérez Gonzalez, 'Una introduccion y dos precisiones', *La Sota. Revista de Naipefilia y Naipologia editada por ASESCOIN*, 19 (1998), pp. 3–18.

25 See especially J. Valverde Madrid, 'Goya y Boccherini en la Corte de Don Luis de Borbón', in *El Arte en las Cortes europeas del siglo XVIII* (Acts of Congress) (Madrid-Aranjuez, 1987), p. 796; P. Gassier, 'Un retrato de Boccherini por Goya', in I. Garcia de la Rasilla and Fr. Calvo Serraller, eds, *Goya. Nuevas Visiones. Homenaje a Enrique Lafuente Ferrari* (Madrid, 1987), pp. 175–81.

26 J. C. Lavater, *Essai sur la physiognomie*, vol. II, p. 30.

27 M. de Garsault, *L'Art du perruquier* (Paris, 1767), pp. 2–3.

28 There is an excellent synopsis on this subject, limited to an English edition: M. Pointon, *Hanging the Head. Portraiture and Social Formation in Eighteenth-Century England* (New Haven and London, 1993).

29 M. Beaumont (J. H. Marchand), *L'Encyclopédie perruquière. Ouvrage curieux à l'usage de toutes sortes de têtes* (Paris, 1762), p. 37. 'Jamais livre ne mérita mieux une Préface et une Postface, qu'un ouvrage destiné à la représentation et à l'ornement des faces. Travailler sur ce beau sujet, c'est livrer ses soins à la plus belle portion de la nature. L'homme presque seul est en possession d'avoir une face. Les autres animaux ont un bec, un museau, une hure et chez la plupart d'entre eux comme parmi nous, c'est un mérite que d'être bien coiffé. Les uns se coiffent du vin, d'autres d'amour, d'ambition, de chimères, d'autres sont nés coiffés, mais heureusement ces différentes coiffures ne les empêchent pas de se coiffer encore de Perruques. Et c'est cette seule coiffure physique à laquelle je me suis borné sans aucune intention de représenter des coiffures morales.' [Translator's note: in this excerpt Beaumont plays with the words: livre/book, livrer/deliver, and the word 'face' as in 'pre-face', 'post-face', 'face', etc. 'Coiffé' and 'coiffure' can refer to 'headgear' (and the wearing of) as well as to 'grooming' and to 'hairstyle' – hence the proliferations of puns at the end of the quotation. These are the most blatant of the puns.]

30 Beaumont, *L'Encyclopédie perruquière*, p. 38.

31 *Ibid.*, pp. 19–20.

32 On this subject, see R. Porter, 'Making Faces: Physiognomy and Fashion in Eighteenth-Century England', *Études Anglaises*, XXXVII (1985), pp. 385–96.

33 J. C. Lavater, *Essai sur la physiognomie*, vol. I, p. 110.

34 A. Cozens, *Principles of Beauty relative to the Human Head*, (London, 1778), p. D^v and F^v.

35 For the significance of the expression 'faire les cheveux', see Garsault, *L'Art du perruquier*, p. 2.

36 For further information on this idea, see V. I. Stoichita, *The Self-Aware Image. An Insight Into the Early Modern Metapainting* (Cambridge and New York, 1997), pp. 198–265.

37 See J. J. Luna's note on the painting, in *Goya 250 Aniversario*, exh. cat. (Madrid, 1996), pp. 343–4. See also the bust-length, profiled portrait of Don Luis, and the similar accompanying label.

38 J. C. Lavater, *Essai sur la physiognomie*, vol. II, p.167.

39 For more information on this, see J. Habermas's classic study, *Strukturwandel der öffentlichkeit. Untersuchungen zu einer Kategorie der bürgerlichen Gesellschaft* (1962; Frankfurt am Main, 1990).

40 For the situation in Spain, see Y. Bottineau, *L'Art de cour dans l'Espagne des Lumières 1746–1808* (Paris, 1986), p. 30ff. and p. 362ff., and M. Moran, *La Imagen del Rey. Felipe V y el arte* (Madrid, 1990), pp. 21–57.

41 For information on the status of this activity and its historical context, see M. Warnke, *Hofkünstler. Zur Vorgeschichte des modernen Künstlers* (1985; Cologne, 1996), especially p. 270ff.

42 T. Gautier, 'Fran^co^ de Goya y Lucientes', *Le Cabinet de l'amateur et de l'antiquaire* (1842), pp. 337–45.

43 See, for example, the painting by Vicente López, *The Visit of Charles IV to the University of Valence* (1802).

44 Crucial to this subject is J. Traeger's article, 'Goyas Königliche Familie. Hofkunst und Bürgerblick', *Münchner Jahrbuch der bildenden Kunst*, XLI (1990), pp. 147–81. See also X. de Salas, *La Familia de Carlos IV* (Barcelona, 1944); F. Licht, 'Goya's Portrait of the Royal Family, *Art Bulletin*, XLIX (1967), pp. 127–8 and G. Anes, '"La Familia de Carlos IV" por Goya', *Reales Sitios*, XXXIII / 128 (1996), pp. 33–9.

45 For information on reactions to this painting, see S. Symmons, *Goya in Pursuit of Patronage,* London 1988, p. 59 ff. and Glendinning, *Goya and His Critics*, pp. 37–8 and 187–8.

46 See M. Rios Mazcarelle, *Vida privada de los Borbónes,* vol. II (Madrid, 1994), p. 880.

47 For further information on this, see L. Hunt, *The Family Romance of the French Revolution* (Berkeley, 1992).

48 For the history of this, we referred to E. H. Kantorowicz, *The King's Two Bodies. A Study in Mediaeval Political Theology* (Princeton, 1957). For the king's role within the context of the absolutist court, N. Elias, *Die höfische Gesellschaft. Untersuchungen zur Soziologie des Königstums und der höfischen Aristocratie* (Neuwied and Berlin, 1969) is essential reading. For the Spanish situation, see J. M. Gonzalez García, *Metaforas del Poder* (Madrid, 1998), pp. 75–95.

49 E. Welsford, *The Fool. His Social and Literary History* (New York, 1935); W. Willeford, *The Fool and His Sceptre. A Study in Clowns and Jesters and Their Audience* (Northwestern University Press, 1969); M. Lever, *Le Sceptre et la Marotte. Histoire des Fous de Cour* (Paris, 1983); W. Mezger, *Hofnarren im Mittelalter. Vom tieferen Sinn eines seltsamen Amts* (Constance, 1981); G. Petrat, *Die letzten Narren und Zwerge bei Hofe. Reflexionen zu Herrschaft und Moral in der Frühen Neuzeit* (Bochum, 1998).

50 On this subject, see S. Billington, *Mock Kings in Medieval Society and Renaissance Drama* (Oxford, 1991).

51 For information on 'El Primo', see J. Moreno Villa, *Locos, Enanos y Niños Palaciegos. Siglos XVI y XVII* (Mexico City, 1939), pp. 55–9. For Velázquez's painting, see D. Davies, 'El Primo', in *Velázquez* (Madrid, 1999), forthcoming.

52 Details in H. Reich, *Der Mimus. Ein literar-entwicklungsgeschichtlicher Versuch* (Berlin, 1903), p. 827.

53 B. Wind, *A Foul and Pestilent Congregation*, p. 77.

54 Gracián, *El Criticón*, vol. II, pp. 141–6.

55 F. Bouza, *Locos, Enanos y hombres de Placer en la corte de los Austrias* (Madrid, 1996), p. 20 and B. Gracián, *Agudeza y arte del ingenio*, E. Correa Calderón, ed., vol. I (Madrid, 1969), 'Discurso V', pp. 74–88.

56 Aristotle, *Generation of Animals*, IV, 770 and Augustine, *The City of God*, XVI, 8. On this subject, see C. Kappler, *Monstres, démons et merveilles à la fin du Moyen âge* (Paris, 1980), p. 208ff.

57 J. Brown and J. H. Elliott, *A Palace for a King. The Buen Retiro and the Court of Philip IV* (New Haven and London, 1980), pp. 253–4. See also J. López-Rey, *Vélazquez Maler der Maler* (Cologne, 1996), vol. I, pp. 83–4 and vol. II, pp. 122–4.

58 Welsford, *The Fool*, p. 55ff.

59 Details in S. Seligmann, *Der Böse Blick und Verwandtes* (Berlin, 1910), 2 vols; Fr. Th. Elworthy, *The Evil Eye. The Origins and Practices of Superstition*

(New York, 1958); T. Hauschild, *Der Böse Blick. Ideengeschichtliche und sozialpsychologische Untersuchungen* (Hamburg, 1979).

60 N. Valletta, *Cicalata sul Fascino volgarmente detto Jettatura* (Naples, 1787; Milan, 1925).

61 Welsford, *The Fool*, p. 74.

62 Details in L. Marin, *Le Portrait du roi* (Paris, 1981).

63 J. K. Eberlein, *Apparitio Regis-Revelatio Veritatis. Studien zur Darstellung des Vorhanges in der bildenden Kunst von der Spätantike bis zum Ende des Mittelalters* (Wiesbaden, 1982).

64 For information on its anthropological context, see R. Girard, *La Violence et le Sacré* (Paris, 1972), especially p. 213ff.; V. Turner, *The Forest of Symbols* (Ithaca and London, 1967), pp. 93–110; V. Turner, *From Ritual to Theatre. The Human Seriousness of Play* (New York, 1982), pp. 22–59 and *The Ritual Process* (Chicago, 1966), pp. 169–203; C. Geertz, 'Centers, Kings, and Charisma: Reflections on the Symbolics of Power', in J. Ben-David and T. Nichols Clark, eds, *Culture and its Creators. Essays in Honor of Edward Shils* (Chicago and London, 1977), pp. 150–71.

65 P. Ariès, *L'Enfant et la vie familiale sous l'Ancien Régime* (Paris, 1960).

66 Details in M. Villa, *Locos, Enanos y Niños Palaciegos*, p. 51 and Bouza, *Locos, Enanos y hombres de Placer*, p. 13ff. See also M. Begeard, *La Folie et les fous littéraires en Espagne 1500–1650* (Paris, 1972).

67 K. F. Flögel, *Geschichte der Hofnarren* (1789; Hildesheim and New York, 1977), pp. 16ff. and 83ff.

68 Dr Doran, *The History of Court Fools* (London, 1858), pp. 380–89.

69 C. E. Merriam, Jr., *History of the Theory of Sovereignty since Rousseau* (New York and London, 1900); J. W. Merrick, *The Desacralisation of the French Monarchy in the Eighteenth Century* (London, 1990).

70 De Baecque, *La Caricature révolutionnaire*; Herding, 'Kunst und Revolution'; Herding, *Im Zeichen der Aufklärung*, pp. 95–126; Duprat, *Le Roi décapité*; A.C. Zijderveld, *Reality in a Looking-Glass: Rationality through an Analysis of Traditional Folly* (London, Boston and Henley, 1982), pp. 92–130; A. de Baecque, 'Les éclats du rire. Le régiment de la calotte, ou les strategies aristocratiques de la gaité française (1702–1752), *Annales*, 52 (1997), pp. 477–511.

71 We drew on Duprat's excellent analyses, *Le Roi décapité*, pp. 88–90 and 166–7.

72 Details in Duprat, *Le Roi décapité*, p. 88.

73 *Ibid.*, p. 90.

74 Kantorowicz, *The King's Two Bodies*, pp. 24–41.

75 See *Carlos III y la Ilustración* (Madrid, 1988), exh. cat., vol. II, p. 40.

76 Details in R. Gruenter, 'Die Mouche', *Kunst und Anitquitäten*, v (1989), p. 31. Eighteenth-century Spanish lyric poetry celebrated the 'mouche' as a fetish-sign of beauty. On this subject, see J. Melendez Valdes's poem, 'El lunarcito', in J. H. R. Polt, ed., *Poesia del Siglo XVIII* (Madrid, 1986), pp. 242–4.

77 For an overview of this, see J.-J. Courtine/Claudine Haroche, *Histoire du visage. XVIe-début du XIXe siècle* (Paris, 1988), p. 66ff.

78 See Gassier/Wilson, *Vie et oeuvre de Francisco Goya*, nos 280, 282, 284, 286, 288.

79 For further information on this subject, see *Le Vocabulaire des institutions indo-européennes* (Paris, 1969), compiled by E. Benveniste; and also Girard, *La Violence et le Sacré*, p. 225ff.

80 It is interesting to note how his contemporaries viewed Goya's message. Vicente López, author of a painting of the *Royal Family*, made two years after Goya's, returned to the question of the Infante Antonio Pascual's double role, but only in the second (and definitive) version of his painting. See E. J. Sullivan, 'Vicente López's "Family of Charles IV" and

Group Portraiture in Spain from El Greco to Goya', *Arts Magazine*, 55 (January 1981), p. 126ff.

81 Gracián, *Agudeza y arte del ingenio*, vol. I, p. 114; Gracián, *Art et figures de l'esprit*, translated into French by B. Pelegrin (Paris, 1983), p. 128.

82 Gracián, *Agudeza y arte del ingenio*, vol. I, p. 124; Gracián, *Art et figures de l'esprit*, p. 132.

8 HA-HA, HO-HO, HU-HU, HE-HE!

1 X. de Salas, 'Sobre un autoretrato de Goya y dos cartas inéditas sobre el pintor', *Archivo Español de Arte*, XXXVII (1964), pp. 317–20. For a synthesis on the dating, interpretations and relationship between these self-portraits, see J. Gallego, *Autoretratos de Goya* (Saragossa, 1990), pp. 69–72.

2 See S. Symmons's observations, *Goya* (London, 1998), pp. 131–6 and those of C. Denk, *Artiste, Citoyen & Philosophe, der Künstler und sein Bildnis im Zeitalter der französischen Aufklärung* (Munich, 1998), p. 140ff.

3 Goya, *Cartas a Zapater*, p. 208, the (slightly modified) English translation was taken from *Francisco Goya (1746–1828). Letters of Love and Friendship in Translation*, p. 129.

4 J.-C. Margolin, 'Des Lunettes et des Hommes, ou la satire des mal-voyants au XVIe siècle', *Annales*, 30 (March–June 1975), pp. 375–93; H. H. Mann, *Augenglass und Perspektive. Studien zur Ikonographie zweier Bildmotive* (Berlin, 1992), pp. 87–119.

5 R. Klein, *La Forme et l'intelligible* (Paris, 1970).

6 Margolin, 'Des Lunettes et des Hommes, ou la satire des mal-voyants au XVIe siècle', p. 388.

7 López-Rey, *Goya's Caprichos*; Levitine, 'Literary Sources of Goya's Capricho, 43'.

8 For an incursion into this motif in Spanish art, see M. Scholz-Hänsel, *El Greco, der Grossinquisitor: neues Licht auf die Schwarze Legende* (Frankfurt am Main, 1991).

9 A. Palomino, *El Museo Pictorico y Escala Optica* (1714–29; Madrid, 1988), vol. III, p. 230. For the English version, we referred to A. Palomino, *Lives of the Spanish Painters and Sculptors*, trans. N. Ayala Mallory (Cambridge, 1987), p. 154.

10 One of many examples can be found at the end of the first *Sueño*: 'Sueños son estos que si se duerme V. Excelencia sobre ellos, verà que por las cosas como las veo las esperarà como las digo.' Quevedo, *Los Sueños* (Madrid, 1991), p. 133.

11 R. Fernández de Ribera, *Los Anteojos de Mejor Vista/El Mensón del mundo*, V. Infantes de Miguel, ed. (Madrid, 1979), pp. 47–8.

12 F. de Ribera, *Los Anteojos de Mejor Vista*, pp. 66–7. For the relationship between the notion of '*desengaño*' and the symbolism of sight, see Schulte, *El Desengaño*, pp. 69–72 and 160-61.

13 De Baecque, *Le Corps de l'Histoire*, pp. 290-92.

14 See W. Hofmann, *Die Moderne im Rückspiegel, Hauptwege der Kunstgeschichte* (Munich, 1998).

15 On this subject, see H. Jansen, *Die Grundbegriffe des Baltasar Gracián* (Geneva, 1958), p. 135ff.

16 Gracián, *El Criticón*, I, IX, pp. 137–8.

17 Gracián, *Oraculo Manual y arte de prudencia*.

18 Gracián, *El Criticón*, I, VII, p. 95ff. See also Schulte, *El Desengaño*, p. 163ff.

19 Licht, 'Goya's Portrait of the Royal Family'.

20 See Hölscher, *Bild und Exzess. Näherungen zu Goya*, p. 66ff.

21 Zeglirscosac, *Ensayo sobre el origen y naturaleza de las pasiones*, p. 95.

22 Plessner, *Lachen und Weinen* (Bern, 1950).

23 Juvenal, *Satires*, X, 28–35.

24 E. Lutz, 'Democritus and Heraclitus', *Classical Journal*, 49 (1954), pp. 309–14; A. Buck, 'Democritus ridens und Heraclitus flens' in *Wort und Text. Festschrift für Fritz Schalk* (Frankfurt am Main, 1963), pp. 167–86; J. Starobinski, 'Le Rire de Démocrite', *Bulletin de la Société Française de Philosophie*, 83 (1989), pp. 5–20; A. M. García Gómez, *The Legend of the Laughing Philosopher and Its Presence in Spanish Literature (1500–1700)* (Cordoba, 1984); T. Rütten, *Demokrit – Lachender Philosoph und sanguinischer Melancholiker. Eine pseudohippokratische Geschichte* (Leiden, 1992).

25 W. Weisbach, 'Der sogennante Geograph von Velázquez und die Darstellungen des Demokrit und Heraklit', *Jahrbuch der Preussischen Kunstsammlungen*, 49 (1928), pp. 141–58; A. Blankert, 'Heraclitus en Democritus in het bijzonder in de nederlandse kunst van de 17de eeuw', *Nederlands Kunsthistorisch Jaarboek*, 18 (1967), pp. 31–124ff.

26 See Denk, *Artiste, Citoyen & Philosophe, der Künstler und sein Bildnis im Zeitalter der französischen Aufklärung*, pp. 43–52 and 191–213.

27 This sonnet, attributed to Don Neto de Silva, is to be found, by way of a prologue in F. de Lucio Espinosa y Malo, *Vida de los Filosofos Democrito y Hercalito* (Saragossa, 1676).

28 We have in mind Alciat's Emblem 151 (*In vitam humanam*). For the Spanish version, see Alciato *Emblemas*, ed. S. Sebastián (Los Berrocales del Jarama, 1985), p. 193.

29 Jansen, *Die Grundbegriffe des Baltasar Gracián*, p. 83ff.

30 Montaigne, *Essais*, I, 50.

31 On this subject, see Hippocrates, *Sur le rire et la folie* (*On Laughter and Madness*), Y. Hersant, ed. (Paris, 1989), pp. 72 and 121.

32 J. Pigeaud, *La Maladie de l'âme* (Paris, 1989), pp. 452–76; D. Bertrand, *Dire le rire à l'âge classique* (Aix-en-Provence, 1995), p. 43ff.

33 P. Mersenne, *Harmonie Universelle* (Paris, 1636), p. 62.

34 L. Poinsinet de Sivry, *Traité des causes physiques et morales du rire relativement à l'Art de l'exciter* (1768; W. Brooks, ed., Exeter, 1986), p. 29.

35 *Ibid.*, p. 29.

36 Bakhtin, *L'oeuvre de François Rabelais*, pp. 69–146.

37 F. Rabelais, *Oeuvres complètes*, J. Boulenger, ed. (Paris, 1938), p. 81; see also Buck, 'Democritus ridens et Heraclitus flens', p. 182 and, for Spain, Garcia Gómez, *The Legend of the Laughing Philosopher*, p. 234ff.

38 A. López de Vega, *Heraclito y Democrito de nuestro Siglo* (Madrid, 1641), p. 5.

39 García Gómez, *The Legend of the Laughing Philosopher and Its Presence in Spanish Literature (1500–1700)*, p. 234ff.

40 Quevedo, *Sueños*, p. 275.

41 For the fortunes of this theme in the eighteenth century, see E. Jollet, *Figures de la pesenteur. Fragonard, Newton et les plaisirs de l'escarpolette* (Nîmes, 1998), with the previous bibliography.

42 R. Caro, *Dias geniales o ludricos* (1626; Madrid, 1977), p. 193

43 Gassier, *Les dessins de Goya. Les Albums*, p. 646. See also T. Lorenzo de Marquez, important observations in *Goya y el espíritu de la Ilustracion*, exh. cat., pp. 476–8 and those of Hölscher, *Bild und Exzess. Näherungen zu Goya*, p. 6off.

44 Always refer to Frazer's deliberations in the chapter entitled 'Swinging as a magical rite' in his book *The Golden Bough*, III. *The Dying God*. For swinging as a carnivalesque custom, see Baroja, *El Carnaval*, pp. 59–61 and 72–4 and Bakhtin, *L'oeuvre de François Rabelais et la culture populaire au Moyen âge et sous la Renaissance*, pp. 166 and 303ff.

45 This ambivalent element reappears in the split executed by the subsequent etching, where the old man depicted on the front of the sheet is the counterpart of the old woman on the back.

46 'Ein böses Kind von hundert Jahren' (Brant, *Das Narrenschiff*, 5, p. 37).

47 For this *topos*, see E. R. Curtius, *European Literature and the Latin Middle Ages* (New York, 1953), pp. 98–101 and J. Hillman, 'SENEX and PUER: An Aspect of the Historical and Psychological Present', *Eranos-Jahrbuch*, 1967 (Zurich, 1968), pp. 301–60. Drawing G. 54 of the 'Bordeaux sketchbook', which shows an old man walking with the aid of croziers and bearing the inscription 'Aun aprendo', is in its turn a reflection on the *senex puer*.

List of Illustrations

All dimensions are given in centimetres.

1 Detail of illus. 8.
2 Italian, *'And This Is the World Upside Down'*, c. 1600, print. Photo: Séminaire d'Histoire de l'Art, Université de Fribourg Suisse.
3 Catalan, *The World Upside Down*, early 19th century, print. Photo: Séminaire d'Histoire de l'Art, Université de Fribourg Suisse.
4 French, *King Janus or the Two-faced Man*, 1791, aquatint, 15.6 x 13.6. Photo: Séminaire d'Histoire de l'Art, Université de Fribourg Suisse.
5 French, *Louis XVI Wearing Liberty Hat*, 1792, print. Photo: Séminaire d'Histoire de l'Art, Université de Fribourg Suisse.
6 Villeneuve, *Food for Thought for Crowned Jugglers*, 1793, print, 16 x 14.1. Photo: Séminaire d'Histoire de l'Art, Université de Fribourg Suisse.
7 French, *The Independent*, after 1792. Photo: Séminaire d'Histoire de l'Art, Université de Fribourg Suisse.
8 Goya, *The Burial of the Sardine*, c. 1816, oil on wood, 82.5 x 52. Museo de la Real Academia de Bellas Artes de San Fernando, Madrid.
9 Goya, *The Burial of the Sardine*, c. 1816, pen and sepia ink, 22 x 18. Museo del Prado, Madrid.
10 Goya, *Mythological Scene*, 1784, oil on canvas, 81 x 64.5. Private collection.
11 *Hercules and Omphale*, 1st century BC. Museo Archeologico, Naples.
12 Lucas Cranach, *Hercules and Omphale*, 1537, beech wood, 85 x 118.9. Herzog Anton Ulrich-Museum, Braunschweig. Photo: Bernd-Peter Kaiser.
13 Goya, *Capricho 35: She Is Plucking Him*, c. 1797–8, etching and aquatint, 21.7 x 15.3.
14 Goya, *'What a Disaster!'*, c. 1800, India ink wash drawing, 20.6 x 14.3. Museo del Prado, Madrid.
15 Goya, *'Blindman Enamoured of His Bulge'*, c. 1800, sepia wash drawing, 20.5 x 14.1. Museo del Prado, Madrid.
16 Goya, *'Aunt Gila's Little Queer'*, c. 1800, India ink wash drawing, 20.5 x 14.1. Museo del Prado, Madrid.
17 Goya, *'Malicious Fool'*, 1824–8, black chalk, 19.2 x 15. National Museum, Stockholm. Photo: Statens Konstmuseer.
18 Studio of Peter Paul Rubens, *Drunken Silenus*, first half of the 17th century, oil on wood, 139 x 119. Gemäldegalerie Alte Meister, Kassel.
19 Jean-Antoine Watteau, *The March of Silenus*, c. 1715, coloured chalks, 15.4 x 21. National Gallery of Art, Washington, DC (Mr Paul S. Morgan).
20 Goya, *Drawing B. 49: Young Woman with a Paunchy Man*, 1796–7, wash on paper, 23.6 x 14.6. Private collection.
21 Goya, *Drawing E. 22: 'This Woman was Painted in Naples by José Ribera Known as the Spagnoletto'*, c. 1640, 1803–12, India ink wash, 26 x 17.8. Location unknown.
22 Giovanni Battista Gaulli (known as Baciccio), *Saint Joseph with the Child Jesus*, c. 1670–85, oil on canvas, 127 x 97.2. The Norton Simon Museum, Pasadena. Photo: The Norton Simon Foundation.
23 Juan Sánchez Cotán, *Brigida del Rio, the Bearded Lady of Peñaranda*, 1590, oil

317

on canvas, 102 x 61. Museo del Prado, Madrid.

24 Sebastián de Covarrubias, *Emblem 64*, from *Emblemas morales* (Madrid, 1610). Photo: Séminaire d'Histoire de l'Art, Université de Fribourg Suisse.

25 Italian, *Harlequin Suckling His Child*, 18th century, print. Photo: Séminaire d'Histoire de l'Art, Université de Fribourg Suisse.

26 Goya, *Woman and Serpent*, 1797–9, pen and sepia wash with reddish scumble over entire sheet, 210 x 147. Museo del Prado, Madrid.

27 Goya, *Dandy and Monkey*, 1797–9, pen and sepia wash with reddish scumble over entire sheet, 206 x 145. Museo del Prado, Madrid.

28 Goya, *Student and Frog*, 1797–8, pen and sepia wash with reddish scumble over entire sheet, 206 x 147. Museo del Prado, Madrid.

29 Goya, *Policeman and Wild Cat*, 1797–8, pen and sepia wash with reddish tint over entire sheet, 210 x 147. Museo del Prado, Madrid.

30 Detail of Goya, *The Washerwomen*, c. 1779, oil on canvas. Sammlung Oskar Reinhart am Römerholz, Winterthur.

31 Charles Le Brun, *The Ram Man*, engraving from Morel d'Arleux, *Dissertation sur un traité de Charles Le Brun* (Paris, 1806). Photo: Séminaire d'Histoire de l'Art, Université de Fribourg Suisse.

32 German, *The Devil and the Woman*, woodcut from *Der Ritter von Turn* (Basel, 1493). Photo: Séminaire d'Histoire de l'Art, Université de Fribourg Suisse.

33 Johann Caspar Lavater, *From Frog to Apollo*, engraving from *Essai sur la physiognomie*, vol. 1 (The Hague, 1781). Photo: Séminaire d'Histoire de l'Art, Université de Fribourg Suisse

34 Goya, *The Dandy Being Tortured*, 1797–8, red wash with touches of sanguine, 190 x 132. Museo del Prado, Madrid.

35 Goya, *Sixteen Caricatured Heads*, 1798(?), pen and sepia, 29.8 x 40.4. Location unknown (formerly Sclafani Collection, Madrid).

36 Goya, *Self-portrait*, c. 1795–7, India ink wash drawing, 23.3 x 14.4. Metropolitan Museum of Art, New York (Harris Brisbane Dick Fund).

37 Charles Le Brun, *Leonine Head*, engraving from Morel d'Arleux, *Dissertation sur un traité de Charles Le Brun*. Photo: Séminaire d'Histoire de l'Art, Université de Fribourg Suisse.

38 Goya, *Blind Man's Buff*, 1788–9, oil on canvas, 269 x 350. Museo del Prado, Madrid.

39 *The Dance of Time*, engraving from Francisco Colonna, *Hypnerotomachia Poliphili* (Venice, 1499). Photo: Séminaire d'Histoire de l'Art, Université de Fribourg Suisse.

40 Goya, *Feminine Absurdity*, 1814–19, etching and aquatint, 24 x 35.

41 Goya, *The Disasters of War* 30, c. 1800–11, etching and wash, approx. 14.2 x 17.

42 Goya, Drawing E 38: *Feats? Be Your Age*, 1803–12, India ink wash, 26.5 x 18.7. Staatliche Museen zu Berlin (Kupferstichkabinett).

43 Goya, Drawing E 39: *Shouting Will Get You Nowhere*, 1803–12, India ink wash, 26.5 x 18.1. Private collection.

44 Goya, Drawing E 6: *Complain about the Weather*, 1803–12, India ink wash, 26.3 x 18.5. Rijksmuseum, Amsterdam.

45 Goya, *A Vision: God the Father and Abraham*, fol. 33r from the 'Italian Notebook', 1770–73, sanguine and black wash highlights, 18.6 x 12.8. Museo del Prado, Madrid.

46 Goya, Drawing C. 101: *We Cannot Look at This*, 1814–24, India ink wash, 20.5 x 14.2. Museo del Prado, Madrid.

47 Goya, *Apparition of the Virgin of the Pillar to Saint James and His Disciples*, c. 1775–80, oil on canvas, 120 x 98. Private collection.

48 Goya, *The Disasters of War* 67: *This One Is No Less*, 1815–20, etching and aquatint, 17.5 x 22.

49 Goya, *The Belvedere Torso*, fol. 61r from the 'Italian Notebook', 1770, black

wash drawing, 18.6 x 12.8. Museo del Prado, Madrid.

50 Goya, *The Disasters of War* 37: *This Is Worse c.* 1812–15, etching and wash, 15.7 x 20.7.

51 Goya, Drawing C. 108: *'Such Cruelty!'*, 1815–20, sepia wash, 20.5 x 14.2. Museo del Prado, Madrid.

52 Goya, Drawing A. b. (2): *Back View of Young Woman Raising Her Skirts*, 1796–7, India ink wash, 17 x 9.7. Biblioteca Nacional, Madrid.

53 Girard Audran, *The Callipygean Venus*, engraving from *Les Proportions du corps humain mesurées sur les plus belles figures de l'Antiquité* (Paris, 1683). Photo: Séminaire d'Histoire de l'Art, Université de Fribourg Suisse.

54 English, *The Man-Wife*, 18th-century, engraving. Photo: Séminaire d'Histoire de l'Art, Université de Fribourg Suisse.

55 Thomas Rowlandson, *The Exhibition Stare-Case, c.* 1800, engraving. Photo: Séminaire d'Histoire de l'Art, Université de Fribourg Suisse.

56 Detail from William Hogarth, Frontispiece of *The Analysis of Beauty* (London, 1753). Photo: Séminaire d'Histoire de l'Art, Université de Fribourg Suisse.

57 The Petrarca-Master, *The Wheel of Fortune, c.* 1500–25, woodcut. Photo: Séminaire d'Histoire de l'Art, Université de Fribourg Suisse.

58 Attributed to Albrecht Dürer, Engraving from Sebastian Brant, *Das Narrenschiff* (Basel, 1494). Photo: Séminaire d'Histoire de l'Art, Université de Fribourg Suisse.

59 Goya, *Capricho* 56: *Ups and Downs*, 1797–8, etching and aquatint, 21.7 x 15.1.

60 Illustration for D.-A.-F. de Sade, *La Philosophie dans le boudoir* (Paris, 1795), engraving. Photo: Séminaire d'Histoire de l'Art, Université de Fribourg Suisse.

61 Illustration for D.-A.-F. de Sade, *La Nouvelle Justine* (Holland, 1797), engraving. Photo: Séminaire d'Histoire de l'Art, Université de Fribourg Suisse.

62 Goya, *Capricho* 71: *We Must Be off with the Dawn*, 1797–8, etching and aquatint, 20 x 15.

63 *Satyr and Young Woman*, engraving from Giovan Battista Della Porta, *Della fisionomia dell'huomo* (Naples, 1610). Photo: Séminaire d'Histoire de l'Art, Université de Fribourg Suisse.

64 *The Lustful Man*, engraving from Della Porta, *Della fisionomia dell'huomo*. Photo: Séminaire d'Histoire de l'Art, Université de Fribourg Suisse.

65 Thomas Rowlandson, *The Court of Statues, c.* 1800, engraving. Photo: Séminaire d'Histoire de l'Art, Université de Fribourg Suisse.

66 Jacques-Louis David, *Mars Disarmed by Venus and the Graces*, 1824, oil on canvas, 308 x 262. Musées Royaux des Beaux-Arts de Belgique, Brussels. Photo: A.C.I.

67 Goya, Drawing B. 7: *The Fainting*, 1796–7, India ink and wash, 23.5 x 14.4. Museo del Prado, Madrid.

68 Jusepe Ribera, *The Bearded Lady*, 1631, oil on canvas, 196 x 127. Fundación Casa Ducal de Medinaceli, Toledo. Photo: Institut Amatller d'Art Hispànic.

69 Goya, *The Straw Man*, 1791–2, oil on canvas, 267 x 160. Museo del Prado, Madrid. Photo: Institut Amatller d'Art Hispànic.

70 Goya, Preparatory drawing for *Merry Absurdity*, 1815–24, sepia on paper, 21.4 x 31.2. Museo del Prado, Madrid. Photo: Institut Amatller d'Art Hispànic.

71 Goya, Preparatory drawing for *Capricho* 52, *Fine Feathers Make Fine Birds*, 1797–8, red ink wash, 23.8 x 16.3. Museo del Prado, Madrid. Photo: Institut Amatller d'Art Hispànic.

72 Goya, *The Sleep of Reason Brings forth Monsters* (first version), 1797, pen and black ink and sepia over charcoal drawing, 23 x 15.5. Museo del

Prado, Madrid. Photo: Institut Amatller d'Art Hispànic.

73 Goya, Frontispiece of the *Dreams* series, 1797, pen and sepia ink over charcoal drawing, 24.8 x 17.2. Museo del Prado, Madrid. Photo: Institut Amatller d'Art Hispànic.

74 Goya, *The Infante Don Luis and His Family*, 1783/4, oil on canvas, 248 x 330. Fondazione Magnani-Rocca, Corte di Mamiano (Parma). Photo: Foto Amoretti-Parma.

75 Detail of illus. 76.

76 Goya, *Charles IV and His Family*, 1800–01, oil on canvas, 280 x 336. Museo del Prado, Madrid. Photo: Institut Amatller d'Art Hispànic.

77 Goya, *Study for a Portrait of the Infanta Maria Josefa*, 1799–1800, oil on canvas, 74 x 60. Museo del Prado, Madrid. Photo: Institut Amatller d'Art Hispànic.

78 Goya, *Yard with Lunatics*, c. 1794, oil on tinplate, 43.6 x 32.4. Meadows Museum, Southern Methodist University, Dallas (Algur H. Meadows Collection).

79 Johann Zoffany, *Cognoscenti in the Tribuna of the Uffizi*, 1772–8, oil on canvas, 123.5 x 154.9. Windsor Castle, Berks. Photo: Royal Collection Enterprises, © Her Majesty Queen Elizabeth II.

80 Detail of illus. 79.

81 Louis Dennel, *Pygmalion and Galatea*, c. 1775, copper engraving. Photo: Séminaire d'Histoire de l'Art, Université de Fribourg Suisse.

82 Etienne-Maurice Falconet, *Pygmalion and Galatea*, 1761, marble. Walters Art Gallery, Baltimore.

83 *Pygmalion and Galatea*, woodcut from *Romaunt of the Rose* (Lyon, 1497). Photo: Séminaire d'Histoire de l'Art, Université de Fribourg Suisse.

84 Goya, *Pygmalion and Galatea*, from Album F, 1815–20, brush and sepia wash, 20.5 x 14.1. The J. Paul Getty Museum, Los Angeles.

85 Goya, Drawing, fol. 147r from the 'Italian Notebook', 1770–73, pencil and wash, 18.6 x 12.8. Museo del Prado, Madrid.

86 Goya, Drawing, fol. 165r. from the 'Italian Notebook', 1770–73, India ink, 18.6 x 12.8. Museo del Prado, Madrid.

87 Goya, *The Madhouse*, c. 1812–19, oil on wood, 45 x 72. Museo de la Real Academia de Bellas Artes de San Fernando, Madrid.

88 Detail from Jacques-Louis David, *The Tennis Court Oath*, 1791–2, oil on canvas. Musée National du Chateau, Versailles.

89 Advertisement announcing the sale of Goya's *Caprichos* in the *Diario de Madrid*, 6 February 1799.

90 Espinosa de los Monteros, Plan of the centre of Madrid in 1769. Servicio Geografico del Ejercito, Madrid. Photo: Seccion de Documentacion del Servicio Geografico del Ejercito.

91 Luis Paret y Alcazar, *The Trinket Shop*, 1722, oil on wood, 50 x 58. Museo Lazaro Galdiano, Madrid.

92 Goya, *Capricho 33: At the Count Palatine*, 1797–8, etching and aquatint, 21.8 x 15.2.

93 Goya, Detail of the copper plate for *Capricho 33*. Photo: Juan Gyenes.

94 Frontispiece of Francisco de Quevedo, *Obras*, vol. I (Antwerp, 1699). Photo: Séminaire d'Histoire de l'Art, Université de Fribourg Suisse.

95 'Empresa 45', from Diego de Saavedra Fajardo, *Empresas politicas* (Milan, 1642). Photo: Séminaire d'Histoire de l'Art, Université de Fribourg Suisse.

96 Detail of illus. 72.

97 Zacarias González Velásquez, *Allegory of the Night*, after 1800, oil on canvas mounted on a wall, 358 x 370. Museo Romántico, Madrid (formerly in the Casino de la Reyna).

98 Goya, *Capricho 43: The Sleep of Reason Brings forth Monsters*, 1797–8, etching and aquatint, 21.6 x 15.2. Museo del Prado, Madrid.

99 Frontispiece of Giuseppe Maria Mitelli, *L'Alfabeto in sogno* (Bologna,

1683). Photo: Séminaire d'Histoire de l'Art, Université de Fribourg Suisse.

100 Goya, 'Francisco Goya y Lucientes, Painter', frontispiece of the *Caprichos*, 1797–8, etching and aquatint, 21.9 x 15.1.

101 Francisco de Paula Martì Mora, *Disprecio* (Contempt), engraving from Fermin Eduardo Zeglirscosac, *Ensayo sobre el origen y naturaleza de las pasiones* (Madrid, 1800). Photo: Séminaire d'Histoire de l'Art, Université de Fribourg Suisse.

102 Martì Mora, *Tristeza* (Sadness), engraving from Zeglirscosac, *Ensayo sobre el origen y naturaleza de las pasiones* (Madrid, 1800). Photo: Séminaire d'Histoire de l'Art, Université de Fribourg Suisse.

103 Catalan, '*The World Upside Down*', early 19th century, print. Photo: Séminaire d'Histoire de l'Art, Université de Fribourg Suisse.

104 German, *The Doctor Curing Fantasy, also Purging Madness with the Use of Drugs*, c. 1630, copper engraving. Photo: Séminaire d'Histoire de l'Art, Université de Fribourg Suisse.

105 Goya, *Capricho* 58: *Swallow That, You Dog*, 1797–8, etching and aquatint, 21.7 x 15.1.

106 Philip Galle after Pieter Brueghel, *Allegory of Temperance*, c. 1600, etching. Photo: Séminaire d'Histoire de l'Art, Université de Fribourg Suisse.

107 Frontispiece of Diego Torres Villarroel, *Nueva folla astrologica* (Madrid, 1761). Photo: Séminaire d'Histoire de l'Art, Université de Fribourg Suisse.

108 Goya, *Capricho* 79: *No-one Saw Us*, 1797–8, etching and aquatint, 21.6 x 15.1.

109 Goya, Drawing B. 63: *Merry Caricature*, 1796–7(?), India ink wash, 19 x 13. Museo del Prado, Madrid.

110 Goya, *Capricho* 13: *It's Hot*, 1797–8, etching and aquatint, 21.8 x 15.4.

111 Goya, *Capricho* 30: *Why Hide It?*, 1797–8, etching and aquatint, 21.8 x 15.2.

112 Goya, *Capricho* 42: *You Who Cannot Do It, Carry Me on Your Shoulders*, 1797–8, etching and aquatint, 21.7 x 15.1.

113 Goya, '*He Puts Her Down as an Hermaphrodite*', 1796–7, India ink wash drawing, 20.9 x 12.5. Musée de Louvre, Paris (Département des Arts Graphiques). Photo: R.M.N.

114 Goya, *Sueño, Masquerades of Caricatures*, 1797–8, pen and sepia ink, 29.2 x 18.3. Museo del Prado, Madrid.

115 Goya, Preparatory drawing for *Capricho* 57, *The Lineage*, c. 1797–98, red ink wash, 19.3 x 12.5. Museo del Prado, Madrid.

116 Goya, *Capricho* 57: *The Lineage*, 1797–8, etching and aquatint, 21.7 x 15.2.

117 Goya, Drawing B. 24: *Lovers Seated on a Rock*, 1796–7, India ink wash, 23.5 x 14.6. Metropolitan Museum of Art, New York (Harris Brisbane Dick Fund).

118 Detail of illus. 114.

119 Goya, Rebus message in an undated letter (1783?) to Martin Zapater. Museo Lazaro Galdiano, Madrid.

120 Goya, Drawing C. 36, 1803–24, India ink wash, 20.5 x 14.1. Museo del Prado, Madrid.

121 Claes Jansz. Clock, *The Glasses Vendor*, 1602, copperplate engraving, 25 x 19. Photo: Séminaire d'Histoire de l'Art, Université de Fribourg Suisse.

122 Goya, *Las Meninas* (after Velázquez), 1778–85, etching and aquatint, 40.5 x 32.5. Photo: Séminaire d'Histoire de l'Art, Université de Fribourg Suisse.

123 William Wellings, *The Austen-Knight Family*, 1783, silhouette painting on paper, 55.9 x 45.7. Edward Knight Collection.

124 '*Reliable and Convenient Machine for Drawing Silhouettes*', from J. C. Lavater, *Essai sur la physiognomie*, vol. II (The Hague, 1783). Photo: Bibliothèque Universitaire de Lausanne Dorigny.

125 A. G. Rämel, *Portrait and Profile of Shadow*, from Lavater, *Essai sur la physiognomie*, vol. II. Photo: Bibliothèque Universitaire de Lausanne Dorigny.

126 *A Prince*, from Lavater, *Essai sur la physiognomie*, vol. II.
127 Detail of illus. 74.
128 Physiognomy of a musician, from Lavater, *Essai sur la physiognomie*, vol. II.
      Photo: Bibliothèque Universitaire de Lausanne Dorigny.
129 Detail of illus. 74.
130 Detail of illus. 74.
131 M. Beaumont [J. H. Marchand], Title page of *L'Encyclopédie perruquière*
      (Paris, 1762). Photo: Bayerische Staatsbibliothek, Munich.
132 Beaumont [Marchand], Examples of wigs, from *L'Encyclopédie perruquière*.
      Photo: Bayerische Staatsbibliothek, Munich.
133 *Four Profiles of Women*, from Lavater, *Essai sur la physiognomie*, vol. I.
      Photo: Bibliothèque Universitaire de Lausanne Dorigny.
134 Alexander Cozens and Francesco Bartolozzi, *Simple Beauty* (profile),
      engraving from *Principles of Beauty Relative to the Human Head* (London,
      1778). Photo: Getty Research Institute, Special Collections, Los Angeles.
135 Cozens and Bartolozzi, *Simple Beauty* (hair), engraving from *Principles of
      Beauty Relative to the Human Head*. Photo: Getty Research Institute, Special
      Collections, Los Angeles.
136 Cozens and Bartolozzi, *Simple Beauty* (profile and hair), engraving from
      Principles of Beauty Relative to the Human Head. Photo: Getty Research
      Institute, Special Collections, Los Angeles.
137 Cozens and Bartolozzi, *Majestic Beauty* (profile), engraving from *Principles
      of Beauty Relative to the Human Head*. Photo: Getty Research Institute,
      Special Collections, Los Angeles.
138 Goya, *Maria Teresa de Vallabriga*, 1783, oil on wood, 47.5 x 39. Museo del
      Prado, Madrid.
139 Goya, *Equestrian Portrait of Margarite of Austria* (after Velázquez), 1778,
      etching and drypoint engraving, 37 x 31.
140 Goya, *Portrait of Maria Teresa of Vallabriga on Horseback*, 1783, oil on canvas,
      132.3 x 116.7. Uffizi, Florence.
141 Detail of illus. 74.
142 Detail of Goya, *Portrait of Count Floridablanca*, 1783, oil on canvas. Banco
      de España, Madrid.
143 *Profile of a Prudent Man*, from Lavater, *Essai sur la physiognomie*, vol. II.
      Photo: Bibliothèque Universitaire de Lausanne Dorigny.
144 Jean Duplessi-Bertaux after François-Louis Prieur, *Last Meeting of Louis
      XVI and His Family*, beginning of the 18th century, copper engraving.
      Photo: Séminaire d'Histoire de l'Art, Université de Fribourg Suisse.
145 Detail of illus. 76.
146 Rodrigo Villandrando, *Philippe IV and the Dwarf Soplillo*, c. 1621, oil on
      canvas, 204 x 110. Museo del Prado, Madrid.
147 Diego Velázquez, *Don Baltasar Carlos with a Dwarf*, 1632, oil on canvas,
      128.1 x 102. Museum of Fine Arts, Boston (Henry Lillie Pierce Fund).
      Photo: Courtesy of the Museum of Fine Arts, Boston.
148 French, *The Mask Removed*, June 1791, etching, 26.2 x 14.2. Bibliothèque
      Nationale de France, Paris (Cabinet des Estampes: Qb1 M 100 735).
149 French, *The Great Anger of Capet the Elder*, June 1791, etching, 14.1 x 22.1.
      Bibliothèque Nationale de France, Paris (Cabinet des Estampes: Qb 1 M
      100 733).
150 French, *Aristocratic Lady Cursing the Revolution*, 1792, coloured engraving,
      28 x 20.3. Musée Carnavalet, Paris. Photo: Photothèque des Musées de la
      Ville de Paris/Bulloz.
151 Detail of illus. 76.
152 Goya, *Self-portrait*, c. 1797–1800, oil on canvas, 62 x 49. Musée Goya,
      Castres. Photo: J. C. Ouradou.
153 Spanish, *Portrait of Francisco de Quevedo*, 17th century, engraving. Photo:
      Séminaire d'Histoire de l'Art, Université de Fribourg Suisse.

154 Goya, *Capricho* 2: *They Answer Yes*, 1797–8, etching with aquatint, 21.7 x 15.1.
155 Detail of illus. 154.
156 Goya, Preparatory drawing for *Capricho* 30, *Why Hide It?*, 1797–8, sanguine, 20.1 x 14.2. Museo del Prado, Madrid.
157 Detail of illus. 111.
158 Francisco de Paula Martì Mora, *Risa* (The Laugh), engraving from Fermin Eduardo Zeglirscosac, *Ensayo sobre el origen y naturaleza de las pasiones* (Madrid, 1800).
159 Philipp Galle, *Heraclitus*, engraving from the series *Variae comarum et barbarum formae*, c. 1600. Photo: Séminaire d'Histoire de l'Art, Université de Fribourg Suisse.
160 Galle, *Democritus*, engraving from the series *Variae comarum et barbarum formae*. Photo: Séminaire d'Histoire de l'Art, Université de Fribourg Suisse.
161 Goya, *Old Man on a Swing*, 1824–8, black chalk on paper, 19 x 15.1. The Hispanic Society of America, New York.
162 Goya, *Old Man on a Swing*, 1825–7, etching and aquatint, 18.5 x 12.